GLOBAL LIBERALISM, LOCAL POPULISM

Syracuse Studies on Peace and Conflict Resolution
Louis Kriesberg, *Series Editor*

GLOBAL LIBERALISM, LOCAL POPULISM

Peace and Conflict in Israel/Palestine
and Northern Ireland

GUY BEN-PORAT

SYRACUSE UNIVERSITY PRESS

The paper used in this publication meets the minimum requirements
of American National Standard for Information Sciences—Permanence
of Paper for Printed Library Materials, ANSI Z39.48–1984.∞™

Library of Congress Cataloging-in-Publication Data

Ben-Porat, Guy.
Global liberalism, local populism : peace and conflict in Israel/Palestine and
Northern Ireland / Guy Ben-Porat.— 1st ed.
p. cm.—(Syracuse studies on peace and conflict resolution)
Includes bibliographical references and index.
ISBN 0–8156–3069–7 (pbk. : alk. paper)
1. Conflict management—Case studies. 2. Peace-building—Case studies.
3. Arab-Israeli conflict. 4. Irish unification question.
5. Northern Ireland—History—1994– 6. Globalization. 7. Geopolitics. I. Title. II. Series.
JZ5538.B46 2006
327.1'72—dc22   2005035938

Manufactured in the United States of America

To Neta, Shira, and Talia

Guy Ben-Porat is a lecturer in the Department of Public Policy and Administration at Ben-Gurion University of the Negev, Israel.

Contents

Preface

LESS THAN A DECADE AGO, Thomas Friedman, the influential columnist, could have not been more optimistic over the future of Israel and the Middle East: "Israel will be a high-tech locomotive that will pull Jordan and the Palestinians along with it. Already Siemens has linked up its Israeli factory, Siemens Data Communication near Haifa, and a Siemens team of Palestinian engineers in the West Bank town of Ramallah, with Siemens headquarters back in Germany. It's just the beginning" (Friedman 1999, 207). Friedman was not alone. The optimism of the early 1990s assumed that the old Middle East of wars, violence, and poverty was going to give way to a "New Middle East" that was prosperous, rational, and peaceful (Ben-Porat 2005). Events unfolded along a different path, however, as the vicious cycles of violence overshadowed the virtuous cycles of peace. A decade after the dramatic ceremonies, the New Middle East has turned from a vision for the future to an example of a pipe dream.

Viewed from different distances, levels of involvement, and ideological perspectives, peace processes offer moments of hope and periods of frustration and despair. In their glorious moments and celebratory events, peace processes promise a bright future in which the removal of the constant threat of violence is accompanied by expectations for a better life. But when the disputant parties fail to resolve their differences and extremists are able to set the agenda, hate and violence seem to take over, erasing all signs of hope and displaying the worst of humanity. Explanations for such swings of the pendulum between peace and war often focus on specific events, on decisions taken or not taken, and on the personalities or skills of leaders involved. A deeper understanding of peace processes and conflicts, however, requires attention to history and also an account of the wider context in which they unfold, a context that structures the constraints and opportunities available to leaders and societies. Globalization is the starting point and the context in which this work is situated as it attempts to understand the developments of conflict and peace in two case studies—Israel/Palestine and Northern Ireland—within the context of two historical periods—early globalization (1880 to 1914) and contemporary globalization (1970 to the present).

The genesis of this work was my personal concern over not only what went wrong but also why things sometimes "go better"—in other words, under what terms the sides to a bitter conflict can make a genuine effort to change their fortunes. Understanding globalization, I argue, is key not only to understanding motivations for initiating peace processes but also for coming to terms with the backlash that such processes often engender. It was the economic historian Karl Polanyi that warned us sixty years ago of the "double movement"—society's reaction to the dislocations caused by liberalization (Polanyi [1944] 1957). This countermovement, according to Polanyi, was more spontaneous than coherent and organized and contained an amalgam of social forces with diverse and, at times, contradictory visions and goals. While the agents of movement toward market economies ranged from the local and national to the global, the agents of the countermovement were largely local and national forces whose aim was the protection of local and national interests (Arrighi and Silver 2002). Thus while the liberal accounts of globalization portray a global world united through a common economic agenda and a global culture that fosters peace, we are often reminded, in various shapes and forms, of Polanyi's "double movement."

The observation of localized social structures, institutions, and political divisions, as well as international relationships between states and societies, provides a unique point of departure to study the dynamics of conflict and peace. Israel/Palestine and Northern Ireland share a legacy of conflicts that came to be described as protracted or intractable, conflicts with roots that can be located in the late nineteenth century (discussed in the first part of the book). In both places, these long-term, ongoing conflicts seemed to permeate all aspects of society and led to a zero-sum mentality that rendered them impervious to conventional methods of conflict resolution (Starr 1999). But in the early 1990s, both conflicts seemed to defy predictions and change their trajectories under the new developments associated with globalization. The emergence of a global economy based on nonterritorial entities—multinational firms, "offshore" economic spaces, and macroregional blocs—created new incentives and opportunities for peace with implications for both conflicts. Indeed, the "unbundling" of territoriality (Ruggie 1993) associated with globalization underscored the new visions for peace and the agreements that followed. According to the new visions of peace, the new incentives to "go global," to be part of the new world and take advantage of new opportunities, overshadow the old concerns over territorial sovereignty. Despite the optimistic visions of the early 1990s, however, history has not reached its liberal-democratic end. Rather, as Northern Irish Protestants and Catholics and, even more so, Israelis and Palestinians came painfully to discover, the visions of peace are yet to come about.

This journey, between two historical periods and between two continents, is an attempt to draw on contexts and histories to understand the trajectories of conflict and peace. While it is situated in the fields of international relations and political science, it draws on sociology, geography, and history to provide a multidimensional explanation for current developments. When I began this project in 1999, the Israeli Labor Party had returned to power with a promise to resume the process shattered by cycles of violence in the preceding five years. Likewise, when I spent some four weeks in Northern Ireland in the summer of 2000, I could feel, in addition to the always necessary caution, optimism in the air. Belfast—whose images to a foreigner, even one from the Middle East, were of fear of violence—was a friendly city that seemed to have shed its violent past. By that time, however, the pleasant atmosphere in Belfast was in sharp contrast to the news coming from home, which seemed cause for despair; the peace summit in Camp David—another potential celebratory moment—failed, and violence resumed, its flames higher then ever. Watching the news from home in a Belfast coffee shop on a quiet street, the different trajectories of the peace processes were striking. Now, as I write these lines in the fall of 2005, the breath of hope that was in the air (again?) after Israel's withdrawal from Gaza has all but vanished with the advent of another cycle of suicide bombings and targeted killing.

Many people, knowingly or unknowingly, contributed to this project. Thanks to its faculty and administrative staff, the Department of Political Science at Johns Hopkins University was a comfortable home and a strong source of support, and I am grateful for the opportunity it gave me and the encouragement it provided before and during the writing of this book. While studying in the United States, I had the opportunity to work as a research assistant in the United States Institute of Peace and the good fortune to work for Idith Zertal and Gadi Wolfsfeld, from whom I learned much. In Northern Ireland, I was fortunate to meet many people who were willing to share with a foreigner their experiences and lessons, and I wish them all the desired peace. They deserve it. In Israel, I enjoyed the cooperation of numerous people who shared with me their knowledge and insights. My sincere thanks to all of them, especially Uri Ram and Michael Shalev. I found a new home in the Department of Public Policy and Administration at Ben-Gurion University of the Negev. I owe much to my colleagues in that department, to the always patient administrative staff, to my colleagues in the School of Management, to the chair, Shlomo Mizrachi, and to the dean, Arie Reichel, for their support.

I was fortunate to have other advisers to guide me through this journey. Siba N. Grovogui from the Department of Political Science at Johns Hopkins University managed the difficult task of being a friend, adviser, and teacher; his influence was key in my decision to make international relations my chosen field of study. I was likewise fortunate that when I embarking on this project Giovanni Arrighi had joined the Sociology Department at Johns Hopkins. Giovanni's work and personality have been nothing less than inspiring, and I hope this work lives up to his standards. Finally, Mark Blyth from the Department of Political Science was the best critical reader one could wish for, and his impact on this work is probably greater than he knows.

Syracuse University Press was very hospitable to this project. Louis Kriesberg, the editor of the press's Peace and Conflict Resolution series, was supportive and encouraging, and Michael P. O'Connor and Glenn Wright of the Acquisitions Department showed skill and patience in answering my many questions over the past two years. In Israel, Karen Oren has done excellent work in proofreading and preparing this manuscript. The images on the cover of this book describe another one of the somewhat odd links between these two conflicts, Israeli flags flying over Protestant neighborhoods and Catholic murals expressing support for the Palestinian cause. I am grateful to Jonathan McCormick who has generously allowed me to use these images from his impressive collection.

Lastly, this project came about only with the strong support and enduring patience of those closest to me. My parents, Amir and Rachel Ben-Porat, made so much possible. My daughters provided me with just enough distraction to keep the work pleasant: Shira was born with this project and grew with it, and Talia came to help in the last stages. Finally, I thank my wife and partner, Neta, whose love and support made this project not only possible but also worthwhile. The book is dedicated to them.

Guy Ben-Porat
November 2005

GLOBAL LIBERALISM, LOCAL POPULISM

I

Introduction

THE CONFLICTS IN ISRAEL and Northern Ireland have oscillated since the mid-1980s between moments of hope, when peace seemed at hand, and (longer) moments of despair when impasses have turned into political deadlocks or new cycles of bloodshed. In Israel/Palestine, the optimism that followed the signing of the Oslo Accords in September 1993 did not last long. Israelis and Palestinians soon found themselves enmeshed in unprecedented levels of violence, including the murder of an Israeli prime minister by an Israeli zealot. In 2005, after three elections ousted Israeli governments with different agendas and even following Israel's unilateral withdrawal from Gaza, no resolution seems at hand. In Northern Ireland, the long road to the Good Friday Agreement of 1998 was paved with moments of both hope and despair—and these moments have continued since the signing of the agreement. Peace has proven illusive as questions of IRA decommissioning, Unionist intransigence, gangsterism, political reform, and continuing violence have left the peace process in an uneasy limbo.

Negotiating peace out of what are seemingly intractable territorial conflicts is never an easy task. All sides to the conflict have to compromise territorial claims, accept security risks, and contend with extremists ready to stir public fears and animosities. Yet those interested in understanding the pendulum swings of peace processes must pay attention not only to internal dynamics and external negotiations but also to the global context in which peace processes unfold and the specific interaction between global and local developments that spells opportunities and incentives for both peace and paralysis.

This book presents a comparative and multilevel explanation for the trajectories of the peace processes in Israel/Palestine and Northern Ireland. These trajectories are explored in two critical periods, early globalization (1870s–1914) and contemporary globalization (from the 1970s), in which, respectively, conflicts were crystallized and peace initiated. An in-depth analysis of each period is undertaken, both at the international level regarding the process of globalization and at the national level, where globalization's more local effects on the social structures, institutions, political divisions, and agencies are expressed. Globalization is key not only to understanding motivations for initiating peace processes but also to coming to terms with the backlash that such processes engender and, consequently, the pendulum swings of the processes. As globalization affects localized social structures, institutions, and political divisions, as well as international relationships between states and societies, it offers a unique point of departure from which to examine not only the commonalties but also the differences between two peace processes that emerged at the same time, drew on global resources, but took different trajectories and reached different outcomes.

Intractable national conflicts are often the result of competing claims for exclusive rights over a certain territory. Therefore, if territoriality is the source of zero-sum intractable conflicts (Agnew 1989) the "unbundling of territoriality" (Ruggie 1993) associated with globalization could be the *deus ex machina* that resolves them. Globalization, in other words, could offer the new economic incentives and political institutions that would change the priorities of those involved in intractable territorial conflicts and incline them toward compromise. Optimism (or pessimism) regarding globalization's consequences depends, of course, on perceptions of what globalization actually means. For some authors, globalization is a clement end of the nation-state in favor of a "borderless world" where the supposedly pacifying logic of markets reigns, but for others it signifies a global crisis manifested in local outbursts of violence and the intensification of conflicts within and between states.

The point of departure for this study, based on Arrighi's work (1994), is the premise that globalization is a systemic change and a transformation of the world system through a "hegemonic crisis." The understanding of this process and its consequences requires attention to its differential effects as well as a broad historical and comparative perspective. While globalization entails an overarching macro-change in the "architecture" of politics and in the organization of social space, it does not "pound everything in the same mold" (Mittelman 2000, 7). The consequences of contemporary global interactions are complex, diverse, and unpredictable and need to be studied in relation to micro, "local" structures and political agency.

Globalization's influence, in other words, is the result of specific interactions between the global and the local. In this respect, globalization is akin to the process of structuration (Giddens 1981) insofar as it is a product of both the individual actions of and the cumulative interactions among countless agencies and institutions across the globe. Globalization, by this definition, structures the field of local politics but is itself shaped (unevenly) by local actions and strategies. It is an evolving structure that both imposes constraints on, and empowers, communities, states, and social forces (Held et al 1999, 27).

Contemporary peace processes are implicated in the dynamics of globalization described above, as they involve complex global-local interactions. Robert Putnam suggested the use of two-level games to solve the theoretical void regarding the relation between domestic politics and international relations in the research tradition of international negotiations. One game is held at the national level between domestic groups and the government, the second is held at the international level between governments that seek to maximize their own ability to satisfy domestic pressures while minimizing the adverse consequences of foreign developments. Both games must be taken into account by decision-makers as long as their countries remain interdependent yet sovereign (Putnam 1988). In periods of globalization, however, politics seem to operate on multiple levels rather than on two. The uncertainty of social space translates into a complex matrix of politics involving governments, business organizations, ethnic and national groups, and international organizations and institutions (Cerny 1997).

The resolution of protracted conflicts is a complex process that must contend with various issues of present, past, and future engaged with grievances, trust and mistrust, security concerns, redistribution of resources and, above all, must provide a formula for transforming the conflict by creating a political framework enabling coexistence and fostering reconciliation. Globalization offers a new economic logic and political structure that is at the core of both the incentives for compromise that sets peace processes in motion and the discontent that undermines peace. It is the specific interactions between global changes and local conflicts that this book seeks to explore.

Israel and Northern Ireland—Unresolved Conflicts?

The partitioning of Ireland and Palestine in the twilight of the British Empire was the pretext for the protracted conflicts that developed in Israel/Palestine and Northern Ireland. The two territorial struggles shared the features of protracted conflicts, being long-term and ongoing and permeating all aspects of society. The apparent total lack of concern the parties had for each other and their zero-sum dynamics rendered them impervious to conventional methods of conflict resolution (Starr 1999). In both cases the asymmetry of power between the powerful group controlling the territory and the weaker group denied recognition and a greater share of power within the same territory created structural conditions that defined the complex nature of the conflict (Rothstein 1999, 6–7). Like other protracted ethnonational conflicts, both extend beyond a specific issue that corresponds to a simple solution and involve not only material interests but also issues of identity and culture.

The similarities led several students of national conflicts in the past to compare the history of these two conflicts, their dynamics, and the attempts to resolve them (Akenson 1992; Giliomee and Gagiamo 1990; Guelke 1988; Knox and Hughes 1995; Lustik 1993). Both conflicts crystallized in what is defined here as the early period of globalization with the development of Jewish nationalism in Europe and the overlap of Irish nationalism with Catholicism, and the development of their counternationalisms, namely Palestinian and Ulster-Protestant. The partitions executed in both cases were at most short-term solutions; each created a large minority whose members consider themselves a majority frustrated by boundaries unjustly and arbitrarily drawn. Thus, Catholics and Palestinians perceive themselves as cut off from, respectively, Ireland and the Arab world (Giliomee 1990).

Israel and Britain poured tremendous resources into the contested territories in order to make their presence into an undisputed fact through settlement. But, despite the efforts to erase the distinction between the core territories and the annexed land, control of the latter remained highly contested and divisive in both Israeli and British politics (Lustik 1993). Neither an internal solution nor an externally imposed solution could satisfy the announced principles of the main disputants (Crick 1990), and because repartition was deemed impossible for Northern Ireland and at best a partial solution for Israel and the Palestinians, the conventional framework of international relations diplomacy, based on mutual recognition, was ill-suited to the task of finding a resolution (Giliomee 1990) so that the conflicts were deemed intractable.

The two conflicts were globalized in terms of political implications beyond their immediate settings. They not only were waged on the local level, between two national communities, but involved wider circles to different degrees and at different periods. Regionally, the Northern Ireland conflict involved Britain and the Irish Republic, while the Israeli-Palestinian conflict was embedded in a wider Israeli-Arab, Middle East conflict. Internationally, both Irish and Jewish communities abroad, especially in the United States, became involved in the two conflicts in the form of either either through economic support or political activity, lobbying government to support their side in the disputed homeland.

The changes of the international setting in the early 1990s had significant implications for the two regions. The end of the cold war, according to some authors, strategically influenced both conflicts, so that each, in this period, entered a new stage of negotiations and agreements into which the United States and other international actors were drawn (M. Cox 1998). But it was wider changes associated with globalization that influenced the perceptions of intractability and created new incentives and opportunities for peace. The visions of peace in Israel and Northern Ireland that emerged in the early 1990s associated conflict resolution with global integration. These ideas were adopted by businesspeople, political elites, and large parts of the middle class, who no longer saw the conflicts as intractable.

Despite the similarities in their historical development and in the changes associated with the contemporary global setting that justify the comparison, the two conflicts were different in several important dimensions that explain their different outcomes. First, the relations between Jews and Palestinians in Israel and Protestants and Catholics in Northern Ireland were differently structured. The Palestinians who remained in Israel after 1948 were granted formal citizenship but those in the territories occupied by Israel in 1967 were not, instead being placed under military control. In Northern Ireland the Catholics received formal citizenship but were discriminated against and politically marginalized, a status resembling that of the Palestinian citizens of Israel. Second, because of the differences in political status, Catholics and Protestants have had more opportunities to interact with each other on an equal level than have noncitizen Palestinians and Israelis in the contested territories encountering each other under terms of military occupation. Third, Northern Ireland's regional setting within the European Union and the third-party involvement of the United Kingdom and the Irish Republic had no parallel in the Israeli-Palestinian conflict.

The structural differences between the two conflicts have had important implications for the resources available and, as a result, for the resolutions suggested for ending the conflicts. The Good Friday Agreement in Northern Ireland was a complex power-sharing model between Protestants and Catholics intended to allow both sides to express their national identity while at the same time building joint institutions that would foster cooperation. The peace process between Israel and the Palestinians, despite rhetoric extolling the globalized "New Middle East," quickly shifted toward an attempted partition that would have created two separate states. When the differences between the sides prevented an agreed partition, violence was renewed and the peace process was replaced by Israeli unilateral partition initiatives.

Globalization(s) in Context

The more skeptical accounts of contemporary globalization point to the fact that much of it is not unprecedented (Hirst 2000; Hirst and Thompson 1999; Wade 1996). Indeed, cross-border flows of trade, investment, labor, and culture occurred in the late nineteenth century in levels comparable to those of the late twentieth. The turn of both centuries was characterized by significant shifts in the perceptions of time and space that followed technological and organizational innovations. Communication dramatically improved in the earlier period with the spread of telegraph lines, transborder telephone communication and radio communications, and in the second period with cellular communication and the Internet. Markets became global in both periods with the development of some systemic transworld distribution, pricing, promotion, and sale of certain commodities. Also, global organizations including market actors, regulatory agencies, and various civil society bodies were formed. Finally, because of all these developments, global thinking was applied to more contexts and to wider circles, including political discourse and imagery (Scholte 2000, 65–72; Maguire 1999; O'Rourke and Williamson 1999).

The comparable patterns between the late nineteenth century and the late twentieth can be explained, using Arrighi's model, by a hegemonic leadership crisis that occurred in each (Arrighi 1994; Arrighi and Silver 1999). Several scholars use the concept of hegemony in different ways to describe the leading and organizing power of a world system able to provide the international public goods of stability and cooperation (R. Cox 1983; Gilpin 1981; Rapkin 1990). In two seminal studies using the concept, Charles Kindelberger (1973) explained the Great Depression as a result of the lack of leadership and Robert Gilpin (1981) compared the U.S. case of hegemony with its nineteenth-century British antecedent. International hegemony, according to this argument, provides stability and decreases both the risks and the costs of international trade. Conversely, the decline of hegemonic power makes international trade more expensive if not impossible. The substantial literature that followed these works has made international hegemony into a common yet contested concept (Rapkin 1990).

World hegemony, as used in this work, is not simply about dominance but also about the capacity of the leader to transform the system by providing system-level solutions to system-level problems and to lead the system in the direction of new forms of interstate cooperation and division of labor (Arrighi and Silver 1999, 28). Hegemony, using Gramsci's definition, is a leadership based not upon coercion but upon the ability of the dominant group to present itself as the leading power. It is "the additional power that accrues to a dominant group by its virtue of capacity to lead society in a direction that not only serves the dominant group's interest, but is also perceived by subordinate groups as serving a more general interest" (Arrighi and Silver 1999, 26). In worldwide, international terms, the formation and expansion of the world system proceeds not along a single track but through several "switches" to new tracks laid by changing hegemonic powers. The hegemonic state exercises a hegemonic function if it leads the system of states in a desired direction and, in so doing, is perceived as pursuing a general interest (Arrighi 1994).

Hegemonic crisis sets in when the hegemonic power loses its competitive edge after it is emulated by competing powers and the competition among the system's units expands beyond the regulatory capacity of existing institutions. The difficulties of the declining hegemon are not necessarily in securing formal agreements with allies but in maintaining the cohesion of the system itself (Cafruny 1990). When the systemic organization that was put in place by the declining hegemonic power disintegrates, a systemic chaos sets in (Arrighi and Silver 1999, 33). Hegemonic crises are characterized by the intensification of interstate and interenterprise competition, by the escalation of social conflicts, and the emergence of new configurations of power. The chaos is resolved when a new hegemonic power, with new solutions for systemic problems, emerges to lay new tracks for leading the system in a direction it designates.

Globalizations Compared

The two periods compared in this study are similar in the hegemonic crisis that occurred in each but differ in both the dynamics of their preceding hegemony and in the nature of the crises. The British hegemony laid tracks for a world order based upon "free-trade imperialism" and the empowerment of nation-states. The system that Britain dominated provided a hundred years of peace that rested on the balance of power, the gold standard, and laissez faire (Polanyi 1957). The crisis of British hegemony began with the Great Depression of 1873–96, during which great power rivalries intensified and a system-wide financial expansion took off. Between the Great Depression and World War I, the marker of the system's final breakdown, interstate relations took the form of fierce competition over territory, imperialism, and a shift from free trade to protectionism. Overall, this period was characterized by contradictions between the global flows—economic, cultural, and political—that reached unprecedented levels and the powerful urge to organize social life in terms of sharp boundaries, national identities, and essentialist cultural categories. The manifestations of the latter were, among others, the rise of modern anti-Semitism, demand for immigration control, and a proliferation of national movements (Calhoun 1997).

The hegemonic order exercised by the United States differed significantly from Britain's laissez-faire hegemony. Leading the Bretton Woods negotiations, the United States explicitly opposed a return to the open, liberal financial order that existed before 1931 and endorsed the use of capital controls to prevent its return. These initiatives described as "embedded liberalism" were designed to protect the new interventionist welfare state and to support the American geopolitical concerns of the early cold war. The transformation of this world hegemony, namely the current period of globalization, is a reversal of the former not only in fostering liberalization rather than protectionism, but also in its mode of deterritorialization rather than territorial expansion. The rise of non-territorial forms of power—multinational firms, offshore economic spaces, or macro-regional blocs—all beyond the control of states, challenge the territoriality of the nation-state. States have largely responded to this challenge by adjusting to what they perceive as a new reality, opening their borders and becoming "competitive" (Cerny 1995).

The decline of the American hegemony is debatable, unlike that of the British, because the United States retains its status as a leading world power. Some regard the globalization of the world economy as a sign of a hegemonic crisis and the relocation of power; others, however, contend that the United States' economy is stronger than ever before (Zuckerman 1998; Krugman 1998). The question of whether the United States is in decline, remains safely in the lead, or carries the potential to renew its power by establishing a new hegemonic order is beyond the scope of this work. My point is that the current period of globalization is the end of the hegemonic order of embedded liberalism set by the United States after World War II and that this change profoundly affects world politics and especially the political construction of space that pertains to the peace processes discussed in this work.

The two hegemonies differed not only in their dynamics of operation but also, and more importantly for this work, in the dynamics of their breakdown and of the globalizations that followed. The two periods of globalization were the contexts in which the Israel/Palestine and Northern Ireland conflicts unfolded: crystallization in the early period of globalization and a turbulent peace process in the second. The decline of British hegemony in the late nineteenth century, when the two conflicts crystallized, was accompanied by a worldwide territorial struggle in which national political elites cooperated with their business elites against their common rivals through territorial expansion. This was the context in which Irish and Jewish-Zionist national identities were formed and encountered their respective Protestant and Palestinian rivals in what would turn into protracted conflicts.

Conversely, with the decline of American-led embedded liberalism in the late twentieth century, the significance of territory came into dispute. For business elites and their allies, territory (or territorial sovereignty) became secondary and at times at odds with economic development and global opportunities. But for significant sectors of society, sovereignty and territorial boundaries remained central to their identity and to a security undermined by globalization. The dynamics of the peace processes under discussion are embedded in the contemporary struggle between *deterritorialization* and *reterritorialization*.

Contemporary Globalization—Agency and Opposition

Agency and political opportunity are significant for understanding not only the evolution of globalization but also the prospects it entails for political agents. The process by which markets are disembedded and borders opened is not the inevitable result of technological changes but the outcome of political actions and decision-making processes. The decisions of most advanced industrial states to disembed markets and to roll back the state were influenced and supported by the dissemination of neoliberal ideas that have made the market economy the optimal solution for society's problems and, consequently, legitimized policies of downsizing and globalizing.

Some scholars have pointed to the emergence and empowerment of a "transnational class" that was both a promoter of the globalization and its main beneficiary. Spread across the globe, this class pursues the project of opening the world, and its respective home states, to global flows and sets an economic neoliberal agenda as a standard (Gill 1990; Sklair 1995). Members of this class are characterized by an "outward perception" regarding their interests and/or the interests of their countries of citizenship, as best served by identification with the interests of the capitalist global system and hold transnational practices to be more valuable than local practices. This class, because of its perceptions, interests, and accrued political power, played a part in the attempts to resolve territorial conflicts in the cases examined here and elsewhere.

Globalization endows the transnational class with significant political leverage but, at the same time, breeds the discontent that undermines its position. The various sources of discontent across the globe raise doubts as to whether this class has achieved the hegemonic position that some researchers suggest. Globalization is not only associated with economic growth and efficiency but also with the deep fault lines exposed between groups who have the skills and mobility to flourish in global markets and those that do not. Inequality between and within nations is growing, the power of labor is undermined, the ability of governments to use compensatory welfare measures is weakened and, consequently, discontent is growing (Devetak and Higgot 1999; Tilly 1995; Sassen 1998; Rodrik 1997).

The sources and motivations of antiglobalization movements are diverse and at times contradictory, as right-wing nationalists and left-wing socialists both react against the dangers they perceive in the process for, respectively, the nation-state and the working class. Karl Polanyi's phrase *double movement*, coined in the 1940s to explain the collapse of the nineteenth-century liberal order, captures well the forces and counterforces of the process of globalization (1957). The creation of a market society based on the disembedding of markets is counteracted by society's protective measures and demands to decommodify the social-economic order. In the context of the contemporary globalization, Polanyi's description of the double movement allows us to come to terms with, on the one hand, the powerful thrust of the neoliberal order associated with globalization and, on the other hand, with the wide discontent and resistance it evokes.

The wedge between groups that flourish in the liberal world order and those who are its victims has important social and political ramifications. For those able to integrate globally and take advantage of global flows, the state is becoming less significant to their success—possibly at times even a burden. But most citizens are still wedded to place and depend upon the state ensuring social justice and protection. The backlash against globalization, as this work will demonstrate, includes not only a demand for decommodification, as Polanyi suggests, but also demands for movement toward reterritorialization and renationalization that oppose territorial compromise and undermine peace processes.

Peace Dividends

Expanding economic ties, goes the liberal argument, will cement the bonds of friendship among and within nations, reducing the likelihood of armed conflict (Barbieri and Schneider 1999). The idea that economic incentives such as trade can become potent forces for peace is an old one. Already at the end of the eighteenth century, the beneficial impact of trade was a crucial element in Immanuel Kant's "perpetual peace." "The spirit of commerce, which is incompatible with war, sooner or later gains the upper hand in every state. As the power of money is perhaps the most dependable of all the powers (means) included under the state power, states see themselves forced, without any moral urge, to promote honorable peace and by mediation to prevent war wherever it threatens to break out" (Kant [1795] 1957, 32).

Later, the pacifying potential of trade was used by international relations scholars of the liberal school begun in the 1970s in critiques of the realist paradigm; they used the term *interdependence* to describe reciprocal, though often asymmetric, political, military, and economic relations among states. Scholars of interdependence have used game-theory methods to examine and suggest payoff matrices under which nations would choose to cooperate even under conditions of international anarchy (Oye 1978; Jervis 1978). According to this theory, when complex interdependence prevails, governments are less likely to employ military force, preferring cooperation between states. This applies particularly to the group of industrialized, pluralist countries that are less concerned about security and who do not see the use of force as an appropriate way of achieving other goals (Keohane and Nye 1977).

The end of the cold war caused a proliferation of studies of peace processes and of conflict resolution methods based on the belief that the potential for peace between the major states had grown (Vasquez 1995). Scholars examined the ability of international institutions and powers to pacify conflicts between minor states by the use of threats and incentives to warring factions (Cortright 1997; Crumm 1995; Solingen 1995). A major inducement for peace, they argued, could be allowing access to the emerging system of political cooperation and economic development among the major states (Cortright 1997, 269). Paul Schroeder described this process, a part of the new world order, as "association-exclusion": that is, international associations "combining the carrot of actual or potential membership with its attendant benefits with the stick of exclusion from the association with the attendant penalties and denial benefits" (1994, 32). The scholarship dealing with peace incentives deliberated over cost-benefit analysis; constructed typologies of the nature of incentives, timing, senders, objectives, and recipients; and examined how incentives can be tailored to increase their value for target states (Crumm 1995). The most powerful incentive has become, according to Cortright, access to the zone of relatively prosperous democratic peace that stretches from Japan and Australia to North America and through much of Europe (Cortright 1997).

The use of the term *peace dividends* became common at the end of the cold war. Studies using the concept examined the effects of "unproductive" defense spending on core economies and the dividends that can be received when a conflict like the cold war ends (O'Hearn 2000; Chan 1995). With a reduced security threat, there is a possibility of "economic conversion," the redirecting of human and capital resources from military—to civilian-oriented activity in order to foster economic renewal (Dumas 1995). Peace dividends are portrayed in win-win terms; namely, that whole regions across communities would benefit from the global integration that follows the end of conflicts (O'Hearn 2000). For example, in local conflicts not directly at the center like Northern Ireland and Israel, core and regional powers can devise peace initiatives that include promises for economic regeneration or growth based on substantial direct aid, investments and regional or global integration.

Most of the studies referenced above considered international organizations and governments using their influence over conflicting parties but paid little attention to internal political dynamics and the varying local reactions to the supposed benefits of globalization and peace. But their attempt to portray peace and globalization as a win-win solution rests on two problematic assumptions: first, that peace benefits are universally available and, second, that they are universally desirable. The first assumption ignores the unequal effects of globalization: the peace dividends associated with globalization can provide incentives to some groups but leave others indifferent or even hostile. The second assumption ignores the possibility that some groups object to the peace agreement proposed on ideological grounds and will oppose any concessions regardless of the economic consequences.

Globalization, Peace, and Discontent

The pacifying potential of dividends related to globalization is portrayed as a virtuous cycle in which peace and economic development cross-pollinate each other. Initial advances toward resolution of a conflict enhance business confidence, foster global integration, and generate economic growth. Economic betterment, or peace dividends, on the behalf of the opposing parties supposedly widens their support for peace moves and facilitates territorial compromises. Indeed, the incentives associated with globalization, promised or real, can help set the peace process in motion but, especially if they are unevenly distributed, might not be enough to bring the conflict to resolution. Peace is a long-term process in which progress is often retarded by disputes and whose outcomes depend on the ability to keep the parties on track and to prevent spoilers from derailing the process.

A successful peace process entails not only an end to violence but also the construction of institutions and support structures that discourage the parties from taking up arms again (Hampson 1996). This requires the parties involved to go beyond conflict management that minimizes violence and transform the conflict from zero-sum to cooperation, recognition and reconciliation. Protracted conflicts are transformed by changes in attitude toward the "enemy," mutual confidence building, mutual security, and a dialogue that will stimulate the wish to settle the conflict. Even when settlements are reached, they are in danger of collapsing if new life is not breathed into them by the will of the parties, their constituencies, and external supporters to make them work. This is especially true if the euphoria that often accompanies the early stages of settlement, with promises of material betterment, turns to disillusionment when expectations, realistic or not, evaporate (Crocker and Hampson 1996; Miall, Ramsbotham, and Woodhouse 1999, 183–84).

In his study of the effects of trade on domestic coalitions, Rogowski (1989) demonstrated that changes in the exposure to trade affects a nation's internal cleavages. Beneficiaries of economic change associated with international trade organize and act politically to continue and accelerate it, while the victims of the same change will endeavor to retard or halt it. Potential or real peace dividends could have similar effects on the making of coalitions. On the one hand, those who seek to exploit the new opportunities created by a liberalizing economy and society are expected to actively support peace (O'Hearn 2000; Shafir 1998; Shafir and Peled 2000). On the other hand, those who feel threatened or set at a disadvantage could embrace local identities and attachments that they see as the only means to obtain status and social justice (Clark 1997). Global-ization, therefore, underscores virtuous cycles of peace but simultaneously breeds the discontent that threatens to undermine them.

Stephen Stedman (1997) uses the term *spoilers* to describe leaders and par-ties who believe that peace emerging from negotiations threatens their power, worldviews, or interests and who use violence to derail it. He argues that peace is bound to create spoilers, either because a negotiated peace has losers or be-cause it rarely satisfies the demands of all parties and factions. Overcoming the challenge that spoilers pose to peace process depends not only on the role played by international actors as "custodians of peace" (Stedman 1997, 6) and on the ability to address the distribution of peace dividends to those who have influence over the recipient government's decision (Long 1996), but also on making the benefits of peace, both material and nonmaterial, available to the public at large so that spoilers will be marginalized by a wide coalition and their violent actions, rather than derailing the process, will be perceived as illegiti-mate by all parties to the process.

The actual implementation of peace settlements demonstrates the limita-tions of economic incentives on the one hand, and on the other, the signifi-cance of the "political"—the interaction between the macro-process and regional and local structures and actors that translate these incentives into more or less stable peace processes. Resistance and support for peace settle-ments cannot be reduced to material considerations. Rather, the argument de-veloped here is that the attempt of political elites to "market" peace as economic betterment ignores both the ideational aspects of territorial com-promise and the unequal distribution of peace dividends associated with glob-alization. The combined projects of globalization, liberalization, and peace are as contradictory as they are complementary. When the great expectations cre-ated by the promise of peace dividends are not fulfilled, or, worse, are fulfilled only for some, the political process might backfire, provoking a view of peace as a particularistic and elite project rather than as a universal interest.

Organization of the Book

In explaining the developments in the Israeli-Palestinian and Northern Irish conflicts in relation to the macro-global developments described above, this work is not designed to provide a historical narrative that spans a hundred years of conflict. Rather, it is intended to make two periodical incursions into critical and formative periods in order to demonstrate how conflict was consolidated and potential resolution emerged, respectively, in the two ages of globalization. An examination of two case studies in the context of these two historical periods offers a framework for threefold comparison. It provides, first, a theoretical-historical comparison between two periods of globalization; second, a historical political comparison within each region across two periods; and, third, a political-sociological comparison of two regions in conflict.

This theoretical framework and the research of the case studies should provide answers to the following questions. First, how did the developments in the period of early globalization, with its territorializing drive, influence the crystallization of Jewish, Palestinian, and Irish national movements? Second, how have the deterritorializing developments in the current period of globalization, by creating new incentives, influenced the resolution of the conflicts? Third, what explains the specific trajectories (namely partition and power-sharing) of the peace processes? Fourth, how does the tension between the forces of deterritorialization and reterritorialization explain the discontent and the impasses the two peace processes face? And, fifth, what different local circumstances and local-global interactions explain the relatively greater difficulties confronting the Israeli-Palestinian peace process?

The two periods of globalization studied in this book provide a framework for understanding, first, the formation the two conflicts in the late nineteenth century and, second, the development of peace processes in the late twentieth century. The purpose of this work, as mentioned above, is to explain not only the relationship between globalization and peace but also the different outcomes of two particular peace processes—the result of specific interaction between globalization and local structures and actions. The first part of the book reviews the earlier period of globalization and the crystallization of the two conflicts. Chapter 2 provides a theoretical-historical framework for the decline of the British hegemony (and the rise of nationalism and territorial struggle) and sets the context for the next two chapters. Chapter 3 examines the development of Zionism and of the Zionist-Palestinian conflict in relation to the global changes described above. Similarly, chapter 4 looks at the crystallization of national identities in Ireland and the emergence of the conflict between Catholics and Protestants. This part of the book is concluded in chapter 5, with a discussion of the partitions—the imposed solution on both regions—that set the conflicts for their next stage.

The second part of the book examines the new opportunities for peace associated with globalization and compares the two peace processes. This part is based on a combination of primary and secondary materials. Primary materials include archival research, review of media reports, and a series of open interviews with leading businesspeople in Israel and Northern Ireland who were involved in the peace process. The purpose of these interviews was to identify the perceptions of businesspeople, to assess their involvement in the peace process, and to gain a general picture of the business community's role in promoting peace. Chapter 6, the opening chapter of this part, provides a theoretical-historical framework for the decline of the American hegemonic order of embedded liberalism and asks what new incentives and disincentives for peace emerged. Chapter 7 examines the development of the Israeli-Palestinian peace process and its impasses. It looks at the formation of a peace coalition in Israel and the emergence of the idea of the "New Middle East" and its failure to engage the Arab world, the Palestinians, and wide sectors within Israel. Chapter 8 looks at developments in Northern Ireland and explains why, despite its own impasses, the peace process in Northern Ireland was more successful than that in Israel.

The dynamics established in the early stages of the two peace processes—power-sharing and reduced violence in Northern Ireland and partition and cycles of violence in Israel/Palestine—and the general instability underscore their recent developments. The concluding chapter will follow the trajectories of the two cases discussed in the previous chapters and will focus on the relationship between the later developments and the early dynamics. Looking closely at the differences between the relatively successful peace process in Northern Ireland and the collapse of the Israeli-Palestinian peace process, it will draw lessons and policy implications from the two case studies examined on the terms under which the incentives associated with globalization can be translated into building blocks of peace.

PART ONE

Early Globalization
and National Formation

2

Globalization and Territorialization

> To open to civilization the only area which it has not yet penetrated, to
> pierce the gloom which hangs over entire races, constitutes, if I may dare to
> put it this way, a crusade worthy of this century of progress.
> —King Leopold of Belgium

IN THE LATE NINETEENTH CENTURY, territory became an epicenter of political life and geopolitics began to define the national interest, first in terms of territorial consolidation and second in territorial expansion. At the same time, however, the world was also "globalized." The stretch of European power across the globe was as much about growing interconnectedness as it was about intensified interstate competition. Global trade and investment soared, transatlantic migrations peaked, and culture and technological innovations diffused across boundaries.

The contradictory trends of pacifying global flows and aggressive territorial expansion and consolidation both relate to the overarching development of this period—the decline of British hegemony. These contradictory developments had important implications for our case studies presented in the following chapters. Both of the national movements discussed below, Irish and Zionist (and their protagonists), were influenced by the opportunities and constraints this period provided and by a zeitgeist in which freedom became associated with or dependent upon national consolidation and territorial sovereignty. But first, let us turn to the theoretical-historical framework explaining the context in which these national movements have developed.

From "Peaceful" Imperialism to Imperialist Struggle

Political conditions in the mid 1800s, when the British hegemony was at its peak, were generally unfavorable to imperialism and discouraged states' territorial expansion. Territorial expansions in this period were usually motivated by private business initiatives, were rarely checked by competing interests, and, therefore, usually did not require government interventions. Britain, with its military dominance and laissez-faire ethos, facilitated an international trade regime that was relatively free, which came to be known as "free-trade imperialism." Britain itself was generally reluctant to formally annex new colonies, believing those would have little, if any, economic value. Similarly, other European powers showed little enthusiasm for expansion. The addition of territories was almost entirely unplanned by European states and was largely a result of the general impact of European industrialization and the local power and interests of the existing "European nuclei" (Fieldhouse 1982, 180).

The relative indifference of European states to territorial expansion, however, did not interfere with the process as European empires continued to grow during the period and added about 6.5 million square miles to their claims between 1800 and 1878 (Fieldhouse 1982, 178). But overall within Europe this was a rather peaceful period, characterized by mild competition among the European powers.

> Annexation was rather selective, regional, lacking an overall pattern: annexation in one place did not necessarily effect the situation elsewhere. Behind it all was the general assumption that areas which no one power chose to annex would remain independent, and that even those that were annexed would remain open to the commercial or other activities of all other countries. This psychology of the "open door" was the precondition of avoiding an international partition. (Fieldhouse 1982, 206)

This atmosphere changed significantly toward the end of the century when territorial expansion became the source of international instability. Territorial expansion between 1883 and 1914 was characterized by growing tension and competition between European powers over territorial possessions. In quantitative measures, the territory added to European powers during that period was not dramatically greater than the previous, 8.6 million square miles compared to 6.5 million (Fieldhouse 1982, 178). But there was increasingly fierce competition for exclusive rights over territories outside of Europe, and the shift to "formal" imperialism became the defining feature of this period during which the world outside Europe and the Americas was formally partitioned into territories ruled by the western powers who sought to extend their exclusive control over new territories. Territorial expansion, therefore, was no longer solely a business interest. The ideas of liberalism and free trade that were an essential part of British hegemony and underscored the belief in mutual benefits were replaced by ideas of "geopolitics" that equated state power with control over territorial space and redefined world politics as the struggle over control of territories across the globe. "To remain a great nation or to become one," explained the French statesman Leon Gambetta, "you must colonize" (Held et al. 1999, 94). Imperialism, therefore, reflected both a nationalist ideology and the ceaseless rivalries between the powers composing the international system of states (Mommsen 1980, 4–5). A variety of economic and strategic incentives can explain each European power's quest for territorial expansion, but it was the overarching crisis of British hegemony and the collapse of the "Pax Britannica" that led European powers to follow their interests unilaterally and, consequently, to the intensification of the interstate and interenterprise competition associated with imperialism.

British Hegemony and World Order

The "Pax Britannica" established toward the end of the eighteenth century provided what the historian Karl Polanyi described as "a phenomenon unheard of in the annals of Western civilization, namely, a hundred years' peace" (Polanyi 1957, 5). Several authors have used the concept of hegemony to describe Britain's provision of the "collective good" of international economic and political stability. The international gold standard, one of the pillars of British hegemony, was, as Gilpin describes, a monetary system whose rules were enforced by Britain upon the world's economies, and in turn provided an effective foundation for the nineteenth-century international and political order.

> The adjustment problem was solved as individual countries adjusted domestic economic activities to a level that maintained the value of their currency relative to gold; the liquidation problem was solved since the production of gold was generally sufficient to meet world demand at the prevailing price in terms of sterling; and the confidence problem was solved because people believed that Great Britain had the power and the will to maintain the prevailing sterling value of gold. (Gilpin 1987, 127)

The leadership exercised by the hegemonic power, as mentioned above, is based not simply on the provision of a public good but on its ability to provide a new direction for the system of states and, in so doing, to be perceived as pursuing a general interest (Arrighi and Silver 1999, 24–26). Thus the British hegemony laid "new tracks" for a world order and provided solutions that addressed system-level problems. After the settlement of the Congress of Vienna of 1815, Britain was both the organizer and the chief beneficiary of a system of universal interdependence in which all successful economies were hooking up to the "British entrepot" (Arrighi and Silver 1999, 63). This system, described as free-trade imperialism, was based on Britain's expansion overseas, on London's becoming the home of *haute finance*—a closely knit body of cosmopolitan financiers—and Britain's unilateral adoption of free-trade practice and ideology. Thus, "by opening their domestic market, British rulers created worldwide networks of dependence on, and allegiance to, the expansion of wealth and power of the United Kingdom. This control over the world market, combined with mastery of the global balance of power and a close relationship of mutual instrumentality with *haute finance,* enabled the United Kingdom to govern the interstate system as effectively as a world empire" (Arrighi 1994, 53–55).

The interstate system the United Kingdom reorganized and went on to govern was novel in several respects. First, a new group of states consisting of national communities of property holders joined the group of dynastic and oligarchic states, and as a result interstate relations began to be governed by collective interests, ambitions, and emotions of national communities. In order to manage the global balance of power more effectively, Britain used the Concert of Europe. Second, Western states expanded into the non-Western world with Britain having the lion's share of this territorial conquest. The recycling of imperial tribute extracted from the colonies into capital invested all over the world enhanced London's comparative advantage as a financial center. And third, this interstate system subjected relations between states to the higher authority of a "metaphysical entity—a world market ruled by its own 'laws,' " Britain being the embodiment of that metaphysical entity (Arrighi 1994, 53–55).

Britain governed the interstate system by providing security and welfare through weilding the political and economic mechanisms of the balance of power and laissez faire. British policy makers perceived the balance of power to be policy rather than system and moved promptly to ensure their control over it (Arrighi and Silver 1999, 58–59). As the "balancer" of the system, Britain took care to counterbalance the emerging powers in Europe by shifting its alliances when necessary. In his seminal account of the balance of power, Hans Morgenthau highlights the British system as a classical example of this system: "Thus it has been said of the outstanding balancer in modern times, Great Britain, that it lets others fight its wars, that it keeps Europe divided in order to dominate the continent, and that the fickleness of its policies is such as to make alliances with Great Britain impossible" (1985, 210). What seems like selfish behavior, however, provides a public good that keeps the system and its members intact. "By making it impossible for any nation or combination of nations to gain predominance over the others, it preserves its own independence as well as the independence of all the other nations, and is thus a most powerful factor in international politics" (Morgenthau 1985, 210).

Between 1820 and 1860, Britain went through major reforms to release its own business enterprises from government influence. The reforms included changes in the banking system, usury laws, poor relief, and most importantly the repeal of the Corn Laws that protected the landed interests and the navigation laws that restricted transportation of goods (Ashworth 1975, 133–35). With the repeal of the Corn Laws in 1948, Britain began its policy of unilateral liberalization of international trade. British policies designed to consolidate its leadership in international commerce and finance pushed for open access to foreign markets rather than special privilege, with the important exception of India. Britain's superiority in industry, transport, and financial organization ensured that the open access to foreign markets it provided strengthened rather than undermined its hegemony.

Nondiscriminatory policies and the government's minimal interference (beyond its initial opening of new markets for trade) were the key to Britain's leading role in organizing world trade and investment (Lipson 1985, 38–40). In earlier periods, during its rise to power in the eighteenth and early nineteenth centuries, Britain did not shy away from endowing its industry with "protection, plunder and protected markets." But once its power was established, protection became a drag on development and its industrialists asked for freedom to trade and new markets rather than protection (Barrat-Brown 1963, 52). Between 1850 and 1870, under the free-trade policy, industrial output in Britain doubled and world trade increased fivefold, with Britain accounting for two-fifths of it (Barrat-Brown 1963, 62). Like the balance of power, free-trade imperialism both empowered Britain and provided a public good:

> By opening up their domestic market British rulers created worldwide networks of dependence on, and allegiance to, the expansion of wealth and power of the United Kingdom. . . . the expansion of the power of British rulers relative to other rulers was presented as the motor force of a general expansion of the wealth of nations. Free trade might undermine the sovereignty of rulers, but it would at the same time expand the wealth of their subjects, or at least of their propertied subjects. (Arrighi 1994, 55)

Britain's power, therefore, rested not only upon its impressive coercive apparatus but also upon its hegemony in the Gramscian sense of the word. It provided leadership by demonstrating its ability to create "orderly progress in organized human affairs" (Imlah 1958, 2). Its coercive apparatus, especially the navy, was used to open the world to trade, providing protection of ocean commerce and surveying and charting the world oceans (M. Doyle 1986, 237–38; Arrighi and Silver 1999, 60), and for security by maintaining the balance of power in Europe. Britain was therefore able to credibly claim that its expansion benefited the whole world, and its ability to keep this argument persuasive and maintain its hegemony was the root cause of the (relatively) long peace between the Congress of Vienna and the First World War.

The Decline of British Hegemony

The depression of the 1870s signaled the beginning of the decline of the Pax Britannica and the consequent change of the structure of world politics. Production and trade in Britain and the world expanded too rapidly for profits to be maintained. Increase of agricultural output in this period flooded world markets and pushed prices down. Because the new and improved production was not matched by the growth of markets for consumer goods, the overall result was a deflationary period with a "cut throat price competition" that reduced both the level of profit and optimism regarding future prospects (Hobsbawm 1989, 36–37). Previous confidence about a future of infinite growth, in Landes's description, "gave way to uncertainty and a sense of agony" (1969, 240).

The depression, on economic measures, may have been less severe than the next depression that would hit the world, yet it had significant effects within Britain and on the structure of world politics. Among Britons, it created a "state of uneasiness and gloom about the prospects of the British economy"; in the wider world, it created a loss of confidence in Britain's leadership that undermined the world order it created. "When the economic sun of inflation once more broke through the prevailing fog, it shone on a very different world . . . Britain ceased to be the 'workshop of the world' and became merely one of its three greatest industrial powers, and in some crucial respects, the weakest of them" (Hobsbawm 1969, 127).

The fierce competition between both firms and nations that followed the depression expressed the loss of faith in open markets and British free-trade order and turned the world economy from a laissez-faire system to a collection of "solid blocs" separated by state frontiers. States began to protect themselves from the social unrest the depression triggered, affirmed their commitment to their populations, and, by so doing, expressed the loss of confidence in the market economy.

> The agrarian crises and the Great Depression of 1873–86 had shaken confidence in economic self-healing. From now onward the typical institution of market economy could usually be introduced only if accompanied by protectionist measures, all the more so because since the late 1870s and early 1880s nations were forming themselves into organized units which were apt to suffer grievously from the dislocations involved in the sudden adjustment to the needs of foreign trade or foreign exchanges. (Polanyi 1957, 213)

European governments pulled away from Britain's laissez-faire world order and responded to internal discontent and popular demands for protection by tariffs and preferential treatment of national economies. This was the basis of Bismarck's famous "iron and rye" coalition uniting the landed aristocracy and the industrialists under a centralized state. The Junker aristocrats were grain exporters who traditionally favored free trade, but when hurt by the fall in the price of grain as a result of imports from Russia and the United States they demanded protection. The industrialists of western Germany, who trailed behind British industry, clamored a long time for protection. Under Bismarck's leadership, the industrialists could join forces with the Junkers and support a new tariff policy. Other countries followed suit and retaliated with their own tariff policies. Austria-Hungary (1876 and 1878), Italy (1878 and 1887), Switzerland (1884, 1891, and 1906), and France (1881) raised tariffs. Only Holland and Britain maintained free-trade policies.

With the rapid industrialization of new competitors, mainly Germany and the United States, Britain gradually lost its competitive edge as the leading industrial power and naval empire, and, consequently, its leadership of the international system. The new powers began in the 1870s to challenge Britain's hegemony and rejected the free-trade imperialism they no longer saw as a public good but as a system operating in favor of Britain. Instead of a universal model of British capitalism, which reigned until the 1870s, three different models for national and international development—British liberal capitalism, U.S. managerial capitalism, and German state-interventionist organized capitalism (Mjost 1990, 25)—competed during this period for world supremacy.

The United States developed a national economy of greater wealth, size, and resources than Britain and pushed south to establish economic and then military presence in Latin America and the Caribbean. This expansion overlapped with Britain's territorial interests, but both governments—thanks to segregated economic interests, the restriction of territorial ambition, and careful diplomacy—were able to avoid conflict. Thus despite the fact that the two countries differed on important issues, each of them was able to assure the other's vital interests in the region (Lipson 1985, 60–61). Between Germany and Britain matters were different. Using its advantage as the latecomer, Germany was able to create new challenges especially to British merchants unused to competition. The industrial growth of Germany turned it, first, from one of the best markets for British manufactures to a self-sufficient industrial country and, second, to a competitor abroad. German merchants entered markets that British merchants had come to look at as a private preserve, and they evoked resentment in Britain because of the allegedly unfair methods they employed (Landes 1969, 328).

The German old regime was modernized into what Michael Mann describes as an "authoritarian national capitalism," changing both domestic and foreign politics.

> Its militarism was deployed domestically—against labor and ethnic minorities, more selectively against others—and geopolitically against rival great powers and foreign capitalists. Its nationalism hastened the regime's drift from liberal conservatism toward a xenophobic sense of community, incorporating concepts of economic interests along the way. Its capitalism had become more repressive, territorial and nationalist than most foreign capitalisms. (Mann 1986, 325)

The German leap forward did not fundamentally change this country's tributary position in the world economy, as it remained behind both Britain and the

United States (Arrighi 1994, 62), but its rise had a deep impact upon world politics. Robinson and Gallagher (1981), discounting the economic motives of British imperialism, may be right in asserting that Britain at this period was more concerned with maintaining the status quo than with expansion,[1] but for Germany this status quo was perceived as a relic of the past and an obstacle for its present development. Germany saw itself as entitled to a share of world power; in Heinrich Von Treitschke's words, it was about Germany becoming a "first rank" state. "Up to the turn of the century Germany has always had too small a share of the spoils in the partition of non-European territories among the powers of Europe, and yet our existence as a state of the first rank is vitally effected by the question whether we can become a power beyond the seas. If not, there remains the appalling prospect of England and Russia dividing the world between them" (quoted in Mommsen 1980, 5).

German attempts to increase their command over world economic resources through territorial expansion, or even their declaration of their intentions and demands, were enough to trigger an escalation of interstate rivalries that further undermined British hegemony. It was not a specific challenge—Britain and Germany were many times able to resolve the disputes—but the general challenge to Britain's imperial position that was important (Joll 1992, 181). By pulling away from the orbit of free-trade imperialism, Germany undermined the general confidence in that system and encouraged other states to follow suit and pull away and eventually undermine this institution.

Not only Britain's industrial supremacy but also its naval supremacy, an essential part of its hegemonic position, was challenged toward the end of the nineteenth century by the European continental powers. Diffused technology enabled other powers to build ships that could challenge British supremacy and, more important, could cut Britain off from the food supplies from abroad it was dependent upon (McNeill 1982). The growth of the arms and naval industries took the shape of a competition between military-industrial complexes, first between the British and the Germans, and then, after 1885, with

---

1. "In the eyes of the real makers of policy, there was obviously a scramble in Africa; but it was hardly for Africa or for the empire for empire's sake. Throughout the partition their over-riding concern was to claim those regions of the continent which seemed vital for security in the Mediterranean and therefore in the world . . . Britain, to sum up the argument, was not trying to build a new empire, but to protect an old one, and was doing so under worsening circumstances, international competition, national upsurges, and loss of faith in the common good of free trade" (Robinson and Gallagher 1981).

French companies that joined in the arms race and the competition of export-ing arms abroad. Government and the private sector joined forces, as a spokesman for the French Schneider-Creusot company explained: "We con-sider ourselves collaborators with the government and we engage in no negoti-ations and follow up no business which has not received its concurrence" (quoted in McNeill 1982, 300–301).

Both Britain and Germany had a hard time financing the armaments race but neither could call a halt to it. The shipbuilding arms race caused the British admiralty, for the first time, to provide the assurances that private firms de-manded to push forward innovations (McNeill 1982, 285). The growth of naval construction continued on an unprecedented scale and was a part of a growing competition between European powers and a struggle over territories outside of Europe. Territorial expansion in pursuit of profitable investments or new markets, as several scholars have noted, was not always beneficial, but much of this cost-benefit analysis could only be made in hindsight. What mattered more to policy makers at the time was the widespread belief that overproduc-tion can be solved by acquiring territories. Under the pressure of the world de-pression, it was difficult to be rational about the relative importance of new markets (Platt 1968).

The increasing interstate competition undermined not only the economic order but also the security order that the British hegemony had established and maintained. New alliances undermined the balance of power, which rested on a combination of economic and political mechanisms and was designed to pre-vent war. In the new atmosphere of interstate competition over territories and economic advantages, alliances were formed not with the purpose of preven-tion of war but to provide the best support for winning a war (Hildebrand 1993). The combination of interstate economic competition with an escalating arms race and a struggle for territorial expansion outside of Europe increased dramatically Britain's costs of protecting its overseas empire. The British at-tempt to secure a (European) public good of a politically stable environment for trade and investment became harder, if not impossible, to sustain once other powers extended their reach outside of Europe and backed their individ-ual merchants in head-to-head competition with the British (Lipson 1985, 42). Rather than rely on the common good of free-trade imperialism for their well-being, European powers began a race to acquire new territories for potential markets and raw materials, and to lend support to their businessmen operating outside of Europe (Polanyi 1957, 217).

Territorial Expansion

By colonizing new territories, European powers hoped to grant their nations' businesses a monopoly position or at least a significant advantage over their competitors. This struggle for national exclusive control over territorial possessions indicated that free-trade imperialism, the British world order, had been deserted (Hobsbawm 1989, 66–67) and that a hegemonic crisis characterized by intensive interstate and interform competition had set in. Africa became the central ground of territorial struggle between European powers for several reasons. First, the Americas and most of Asia were not open to colonial acquisition, the former because of the Monroe Doctrine and the latter because most Asian powers were relatively independent (China and Japan). Second, while economic gains were marginal, strategic interests in Africa helped defend economic interests elsewhere. And third, international prestige and national pride were important motives for the expansion into Africa as the glory of colonies was displayed in popular exhibitions in Europe and North America.

But the scramble over Africa was first and foremost a part of the changing world economy and must be understood within that context. Nobody in the early 1880s could have made reliable predictions for trade and economic prospects in the region (Platt 1968), and this uncertainty, combined with the zero-sum political economy of the time, was enough to motivate the European powers to secure themselves a position in this region. In West Africa and the Congo, the struggle was over concrete economic advantages found within these regions (Hobsbawm 1989, 68–69). The conference in Berlin in 1885, where European "rights" over Africa were debated, has made it clear that imperialism was the new zeitgeist, and not to be imperialist was equal to not being present (Thornton 1959, 62).

While territorial expansion was always a part of British policy, formal imperialism was undoubtedly a step back for Britain. In the territorial competition that emerged, Britain exchanged its informal empire over most of the underdeveloped world for a formal empire over less than a quarter of it and for a higher cost (Hobsbawm 1969, 150). But imperialist expansion was perceived in Britain, in light of the new competition, as "economic necessity," so the old debates over the value of the empire all but ended. The Royal Commission on the Depression of Trade and Industry reported in 1886 that Britain had lost its advantage in production and that the Germans' superior adaptability was putting them ahead in markets in the East. British officials were not easily persuaded by the mere fact of foreign competition to abandon their laissez-faire tradition. But the policy of "fair field and no favor" was threatened by "unfair" pressure by foreign diplomats at Oriental courts on behalf of their nationals and by the closure of international markets by revived protectionism (Platt 1968).

New (and exclusive) territories, therefore, were sought by Britain in order to compensate for tariffs imposed in Europe, and from those that might soon be imposed in the periphery. Lord Salisbury eloquently stated this position:

> If you are being shut out by tariffs from civilized markets of the world, the un-civilized markets are becoming more and more precious to you, and they threaten to be the only field which will offer you a profitable business. At all events they are fields which will offer the most profitable business, and as civilization goes on, as exportation increases, these uncivilized markets would be open to you, if only no foreign power is allowed to come in and interpose its hostile tariffs between you and the benefit for which you look. (quoted in M. Doyle 1986, 274)

Once the late industrialized nations, determined to exploit all available opportunities, began to establish claims for territories and to withdraw from free trade, Britain was bound to change its policies and join the territorial struggle. Ironically, as Platt noted, it was the fact that Britain was bound by her free-trade principles that pushed her imperial expansion. "Unless Britain was prepared to manipulate her tariffs as a bargaining-counter in obtaining fair terms for British trade in the new, protected colonial markets, the alternatives (in the 1880s and 1890s) seemed limited to taking a share in the colonial scramble or losing the markets of the underdeveloped world altogether" (Platt 1968, 126).

For Britain, the drive to maintain control for territories was perceived as defensive in nature, a struggle against its exclusion from spheres previously open to free trade and an attempt to preserve its position in the world rather than extend it. As much as one should be cautious using the term *defensive* for an empire that, despite the challenges, included by 1900 about one-fifth of the world's territory and one-quarter of its population, Britain's policy alternatives were narrowed. Expansion seemed for many policy makers no longer a matter of choice, as Lord Rosebery, the Liberal prime minister, explained in a speech before the Royal Colonial Institute in March 1893: "It is said that our Empire is already large enough and does not need an extension. That could be true if the world were elastic but unfortunately it is not elastic, and we are at the present moment, in the language of mining, in 'pegging out claims for the future.' We have to consider not what we want now, but what we shall want in the future" (Beloff 1987, 40).

With the decline of the Pax Britannica and, consequently, the rise of interstate competition, trade and national security—or power politics and economic motives—could no longer be separated in theory or practice. The new economic competition changed the structure of world politics as a number of developed economies simultaneously felt the need for new markets. Not feeling strong enough to compete in an "open door" policy, partition and exclusive rights over new territories was the logical thing to aim for (Hobsbawm 1989, 66–67). Britain, on its behalf, had to retaliate in order to maintain the advantages it drew from its free-trade regime and to exploit whatever economic advantages it had left. The result was an outward surge of territorial expansion but at the same time an attempt to exploit any potential opportunities left in the old free-trade order.

Globalization

Despite the tensions mentioned and the boundaries drawn, this period was also a period of globalization in terms of extensive flows across boundaries, growing interconnectedness between states, and the formation of international organizations. The growing connection between business and national politics over territorial expansion and consolidation was counteracted by the growing interdependence of the world economy, or its "globalization." Several economic historians have argued that in the late nineteenth century, due to a dramatic expansion of production and commerce, an integrated global economy was achieved, "binding the whole world into something very close to an economic unit" (Ashworth 1975, 219). The globalization of the world was indicated by measures of trade, finance, immigration, and the development of international organizations, all facilitated by technological developments in transport and communication, and all attesting to the growing interconnectedness.

The national industrialization of the leading economies of the period led to a rising demand for raw materials and created a more extensive international trading system. Indicative of the increasingly integrated nature of the world system is the ratio between production and international trade. Trade, despite all the protectionist measures, continued to increase faster than production:

the annual rate of world trade rose by 3.4 percent while production only by 2.1 percent (Pollard 1974, 121–22). The high levels of trade led to a marked convergence in the prices of internationally traded goods and wages, rent and profit rates. The market for key goods began to acquire a global dimension, resulting in country specialization and national production influenced by global competition and subjected to global market discipline (Held et al. 1999, 161–63).

Finance was also globalized. As the leading economies matured, their saving levels exceeded domestic demand for investment, and markets beyond the state boundaries were sought. In many emerging economies, the situation was exactly the opposite: capital being scarce, overseas investment offered, at a higher risk, higher returns than those available domestically (Held et al. 1999, 192–93). The globalization of finance was facilitated by a stable exchange-rate system based on the gold standard formally established in 1878 (Clark 1997, 44). The general worldwide acceptance that the maintenance of exchange stability should be the chief aim of banking policy left Britain in control with the London market setting the pace of the flows of money and trade. "Governments and business circles agreed that they had more to gain than to lose by stabilizing their financial relations with each other, submitting to a common international discipline in monetary policy and not upsetting trade by arbitrary, unilateral actions which must create uncertainty about the future value of mutual debts and credits" (Ashworth 1975, 212).

Immigration rates were high throughout the nineteenth century. With a large surplus of agrarian workers after the industrialization of Europe and the growing demand for workers in the industrializing United States, some 50 million immigrants crossed the oceans between 1850 and 1914, the bulk of them after 1880. These migratory flows were encouraged both by governments in Europe wishing to export their rural poor and by colonial administrations seeking immigration (Held et al. 1999, 292–93).

Finally, another indicator of globalization was the development of new international organizations throughout this period, cutting across boundaries and bringing states together. The universal postal union was formed in Berne in 1874; it handled 144 million letters in 1875 and 2,500 million in 1913. Other international initiatives included an international sanitary convention (Venice 1892) that united the efforts of fourteen countries to stop the import of disease through the Suez Canal; the Dresden Convention (1893), gathered to stamp out cholera in Europe; the Paris Convention (1894) to fight cholera at its countries of origin. In addition, international initiatives were taken to prohibit drug trade (1909 and 1912), to protect labor, handle extradition of criminals, and manage the treatment of POWs; there were economic, scientific, sports, and other conventions (Pollard 1974, 124–26). To all the above we must add the operation of international business forging links across the globe for reasons of technical logic and real costs.

Sports serve as a good example for the ambiguity of this period, being both a national expression and structured globally. Sports provided new expressions of nationalism through the choice or invention of nationally specific sport, but they also served as an arena for international competition (Hobsbawm and Ranger 1983, 300). On the one hand, this was an arena in which nations competed against each other, but, on the other hand, it required international institutions and codes of conduct. Therefore, the establishment of international sports organizations, the growth of competition between national teams, the worldwide acceptance of rules governing specific sport forms, and the establishment of global competitions such as the Olympic Games developed simultaneously and were interdependent (Maguire 1999, 83).

Globalization and Fragmentation

The period between 1870 and 1914 was characterized by the paradox of a world integrating and disintegrating at the same time (Clark 1997, 48). Underlying these two seemingly contradictory processes was the change in the structure of world politics—the declining hegemony of Britain—and the role Britain still fulfilled—its insistence on maintaining a unilateral free-trade policy. The former, discussed above, was related to the rise of new competing powers, the latter to the continuous growth of global flows. Britain throughout this period not only kept its markets open, regardless of many other states' policies of raising tariffs to protect their agriculture and industry, but also avoided adopting a path of systemic economic concentration that might enable it to outcompete its new industrializing rivals. These decisions, to maintain free trade and avoid industrial competition, were not irrational but based on an economic logic. Britain escaped from the depression (1873–96) not by modernization of its economy but by exploiting the remaining opportunities of the system it had created that was now falling apart. British manufacturers lost their competitive edge, and it was now the turn of the financiers to assume leadership and reap profits. Britain made the most of its new stance, compensating for industrial

decline by financial expansion. "The British economy as a whole tended to retreat from industry into trade and finance, where our services reinforced our
actual and future competitors, but made very satisfactory profits. . . . Britain,
we may say, was becoming a parasitic rather than a competitive economy, living
off the remains of world monopoly, the underdeveloped world, her past accu-
mulations of wealth and the advance of her rivals" (Hobsbawm 1969, 151). At
the heart of this period was a beginning of a financial expansion centered on
Britain. Precisely at the time its industrial and imperial supremacy waned,
Britain was benefiting from being the nerve center of world commerce and finance (Arrighi and Silver 1999, 67). Material expansion was switched, due to
decreasing returns, into financial expansion that provided higher returns. With
growing British investments abroad, London became a market for international funds, and Britain grew in importance as banker, moneylender, insurer,
shipper, and wholesaler to the world at large (Cain and Hopkins 1993, 177).
Britain was no longer the workshop of the world in face of the industrialization
of other countries, but its superior command over surplus capital enabled it to
profit from the competition for capital among the new industrializing powers.
Yet this was the twilight of the empire; in a short time these new powers, serv-
iced by Britain, would challenge British naval supremacy and undermine the
balance of power.

What enabled Britain to continue keeping its markets at home open was its
exclusive possession of India, which provided raw materials and was a market
for British products.

> Railroads, steamships and the opening of the Suez Canal in 1869 transformed
> India into a major source of cheap food and raw materials for Europe—tea,
> wheat, oil seeds, cotton, jute—as well as into a remunerative outlet protected
> by administrative action for the products of British capital goods industry
> and for British enterprise. What is more, in the late nineteenth and early
> twentieth centuries the large surplus in the Indian balance of payments be-
> came the pivot of the enlarged reproduction of Britain's world-scale process
> of capital accumulation and of the City's mastery of world finance. (Arrighi
> 1994, 263)

No less important, the possession of India supplied Britain with a surplus of
military labor organized in the British Indian army. The exclusive possession of
India and the Indian surpluses of money and labor endowed Britain with an
exceptional freedom first to convert to free trade and later to maintain it.

In the new structure of the world economy, business enterprises that operated within the domain of a large and diversified territory had better opportunities. Britain's expansionist policy and free-trade policy were two sides of the same coin. The decision to maintain the free flow of goods and capital and the continued and expanded possession of formal empire were widely viewed as the means to ensure Britain the predominance that allowed it to discharge its traditional world role. The geographer Halford Mackinder explained, "Under conditions of universal free trade, the dream of the sixties of the last century, industrial life and empire may be dissociated, but when competing industries seek to monopolise markets by means of customs tariffs, even democracies are compelled to annex empires. In the last two generations . . . the object of vast British annexations has been to support a trade open to all the world" (Gamble 1994, 57).

Empires in rise or decline, as Michael Doyle argues, are neither the inevitable product of competing national interests nor the straightforward sum of the economic interests that they may incorporate (1986, 305). Rather, they are the products of the interests, material and ideal, of the dominant domestic coalition. Doyle himself seems to underplay the role of finance, yet financial interests and actors are central for the understanding of the coexistence of national competition and globalization. Karl Polanyi underscored the role of haute finance, a closely knit body of cosmopolitan financiers who were independent from political powers but closely connected with them, as a force behind the Pax Britannica (1957, 11). Making London their home during this period, their backing of peace was based on economic rationality. A fortune was made in the financing of wars, and minor, short, local wars could be beneficial. But a general war between the great powers could interfere with the monetary foundations of the system.

Haute finance has, therefore, played an ambiguous role reflecting its conflicting interests of serving the system and exploiting it. On the one hand, national rivalries sabotaged long-term investments and therefore were contrary to the interests of finance. On the other hand, there were benefits to be reaped from national aggressiveness: "*Haute finance* just as often was not the victim, but the beneficiary of *dollar diplomacy* which provided the steel ribs to the velvet glove of finance. For business success involved the ruthless use of force against weaker countries, wholesale bribing of backward administrations, and the use of all the underhand means of gaining ends familiar to colonial and semicolonial jungle" (Polanyi 1957, 13). By its pursuit of free-trade policies, Britain was able to become the center of a financial expansion and remain the home of haute finance. But while Britain was able to retain some of its power, with the shift to finance it gradually lost its hegemony and, consequently, the world order it established reached its end. Haute finance could not help avert the decline as capitalists themselves tried to take advantage of both international trade and national competition (Joll 1992, 148) and were torn between being nationalist or cosmopolitan. Essentially they promoted both national aggression and international peace by investments that backed international competition over territories and consolidation of alliances in Europe and attempts to prevent major conflicts in Europe (161). In an international system that changed from peaceful commerce between businessmen to aggressive competition between nations, free-trade imperialism still enabled a profitable globalization of business and politics. But whatever profits were to be made in the short run, the British hegemony exhausted itself. It was one of the great ironies, concludes Kern, that a world war became possible only after the world had become so united (Kern 1983, 234).

Boundaries, Nations, and "Others"

An important political ramification of the competition between states was the strengthening of the relations between the state and its people, making this a competition not only between states but also between nations. The rivalry between European states and the need to mobilize their populations required each to negotiate rights with its subject people in order to strengthen their loyalty. Consequently, state activities were extended to the welfare, culture, and daily routines of ordinary Europeans.

> Government now reached down directly to each citizen on their territory in everyday life, through modest but omnipresent agents, from postmen and policemen to teachers and (in many countries) railway employees. They might require his, and eventually even her, active personal commitment to the state: in fact their "patriotism." Authorities in an increasingly democratic age, who could no longer rely on the social order submitting spontaneously to their social superiors in the traditional manner, or on traditional religion as an effective guarantee of social obedience, needed a way of welding together the state subjects against subversion and dissidence. "The nation" was the new civic religion of states. (Hobsbawm 1989, 149)

Facing social and economic pressure, from external competition and internal discontent, states were more and more concerned with consolidating the relationship between national identity and territorial boundaries. The rising level of literacy and technology facilitated interclass communication and the diffusion of national histories and culture across state boundaries. But the growing nationalism was a process of divergence and tension as much as of convergence. The homogenization of life within the state through the imposition of a national language and education encountered resistance from those who sought to maintain their identity or those who were found to be "unassimilable" but remained part of the state. Because state power was thought to rest on its "organic" unity, those who did not belong were perceived as a threat and therefore, from the state's "point of view," had to be assimilated or excluded.

With the growing political influence of the masses, as Carr argues, not only was the nation socialized but socialism was nationalized. Civil and economic rights became linked to citizenship and national identity, and the nation-state, on the one hand, privileged its members and, on the other hand, competed against or excluded nonmembers. "Nationalism had invaded and conquered the economic domain from which the nineteenth century had so cunningly excluded it. The single world economy was replaced by a multiplicity of national economies, each concerned with the well-being of its own members" (Carr 1945, 22).

In that period in which rival national economies were protecting themselves from each other, politics and economics were inseparable. Rapid economic and territorial expansion was accompanied by the urge to organize social life in terms of sharp boundaries, national identities, and essentialist cultural categories of inclusion and exclusion. As national differences became clearly demarcated, movement across borders was controlled, and a rise of nationalism in the sense of heightened commitment to the state's international strategy, or as a counterreaction of groups to the imposition of nationalism, became a common phenomenon (Tilly 1975, 115–17). Overall, the desire to organize social life in essentialist categories led to a demand for immigration control, a proliferation of national movements, and the rise of modern anti-Semitism (Calhoun 1997).

Nationalism was certainly not a novel phenomenon, but in this period its character changed. E. H. Carr described this nationalism as totalitarian in nature and a result of the combination of three factors: the socialization of the nation, the nationalization of economic policy, and the geographical extension of nationalism (1945, 24–26). Eric Hobsbawm suggested three different major respects in which the nationalism of the late nineteenth century was different from that which had gone before. First, the "threshold principle" was abandoned in favor of the assumption, foreign to the prior liberal phase, that national self-determination was open for all groups claiming to be a nation, and that it could not be satisfied by anything short of full state independence. National movements during this period were established among peoples considered to be "unhistorical" (with no history of independent statehood) and among peoples that previously were not considered to have the potential to become national. Second, ethnicity and language became the central and decisive criteria of potential nationhood. And third, nationalism became an ideology of the political right (Hobsbawm 1990, 102).

Nationalism manifested itself either by the consolidation of a nation within the boundary of the state or by the upsurge of national movements demanding a territorial state based upon a common language, culture, or heritage. The territorial state of the French revolution was the model to emulate, and national groups sought to achieve the nearest thing to complete control over a clearly defined territory and its inhabitants that was available in practice (Hobsbawm 1990, 147). Unlike earlier forms of nationalism that had some prospects of being harmonized within a federated Europe, the new nationalism was based on political and economic separatism, national rivalry, and on popular support (Hayes 1963, 253). National conflicts under these conditions were all but inevitable. First, because national/ethnic and territorial boundaries rarely overlapped, especially after the migrations of the century and before, territorial control became a zero-sum game between would-be nation-states. And second, with the economic depression, scarce resources were another cause of frictions between national groups. The control of territory overseas was both a potential for economic advantage and a symbol of national prestige.

The empowerment of nationalism was a political phenomenon as it had much to do with the development of mass politics and the attempt of regimes to maintain their legitimacy through appeals to national identity and of their competitors to undermine it. Rulers and observers of the late-nineteenth-century politics discovered the "irrational element" in mass politics as political life became obsessed with symbolism, ritual, and identity construction (Hobsbawm 1983). Attempting to cement loyalty by making nationalism a counterweight to all contesting identities, the state found out that this was a double-edged strategy. Nationalism alienated those who did not belong to the nation, and they refused to assimilate if they were not allowed to become full members of the official nation. It also exposed the problem of those who wanted to assimilate but their assimilation was perceived by nationalists as undermining national boundaries. As rising anti-Semitism proved, even middle-class Jews who perceived themselves to be members of the French or German nation discovered they were not perceived as such by others.

The rise of nationalism of this period was reinforced by a "scientific" discussion of nation and race. Theories that conceptualized the state as an organic phenomenon subjected to laws in its territorial growth and development attributed the success of states as dependent on their ability to secure an adequate and suitable *Lebensraum,* or "living space" (Parker 1998, 17). Theories of social Darwinism pushed states to consolidate their boundaries and compete with other states over resources, a competition in which the fit would survive at the expense of the less fit. States became fixated on territoriality, arguing that not growing meant stagnation and decline, as the influential French political economist Leroy-Beaulieu explained:

> Colonization is the expansive force of the nation, its power of reproduction, its dilation and multiplication across space; it is the submission of the universe or of a vast part of it to the language, the manners, the ideas and laws, of the mother country. . . . Either France will become a great African power, or in a century or two she will be no more than a secondary power; she will count for about as much in the world as Greece or Romania. (Kern 1983, 234)

Most European nations acted as if the choice was between expanding toward greatness or falling into mediocrity. Translated into expansionist policies, this had grave implications for non-Europeans. While scientific theories of the nation as an organ depicted the competition between European powers as a struggle between potential equals, their treatment of non-Europeans was based on a racial hierarchy that depicted them as inferior. Racial categories were employed to justify territorial integrity and legitimize exclusion within Europe, but more directly to establish claims over non-European peoples and territory. Non-European peoples, in general, were excluded from the right to self-determination as their territories were open to European competition and were divided between European powers without their consent. The European scramble over and the ruling of African territories, denying their native inhabitants the right to rule themselves, was based on defining Africans as "tribes-men" or "savages" that "happened to occupy specific geographical spaces that they could not legitimately claim as their own" (Grovogui 1996, 87).

James Blaut describes this spatial division of the world into occupied and empty areas as "the diffusionist myth of emptiness" (1993, 15–16). This propo-sition of emptiness made a series of interrelated claims that justified European conquest. First, non-European regions are empty or nearly empty of people, so European settlement does not displace any native people. Second, the region is empty of settled population: the inhabitants are nomadic and mobile and therefore have no sovereignty. Third, the culture of this region does not possess an understanding of private property. And fourth, the region is empty of intel-lectual creativity and spiritual values, so European settlement benefits the region's native inhabitants.

Europeans had been exploiting and conquering territories long before this period, and the perception of European superiority was entrenched by 1870 (Blaut 1993, 22). But in this period, economic pressures and national compe-tition exacerbated the discourse of inferiority/superiority and, more impor-tant, practices of territorial annexation of a different scale. The conquest of territories as a demonstration of national superiority was related to domestic politics, providing the masses with national pride by encouraging the poten-tially discontented to identify with the glory of their nation. International ex-hibitions and military parades in Europe and in the United States proudly presented the "exotic" to the masses, exhibiting what was considered bar-barism in the service of civilization (Hobsbawm 1989, 71). This sense of supe-riority demarcated Europe as a zone of "civilized behavior" and the realm beyond Europe as a zone where no standard of civilization applied. The rights of Western nations to pursue wealth were elevated above the absolute rights of non-Western people and governments (Arrighi 1994, 63). This discourse of possession based on superiority that Edward Said (1979) termed *Orientalism* became practice in the Berlin conference of 1886, which provided the legality to new and past colonial claims by legitimizing all forms of European author-ity in Africa: zones of influence, protectorates, and colonies (Grovogui 1996, 85).

Thus the conquest and division of the world between European powers was legitimated not only by the "necessity" to compete against rivals but also by the perception of non-Europeans as inferior, bolstered by "scientific" theories and the recurring depiction, since the conquest of America, of their lands as "empty" (Connolly 1996).[2] The right of Europeans to rule was based both on their "necessity," derived from the power struggle in Europe, and the belief that natives were unable to rule themselves, rendering imperialism the carrier of progress for the benefit of Europeans and natives alike. Territories outside of Europe became a space of interstate competition that provided the winners with glory, wealth, or both. It was also hoped that these territories would be useful for diminishing discontent in Europe by providing new opportunities and outlets for immigration. The idea that immigration to colonies would provide a safety valve for overpopulated European countries was, as Hobsbawm argues, little more than a fantasy (1989, 69). Yet, as will be discussed below, many in Europe believed (and acted upon that belief) that emigration could solve social tensions and especially could provide a solution for the so-called Jewish problem.

Conclusion

Until the depression of the 1870s, an international order was maintained by Britain's hegemony with a unique combination of economic and political institutions that provided an unprecedented pacific era. The pillars of the system established by Britain, the balancing of power on the one hand and global trade on the other, seemed to benefit all European powers. But from the 1870s, the system was no longer perceived as universally advantageous, and Britain lost its hegemonic stance. As a result, free trade was replaced by protective tariffs, and the alliances of the balance of power system that were designed to prevent war were replaced by alliances whose purpose was to provide the best coalition for winning a war.

Britain's unilateral insistence on free trade enabled global flows and international organizations to coexist until the onset of the first world war when boundaries closed and interstate competition undermined international order. This combination of global flows and intensifying interstate competition had three important ramifications for our study. First, more than before people began to identify themselves with a nation and territory, excluding, demarcat-

2. Tocqueville, for example, explains that "North America was only inhabited by wandering tribes who had not thought of exploiting the natural wealth of the soil. One could still properly call North America an empty continent, a deserted land waiting for inhabitants" (quoted in Connolly 1996, 168).

ing, and encouraging others to do the same thing. Second, the world was perceived as made of "organic" nations competing against each other for survival. And third, as part of that competition the world beyond Europe was perceived as a legitimate field for European nations to expand into. The global dynamics and the nationalist reactions described in this chapter had important effects on our two case studies. The first, Jewish nationalism, was a reaction to the exclusion of Jews from European nationalism. The second, Irish nationalism, was a demand to separate from the British state and establish sovereign territoriality. Interstate competition and rising nationalisms provided powerful incentives for the Irish (Catholic and Protestants) and Jews (and, consequently, Palestinians) to define themselves in national terms with territorial demands. Globalization—flows of capital, people, technology, and ideas—provided the tools to achieve those national desires.

3

The Rise of Zionism

An International Context

THE STUDY OF ZIONISM in relation to colonialism and imperialism has been a part of a wide debate in Israel and elsewhere over the foundations of Zionism. Since the late 1980s, Israeli scholars have been engaged in a heated and politically charged historiographic debate over the history of Zionism that pertains to contemporary questions of territorial rights and justice. The major issue debated is the war of 1948 and its consequences, specifically whether there was a systematic expulsion of Palestinians by the Israeli army. Another important question, somewhat more theoretical, was whether Zionism can be explained as a colonialist project, similar to other encounters between Europeans and natives, or as a unique case that cannot be categorized as colonialist. This controversy, known as the "historian's debate," has been more than academic as, according to several of its participants, it has important contemporary political implications. For revisionist (or "new") historians and scholars, a critique of Zionism is a necessary step for reconciliation with the Palestinians. For mainstream (or "old") historians, the debate undermines the legitimacy of Zionism to a point that some describe it as "collective suicide."

> What we are witnessing is the rewriting of the past hundred years of Zionism, in the spirit of its enemies. . . . all those beautiful phrases we honestly believed in, and were educated by—"redemption of the land," "conquering labor," "merging the exiles," etc.—were hypocritical and deceitful . . . these claims are not new, of course . . . only this time they are iterated by Israeli academics and publicists . . . if this rising tide in our midst, which questions our being here in our historical homeland, which slowly degenerates our body and weakens our hands, will not cease [then] we will not have the strength to face the dangers which threaten our very existence. (Megged 1994, 20)

43

Edward Said, who wrote about Zionism from what he called "the stand-point of its victims," stressed the cultural, discursive, and eventual political semblance between Zionism and colonialism, as both erased the presence of the native. It was this epistemological resemblance, according to Said, that enabled Zionism to establish a powerful position in world politics as it took part in the European expansion into what was described as "uselessly occupied territory" (1979b, 77–78).

Within the Israeli historians' debate, Ran Aharonson (1999) suggested that when engaging with the history of Zionism one should make the analytical distinction between "colonialism" and "colonization." Colonialism is defined by Aharonson as a political and economic phenomenon, which is about a takeover by force of a territory and a population by a state who desires to exploit it for its own purposes. Colonization, on the other hand, is a geographic phenomenon, which is about immigration and settlement in a new territory. Colonialism and colonization can appear together in different combinations, but Jewish settlement in Palestine, he argues, was colonization without colonialism for several reasons. First, in Zionism, unlike colonialist projects, profit motives played little if any part. Second, Zionist settlers were more concerned with distancing themselves from the local population than with exploiting it. And third, unlike most colonialist projects, there was no support of a home country behind Zionist immigration.

Several revisionist Israeli scholars have found the comparative framework of colonialism useful for the study of Zionism. Baruch Kimmerling uses Turner's "frontier theory" to describe the relationship between the Zionist immigrant-settler society and the physical, political, and economic environment that it settled (1983, 5–7). Translating the concept of the frontier into quantitative terms, as the measure of free territory ("frontierity"), the settlement of Palestine is compared to other colonizing efforts. The fact that Jews settled in a land with a very low degree of frontierity, according to Kimmerling, shaped the dynamics of settlement and the relations with Palestinian natives. For example, in contrast to most colonizing projects, until statehood in 1948 Jewish settlers had to purchase the land for increasingly high prices. Gershon Shafir (1989) argues that the development of the conflict between Jewish immigrant settlers and Palestinian inhabitants at the end of the nineteenth century shaped the development of the *yishuv* (the prestate Jewish settlement) and later of Israeli society. Shafir delineates the development of different modes of colonization. Initially a model similar to the French agricultural colonization in Algeria and

Tunisia was pursued, but when this model failed others were attempted. Attempts finally synthesized into a "pure settlement strategy," direct control of the land and a European community that maintains cultural and ethnic homogeneity and separation from the native population.

While drawing on all the above, the purpose of this work is different. Rather than examine whether Zionism was colonialist or not, or attempt a different typology of its colonialist method, I wish to examine, based on the theoretical framework of the previous chapter, what incentives, opportunities, and constraints developed during this period for Jews and Jewish nationalism. It is impossible, I would argue, to understand Zionism outside the international context in which it developed. In "the age of imperialism" and the decline of the Pax Britannica, described in the previous chapter, the position of Jews in Europe was undermined, providing Zionism with ideological material, legitimacy, and motivation.

This chapter therefore is not an historical account of Zionism between 1880 and 1914 but rather an attempt to outline three central influences of international politics on the development of Zionism. First, the consolidation of national identity in Western Europe and political and economic turbulence in Eastern Europe undermined the position of Jews and motivated a minority of them to find a national solution for the so-called Jewish problem. Second, the forming Zionist movement sought to take advantage of the imperial struggle and territorial expansion and used diplomatic means to receive a charter from a European power. And third, the Jewish settlement of Palestine drew on "technocratic" ideas of European colonial administration (Pensler 1990, 143–60) and European ideas of, and attitudes toward, indigenous populations.

Anti-Semitism and Jewish Nationalism

> I would call anti-Semitism a poor man's snobbery.
> —Jean-Paul Sartre, *Anti-Semite and Jew*

The rapid modernization of Europe, and the consequent international competition discussed in the previous chapter, had important implications for European Jews, especially for those in Eastern Europe. If in the progressive countries of the West the condition of Jews was generally tolerable (though not without difficulties), in the East, where hopes for liberalism and amelioration diminished, life for Jews was becoming more and more intolerable (Vital 1988, 4–5).

Overall, Jews in East and West could not remain indifferent to a zeitgeist that emphasized national identity and consolidated bounded territories, undermined their position, and motivated, among other changes, the rise of a Jewish national movement.

In premodern Europe, a society divided into estates or castes, the Jews, being one caste among many, could in theory at least be accommodated as long as they were segregated in their own communities. But because their image was construed as compromising and defying the (Christian) order of things and therefore as a potential danger for the existing social order, Jews were not like most other groups (Bauman 1989, 37–39). This image of Jews as a "social danger" that developed in medieval Europe was easily adapted to the modern period. "The age of modernity inherited 'the Jew' already firmly separated from the Jewish men and women who inhabited its towns and villages. Having successfully played the role of the alter-ego of the Church, it was prepared to be cast in a similar role in relation to the new, secular, agencies of social integration" (Bauman 1989, 40).

Modernity exposed the inherent tensions between the Jews and the community surrounding them and changed their vulnerable status for the worse. The Jews, or rather the image of the Jews imported from premodern times, were an instrument used for the drawing of new boundaries and identities that placed them on the outside. Like other minorities, liberalization freed Jews from some of the restrictions placed upon them during the ancien regime, but at the same time they lost their monopoly over certain trades and the relative protection that the old order provided them with. This change placed them in a precarious position within nationalizing societies busy protecting themselves from the ravages of international development and erecting boundaries. The age-old image of Jews as rich and disloyal made them a target for the propaganda of nationalist movements. Economic superiority, real or imagined, and cultural distinctiveness, as Ernest Gellner (1983, 105) notes, had disastrous and tragic consequences.

European Jews were caught in the middle of the conflict between the premodern and the modern world. On the one hand, Jewish distinctiveness could be resolved within the nation-state through assimilation, a demand often placed upon Jews. But on the other hand, the move of some Jews into social and economic positions of influence signified for anti-Semitic nationalists hostile to assimilation the uncertainties and instability of the period. In the depression, the Jew as the foreigner came to symbolize the disruption of old ways and the capitalist system of economic expansion that undermined the traditional social order. The new anti-Semitism that emerged in that period was directed against Jews as a symbol of capitalism (an image that had nothing to do with the actual number of Jews among capitalists) and was associated with right-wing nationalism. This nationalism, as Hobsbawm notes, "lent itself exceptionally well to expressing the collective resentment of people who could not explain their discontents precisely. It was the foreigners' fault" (1989, 160).

The dynamics of the relations between Jews and the rest of society were different in Western and Eastern Europe. In his speech in the First Zionist Congress, the Zionist leader Max Nordau explained the difference:

> Jewish misery has two forms, the material and the moral. In Eastern Europe, North Africa and western Asia—in those very regions where the overwhelmingly majority, probably nine-tenths of all Jews, live—there the misery of the Jews is to be understood literally. It is a daily distress of the body, anxiety for every day that follows, a tortured fight for bare existence. In Western Europe . . . the question of bread and shelter, and the question of security of life and limb concerns them less. There the misery is moral. It takes the form of perpetual injury to self-respect and honor and of a brutal suppression for the striving of spiritual satisfaction which no non-Jew is obliged to deny. (Vital 1975, 363)

Jews of Western Europe made great political, social, and economic advancements during the nineteenth century, but their integration, predicated on acculturation and assimilation, was not a steady and irreversible process. The extension of legal rights did not lead to their full acceptance into society, a fact demonstrated by the proliferation during the period of anti-Semitic literature, movements, political parties, and riots(Rogger 1986, 1–4). Jews, by the very fact of their territorial dispersion and ubiquity, constituted an inter-national—or non-national—nation. As nationhood and territoriality were becoming the political manifestation of self and collective identity, Jews undermined the most basic difference—between "us" and "them" (Bauman 1989, 54). Moreover, the difference between Jews and the rest of society lost the "naturalness" of the premodern era during which they were easily distinguished from others. The fact that some Jews were willing to embrace the new opportunities afforded and to assimilate, therefore becoming truly indistinguishable, threatened to wipe out boundaries. The distinctiveness of the Jews had, according to right-wing nationalists, to be laid on new foundations from which no escape was possible. Racism in its modern pseudo-scientific form, which as earlier mentioned was inseparable from the age of imperialism, was to fill up this void and stand in the way of Jewish assimilation.

Once emancipated by the state, observed George Mosse, it was the nation that Jews had to face (1993, 121–24). The problem for Jews was that the creation of a "national character" was drawn upon a distinction between insider and outsider, the Jew castigated as the latter and the opposite of the national ideal. The stronger the nationalism, the greater the need for external and internal enemies, and the more the Jews would become the target for eradication that would enable the "purification" of the nation-state. The precarious position of Jews was especially evident during the great depression when a critique of the liberal order was often linked to anti-Jewish feelings.

Anti-Semitism was on the rise in various countries, led by nationalist groups that advocated patriotism, purity, and the need to consolidate the nation's boundaries. An influential incident that made its impression on Theodor Herzl, the future leader of Zionism, was the Dreyfus case in France. Alfred Dreyfus, a Jewish officer in the French army, was falsely charged and convicted of treason. His trial was conducted amid a wave of anti-Semitism that argued that his treason was an example of the wider "Jewish threat" and of the disloyalty of the Jews. In Germany, anti-Semitic movements protested against the achievements Jews supposedly made at the expense of "true" Germans and demanded to reverse the emancipation of the Jews and place them in a position of "tolerable aliens." Anti-Semites enumerated the dangers that Jews posed to the spiritual and material status of German society they were not a part off (J. Katz 1979, 249–50). When Jews who escaped the pogroms in Russia sought refuge in Western Europe, even liberals joined right-wing nationalists in demands for a restrictive immigration policy.

The new anti-Semitism that sought to reverse the results of emancipation signaled to some Jews that Europe's dominant national groups refused to accept them as equals due to a combination of popular prejudice and fear of economic competition (Peled 1989, 17). But despite the setbacks in the process of assimilation, the continued attempts of Jews to assimilate and their relative success caused worries among Jewish leaders over the fate of the Jewish people (Sternhell 1998, 49–50). Among Jews there was a debate over the benefits of emancipation and a deep cleavage was drawn between those who took advantage of the new opportunities and attempted to assimilate and those who maintained tradition and identity. The process of assimilation also differentiated the Jews of Western Europe who had access to those opportunities from the Jews of Eastern Europe who did not and remained more traditional.

In Eastern Europe, where most Jews lived, the political and economic instability was the worst and anti-Semitism had the most devastating results. In the premodern period, being middlemen minorities, Jews were often expelled from areas in Western Europe where the development of capitalism gave rise to a mercantile class belonging to the dominant ethnic group. Many Jews were pushed into Eastern Europe, where modernization finally caught up with them in the middle of the nineteenth century (Peled 1989, 17). In 1880, world Jewry numbered between 7.5 and 8 million; at least 75 percent of them resided in Eastern Europe (Vital 1975, 26). The uneven modernization of the peripheral states, whether it was in North Africa, the Ottoman Empire, or especially Russia, worsened the condition of Jews and made life more and more difficult for them.

In Russia, Jews since the eighteenth century were concentrated in the Pale of Settlement, an area stretching roughly from Lithuania in the north to the Black Sea in the south, and from Poland and Serbia in the west to White Russia and the Ukraine in the east. Jews constituted a high proportion of the population in the Pale; most of them lived in miserable conditions in the towns where they were forced to settle. Their relationship with the rural population was also tense. Their religious and traditional distinctiveness and their economic role of tradesmen or middleman made them distrusted, and often resented, by the peasantry.

Unlike their brethren in the West, very few of the Jews of Eastern Europe advanced and integrated in the society surrounding them. In the middle of the nineteenth century, a modernist movement among Russian Jews arose with the hope of assimilating into Russian society by joining the modernizing forces and achieving a status similar to Jews in the west. During the reign of Czar Alexander II, this seemed a promising strategy as some restrictive laws were relaxed and Jews were allowed to attend universities in Moscow and elsewhere. But progress was short-lived: the Czar's assassination in 1881 reversed Jewish fate as the new regime proved hostile to Jewish modernization and assimilation.

The economic conditions in the Pale steadily worsened after the emancipation of the Russian peasantry in 1861. The construction of railroads across the empire hurt the status of the petty traders and small craftsman who could not compete with the industrialized goods that became available. Some Jews

successfully adapted to the changes, but, as they moved to exploit new opportunities, they became a target for the mounting pressures of the Russian unemployed as well as their Russian competitors. The overall result was that the
decade preceding the pogroms was characterized by a growing concern among
Jews over their future. Russian statesmen, goaded by an increasingly militant
Judeophobe press, clung to their old prejudiced views of Jews as a serious economic, political, and social problem (Klier 1992, 11).

The hatred toward Jews, both by peasants and by men of position in Russia, was several times translated into violent pogroms during the nineteenth
century. But a series of pogroms unprecedented in scale and spread occurred
between 1881 and 1884, in which almost all of the major Jewish communities
were attacked by mobs. By the end of 1881 alone, 215 communities had been
attacked, driving 20,000 Jews out of their homes, ruining the means of living of
100,000 Jews, and destroying an estimated $80 million worth of property (Vital
1975, 51–52). While there was no proof that the government instigated and coordinated the pogroms, its reaction was ambivalent, often doing little to prevent the pogroms and showing little sympathy toward the Jews' plight. In May
1882, a new series of edicts was published (known as the "May Laws") principally designed to harden and broaden existing legislation that limited Jews'
right to own land and reside outside the towns of the Pale (Vital 1975, 56–58).
In addition, various quotas were set that restricted Jewish entry into professions like medicine or brokerage (Rogger 1986, 67–69).

What motivated anti-Jewish legislation, according to Rogger, was a genuine fear among the Russian political elite of Jewish radicalism and the expanded role (or potential role) of Jews in the professions, the economy, and in
the public sphere. Because Jews, it was argued, were better equipped to take advantage of modernization, restrictions upon them were necessary for the protection of the lower classes, especially the peasants. Amid nationalization and
social unrest, Jews were depicted as a danger to society either because they were
subversive and disloyal or because they were "parasites," becoming rich at the
expense of the wider native society. Russian minister of the interior Phleve explained in his meeting with Theodor Herzl that the restrictive policy toward
the Jews was justifiable because they endangered Russia's social fabric and political order (Gutwein 1994, 197–221).

A second series of pogroms that began in 1903 shocked world Jewry and
elicited strong responses against the Russian government deemed responsible.
The pogroms were a combined result of an active anti-Semitic press, deep-

seated anti-Semitic feelings, and the mismanagement and irresponsibility of the local government. In the background was the faltering economy, with rising unemployment and poor harvests in 1902–03 that produced social unrest and a cycle of violence of which Jews were its main victims. Two rumors inspired the mob in Kishinev, where the most infamous pogrom took place: the first that the Czar himself gave permission to abuse the Jews (a similar rumor played a part in the 1881 pogroms), and the second that the Jews played a major role in the revolutionary movement. More pogroms occurred within the next two years, with a growing number of casualties (Lambroza 1992).

The Jews of Romania were also in a dire situation. The Romanian regime was worse than the Russian in refusing to allow Jews any form of citizenship, and Jews were subjected to anti-Jewish laws and an anti-Semitic campaign in the press (Vital 1975, 89–91). Unlike the Jews in the west, where anti-Semitism did not pose an immediate threat and Jews could hope for a better future, Jews in Russia and Romania required an immediate solution as their lives became intolerable. The combined effect of the violence and the anti-Jewish legislation was a loss of faith in future prospects for Jews in Russia, even among many of those who previously believed in that possibility. These feelings grew stronger after the second wave of pogroms, when it was proven again that the government was uninterested or unable to defend its Jewish subjects. This loss of faith caused Jews to take part in the extensive global migrations characteristic of the period. A large number of Jews left Russia and emigrated to America and Western Europe, and a small number, several thousand, inspired by a national ideology, chose to move to Palestine. This group, who later came to be known as the "second aliyah," was made of young Jewish people, many of whom leaned toward socialism or other radical ideologies, who became convinced that these ideologies could not be realized in Russia or Romania but only in a land of their own (Vital 1988, 392).

The immigration of Jews from east to west had also an effect upon the Jews living in the west. More involved with the society surrounding them, dispersed in small communities, speaking the language and identifying themselves as a part of the nation, Jews in Western Europe suffered from anti-Semitism but felt secure enough to believe integration was possible in the near future. The arrival of masses of Eastern Jews caused great discomfort and anxiety for those who feared that the modernized and halfway assimilated Jews could be associated with those traditional Jews from Eastern Europe that corresponded to the anti-Semitic image (Vital 1975, 208–9). The Eastern Jews' problem seemed for many of the Jews in Western Europe as a problem that could be solved through philanthropy, and that did not indicate a more general "Jewish problem" in need of a national solution.

Neither in Western Europe nor in Eastern Europe had the national idea gained the support of the majority of Jews. In Western Europe, most Jews firmly believed that assimilation would prevail over anti-Semitism. The overwhelming majority of Eastern European Jews who decided to emigrate chose to resettle in countries that offered better opportunities rather than seek a national solution. Yet several influential Jews across Europe, in the spirit of the time, reached new and different conclusions. The two most important thinkers, Theodor Herzl and Leon Pinsker, one in Western Europe the other in Eastern Europe, both identified the "Jewish problem" as a national one, and they composed what would soon become two of the founding texts of Zionism.

Leon Pinsker, a Russian Jew and formerly an advocate of assimilation, published after the pogroms of 1882 a short and provocative text titled *Auto-Emancipation: An Appeal to His People by a Russian Jew*. Pinsker urged his compatriots to seize the moment and commit themselves to the making of a national movement. The only solution for the Jews, he argued, was "the creation of a Jewish nationality, of a people living upon its own soil, the auto-emancipation of the Jews; their emancipation as a nation among nations by the acquisition of a home of their own" (Sicker 1992, 102). Anti-Semitism was not a temporary phenomenon, Pinsker observed, because Jews qua Jews could not fit within the new Europe of nations. There was something "unnatural" in a people without a territory that inspired fear and hatred against the Jews: "For the living—the Jew is dead, for the natives of the land—a foreigner, for its residents—a vagabond, for the rich—a pauper, for the poor—a millionaire and exploiter, for the patriot—stateless, and for all classes—a despised competitor" (Pinsker 1951, 46).

Jewish hatred or "Judo-phobia," he argued, is entrenched within the nations as an incurable psychosis, and emancipation, which accorded a legal status to the Jews, could not provide an answer to the deeper roots of the problem. Jews must not rely on possibilities of assimilation, therefore, but emancipate themselves through a national-territorial solution that will "normalize" the relationship between Jews and non-Jews (Sachar 1996, 14–15).

> The Jews are not a living nation; they are foreign everywhere and therefore despised. The equalization of their civil and political status is not enough to

make them worthy in the eyes of the nations. The only true remedy is, the creation of Jewish nationalism, a people dwelling on his own land, autoemancipation of the Jews, equalization of their status among nations by purchasing their homeland for themselves. (Pinsker 1951, 65)

Only when this foundation would be established, when the equality of value between Jews and the rest of the nations becomes a matter of fact, only then could we see the Jewish question as resolved. (39)

When Jews become a nation, Pinsker concluded, their suffering will come to an end as they would enjoy the respect of other nations.

Theodor Herzl, an Austrian Jew who worked as a journalist in France, reached a similar conclusion. Herzl became concerned with the rise of anti-Semitism in Europe and in his native Vienna where the anti-Semitic Christian-Social Party was on the rise. The destabilization of the multiethnic Austro-Hungarian empire, whose stability had been a guarantee for Jewish safety, placed Jews in the midst of national struggles across the empire (Avineri 1997). Unfamiliar at the time with Pinsker's work or with the Zionist movement of Hibbat Zion in Russia, Herzl pointed to the anomaly of the Jews and the need of a territorial solution for the Jewish "problem," and traced anti-Semitism to the statelessness of the Jews: "We have honestly endeavored everywhere to merge ourselves in the social life of surrounding communities and to preserve the faith of our fathers. We are not permitted to do so. In vain we are loyal patriots . . . In countries where we have lived for centuries we are still cried down as strangers" (1988, 76).

Anti-Semitism, Herzl concluded, is deeply entrenched and wide in scope because all the nations in whose midst Jews live are either covertly or openly anti-Semitic (1988, 86). Although his analysis of anti-Semitism was focused on the Jews of the West, his predictions were as pessimistic as Pinsker's were. Jews, he argued, were emancipated in a stage where they were already "a bourgeois people" and found themselves in competition with the middle classes who could not withdraw their rights but refused to accept them as equals. Prospects for positive change were unlikely: "We might perhaps be able to merge ourselves entirely into surrounding races, if these were to leave us in peace for a period of two generations. But they will not leave us in peace. We are one people—our enemies have made us one without our consent, as repeatedly happens in history. Distress binds us together, and, thus united, we suddenly discover our strength. Yes, we are strong enough to form a state, and, indeed, a model state" (Herzl 1988, 86). Influenced by international politics, Herzl sought to seize the moment he thought was ripe for Jewish sovereignty. "The Jewish State," he declared, "is essential to the world; it will therefore be created" (72). In a short work entitled *The Jewish State,* Herzl outlined a plan for the mass immigration of Jews to Palestine and the creation of a state with the financial support of wealthier Jews. The immigration of the poor Jews, he argued, was in the interests of the rich. Such rich Jews, already more acceptable because of their economic status, would have an even better chance of being assimilated once the poor Jews had emigrated; therefore, they should support the plan.

The Jewish State prompted mixed reactions, generally arousing reluctance in Western Europe and finding more favor in Eastern Europe. While Russian Zionists found little that was new in the text itself, at least in its theoretical argument, they were delighted with what they perceived as a "reawakening of western Jewry" (Vital 1975, 276). What mattered to them was the idea that Jews in Western Europe could be potential partners in the making of a national movement that would, as the two texts advocated, "normalize" Jewish existence. But even in Russia, only a minority of Jews were attracted to the idea of Jewish nationalism. Some even warned that by declaring that Jews were a nation deserving a state, Zionism would undermine the position of all Jews, Zionist or non-Zionist.

The historian S. M. Dubnow, who advocated communal autonomy in the diaspora, was skeptical regarding the ability of Zionism to solve the Jewish problem. Dubnow argued that because only a minority could settle in Palestine, this solution was less than partial and unfair to those who would stay behind. "What do you say of this original [plan for a] settlement of the Jewish Question which sentences the whole of the people, with a possible exception of a twentieth part of it, to national extinction?" (Vital 1988, 175). Those Jews, he argued, are doomed for destruction through either assimilation or socioeconomic degeneration. An independent Zionist state would provide a limited solution and undermine the position of Jews, as the answers to their distress or complaints of discrimination would be "if you don't like it here, why don't you go away and live in your own state?" (Vital 1988, 175)

Western European Jews, especially the wealthy who were supposed to back the plan financially, were even less sympathetic. When Herzl approached the Baron Edmond Rothschild seeking support for the program, Rothschild responded coldly. In a letter to Herzl he explained why he thought the idea of a Jewish state was wrong:

> I should view with horror the establishment of a Jewish Colony pure and simple; such a Colony would be Imperium [in] Imperiu; it would be a Ghetto with the prejudices of the Ghetto; it would be a small Jewish State, Orthodox and illiberal, excluding the gentile and the Christians. And what would be the result; ten, fifteen or fifty thousand Jews would live in comparative happiness and ease, their habits and their example would be quoted and their co-religionists and brethren at home would be more oppressed and more ground down by others on the principle of "Do unto others as you would be done by." (quoted in Vital 1988, 175)

Both anti-Semitism and assimilation, two seemingly contradictory forces, motivated Zionism. It was not only that Zionism encompassed a pessimism about prospects for assimilation, but also that as national movement it abhorred the possibility of assimilation, which would entail the loss of identity.

Zionism has been characterized as a reactive or a "secondary" nationalism (Trevor-Roper 1961), responding to the developments in Europe. But its emergence in the late nineteenth century was not only a result of external forces but also an expression of much older needs and desires, a movement with deep roots drawing on a large reservoir of collective memories, shared myths, and religious yearnings of a return to Zion (A. Smith 1999). The external constraints imposed upon and the opportunities provided to the Jewish people during this period motivated a Zionist movement that drew also on Jewish history and tradition to mobilize Jews. This combination of present needs and past commitment directed the Jewish quest for territorial sovereignty toward Palestine and cooperation with European powers to take advantage of imperial expansions.

Zionism and the Imperial Powers

The Zionist movement, led by Herzl, sought to seize the opportunities created by the extensive European expansion and operated politically in an attempt to receive a "charter" from the great powers to establish a Jewish state in Palestine or, as some were willing to consider, in any available territory. The integration of the Middle East into the modern world economy and the modernizing reforms of the Ottoman Empire enabled Jewish immigrants after the 1880s to settle in sparsely settled regions of Palestine, despite the reluctance of the Ottoman government. Herzl, who for a long time was unaware of the attempts of the Eastern European Hibbat Zion movement to settle Palestine (Avineri 1997), opposed this "infiltration" of Jews into Palestine against the wishes of the Ottoman government, arguing that it was both demeaning and inefficient.

Zionists contemplated which method would best establish ownership over the land. Menachem Usishkin, a rising leader of Hibbat Zion, outlined possible methods of acquiring property: "by force—that is by conquest in war, in other words, by robbing land of its owner; by forceful acquisition, that is, by expropriation via governmental authority; and by purchase with the owner's consent" (Shafir 1989, 42). Because conquest of the land by force was unrealistic, the Zionist movement was divided between those who advocated purchase, settlement, and establishing of a foothold in Palestine, dealt with in the following section, and those, like Herzl, who believed that only by a diplomatic effort that would grant the Jews a formal authority could the Zionist enterprise become real.

In his effort to turn the Zionist movement into the representative of the Jewish people, Herzl's diplomatic activity was a continuous search for the Archimedean point that would open the road to territorial sovereignty. He used both anti-Semitism and imperialism as the means to convince European powers of the double advantage in granting the Jews a state of their own, transforming what constituted a problem—unassimilable Jews—into an advantage—a European outpost in the Levant. Diplomacy was a not a readily accessible path for Zionists who were clearly at a disadvantage. First, Zionists represented only a fraction of the Jews and even less of their wealth, which made it difficult to speak on behalf of the Jewish people. Second, they had to deal with cautious European statesmen used to engaging with officials of the same status rather than with stateless people. And third, because Jews presented only little danger to the existing social order and were not perceived as an acute political problem, they could simply be ignored (Vital 1988, 94–96).

The attempt to recruit Jewish financiers to the Zionist cause in its initial stages failed miserably. Because many of them were part of the circle of cosmopolitan haute financiers, they were willing to support their brethren as philanthropists but not as conationalists. Herzl met with Baron Maurice Hirsch, who financed and initiated settlement of Jews in Argentina, on May 1895, but the baron was unconvinced and according to Herzl's memoirs even cynical (Herzl

1997). In the following month, Herzl approached the Rothschild family with no better results. The Jewish financiers were engaged in philanthropy but refused to commit themselves to a national cause. Edmond Rothschild, who already had invested a fortune in the Jewish colonies in Palestine, was disenchanted by the visions of Herzl. He saw Palestine, as his biographer explains, for what it really was: "a real territory, with a real domestic economy, a punishing climate, a government beset by corruption and anarchy and an indigenous population that could not be wished away by messianic optimism" (Schama 1978, 146). Herzl perceived Rothschild as having different and selfish motives. On May 18, 1896, after a second failed attempt with Rothschild, he wrote in his diary, "Rothschild does not want to have anything to do with this, he does not believe we can get anything from the Sultan. My actions seem to him dangerous, because they might raise doubts regarding the patriotism of the Jews, and harmful to his colonies in Israel" (Herzl 1997, 313).

Giving up on the support of the Jewish financiers, Herzl followed the diplomatic course in hope that the European powers could be convinced of the advantage of a Jewish sovereign entity. The natural place to go was the Ottoman government. Palestine constituted a part of its empire, and the Ottomans firmly objected to Jewish settlement attempts. The Ottoman government perceived European immigration in large numbers as a potential threat of a new ethnic tension like the ones that undermined their hold of the Balkans. It was therefore reluctant to have Jews settle in large numbers in Palestine and restricted immigration and settlement. The attempts of Jewish settlers in Palestine to use European governments or the capitulation system (granting an exterritorial stance for Europeans in the Ottoman Empire) to protect them may have been counterproductive. The involvement of European diplomats on the behalf of Jewish settlers bolstered the Ottomans' concerns that Jewish settlement would undermine their control and confirmed their suspicions that the settlers were being used as pawns by European powers to the detriment of Turkish sovereignty (I. Friedman 1977, 42–43). Their conclusion was that the number of Jews entering and settling in the country must be severely limited (Vital 1988, 51). Measures taken by the Ottoman government against Jewish immigration included restrictions, not always successfully employed, on foreign Jews from purchasing land or for staying in the country for more than three months (I. Friedman 1977, 44). While a total ban on Jewish immigration was never imposed, immigration was limited to small numbers that bypassed the restrictions of the Ottoman government and confirmed Herzl's skepticism toward settlement by infiltration (Vital 1988, 52).

Herzl's negotiations with Turkish authorities proved difficult and frustrating, and his first voyage to meet with the sultan in June 1896 brought no results. Only vaguely familiar with the Ottoman Empire, he failed to understand the sensitivity and, consequently, the straightforward opposition, to the creation of another national minority within the empire. Moreover, as the sovereignty over much of the Muslim world and over all Muslim holy places was key to their legitimacy, it was improbable that any concession in Palestine could be made (Vital 1975, 289–90). Herzl managed, nevertheless, to put forward a bold proposition of buying out the Turkish debt in return for a Jewish homeland of some sort. This tactic—relying on the image of the Jewish financiers with international capabilities, reminiscent of the anti-Semitic view of the Jews—had its own disadvantages. It helped to make some progress in Constantinople but was immensely disturbing to the Jews of Western Europe, especially among the notables whose support he was trying to win (290–97).

The determination of the Ottoman government to modernize the army, infrastructure, and administration required large sums of money that European governments and private business seeking foreign investments were initially happy to lend. But as confidence in the empire's financial future waned, the terms on which Turkey was able to borrow progressively worsened. Between 1854 and 1875, the Ottoman government obtained fourteen foreign loans and amassed a heavy external debt, becoming bankrupt in 1875. In 1881, under pressure from the European powers, an agreement was reached between Turkey and its creditors on the establishment of an Ottoman Public Debt Administration that limited its economic independence (Owen 1981, 101–10). With the decline of British hegemony and the emergence of world rivalry, the Ottoman Empire became an intense site of contention and part of the imperial struggle. Britain continued to hold the largest share in Ottoman foreign trade, but Germany and France, whose capital was invested in the construction of railroads, also obtained influence and partitioned the Ottoman Empire into spheres of influence (Pamuk 1987, 14).

The weakness of Turkey in face of the European powers and the Debt Administration was the key, Herzl believed, for fruitful negotiation. "The role of the financial plan," he wrote in his diary on May 7, 1896, "is to liquidate the European Commission and take into our hand the payment of interest, so that the Sultan can get rid of this humiliating inspection and take new loans ad libitum" (Herzl 1997, 309). As mentioned above, his first voyage brought no results. An emissary to the sultan, who refused to meet Herzl, delivered the sultan's negative response: "The Turkish Kingdom does not belong to me but to the Turkish people. I could not give any of it. Let the Jews keep their billions for themselves" (332). Herzl continued to try and obtain some concessions from the Ottoman government using new contacts and offering new ideas to win support. At the same time, he also sought new alternatives. "I am contemplating to establish before the movement a closer territorial destiny, although Zion will remain our goal. The poor masses need help and Turkey is not desperate enough to respond favorably to our wishes . . . Maybe we could demand Cyprus from the British, consider South Africa or America—until Turkey will fall apart" (528).

In a letter to the Turkish ambassador in Vienna, he explained that time was running out: "Turkish statesmen must see clearly the advantages lost if you will not have a Jewish settlement in Israel, which could bring you a lot of money immediately, and for that you will miss a complete financial settlement, a modern navy, industry and commerce, that is the empire's well being" (Herzl 1997, 150).

It took almost five years of meeting with Turkish bureaucrats and the use of various contacts until in May 1901 Herzl managed to receive an interview with the sultan, although he was forbidden to speak directly on Zionism or about a charter. Herzl tried to offer the sultan services that he and his "friends" could perform for him. In a letter to the sultan a month later (June 15), he suggested establishing an economic company for the development of Asia Minor and Palestine, to which the sultan would grant charters. In return the company would provide a loan in favorable terms that would solve Turkey's financial problems. The offer was declined as the Ottomans again refused any form of sovereignty for the Jews. In February 1902, the sultan offered that, in return for annulment of the debt, Jews could become Ottoman subjects and settle in the empire, but not in Palestine (Herzl 1997, 2:387–88). Initially declining the offer, Herzl returned home to contemplate it. Soon he was informed that the sultan had backed off from the offer; Herzl suspected he had been used by the Ottomans to bargain loan conditions with other businessmen and states (413).

Another route to Palestine pursued by the Zionist movement was Germany, who had its own interests in the Middle East that Zionists were hoping to tap onto. A German-sanctioned Jewish settlement in Palestine, Herzl argued in his meetings with German statesmen, would have a double advantage for Germany, solving the "Jewish problem" at home and establishing German influence in the Middle East. This Jewish protectorate would introduce a German cultural element into the Orient (Sachar 1996, 47): "As the bearers of Western culture we wish to bring into this neglected and ill corner of the Orient, cleanliness, order and the Virtues of the West," he wrote to one of his correspondents (Herzl 1997, 2: 306). Through William Hechler, the chaplain to the British embassy in Vienna and a devoted believer in Jewish redemption, Herzl hoped to gain access to the German authorities, as well as to the British and the Ottomans. Hechler, who had served in the past as a tutor to the son of Friedrich, the grand duke of Baden, managed to get Herzl an interview with grand duke in April 1896. The meeting with the grand duke in the summer of 1898 led to meetings with Count Eulenburg, one of the most influential men in Germany and an intimate of Kaiser Wilhelm, and with Bülow, the German secretary of state for foreign affairs. Through these men Herzl hoped to get an interview with the German kaiser.

In his engagement with German statesmen, Herzl tried to convince them that Zionism could aid Germany in the imperial struggle. First there were the benefits German society would derive from the departure of its "superfluous" Jews. Second, there were the benefits to Turkey, Germany's ally, from the "influx of an intelligent, economically energetic national element." The large sums of money it would get from the Jews could help in the "restoration to health of this neglected corner of the Orient." Finally, there was the role that the Jews could play in the building of a great railroad from the Mediterranean to the Persian Gulf, another German imperial interest (Vital 1988, 83). "From the Mediterranean coast to the Persian Gulf a railroad will be, and must be, built, and only the Jews can build it. The solution to the question of the land of Israel—not just the Jewish-question—is an act that complements the latest developments in Asia" (Herzl 1997, 2: 90).

The kaiser, Wilhelm II, was warm to these ideas, first in agreeing to meet with Herzl and then, after the meeting, to intercede with the sultan on the Zionists' behalf. In their meeting on October 18, 1898, Herzl asked that the kaiser request from the sultan a "Chartered Company" for the Jews under a German protectorate (Herzl 1997, 45). Generally, the kaiser saw the benefits of the plan that might save the Ottoman Empire from bankruptcy and help it recover. In addition, the plan could bring direct benefits for Germany, with Jews immigrating to Palestine and the Jewish people becoming indebted to Germany: "In view of the gigantic power (very dangerous in a way) of international Jewish capital, would it not be a great achievement for Germany, if the world of the Hebrews looked to her with gratitude?" (I. Friedman 1977, 66).

While the kaiser was critical of anti-Semites, his support of Zionism replicated some of their arguments. To Herzl he said, "There are elements among your people whom it would be a good thing to settle in Palestine. I am thinking of Hesse, for example, where there are usurers at work among the rural population" (Vital 1988, 89). Herzl was not only undeterred by anti-Semitic remarks but was instrumental, and in his negotiations with European statesmen he used anti-Semitism to gain support for his plan. He mentioned the need to "draw to our enterprise decent anti-Semites" (Herzl 1997, 161), and wrote that some "anti-Semites treat me fairly" (Vital 1975, 268). What mattered was that winning German support seemed to be at hand. But the meeting with the kaiser in Palestine revealed that the Germans had backed off from their position, probably after encountering the sultan's dislike of the whole idea. The Germans, who gave relations with Turkey high priority, were unwilling to risk this relationship even for the German Templars who had established colonies in Palestine. Herzl continued to press for German support and repeated the arguments that Jewish settlement in Palestine would bolster Germany's world power. In creating this settlement, Germany would "secure for itself future influence and secure for itself a first rate industrial market" (Herzl 1997, 84). But the Germans retreated from support and henceforth remained cold to Zionism.

The final disengagement of the Germans from the Zionist idea (until the war) was in 1904, at the same time when Zionist prospects in East Africa had vanished. The Germans concluded that they had no interest in Zionism because it would risk their relations with Turkey. Von Richtofen, the foreign minister, explained the German preferences:

> For years Turkey has been in conflict with the great powers in order to prevent the establishment of national autonomy, or even a nucleus of such autonomy, in Macedonia. She is also strongly opposed to the introduction of reforms under European supervision. There is, therefore, a danger of international complications and even a threat to world peace . . . time is not ripe for political intervention on behalf of Zionism. Such intervention can only do harm to Zionism and diminish the prospects for the realization of Dr. Herzl's ideals. It would also damage other German interests in Turkey. (I. Friedman 1977, 115)

In 1902, giving up hope on the possibility of influencing the Ottoman government and frustrated with the Germans, Herzl and the Zionist movement shifted their attention toward the British Empire. They hoped that the idea of a Jewish colony in Palestine would appeal to the British, who were at the time already established in the region and involved in competition with the other powers. "England the mighty, England the free, the England that looks all over the seas, will understand us and our endeavors," Herzl told the Fourth Congress (Vital 1988, 139). A British committee was at the time looking into the issue of immigration into Britain, mostly of Jews from Eastern Europe. While within Britain a large opposition to immigration was forming, formal restriction was contrary to the liberal tradition still valued in Britain. When British Zionists persuaded the committee to invite Herzl to give evidence, he presented the committee with the arguments he has used before, reiterating the advantages of Jewish settlement for Europe and for European imperialism. "The Jews of Western Europe cannot stay where they are—where are they to go? If you find that they are not wanted here, then some place must be found to which they can migrate without by that migration raising the problems that confront them here [in England]. These problems will not arise if a home be found them which will be legally recognized as Jewish" (Vital 1988, 143).

Where Herzl found an attentive ear was with the colonial secretary, Joseph Chamberlain. Though not devoid of anti-Semitism, Chamberlain, according to his biographer, was the first among British statesmen to see in Zionism both a solution for the ancient Jewish problem and a means for advancing the interests of the British Empire (Amery 1951, 256). Britain had been the destination for nearly one hundred thousand Russian Jews in the first years of the century, and labor unions were agitating out of fear from the competition of these newcomers. In other words, the "Jewish problem" became a British internal political issue. Herzl's arguments strengthened his position that supporting Zionism would both enlist the sympathies of world Jewry and develop an area in which Britain had a strategic interest (261).

In his first meeting with Chamberlain, Herzl presented him with the idea of a Jewish settlement in Cyprus or in the Sinai Peninsula. Chamberlain thought Cyprus, already populated, was unsuited for Herzl's purposes and sent Herzl to meet with the foreign secretary, Lord Lansdowne, whose office was responsible for the Sinai area. These successful meetings resulted in an expedition to the area to examine the feasibility of settlement. The project, however, never took off because of the pessimistic conclusion of the expedition—that the lack of water made settlement of the area unfeasible—and the objections of Lord Cromer, the British governor of Egypt. Chamberlain's journey to Africa yielded a new idea. Settling a European population in the land between Nairobi and the Mau Escarpment seemed to him an attractive project that would require settlers and capital. The Jews, he suggested, could secure the British possessions in Africa through a protectorate: "If Dr. Herzl were at all inclined to transfer his efforts to East Africa," he noted, "there would be no difficulty in finding land suitable for Jewish settlers" (Vital 1988, 158). The only question, of course, was whether the Jews would accept this substitute for Palestine. The offer was presented to Leopeld Greenberg, a British Zionist activist. Chamberlain suggested that the Zionists send a commission to inspect the area and then decide whether the offer should be accepted (Weisbrod 1966, 77).

Although Palestine was the agreed destiny of the Jewish people, under the circumstances of pogroms in Russia, Herzl was willing to consider the offer, which mistakenly came to be known as the "Uganda Plan." But the presentation of the idea of settlement in Africa at the Sixth Zionist Congress, assembled in August 1903, was a complete failure and the ensuing debate threatened to split the movement. Herzl was called a traitor to his face and the Zionist leader Max Nordau, who supported the idea, was almost assassinated. The decision to send an expedition to evaluate the project, a gesture considered necessary if only not to offend the British, was just barely approved and with an opposition that was difficult to appease. In his closing speech, worried about the fate of the Zionist movement, Herzl reaffirmed his commitment to Palestine, stating, "If I forget thee, O Jerusalem, may my right hand wither." Secular Zionists had quickly learned that their ability to depart from Jewish tradition was limited, that the "Land of Israel" (Eretz Israel) was the only territory that could evoke sentiments among a critical mass of Jews, and any solution outside of Palestine was unworkable (Ben-Porat 2000, 223–45). Herzl, however, saw the Uganda plan, despite the unpleasant events at the congress, as a potential starting point, a charter received from the power. After the congress he wrote to Nordau, "Our road to Zion will have to be paved with charters. And, I can present this state treaty as a model—particularly to the Sultan!—and that will carry enormous weight" (Vital 1988, 275).

Herzl's death a short time after the East African episode and the inability of diplomatic Zionism to achieve progress allowed "practical Zionists," who advocated the settling of Palestine without waiting for a charter, some leverage in the Zionist movement. Zionism's center of gravity shifted to Eastern Europe and gradually to the leadership of the settlement supporters (Vital 1988, 367–68). While the political transformation within the Zionist movement was gradual, significant changes were happening in the immigration to Palestine. Between 1904 and 1914, a group of perhaps two thousand young immigrants with strong political motivations who came to be known as the second aliyah emerged. This movement, which developed in the turbulent Russia of the early 1900s with its socialist-revolutionary rhetoric and inclinations, reinvigorated the pace of settlement of Palestine. Zionism from that period onward attempted to synthesize political maneuvers for a charter with creating facts or a presence through settlement and land purchases in Palestine. Haim Weizmann, an active political Zionist, explained in 1907 that diplomatic Zionism on its own had failed. To succeed, he argued, it must be supplanted by action. "The charter is to be aimed at, but only as a result of our endeavors in Palestine. If the governments give us a charter to-day it will be a scrap of paper. Not so if we work in Palestine; then, it will be written and indissolubly cemented with our blood" (quoted in L. Stein 1961, 63).

The relationship between the Zionist movement and Britain gained a new momentum during World War I. At the onset of the war, the British declared their new aim: dismemberment of the Ottoman Empire. Herbert Samuel, a British Jew and at the time a member of the cabinet, discussed in November 1914 the idea of Zionism and a Jewish state in Palestine with Lloyd George and the foreign secretary, Edward Grey. Samuel argued that it would be difficult to allot Palestine to any European power, and therefore a Jewish state loyal to Britain, in proximity to Egypt, would be of importance to the British Empire. Both George and Grey responded favorably to the idea (L. Stein 1961, 104–5). Samuel, despite his sympathy to Zionism, realized its inherent weakness and its minority position in Palestine. In January 1915, he moved to press Grey and Lloyd George for British control of Palestine after the war, arguing that Great Britain could not afford any other power to take control of Palestine nor share the control of the area. The Zionists, he believed, could help Britain consolidate its control of the area. In a memorandum he circulated between Cabinet members, he explained that

> under British facilities [permission] would be given to Jewish organizations to purchase land, to found colonies, to establish educational and religious institutions, and to co-operate in the economic development of the country, and that Jewish immigration, carefully regulated, would be given preference, so that in course of time the Jewish inhabitants, grown into a majority and settled in the land, may be conceded such degree of self-government as the conditions of that day might justify. (L. Stein 1961, 110)

Prime Minister Asquith, however, was unimpressed with the idea and Lloyd George and Grey, despite their initial interest, were reluctant, worried of both antagonizing the French and internal opposition in Britain, to pursue the idea.

The outbreak of the war in 1914 caused some changes in German perceptions of Zionism. While taking care not to alienate their Turkish ally, German delegates in Constantinople and Palestine intervened on behalf of Jews with the Turkish government. Among other things, these interventions saved Jews of prominent positions in Palestine from imprisonment or expulsion. Like the British, the Germans also thought about the end of the war and the possibility that Turkey would become a German satellite and the Near East open to German enterprise. The Zionist office in Germany stressed the benefits that Germany could gain from a German protectorate. Because "in a certain sense the Jews are a Near Eastern element in Germany and a German element in Turkey," Jews, whose native language was closely akin to German, were the natural intermediaries between Germany and the East. In July 1915, a document circulated to German consulates in Turkey stated that the German government looked favorably on "Jewish activities designed to promote the economic and cultural progress of Jews in Turkey, and also on the settlement of Jews for other countries." Accordingly, the consuls were authorized to adopt a "friendly attitude" toward such Jewish activities (L. Stein 1961, 211–12).

The interest the Germans were taking in the Zionist movement did not amount to a full commitment but had important implications for improving the Jewish bargaining position with Britain and may have been decisive in pushing the British to make their own initiative. Initially, in a struggle over the support of the Jewish community in America, an unsuccessful attempt was made to deliver a joint statement of support for Zionism by the allies. During the war, Britain and France argued over the division of the Turkish empire after the war, and the result was the Sykes-Picot agreement that divided the area into spheres of influence, areas of direct control, and of international administration. This latter was to be the status of most of Palestine. Toward the end of the war, British statesmen encouraged Zionist leaders to declare their desire to have Palestine united under British rule. Zionists leaders, who sought wider support, traveled to France, Russia, and the United States to popularize the idea of British protectorate over a Jewish Palestine.

The British war cabinet was reluctant to officially declare its support for Zionism, persuaded among other things by the negative reactions toward Zionism of several prominent British Jews. Speaking to the cabinet in October 1917, Balfour warned that the delay of authorizing a pro-Zionist statement would allow Germany to win Zionist sympathies and the support of Russian

Jewry in the midst of the war. Another reason to declare British support of Zionism, he argued, was to impress upon the French, first, that in any settlement the Zionists must be taken seriously into account, and, second, that they were in favor of British trusteeship over any other settlement. On November 2, 1917, Balfour wrote to Baron Rothschild what would be known as the "Balfour Declaration," considered to be the greatest achievement until that time for political Zionism as well as a founding text for the legitimacy of Zionist claims in the years to follow. Balfour wrote, "His Majesty's Government view with favour the establishment in Palestine of a national home for the Jewish people, and will use their best endeavors to facilitate the achievement of this object . . . it being clearly understood that nothing shall be done which may prejudice the civil and religious rights of existing non-Jewish communities in Palestine, or the rights and political status enjoyed by Jews in any other country" (quoted in L. Stein 1961, 548).

The Zionist movement that grew out of the constraints this period created for Jews in Europe was able toward the end of the period to take advantage of the opportunities it provided. The diplomatic efforts of Zionism used two arguments that fit the political spirit of the time: first, that a Jewish sovereign territory could be beneficial to European expansion and, second, that it would rid Europe of the "problem" of strangers in its midst. Shifting from "diplomatic" to "practical" Zionism had to take advantage of the financial and organizational resources at hand.

In Palestine

Herzl's death and the failure to achieve a charter through political means gave momentum to "practical Zionism," the acquisition of Palestine by piecemeal action of land purchase and settlement. Nachum Sokolov, the editor of the newspaper *Ha'Olam* and a central figure in the Zionist movement, explained the change of mind: "If there were people who thought that political Zionism meant that a special and unique person would be able to get us some extraordinary permission—this was a mistake" (1907). Another important Zionist leader, Menachem Usishkin, emphasized to the Eighth Zionist Congress held in 1907 that time was working against the Zionist movement: they must seize the moment and take concrete action.

If we will not redeem the land, others will . . . land is becoming more and more expensive and the conditions of settling Israel more difficult. And the man who looks ahead will see that in twenty years the redemption of the land will be even more difficult. Turkey is moving toward release from European dependency. And its best pupils aspire a national revival. And then, undoubtedly, they will object even more to the entry of foreign elements. The Arab peasants who will develop and become educated would also object. (Usishkin 1907, 000)

The settlement of Palestine without the official backing of a major power and with the objection of both the ruling Ottoman Empire and the indigenous population was an ambitious project. Lacking in military force and politically weak, Zionists had to rely on land purchases to establish themselves in Palestine. With the help of Jewish communities in Europe and, more important, of Jewish financiers, the Zionist movement was able to purchase tracts of land and settle immigrants. Between 1880 and 1900, various local Zionist groups of Hovevi Zion in Eastern Europe organized to purchase land in Palestine. The more successful among them, like the Menuhah ve-Nahalah Company, consisted of relatively affluent Jews and purchased land and settled with detailed planning. The major investments in Palestine, however, were Baron Rothschild's, who by 1900 had invested 40 million francs; Hovevi Zion contributions amounted to less than 2 million (Katz 1994). In the shift of emphasis from diplomatic maneuvers to an active process of settlement, the Zionists faced an indigenous population that could not be ignored and, consequently, were forced to recognize that their description of Palestine as "a land with no people for a people with no land" was at best wishful thinking (Gorny 1987).

Back in Europe many Zionists, like many European colonizers, believed that the native population would benefit from the progress Europe would bring to them and therefore would not object to their presence. Sokolov, in the article quoted above, outlined the approach to be used vis-à-vis the local population. First, he argued, "We should act with the best of manners, with political tact . . . in order to build strong foundation for peace and harmony with all nations there." And second, the Jewish settlers should make use of their European skills to find ways to reassure the Arabs of Zionism's benefits: "In the West, among the highly educated nations there is no place for us to be teachers . . . in the East—the situation is entirely different . . . we come there armed with new power, new knowledge—and a above all with political skills" (Sokolov 1907, 466–67).

Herzl, in the few occasions where he addressed the issue of the native population (who he acknowledged would have to be dealt with after the charter was received), made similar arguments. In *The Jewish State,* his detailed plan for Jewish settlement, he called for tolerance toward those of different nationalities coming to live among the Jews in their state, but he ignored the Arabs who already lived there. Where he did acknowledge their presence is his utopian novel *Altneuland.* His solution, very much motivated by the universalistic, humanistic ethos of the novel, proposes that all Arab inhabitants could join the new society as equal members. But not only did he not explore the possibilities and problematics of such equality within a Jewish state, the solution proposed overlooks the possibility that Arabs might wish to establish their own national movement. The fact that nothing in *The Jewish State* and only seven of the three hundred pages of *Altneuland,* describing the future Jewish community in Palestine, were devoted to the Arab issue could attest to the relatively little attention Herzl paid to the question. While Rashid Bey, the Arab character in the novel, rejects the assertion of his Jewish friends that they have brought culture to Palestine, he concedes that in the wake of the accelerated technological and commercial development that Jewish settlement created, the economic situation of Arabs has drastically improved. Thus Arab farmers who "had lived in poor clay houses which were not fit to serve as cowsheds" and whose babies "lay out naked and uncared for and grew up like beasts and animals," now, after Jews have established themselves, "make a respectable living, their children are healthy and studying" (Gorny 1987, 32–33).

The claim that Jewish settlement would bring with it progress to the land and its inhabitants was also used by Herzl in the brief encounters he had with the land and its people. In March 1899, Yusuf al-Khalidi, an elderly Jerusalem notable, sent a letter to Zadoc Kahn, the grand rabbi of France, that was forwarded to Herzl. Palestine, argued al-Khalidi, was no place for large numbers of Jews. It might be better, he suggested, to search for a different place where "millions of poor Jews could be settled and perhaps be happy and some day constitute a nation . . . But in the name of God, let Palestine be left in peace." Herzl responded that the local population had no reason to worry from the Zionist enterprise; on the contrary, "They will acquire an excellent brother, just as the Sultan will acquire loyal and good subjects, who will cause the region, their historic motherland to flourish" (Vital 1988, 381).

Herzl's conviction in the benefit of Jewish settlement for the native population reflects his background and his time. He was a liberal and aesthete, and what he found in Palestine in his visit was far from his liking. When visiting Jerusalem in 1898, he was unimpressed, neither by Jews nor by Arabs, noting "the decayed sediment of thousands of years of worthlessness, dark fanaticism, uncleanliness lurking in all the streets with their stench" (Gorny 1987, 30). His famous picture of his meeting with the German emperor in Palestine was symbolic of his foreignness, as the historian Anita Shapira describes: "It was a meeting of two Europeans in an Asian country. They are conscious of their being representatives of a higher civilization than the Oriental one . . . for Herzl this was an affirmation of one of his underlying assumptions: that the Jews are the bearers of European progress and culture to the Orient. Jews will function as a civilizing element, bringing progress and development to the heart of an unstable and volatile area" (1999, 15).

The optimism of the Zionist writers at the early stages of planning and settlement was based on a stereotype of the Arab and on European "Orientalist" conceptions typical of this period. The Arab was portrayed as primitive, backward, and childish, potentially violent but also with some good qualities: hospitable, responding positively when positively approached, and appreciative of the fearless. This stereotype helped to sustain the belief that a conflict would not occur (Shapira 1992, 83). But there were dissenting voices that warned against patronizing attitudes toward the Arabs. The writer Ahad Ha'am, a critic of Hibbat Zion and of Herzl, saw formidable external obstacles to Jewish national purposes after two visits to Palestine. In an article he published, titled "Truth from the Land of Israel," he warned against the illusions other Zionists held in regard to the settlement in Palestine. First, there was little cultivated land that could be purchased and what land could be purchased required much effort and was of limited use. Second, the Arab population, contrary to what Zionists thought, understood precisely what the Zionists were aiming at.

> Particularly the town-dwellers among them do see and understand what we are about, but they keep their own counsel and pretend to ignorance because they see no future danger to themselves in anything we do. On the contrary, they exploit us as best as they can. . . . The peasants are glad enough to have Jewish settlements set up among them because they are well paid for their labor . . . But if ever there comes a time when we shall have developed our lives in Eretz-Israel to the point where we shall be encroaching upon them in a greater or lesser degree [then we should not expect them] to yield their place easily. (Ahad Ha'am 1931, 28)

Third, he concluded, the Turks, whom the Jews wrongly assumed could be bribed out of Palestine, were unlikely to allow massive immigration and should have been expected to remain opposed to Jewish settlement (Ahad Ha'am 1931).

Several years later, in 1907, Isaac Epstein, a Jewish settler in Palestine, published a similar critique of the obliviousness of Zionism to the Arab question. Epstein's article "The Hidden Question" reflected the moral tensions between the belief in the necessity of Jewish settlement in Palestine and its consequences for the Arab native population. "There is one question that outweighs all the questions related to our national revival: our relation to the Arabs. This question has not only been forgotten but was completely alien to Zionists . . . we have forgotten that there is a people in our land who has been there for hundreds of years and never intended to leave it" (Hareven 1978, 111–20).

A major transformation of landholding patterns occurred in Palestine before Zionist immigration began. Title deeds were acquired by relatively few people or families, some of them outsiders, while the peasants who lived on much of that land assumed they had customary rights to its use (C. Smith 1992, 20–22). Zionists' purchase of lands from absentee landlords required the tenant farmers who had cultivated the land for generations to be evacuated (Gorny 1987, 17), and these evacuations were a major source of conflict between Jewish settlers and the Arabs. Isaac Epstein alerted his readers to the fact that the problem was not only about ownership but also about belonging and attachment: "When we feel the love to our country with all our heart we forget that the people who live in it have strong emotions for it. The Arab, like any human being, has strong ties to his country" (1907).

This tension was inevitable, but the only solution Epstein, who expected that an Arab national consciousness would form, could find was the one Herzl and others had came up with, modernization in exchange for cohabitation. Epstein hoped that the spread of agricultural knowledge, medical services, quality education, and other advantages of European civilization would provide sufficient compensation for the Arabs and incorporate them within the Zionist enterprise. Epstein's article elicited many responses from fellow settlers. Zeev Smilansky, for example, denied the national consciousness and the rights of Arabs to the land and argued that this was a zero-sum game in which Jews could not afford any concessions. As competition between the two was unavoidable, the Jews should treat Arabs with justice, but they could not afford to share their wealth and knowledge with them (Smilansky 1909). In a similar vein, Nehama Puchachevsky argued (1908) that the Arabs already had only benefited from Jewish settlement and that Jews at this time should be con-

cerned with the success of their own enterprise. These writers and others advocated a "separatist" (contrary to Epstein's "integrative") approach toward the
Arabs, arguing that their backward culture was incompatible with the European settlers' European culture (Gorny 1987, 54–57).

Zionism, as a result of disillusionment with the prior perceptions of the
(empty) land, changed not only its ideological perception but, more importantly, the strategy of colonization. Most of the first aliyah immigrants,[1] who
came between 1880 and 1904, settled in colonies that, after they foundered, became dependent on the funding of Baron Rothschild, who injected French
colonial technology into Palestine (Pensler 1990). Small in numbers, they required Arab workers for their vineyards and orange groves, and like many other
colonialist societies, a few settlers had contact with the local workforce but kept
distant from their communities as a whole. This form of colonization, according to its critics, led to a patronizing attitude and to a stereotyping of Arabs as
dishonest and lazy, reminiscent of other colonial descriptions of natives
(Shapira 1992, 91–93). Ahad Ha'am in his critique described above accused the
settlers of abusing the Arabs. They "treat the Arabs with hostility and cruelty
and trespass unjustly, beat them shamefully without good reason, and even
boast of having done so, and nobody stands in the breach to check this con-
temptible and dangerous tendency" (Ahad Ha'am 1931).

Migrants of the second aliyah differed from their predecessors both in
their ideology and their practices of settlement. Some 35,000 immigrants arrived between 1904 and 1914 and several thousand of them became the ideological and political core of this wave of immigration. Generally, this core was
made of young people with a socialist and a collectivist orientation and a romantic nationalist ideology. The political objectives of this group clashed with
the nonpolitical objectives of the JCA (Jewish Colonial Association) that assumed control over the Rothschild colonies in 1900 and refused to associate its
enterprise with an assertion of sovereignty over the land. The second aliyah
perceived Jewish sovereignty as the present goal of Zionism and settlement the
means of achieving it. The nationalist drive of the newcomers had important
consequences. Perceiving themselves as workers, rather than farmers like their
predecessors, they demanded to replace the Arab workers, regardless of
economic considerations. They also had different perceptions of the Arabs.
Contrary to the more optimistic views of the early settlers who believed ac-

1. *Aliyah* is the Zionist term for immigrating to Israel, literally meaning "ascent."

commodation was possible. The newcomers saw conflict with the Arabs as inevitable. Accordingly, while the veterans advocated caution and restraint, the newcomers romanticized heroism and practiced an activist approach that did not avoid confrontation when necessary (Eh'ad Ha'Am 1931, 105–7).

Shapira concludes that this new approach substituted a semicolonial model with a settlement model based on the construction of a separated Jewish community with minimal ties with Arabs (Shapira 1992, 120–21). It is debatable, however, whether Zionism shed its colonial characteristics at this period or only shifted to a different type of colonialism based on a change of political reality rather than of ideology. It is obvious that at this stage, using Kimmerling's terms, Zionists realized the degree of *frontierity* (the available territory) was lower than early expectations indicated. Not only was there little uninhibited land, but almost every tract of land available for settlement had an economic value and the settlers had to pay high prices for it. Unlike in other settler destinations, the people of Palestine had already developed a sense of ownership, so the only way for Jews to acquire land was by purchasing it (Kimmerling 1983, 10–14).

Already in 1904, Usishkin described the project as one of ownership: "it is essential that all the land of Palestine, or at least most of it, be the property of the Jewish people." Until Israeli statehood, lands could not be taken by force and Zionists had to rely on purchase (Kimmerling 1983, 14). What changed during this period of the second aliyah were the dynamics of settlement and the relationship with the local population. Unable to compete with Arab workers in skill or wage, Jewish laborers fought for a segregated labor market under the slogan "conquest of labor" (Shafir 1989, 56–58). This created a split between farmers and laborers, as the former were concerned with the economic base of the enterprise (as well as with maintaining good relations with the Arabs) and the latter with the demographic base as a condition for national liberation (88–89).

When the "conquest of labor" as a strategy to exclude Arab laborers and protect Jewish ones failed to achieve the expected results, other methods that would not be subjected to market forces had to be used to realize the demographic/national interest. The organizational innovation that provided the infrastructure for effective colonization was cooperative settlement. This "pure settlement theory" adopted by the World Zionist Organization drew on similar experiences in Germany. Its basic principles were that the political question of Palestine would be solved once Jews owned most of the land, dominated the economy, become the majority of the population, and could legitimately demand autonomy (Shafir 1989, 154). Several Zionist organizations began to purchase land, train Jewish immigrants for agriculture, and settle them on the land. The combined effect was a settlement largely sealed off from the labor market that guaranteed exclusive Jewish employment.

Lacking the political or military power to take over the land, the Zionist strategy continued the attempts to extend ownership of land and developed models of exclusive collective settlement as the basis for future political maneuvers. Between 1900 and 1914, major changes in the pattern of land acquisition took place. First, Baron Rothschild, frustrated with the economic failure of the settlements in Israel, transferred them into the hands of the JCA whose policy in the old and new colonies was based on making them economically sustainable. Second, the Zionist movement through the Anglo-Palestine Company (APC) became involved in land purchase in Palestine. And third, Zionists succeeded in drawing private capital for land purchase in Palestine, despite the meager profits involved. These were, according to one Zionist leader, "companies for the public benefit operating on a commercial basis" (Shafir 1989, 313). By 1914 Jews owned more than four hundred thousand dunams of land in Palestine and had established forty-four settlements, fourteen of them sponsored by the World Zionist Organization.

Palestinians: Resistance and Identity

The Zionist enterprise in Palestine did not develop in isolation as Arab reactions to Jewish immigration and land acquisitions demonstrated. Implicitly or explicitly, Zionists had to recognize the existence of another nation or would-be nation on the same territory with competing claims to it. Arab attacks gradually grew in number and became explicit in their aim so they could no longer be explained away as local feuds or misunderstandings of cultural differences. The question of Palestinian nationalism and its time of appearance, like that of the relation between Zionism and colonialism, pertain to the contemporary debates over territorial rights. Palestinian nationalism has often been discounted by Israeli statesmen as well as scholars who argued that the Palestinians are part of the wider Arab nation rather than a separate nation deserving political sovereignty.

Most scholars, however, seem to agree that by 1914 a Palestinian national movement existed and that this movement challenged the Zionist project with its territorial claims. In his seminal study of Palestinian nationalism, Yehoshua Porath argues that the external pressure of Zionism endowed the nonpolitical concept of Palestine that developed during the first half of the nineteenth century with a political significance as the desire to prevent Zionism from realizing its goals motivated the Arabs of Palestine to organize politically and formulate their claims on a nationalist base (Porath 1974, 304). Indeed, Palestinians had to fashion their identity and independent political existence not only in opposition to British power but also against the Zionist movement that challenged their rights to the land. Yet, as Rashid Khalidi suggests, Palestinian identity cannot be reduced to a reaction to Zionism as this ignores the process of nationalism and identification that unfolded throughout the Middle East with the new states created after World War I: "In every case, these new identities can be shown to have been contingent, conjunctural, and dependent on circumstances rather than essential or primordial. As part of this universal process, moreover, Lebanese, Syrians, Egyptians and Jordanians all managed to develop their respective nation-state nationalisms during the same period without the dubious benefit of a Zionist challenge" (Khalidi 1997, 21).

Kimmerling's differentiation between a national identity and a "collective identity" that necessarily preconditions it provides a useful framework to understand the development of Palestinian nationalism. The collective identity crafts physical and social boundaries, a domestic social order, and accepted rules of the game that govern the collectivity (Kimmerling 2000). Accordingly, Kimmerling and others describe a Palestinian collective identity that preceded the formation of a modern national consciousness and underscored early opposition to Zionism. This collective identity also underscored the resistance of the Arabs of Palestine to the invasion of Muhammad Ali in 1834, which has been described as the first Palestinian revolt (Kimmerling and Migdal 1993, 6). Enduring regional and local loyalties that involved the intense attachment of the urban population to their towns, of the peasantry to their villages and lands, and of both to their home regions preceded more modern national sentiments and served as its building blocks. Thus the threat to the Holy Land, to take one example, provided a locus of identity for local Palestinians and was the forerunner of modern Palestinian consciousness so that Zionism was depicted as a threat even before modern nationalism had set in (Khalidi 1997, 32). In a short time, due to global, regional, and local transformations, sufficient demands for political rights based on "objective factors" were voiced to argue that the transition from Arab consciousness to Arab/Palestinian nationalism had begun (Porath 1974, 20).

Several overlapping senses of identity operated in the way Palestinians came to define themselves as a people at the turn of the century. Khalidi finds that major currents that swept the Middle East during the early twentieth century—Western powers' definition of state boundaries as well as Arabism, Islamic trends, and Zionism—along with more parochial (and long-term historical) factors—strong religious attachment to Palestine, the impact of long-standing administrative boundaries, and enduring regional and local loyalties—shaped the Palestinian national identity (Khalidi 1997, 21). In the earlier period of Zionism, manifestations of Arab collective identity vis-à-vis Jewish immigration were largely sporadic and uncoordinated. On the one hand, Palestinian-Arab notables already in 1891 petitioned the Ottoman government demanding the prevention of immigration of Jews to Palestine and purchase of land by them. On the other hand, Arab peasants "locally" protested the sale of the land by their absentee landlords to the Jewish settlers when the change of owners entailed their expulsion from the land.

Manifestations of anti-Zionism became more systematic after the 1908 young Turks' revolt in the newly established Ottoman parliament. The temporary removal of censorship enabled the anti-Zionist movement to express its discontent with Jewish immigration and land purchase (Mandel 1976, 80). The local Arab elites that adopted an Ottoman identity shared with Turkish ministers the view of Zionism as a nationalist "separatist" movement and as the vanguard of Russian or German influence in the region (226). For example, on the eve of the elections of 1914, candidates from the Jerusalem district vowed to fight the "threat of Zionism" (Lesch 1979, 27). Ottoman loyalism, however, was gradually translated into a local patriotism as Zionists came to be seen not only as a general threat to Ottoman rule but also as a particular threat to Palestine. Accordingly, local Arabs began speaking of themselves as "Palestinians" and organizing around a Palestinian identity.

The continued land purchases by Jews helped the Palestinian national movement to consolidate the local struggles into a wider resistance. The purchase of al-Fula marked the beginning of an overt and articulate anti-Zionist campaign, supported by Arab elites and receiving high attention in the press, that indicated the intention of the Jews to take control of the country (Khalidi 1997, 107). Gradually, opposition to Zionism and to land sales by absentee landlords created an important shared element that cemented the link between Palestinian elites who opposed Zionism on grounds of principle and peasants whose resistance played a vital role in mobilizing opinion in Palestine and the wider Arab world. These trends were also influenced by developments in the

Zionist movement and its strategies of land purchase and settlement. The new settlers who arrived in the second aliyah, unlike their predecessors who employed Arabs, developed an ideology and practice of "Jewish labor" and "Jewish defense" with an aim of nationalist exclusivism. This new strategy of colonization entailed the exclusion of Arab workers from the colonies and the replacement of local "strongmen" protection by Jewish armed guards (Kimmerling 2000). The limited success of outcompeting Arab workers led to a new strategy of a "pure settlement colony" aimed at control of land, employment that ensured a European standard of living, and massive immigration (Shafir 1999). The removal of land and labor from the market by the establishment of "settlement-cooperatives" closed them off to Palestinian Arabs and sharpened the perception among Arabs of the zero-sum nature of the conflict.

The combination of anti-Zionist arguments and claims of historical continuity of the Palestinians, according to Porath, "came close to the fundamental principle of the national independence movements in Europe" (1974, 41). In the late nineteenth century Ottoman loyalism, Arabism, religion, and local patriotism overlapped in the identity of the Arabs in Palestine. With the collapse of the Ottoman Empire after World War I and the diminishing role of religion as a source of identity across the Arab world, nationalism grew rapidly. Early on in the British mandate, the Arab residents of the country increasingly came to "imagine" themselves as part of a single community, although Arabism, religion, and local loyalties remained highly relevant (Khalidi 1997, 145–58).

The global changes of the period have had important influences on the development of Palestinian national identity and strategies. In the wake of World War I, the Arabs of Palestine were caught between the Balfour declaration committing Britain to the Zionist cause and the Sykes-Picot accords of 1916 in which Britain and France divided the Arab provinces of the Ottoman Empire between them. "These upheavals in the world around them, upheavals that impinged directly on the structure of the lives of the entire population, made possible, and at the same time necessitated, extremely rapid changes in attitudes and consciousness on part of the people of Palestine" (Khalidi 1997, 160).

These attitudes were translated for a short period into a wider Arab identity. This short episode began in 1918 when Amir Faysal ibn Husayn proclaimed in Damascus an "independent Arab constitutional government" in hope of being included in the new world order of self-determination. Arabs of Palestine, especially the elites, hoped to be a part of the greater Syria (including present-day Syria, Lebanon, Jordan, and Israel) that would remain a united

Arab state. Palestinian notables and intellectuals petitioned the British government and other powers and expressed their will to be included under Syrian
rule and their belief that Palestine was part of Syria. This collective identity,
however, almost disappeared after Faysal's fall when the French took over
Damascus. Afterward, it was the British mandate and its boundaries that
shaped the Palestinian collective identity. The regional political reality created
after the war—the creation of Arab independent or would-be independent
states, the British mandate, and the fast development of the Jewish settlement—enhanced the consolidation of identity among various groups and
strata and accelerated institutional building (Kimmerling 2000).

The political arguments raised by the Palestinians after World War I
tapped into Woodrow Wilson's peace program based on the right to self-
determination. Article 22 of the Covenant of the League of Nations, which
stated that the wishes of certain communities formerly belonging to the Turkish empire should be recognized as potential states in need of temporary guidance, was used by Palestinians to demand a status similar to that of Iraq and
Transjordan, who attained a more independent form of government (Porath
1974, 44). Against the Balfour declaration, Palestinian Arabs presented the correspondence between Sir Henry McMahon, the British high commissioner in
Egypt, and Sherif Husayn, the emir of Mecca in which the latter agreed to join
the allies if they would uphold the Arabs' claims for independence. Britain, in
its struggle to establish control of the region, it appeared, had made commitments that were contradictory (Lesch 1979, 33). The struggle with Zionism was
presented by the Arabs as zero-sum. Palestine, it was argued by the Arab Executive Committee in 1921, could only remain tranquil if it would be inhabited by
one people, possessing one language, one nationality, and one interest. In a letter to Herbert Samuel, the committee explained its position: "We cannot pa-
tiently watch our homeland pass into others' hands. Either us or the Zionists!
There is no room for both elements struggling together in the same area. The
laws of nature require that one side be defeated. We want life and they are striv-
ing for it, but life is indivisible. There is no escaping the fact that one of us must
win" (Porath 1974, 50).

The realization of the Arabs that Zionists' aim was a Jewish homeland in
Palestine underscored the consolidation of national identity based on elements
of collective identity that had developed earlier. Initially, Arab resistance was in
the form of local unrest with peasants protesting their evacuation from the
land and elites appealing to the Ottoman government to prevent Jewish settle-

ment. But in a short time, a Palestinian national movement with leadership and organization was facing the Zionist movement. Despite the consolidation of a national identity between 1919 and 1948, however, Palestinians had difficulties transcending local, family, and regional rivalries to unify their efforts (Khalidi 1997, 25).

Conclusion

The turbulent period described in chapter 2 provided the context for the rise of Zionism and Palestinian nationalism. For Zionism the global changes provided the motivating force, the opportunities, and the logic of operation. The development of exclusionary nationalism in Europe imposed new constraints upon Jews, mainly in Eastern Europe but also in the West, and was a powerful incentive for Jews to find a political solution. For a minority of Jews, this solution had to emulate the developments in Europe and follow the nationalist zeitgeist, namely making the Jews a (territorial) nation like all nations. The international arena, where powers struggled for territorial expansion and control, provided opportunities that Zionists attempted to exploit in order to achieve territorial sovereignty in Palestine.

The Zionist campaign consisted of a wide-reaching diplomatic move that attempted to receive international support in the form of a charter to the land and a piecemeal settlement and purchase of land in order to make the Zionist enterprise into a fact. The diplomatic effort resulted in the Balfour declaration that committed Britain to the Zionists' cause. The settlement effort developed new strategies for conquering the land and created the infrastructure for future massive Jewish immigration. Zionism, however, soon had to face the reality of a protagonist Palestinian national movement with competing territorial claims. Shortly after World War I, the two national movements were facing each other and the protracted Israeli-Palestinian conflict began its long journey.

4

The Making of Irish Nationalism

IRISH NATIONALISM entered the period of early globalization in a more developed stage than Zionism. To start with the obvious, unlike Jews who were a diaspora nation, Irish Catholics were living on their own land in a status they defined as an "oppressed majority." In addition, Irish nationalism had a history of political struggles under different forms and for different causes that had important influence upon its state in the late nineteenth century. Therefore, the effects of external influences and the general impact of the international changes of the globalization period previously discussed were less profound than in the Zionist case. Yet the changed international setting had some important influences on the developments in this region. Nationalism, as John Hutchinson argues, is a global phenomenon, and therefore Irish nationalism, like any other nationalism, can only be understood within an international perspective (Hutchinson 1996).

During this period, and in line with the zeitgeist of the time, the Irish conflict crystallized along clearly defined ethnic-religious lines, Catholic and Protestant, and around two different territorial agendas, political independence or unification with Britain. The developments in nationalism in Ireland paralleled developments elsewhere as the ideas of territoriality and homogeneity, cultural revival, historicism, and nationalism based upon mass participation that evolved in Ireland were all features of late-nineteenth-century nationalism elsewhere. The general developments of British imperialism and the related developments in British domestic politics influenced the dynamics of this national struggle. Opposition to British rule in Ireland can be traced back to the beginning of the English occupation and colonization of the island in the sixteenth century. Earlier struggles against British rule, however, were not exclusive to Catholics or even dominated by Catholic identity. Rather, in the late eighteenth century it was the settler Protestant minority that sought to secure legislative independence from Britain that led the struggle and developed an idea of Irish nationalism.

Until the late nineteenth century, both the opposition to British rule and the support of the British union crossed religious lines. Nothing, therefore, in the development of Irish nationalism in the late nineteenth century during which it overlapped with Catholicism was predestined or inevitable. While Irish nationalist narrative retrojected modern nationalism into the Gaelic past to make current politics its simple continuation, various revisionist historians sought to argue the opposite. George D. Boyce, for example, highlights the discontinuities between the different periods of nationalism. Irish nationalism, he argues, has gone through different phases in which it was characterized by race, religion, and a sense of territorial unity and integrity and was influenced by the power and proximity of Britain (Boyce 1991, 19). In this and other works, the nation is seen as constructed out of diverse and often contradictory interests with Gaelic history being a resource drawn upon at different periods by different political agendas (Hutchinson 1996).

Similar to the Zionist case, it was a group of activists that reached the conclusion that nationalism (through elimination of British rule) would be a solution to the Irish people, that Catholicism overlapped with Irish nationalism, and, thus, ended up revolutionizing Irish life.

> In the wake of famine, a radicalized generation of young men, most of them Catholics and of modest social origins, put together an almost open and certainly very widespread, conspiracy to eliminate British rule in Ireland. Much derided at the time, this conspiracy persisted for over sixty years; some would argue that it still exists. There was nothing spontaneous about the Irish revolution; it was created by the strenuous efforts of many activists over two generations. (Garvin 1987, 5)

Like in the previous chapter, the purpose here is not to provide a historical account but to trace the influence of early globalization on local developments in Ireland. Moving from the macro, changes in the international system, to the micro, the ethnic conflict in Ireland, I am interested in the opportunities and constraints created by the international developments and their translation into domestic agendas. Accordingly, I will, first, outline the similarities between the developments in Irish nationalism and the general ideas of the period and its zeitgeist. Second, I will describe how the development of Irish nationalism at the turn of the century was influenced by world politics, especially Britain's interests and concerns. And third, I will show the competition the new Irish nationalism was soon faced with from a self-conscious Protestant community.

Inclusive Nationalism

The development of Irish nationalism associated with Catholicism that "exploded" at the end of the nineteenth century had roots in earlier developments. These precursors can be found in other national expressions such as Wolfe Tone's "Society of United Irishmen," in the formation of Daniel O'Connell's Catholic Association in 1823, in the secret Irish Revolutionary (later Republican) Brotherhood in 1858, or in Parnell's Home Rule Party of the late 1870s. What separates these early expressions of nationalism from their modern form was that they did not overlap with the Catholic-Protestant divide. Rather, this early nationalism was essentially anti-British and relatively inclusive regarding participation. A Catholic separate identity was not consolidated until the late nineteenth century, and only then did Irish nationalism take its modern form, becoming exclusively Catholic with an agenda of territorial sovereignty for Irish Catholics.

Wolfe Tone's national ideas in the early nineteenth century were strongly influenced by the French revolution and its ideas of liberty. This nationalism appealed mainly to the Irish Protestant middle class but also to the Catholic middle class in Belfast and Dublin. Tone called for the unification of all Irish in order "to subvert the tyranny of our execrable government, to break the connection with England, the never-failing source of all our political evils, and to assert the independence of our country—these were my objects. To unite the whole people of Ireland, to abolish the memory of all past dissensions, and to substitute the common name of Irishman in place of the denominations of Protestant, Catholic and Dissenter—these were my means" (Cronin 1980, 44).

Tone's nationalism was a product of the Enlightenment, the French Revolution, and the American Revolution. Its protagonists, mainly Protestant business and professional men, were not concerned with national origins and the past, but with the present and the future. They were interested in creating a socially progressive and tolerant society in which all Irish would find their place: "If we are still illiberal and blind bigots, who deny that civil liberty can exist out of the pale of Protestantism, if we withhold the sacred cup of *Liberty* from our Catholic brother, and repeal him from the communion of our natural rights, let us at least be consistent and cease to murmur at the oppression of the government that grinds us" (Cronin 1980, 46). But despite the unifying rhetoric, the early nineteenth century was a period of sectarian conflicts, and Tone's republicanism—and more importantly secular nationalism—was not a set of principles that could give life and meaning to everyday politics and life. Therefore its agenda appealed only to a minority of the Irish and had limited political significance (Boyce 1991, 132–33).

Daniel O'Connell's "Young Ireland" movement of the 1820s was also a liberal form of nationalism and advocated an amalgamated Ireland to repeal the union. The British union, he argued, could be defeated only by a concerted effort of all Irishmen, Catholic and Protestant (Boyce 1991, 135). "Let us . . . endeavor to amalgamate the Catholic, the Protestant, the Presbyterian, the Dissenter, the Methodist, the Quaker, into the *Irishman*—and, forgetting our individual wrongs, let us call upon Irishmen of every description to combine in a noble struggle for the natural and inherent rights of our wretched country" (Flynn 2000, 59). But O'Connell's message was ambiguous regarding the boundaries of Irish nationalism. The root of the difficulty, which will repeat itself later on, was the inability to decide or to spell out whether the Protestants were part of his vision of Ireland.

O'Connell gave different messages at different times and for different audiences. He revived the confederate concept of the Catholic Irish nation loyal to the British crown, and the Catholic Association he has founded in 1823 advocated national pride, self-respect, and the right of the Irish nation to its land (Boyce 1991, 137–41). But although it became more and more clear that the Irish nation overlapped with Catholicism, out of O'Connell's thirty-nine members of Parliament, thirteen were Protestants. Also, Irish Protestants within the movement like Thomas Davis attempted to create an Irish nationalism that would be more inclusive (154). Davis advocated making linguistic and cultural barriers between Ireland and England and breaking the barriers between Catholics and Protestants. Irishness, he argued, was not a product of race but of an environment (157–58). Despite not having sectarian intentions, O'Connell's movement drifted away from Davis's concept of nationhood and increasingly slipped into identifying Irishness with Catholicism and ended up alienating most of the Protestants who were a part of the movement (Girvan 1999).

The famine of the mid-nineteenth century and its legacy had profound influences on the development of nationalism and the relationship with Britain.

Most importantly, the neglect by the British government and its slow intervention in the deep crisis, intentionally or not, signaled for many Irish that they were not considered equals by Britain and therefore could not be regarded as British. The famine crisis, argues Girvan, restructured Irish society and led to the consolidation of a Catholic identity with a nationalist agenda. "This new society was more uniformly Catholic, English speaking and middle class than the society that preceded it. Whereas there had been serious competition for power and resources within the national community in prefamine Ireland, the characteristic feature of the post famine conflict was competition between the Catholic-nationalist community on the one hand and the British state and Irish landlordism on the other" (Girvan 1999).

The famine and the following mass migration eventually changed the structure of Catholic society itself. The decimation of the poorer classes, British reforms, and the growing influence of the Church all contributed to the formation of nationalist identity. In the years that followed the famine, increasing levels of literacy, commerce and urbanization, wider employment opportunities, and the availability of a popular press made it more likely that the Irish public would be influenced by ideas from outside their immediate communities (Flynn 2000, 85). Thus in Ireland, like in other cases of developing nationalism, a modernizing ethnic group, dominated by a younger generation frustrated with its limited mobilization opportunities, gradually led the nationalization of society.

Irish Americans supported a more radical separatist idea called Fenianism, whose central motivation revolved around the view of England as a "satanic power," a mystic commitment to Ireland, and a belief in a superior moral authority of a future independent Irish republic (Foster 1988, 391). This political agenda had limited appeal within Ireland, as the failed 1867 rebellion attested. Home rule—the demand for devolution and an Irish parliament—was a theme that could potentially unite Catholics with Protestants unsatisfied with British rule, and it was by far more popular. The leadership of Protestants like Isaac Butt (of the Home Government Association in 1870) and later of Parnell demonstrated that it was not only Catholics who were unsatisfied with the union and, therefore, that the national idea had the potential to cut across the religious divide. Butt, a typical member of the Protestant class, converted from British unionism to devolution, or "home rule." Like other Protestants, he believed that a true union would require a properly functioning representative institution that eventually would be a better alternative to a coerced union. This institution, he argued, could eventually bind England and Ireland in mutual harmony. In a meeting in May 1970, a committee was established to advance the cause of a devolved government that included thirty-five Protestants and twenty-five Catholics (Boyce 1991, 193). Parnell, who replaced Butt as the president of the Home Rule Party, was more decisive than Butt in his criticism of British rule and was supported by both the Catholic Church and constitutional Fenians, a support base that required constant negotiations and compromises between the parties and was not devoid of tensions. What united all these forces was hate toward British rule, but the attempt to bring together moderate nationalists, Fenians, the Catholic Church, agrarian radicals, and even unionists was a difficult endeavor.

The agricultural crisis of 1879–82 reawoke among Irish farmers, especially the Catholics, the feeling of resentment toward the existing British social order. This crisis strengthened their belief that the former famine was not an act of God or an accident but a conspiracy of landlords, as was the present crisis (Boyce 1990, 16). Cooperation with Protestants disenchanted with Britain's rule, however, still operated at this stage. Therefore, it was Parnell who led the Irish National Land League that was formed in 1879. Its agenda brought together home rule and economic rights for the rural population and demanded that the farmers be made owners of their lands. The diverse elements that made the league (tenants, laborers, priests) united in a communal struggle of "the people" versus "the landlords" or "the state." The union, they believed, was a poor political arrangement for the nation, now defined as non-landlord, and the Home Rule Party became synonymous with nationalist Ireland (172). The struggle successfully used the technological innovation of print capitalism, as newspapers became widely read and a source of information (McCall 1999, 30). This combined agenda of anti-rent and nationalism that drew both constituencies together was a result of a conjuncture of interests and opportunities. "Sudden economic shifts made an anti-rent campaign financially attractive, and cultural changes made a nationwide campaign organizationally feasible. Cultural continuity, on the other hand, supplied the folk memories that questioned the property rights of the landowner, excused agrarian crime and strengthened local solidarity against the outside" (Garvin 1981, 70).

Not only did the issues of political independence and land reform cut across the Protestant-Catholic divide, but in the cultural revival Protestants were active in the attempt to create an inclusive Irish identity. The Gaelic League was initially made of both Catholics and Protestants like Douglas Hyde, all united in the belief that Ireland must "de-Anglicize" and in the rejection of the intrusion of English culture. Hyde even used the rhetoric of purity and argued that those refusing to use the Irish language not only were untrue Irishmen but were not even English. Rather, they were stranded in a no man's land between two distinct nations (Boyce 1991, 237–39). This process of de-Anglicization, in which Irish intellectuals were busy revitalizing the Celtic language and history, began as a nonexclusive movement. Hyde, a Protestant and a unionist in his politics, explained, "Our once great national tongue must be revived and the spiritual Irish nation saved. In order to de-Anglicize ourselves we must at once arrest the decay of the language" (Cronin 1980, 97).

The Home Rule Party competed in the elections of 1874 with land and educational reforms in its political platform standing above self-government. The party won sixty seats and went to Westminster to bargain for those it defined as the "Irish people" (Boyce 1996, 24–25), but the issue of "who are the Irish people" was yet to be clearly defined and soon split the party. Similar deliberation over the boundaries of Irishness accompanied the political developments of the Gaelic revival and the noninclusive arguments raised by some of its Catholic leaders caused it to gradually shed its early rank-and-file Protestant supporters. D. P. Moran, a journalist and the founder of the *Leader* journal, spelled out the fundamentals of Irish nationalism and the split between Catholics and Protestants: "In the main non-Catholic Ireland looks upon itself as British and as Anglo-Irish," but even the Protestants who see themselves as nationalist, he argued, "must recognize that the Irish nation is *de facto* a Catholic nation" (quoted in Boyce 1991, 242–43). Nationalism had now to contend with the difficult questions of who constituted "the Irish people" or "the nation" and of how to "reconcile their notions of a dispossessed people with their purpose to create an Ireland in which the dispossessed and those who [in nationalist ideology)] did the dispossessing could live together" (Boyce 1990, 183).

Parnell attempted to hold the movement together across the deep divisions, but the split between Parnell and the church and the breakup of the national league permitted other organizations to emerge and capture the imagination of the young (Garvin 1981, 97). New forces began pulling nationalism toward the direction of national exclusiveness. The Gaelic League, the Literary Revival, and the Gaelic Athletic Association, founded to revive the traditional sports of hurling and Gaelic football, all launched between 1886 and 1893, sprang from discontent at Ireland's drift toward British cultural and social forms (MacDonagh 1977, 73). The successful Gaelic and Christian past was revived and played a central role in the transformation of the Irish from an ethnic group into a nation. The message of all those groups was that a distinctive national cultural and linguistic tradition separated the Irish from the English.

Different past injustices and grievances, especially the famine, combined with the cultural movements described above to push nationalism forward (McCall 1999, 22–23). Protestants who initially took part of this cultural revival no longer had a place. Douglas Hyde, a Protestant and founder of the Gaelic League, expressed his frustration with the development—or the lack of it. "The Irish race at present is in a most anomalous position, imitating England and yet apparently hating it. Just when we should be starting to build anew the Irish race and the Gaelic nation—as within our recollection Greece has been built up anew—we find ourselves despoiled of the bricks of nationality" (MacDonagh 1977, 73). Hyde and Protestants like him, however, were now at the margins of the national revival, which, toward the end of the nineteenth century, overlapped with Catholicism.

Irish Nationalism

The nineteenth century in Ireland witnessed a gradual rise of a Roman Catholic middle class which was the driving force behind nationalism. Catholics were making important advances in social status, economic betterment, and political power (Boyce 1988), but they were not satisfied with their achievements and attributed the limitations to the British-imposed and Protestant-dominated social order. It was modernity, therefore, that provided the conditions for the development of Irish nationalism both negatively, by grievance and historical memory, and positively, by providing the means by which an "imagined community" could be developed. As in the Zionist case, it was the limits of modernization that caused this middle class to realize its identity: "In Yeats's classical phrase, many of them indeed possessed great hatred and suffered from little room; little room was accorded them by Irish society or by the Anglo-Irish establishment, and great hate was commonly the consequence" (McCall 1999, 35).

The elections of 1885 and 1886 marked both the turning point and the future of Irish politics. Not only were these elections characterized by the rise of modern political parties based, like elsewhere, on a new mass electorate, but also a distinct nationalist/unionist division overlapped with the

Catholic/Protestant divide. In previous elections, the divide was less clear as the British parties were able to appeal to different constituencies: Catholics at times voted for the Conservatives and Protestants for Liberals (Walker 1994, 5–7). When nationalists in the 1880s began reorganizing themselves through nationalist parties, a patriotic union was formed in the south in response, uniting Liberals and Conservatives behind a platform of preserving the union with Britain. Denominational ties and identities became the main determining factor in political behavior, regardless of regional and class differences. The divide between Protestants and Catholics was overriding all other divisions.

National consciousness in Ireland had been brewing since the middle of the nineteenth century, and toward the century's end it became a typical product of the period. Like other nationalisms, it was based upon territorial logic, mass participation, and cultural-historical revival. This new nationalism fused Catholic religious identity, demand for democratic rights and social justice, and resentment for what it considered a long history of dispossession, discrimination, and inequality. Garvin describes the leaders of the revolution as "children of their time" who, like their contemporaries elsewhere in Europe, sensed that the twentieth century was going to bring great changes (1987, 57). Much of this movement, he argues, was antimodern and tended toward a romantic and messianic nationalism. At its extreme, this nationalism expressed fear and dislike of Freemasons and Jews that were imagined as part of an international conspiracy. A preacher in Limerick in 1904 incited Ireland's only pogrom. The source of anti-Semitism, according to Garvin, was the "fear of the modern, the fear of change, and the belief that the Catholic Irish were not well-equipped to survive and compete in the modern world" (71).

John Redmond, Parnell's successor in the Home Rule Party, regarded the "normalization" of Ireland as the goal of political nationalism, namely attaining an independent status. Political nationalists held a moderate stance toward nationalism; they wished for an Ireland modeled on British liberal lines that would be a partner in the British imperial mission. Redmond's moderate position on political nationalism, however, was challenged not only by unionist opposition but also by more radical demands for cultural nationalism. This nationalism, represented by Sinn Fein, aimed at the moral regeneration of the historic community and the re-creation of distinctive national civilization (Hennessey 1998, 24–25, 28).

Compromises like home rule and equal rights through British citizenship no longer satisfied growing numbers of the Catholic Irish whose aim was secessionist, demanding an independent Irish state completely separated from Britain. The Catholic middle class, who had grown in numbers since the middle of the nineteenth century, made advances, especially in education, but their upward mobility was increasingly blocked as employment opportunities satisfied neither their expectations of self-fulfillment nor those of prosperity. The fact that Protestants were proportionally overrepresented in higher posts in government and commerce led Catholics to the conclusion that the modernization process Ireland was going through brought them poor material prospects and added little to their self-esteem. Their reaction was what one author described as a "Social Darwinist inspired patriotism," highlighting the superiority of the Catholic or Gaelic nation and the alleged unfairness of the contemporary social order.

These ideas of national goals and international competition, like in other places, opened space for intellectual and cultural work, and a transcendental idea of superiority crystallized around Irish culture. The main cultural achievements of this new nationalism were, negatively, demarcating Irishness as non-Englishness and, positively, creating a new "race project" that answered the psychological needs of the time for a solidarity based on primordial and quasi-egalitarian feelings of collective identification before the nation (O'Mahony and Delanty 1998, 77). The Gaelic League was founded in 1893 with the purpose of reviving the Irish language. Although its founders declared that the league was apolitical (and its membership included Protestants), its campaign did have significant political ramifications and eventually the league became a major part of the nationalist struggle. In time the league grew larger and became more Catholic and more clericalist to the point where its publication, the *Leader,* raised the question whether a Protestant could be Irish. Its answer ridiculed this possibility.

> The type of Non-Catholic Nationalist to whom we refer to has been pampered in vanity. He could not be a mere home ruler, so he found it necessary to differentiate and be a Protestant home ruler; he thinks that Ireland practically never had a leader who was not a Protestant—that is one of the fruits of commencing Irish history at the year 1782. . . . he does not understand Ireland— a fact which would not be of much import if he did not firmly believe that he is a philosopher. (Garvin 1987, 85)

Irish cultural revival was now almost exclusively a part of a Catholic political agenda. Accordingly, the very concept of Irish history became an "ideological football" between two evolving competing accounts of history: one Protestant and unionist, the other Catholic and nationalist, each telling a different version of history, which also served as a model for the future Ireland (Garvin 1987, 112). The use of culture and especially language had important consequences. Like Zionism, this national revival was both modern and nostalgic (or even antimodern as mentioned above), drawing on past resources (real or fabricated) for present and future purposes. Mainly, if successfully implemented, it was believed, this revival of culture could provide the Catholic aspiring middle class with the equality or superiority it could not hope to achieve under British rule and Protestant dominance.

> To preach to the return of Ireland to its ancient language would no longer be a propagandist slogan for men and women studying Gaelic in Dublin evening classes and teaching what they had just learned to other militants. As the history of the Irish free state was to demonstrate, it would become the qualification for all but the most subaltern civil service jobs and passing examinations in Irish would therefore be the criterion of belonging to the professional and the intellectual classes. (Hobsbawm 1990, 112)

Where Zionism—which was, as described earlier, a diaspora nationalism—was directly affected by events in Europe and the zeitgeist—Irish nationalism was less exposed to external influence but not immune to it. Arthur Griffith, one of the founders of the Republican Sinn Fein, defined the aims of Irish nationalism through comparison with Magyar achievement. Irish nationalism, he argued, could reinforce its strength and broaden its inspiration by relating to other nationalist movements in Europe. Griffith was also influenced by the ideas of economic autarchy pioneered by the German economist Friedrich List, thus bringing together cultural and economic separatism.

> "My object," said List, "is at all costs to save Germany from the destruction which the commercial policy of England designs for her." Our object is, at all costs, to save Ireland. "On the development of the German protective system," List wrote, "depends the existence, the independence, and the future of German nationality. Only in the soil of general prosperity does the national spirit strike its roots, produces fine blossoms and rich fruits—only from the unity of material interests does mental power arise and again from both of them national power." The fruits of List's teaching is the Germany of today. It is part of the policy of the National Council (Sinn Fein) to bring about that unity of material interests which produces national strength. (Cronin 1980, 119)

This was translated into a political agenda advocating abstentionist tactics and the withdrawal of support from all British institutions from Parliament down (Foster 1988, 457).

The developments within Republicanism of separatism, cultural revival, and a "youth culture" had parallels elsewhere in Europe. Tom Garvin refers to what he defines as the "generation of 1914" as a European phenomenon that had ramifications on the formation of nationalism in Ireland.

> The "generation of 1914" saw itself as a cultural and political renewal. The recent past was disavowed and romanticized versions of medieval society were reconstructed and forwarded as blueprints for the future. Age came to be associated with degeneration and a society, which was materialistic, crass and unjust. War came to be seen as a cleansing thing and young intellectuals bewailed their fate of having been born into a selfish and hateful society. (Garvin 1988, 100–101)

The radicalization of Irish politics in general and nationalism in particular was also influenced by the Boer War around 1900. This war signaled for many nationalists that British rule could be fought and boosted the membership of the Gaelic League, from 107 branches in 1899 to nearly 400 by 1902. In Belfast, Catholic gangs took the names of Boer generals (Foster 1988, 458).

If Irish nationality has been assumed rather than defined throughout most of the nineteenth century, the Gaelicizing movements were creating something new. A Gaelic Ireland that spoke a different language, played different games, and fostered a different culture was deepening the gulf between the northeast and the rest of the island. In the spirit of the time, nationalists advocated cultural distinctiveness and economic independence by calling upon people to "buy Irish" (MacDonagh 1977, 74). Sinn Fein, established in 1905, meaning "ourselves," was becoming the dominant Catholic political movement, pushing forward the ideas of self-reliance and cultural distinction. Griffith, who was as already noted influenced by the ideas of the German economist List, argued in that spirit that isolation would be the way to solve Irish poverty. A sectarian, if not a racial, tone distinguished Sinn Fein's ideology from that of its national predecessors, making "Gaelic" and "Irish" synonymous terms and then making "Gaelic" and "Catholic" synonymous, although neither overlapped completely in reality. Finally, Irish history was also interpreted in racial/ethnic terms of Gaelic civilization versus Anglo-Saxon (Cronin 1980, 99). The combined influence of the antimodern romanticism of the period and a specific Catholic worldview led to a strain of xenophobia and even anti-Semitism, culminating in 1904 in a pogrom against Jews in Limerick (Garvin 1981, 57–59, 70).

The rebellion of 1916 was an especially important mark in the development of nationalism, despite the fact that it was taken by a small group of nationalists against the wishes of the majority of Catholics who, for several reasons, remained loyal to Britain during the war. First, the rising was strategically timed not only to take advantage of Britain's involvement in the war, but also—so its planners hoped—to win recognition for Ireland's claim to independence and representation for Ireland in the envisaged postwar conference (Hennessey 1998, 130). Second, unlike the rebellions of 1848 and 1867, it was not a complete fiasco; the rebels were able to cause some difficulty for the British before the rebellion was put down. And third, whereas the 1848 rebellion was Anglo-Irish and the 1867 rebellion met with strong opposition from the Catholic Church, the 1916 rising was a rebellion by members of the Catholic nation—the "Irish properly," so called—for the Catholic nation. It was not only that the leaders were all Catholic, but many were also attached to the church and believed in the special nature of the Irish Catholic people. While the rising was not directed against Protestants, it was a rising without Protestants in influential positions. Previously mostly Anglo-Irish movements and leaders had shaped the ethos of Ireland and Irish nationalism. The new nationalism had taken a different turn; nationalist Ireland no longer required Protestant leadership (Boyce 1991, 309–10).

The rebellion itself was the act of a minority since most Catholics were reluctant to join the rebels. Measures taken prior to the war to ameliorate some of the Catholic grievances and offer a moderate alternative to home rule were enough to curb disloyalty to the point that many Irish volunteered for the army during the war. But the aftermath of the rebellion gained the rebels, in retrospect, sympathy and admiration of the wider populace. The execution of the rebels themselves and the harsh measures the British government took against those suspected to be connected to the rebellion backfired and turned an unpopular revolution into a founding act of the Irish nation. Sinn Fein, reaping the popularity of nationalism, became the dominant national organization; it declined to settle for home rule and instead demanded full independence for Ireland. In its direct appeal to what it called "our people" (namely, Catholics) and its enlistment of the support of Roman Catholic bishops, Sinn Fein excluded Protestants, practically if not formally, from its ranks. After its electoral victory in 1918, Sinn Fein's chosen members for Parliament refused to take their seats in Westminster.

The International Dimension of the Conflict

For Zionists during this period, British rule over Palestine was considered as potentially liberating, but for Irish nationalists, being part of the British Empire and in many regards still a colony, British imperialism was far from desirable. The "Irish question" entered British politics in 1844, and its essence was the difference between what England could consent to regarding Irish self-rule and what Ireland would be content to receive. Britain's approach to the Irish question, according to Boyce, was determined by the exigencies of her own politics and depended very much on the state of public opinion in Britain. Toward the end of the century, however, international developments and Britain's changing international position and concerns also influenced policies toward Ireland (Boyce 1996, 1–2).

Several authors argue that colonialism is a useful theoretical concept to explain the relations between Britain and Ireland. Hechter's "internal colonialism" model explains the relations between the English core and the Celtic periphery as exploitative, similar to other colonialist relations. Thus, Ireland since the seventeenth century was developing according to the desires of the English core.

> In 1600 Ireland was largely a woodland society in which there was very little production for export. However, during the seventeenth and eighteenth centuries, English markets penetrated Ireland to much the same effect as they had the economies of Wales and Scotland. While fully one-eighth of Ireland was covered with forests in 1600, a century later the country was virtually cleared. Irish timber was exported to England, and an Irish controlled iron industry was also developed. Once the supply of timber ran out, the industry disappeared. As English demand for marketed food rose, the Irish economy quickly responded by concentrating on cattle-breeding. (Hechter 1975, 84)

This relationship of "internal colonialism" had two main characteristics. First, Irish society was predominantly agrarian, and because its production was geared toward exports for the British market it was dependent on demands and prices dictated by Britain. And second, cadres not recruited from among those constituting its major sociocultural group, Irish Catholics, politically dominated Ireland (Hechter 1975, 53–54). Initially, this system enabled Britain to rule Ireland effectively, but the developments in the nineteenth century described above made the ruling of Ireland more difficult. Politically, the liberal ideals Britain introduced to Ireland, such as representative government and civil liberties, collided with other popular ideals of this age such as popular sovereignty and self-determination.

> This encouraged an eventual splintering of the union on its periphery. It was not that British political ideals could not apply to Ireland. Rather these ideals were enacted in a way which many Irishmen came to view as antithetical to another liberal tenet, that of popular sovereignty, central to the nascence of nationalism and the ideal of national self-determination in Europe. By relying on liberalism as the doctrinal foundation for the British system, the British state provided the potential basis for Irish nationalist dissent, mobilization, and rebellion. (Flynn 2000, 43)

Britain had its own interests in Ireland especially during this period, however, that prevented it from compromising. First, there was the determined opposition of Protestants, especially in the north, to separation from Britain that could not be ignored because of their political influence in Britain. Second, for the British government, Irish issues were considered to have implications beyond local significance for the British Isles and the empire at large (Kearney 1989, 176–77). Thus, British sensitivity toward Ireland was divided between, on the one hand, the desire to maintain the empire intact and the pressure put by the unionists, and, on the other hand, the growing difficulty of governing the island and the international power the Irish nationalists could exert through the Irish diaspora.

Gladstone, who favored a political settlement in Ireland, argued that the Irish possessed what he called "elements of nationality . . . collective or corporate individuality, tested by reason, and sufficiently confirmed by history." His political conclusion was drawn from developments elsewhere in Europe, whose map "shows us that in cases like those of Hungary or Norway, a vigorous sense of nationality is compatible with effective organic Union tempered by autonomy." The alternative, he feared, was social chaos in Ireland and the undermining of the stability of the British political system (Boyce 1996, 33). Autonomy to the Irish, he believed, would grant them an opportunity to express their patriotism in a way compatible with remaining a part of the British Empire. "The Irishman," he told Parliament, "is more profoundly Irish, but it does not follow, that because his local patriotism is keen, he is incapable of Imperial patriotism" (Mansergh 1965, 137).

In the following years, the debates over home rule led to several political crises in Britain over the future of Ireland and an overall inability to decide. Because home rule signified more than administrative reorganization, British statesmen debated their interests in Ireland and were unable to formulate a coherent policy. Home rule was defeated twice, in 1886 and 1893, in the parliament in London. In 1910, after the election of a liberal government, Parliament was due once again to vote on home rule, but reluctance to open such a volatile issue was so great that a third home rule bill wasn't even introduced until 1912. The bill passed in May 1914, but with Ireland on the verge of civil war and with the advent of World War I, it was not implemented. The political parties, caught in internal dilemmas and an external relationship with the electorate, found it easy to choose paths that led nowhere but entailed the risk of civil war or anarchy (Boyce 1996, 57). The debate itself signaled the significant change in the hegemonic status of the belief that Ireland was a permanent and necessary part of the British state.

The question of political autonomy for Ireland was again open to legitimate public debate. The developments of Irish nationalism found their match in new British perceptions, themselves influenced by European cultural and intellectual developments of historical-cultural determinism, that encouraged the perception of Ireland as crucially distinct from Britain and references to Ireland as Celtic, rather than either Anglo-Saxon, British, or English. These developments led some British imperialists to conclude that their English institutions should not accompany their rule over non-Anglo-Saxon peoples and, henceforth, that Ireland justified no more intimate ties than the other white dominions. Moreover, the autonomy granted to Canada, Australia, and South Africa was increasingly perceived as contributing to the unity rather than the disintegration of the Empire and made it possible to view a similar solution for Ireland (Lustik 1990).

These developments, however, did not resolve the main issue. While British statesmen were in agreement that the government of Ireland was in need of reform, they were split on whether reform necessitated the repeal of the union. The nexus between compromising on the possession of Ireland and imperial security was spelled out through a "Victorian Domino Theory" outlined by Salisbury. Salisbury argued that if the "forces of disintegration" would be allowed to succeed on Britain's doorstep, it would send signals across the empire and a cause a chain reaction that would bring down the whole empire (Brasted 1983).

In this period of intensive international competition, Salisbury's concerns for the fate of the empire were shared by many other statesmen and bureaucrats. "If we lose Ireland we have lost the empire," predicted the chief of the imperial general staff, Field Marshal Sir Henry Wilson. Britain had to wrestle with unrest in India, Egypt, and Ireland, and British statesmen perceived them all to be interlinked. This had some resonance in Irish nationalists' statements, as they themselves had expressed interest in other points of conflict in the empire and support for the Boer War (McMahon 1999).

Conservative politicians and others opposing home rule agreed that Irish governance was in need of reform but argued that this could be accomplished within the empire. Since the 1870s, British statesmen had made various reforms regarding land and employment opportunities to ameliorate tensions in Ireland. The attempts between 1880 and 1900 to appease Ireland by solving its economic and social problems, especially the issue of land ownership, came to be known as "killing home rule by kindness." British statesmen calculated that a nation of peasant proprietors would become conservative in outlook and that this would undo the nationalist movement. The reforms, however, either came too late or failed to appreciate the nonmaterialist elements in nationalism. For the nationalists, the crux of the matter was the feeling that they were treated unfairly within Britain and, therefore, a solution within Britain fell short of their desires. "For while they were the majority in Ireland, the 'Irish people,' they remained a minority in the United Kingdom as a whole; and they were subject, at one and the same time, to veto also of the non-Catholic Irish minority. Thus their majority status in Ireland was not recognized, and this in a century which saw the inexorable advance of politics almost everywhere in Western Europe" (Boyce 1991, 271).

For the British, the issue of Irish nationalism could not be separated from the larger issues of empire. Irish nationalists were able to internationalize the struggle by an effective use of the diaspora on their behalf. The Irish diaspora has been involved in the political developments in Ireland since the 1850s. This diaspora, especially in America, gave the conflict an international dimension for many years to come. Fenianism, an ideology of uncompromising nationalism, was bred in America and exported back to Ireland where it drew its membership from the laboring poor, younger sons of tenant farmers, and rural teachers (Cronin 1980, 91). Their political ideas were heavily influenced by the American and French tradition, as was their model constitution of an independent Irish republic (Garvin 1981, 35). In numbers this movement did not amount to much, and Britain suppressed their attempted revolt in 1867 with little difficulty. Their importance lies in their contribution to the renationalization of Ireland after the collapse of nationalist politics that followed the great famine and their help in directing politics back to the "England versus Ireland" framework (Boyce 1991, 183). The strategy of John Devoy, one of the founders, involved building a great movement of Irish exiles and unsuccessful attempts to seek assistance from Russia and Spain; both declined since they perceived Fenianism, probably correctly, as too weak at this stage to be taken seriously (Cronin 1980, 92–93).

Efforts to internationalize the conflict were more effective during World War I through the ability to affect American public opinion with the help of the Irish diaspora and the British belief that good relations with America were essential to British security. In a letter to Robert Cecil, Winston Churchill encouraged him to consider this matter and push forward the home rule bill in the British parliament. "I beg you to consider as a military measure the importance of giving the Irish their bill and so bringing them in England and America to our side. The denial of this will certainly be paid with disloyalty and rancor and an element of weakness and discord introduced into our affairs" (Beloff 1987, 168).

Toward 1914, the tension in Ireland and especially the growing resistance of Ulster unionists to home rule evoked more concerns among British statesmen that instability in Ireland would influence Continental assessment of Britain's credibility in any European crisis. A high point of those tensions was the Curragh Mutiny, in which British army officers warned that any order for army action against Ulster unionists might be refused (Hartley 1987, 8–9). Lord Cromer, former high commissioner of Egypt, warned of the implications of the loss of control of Ireland due to the restlessness among both nationalists and unionists, alluding again to the domino theory. He went on to conclude that the Irish situation would affect the German decision to go to war: "The Germans are always on the lookout with a view to taking advantage of any dissension which may occur in this country. I hope this point will not be forgotten" (Hartley 1987, 10). David Lloyd George in his memoir also related the developments in Ireland to the events leading to World War I: "There can be little doubt that the expectation that Britain had for the moment sunk so deep in the quagmires of the Irish bog as to be unable to extricate her feet in time to march eastward, was one of the considerations which encouraged Germany to guarantee Austria unconditional support in her Serbian adventure" (Hartley 1987, 16).

British imperial interests made it difficult to compromise on the Irish question as it became, in perception at least, part of the international struggle of that period. Nationalists hoped that the war would advance their cause, and many of the Catholics joined the British army in hope that home rule would be implemented after the war. The war split the nationalists over the question of enlisting in the British army. For the moderate constitutionalist Irish Parliamentary Party under the leadership of John Redmond, World War I was a moral struggle for the rights of small nations. Thus, they argued, by aligning with Britain in the war, Irishmen were defending the principles of Irish nationhood and advancing the nationalist cause. The war, it was hoped, would not only improve the relationship between the Irish and Britain but would also reconcile the relationship within Ireland and enable a compromise between Catholics and Protestants after they fought together for the same cause. Separatists, represented by Sinn Fein, objected to Irish participation in the war and dismissed the idea of reconciliation between Ireland and Britain. Sinn Fein maintained that Irish loyalties should be to Ireland alone and that the idea of a dual sense of national identity was anathema to the principles of nationality. It was impossible for an Irishman to join the British Army, the separatists argued, because to enlist was to forsake one's nationality. "England Wants Men!" exclaimed an antirecruitment leaflet, "but by God they will not get Irishmen!"

While Sinn Fein had limited support in the early stages of the war, in the aftermath of the 1916 rebellion it gained increased popularity. Sinn Fein's sweeping victory in the general election of 1918 signaled a shift in nationalist perceptions. The vision of a semiautonomous Irish nation existing in harmony within a multinational British state was replaced by an alternative vision of an Irish nation-state that would be Gaelic, Catholic, and independent (Ellis 2000). Thus the moderate views of Redmond and the Irish party that aimed at some form of Irish self-government within the British Empire had given way to the more determined views of Irish republicanism that struggled for a complete dissociation from Britain. Sinn Fein hoped to take advantage of the new developments after World War I to achieve its aims. Arthur Griffith, one of its leaders, claimed in 1917 that Ireland had ceased to be an English domestic affair.

Like Poland, who had no government before the war and was not recognized by the powers, Ireland should present itself as an international problem and refuse to send its elected representatives to Westminster. "It was Sinn Fein's contention that Ireland's geographical position rendered her independent sovereignty essential to Europe and the World's peaceful development, and it appealed to the great powers to recognize this, especially as most of those powers in the current war had publicly declared for the rights of small nations" (Hennessey 1998, 164–65).

Irish nationalists made a strong case for independence before and after the war, and their pressures combined with other developments across the empire to change British perceptions. While immediately after the war British statesmen contemplated the extension of their territorial overseas possessions, in a short time reality forced them to rethink the empire. "Ireland, Egypt, India: one by one these hammers beat upon the anvil of empire," so in order to keep those important bastions others had to be given up as Britain faced a shortage of troops (Gallagher 1981, 365). In 1920 the chief of the imperial general staff warned, "our small army is much too scattered . . . in no single theatre are we strong enough—not in Ireland, nor England, not on the Rhine, not in Constantinople, nor Batoum, nor Egypt, nor Palestine, nor Mesopotamia, nor Persia, nor India" (365). While nationalists were drifting away from Britain, the growing overlap between nationalism and Catholicism engendered strong opposition especially from the threatened Protestant community around Belfast.

Unionism

The formation of an exclusionary nationalism with a territorial dimension, like in the Israeli case, influenced the formation of a competing nationalism whose main aim was to maintain the union between Ireland and Britain but that developed its own concepts of identity and belonging. The decision of Gladstone to grant home rule caused a reaction among Protestants who perceived the decision as a step toward the independence of Ireland and, consequently, their relegation to minority status vis-à-vis the Catholics. Thus home rule was countered, among other responses, by the revival of the Protestant Orange Order, originally formed in 1795 against a background of sectarian faction fighting (Hennessey 1998, 1). Threatened by the idea of home rule, or secession, and unwilling to relinquish their preferred status, the Protestants developed a counteridentity that sought to preserve the union.

Protestants were initially concerned with the defense of the union and later, when home rule seemed inevitable, they concentrated on defending the right of Ulster to remain part of the United Kingdom. During this struggle, unionism developed its own political agenda based on what it defined as civil and religious liberty as well as its own nationalist legacy, myths, and traditions going back all the way to the Siege of Derry (Fraser 1994). Unionists used the general language of British patriotism and imperial sentiment to further their cause within the Protestant community of Ireland and in Britain against nationalist aims. William Moore, MP for Northern Armagh, rejected the nationalist case put forward by John Redmond, Parnell's successor, declaring for the Protestants' concept of nationalism: "We are West Britons . . . we regard the term Briton as the emblem of liberty. We have prospered under it and we will take nothing less. And instead of the sentimental humbug about Ireland's well-being . . . we maintain our own ideals because we are connected with Britain by ties of blood . . . religion and history; and we object to being swallowed up in the claim that . . . we should come into his [Redmond's] fold because we live in Ireland" (Hennessey 1998, 10).

In Belfast, despite its mixed population, an overwhelming majority of businessmen were Protestants who were not only culturally but also economically linked to Britain and enjoyed a growing prosperity in the late nineteenth century. This fusion of business and political interests in the north was vital to the formation of Ulster unionism, offering sound economic arguments against home rule (Boyce 1990, 203–4). Social and economic forces had influence on both parties of the dispute. Where nationalists saw an economic decline that was linked to the union with Britain and their unjust treatment, Ulster Protestants were reaping the benefits of the industrialization of Belfast (Walker 1994, 9).

The Ulster unionist business class used their power, money, and political expertise to counteract home rule. The experience of some important unionists in the war in South Africa shifted them toward a more resolute militancy. Also, the more dangerous atmosphere in Ireland, Britain, and Europe generally on the eve of the World War I helped break down the inhibitions and constraints of the bourgeois, previously reluctant to fight (Boyce 1999). From the 1880s, the Orange Order formed a powerful cross-class alliance of Protestants against home rule (Hennessey 1998, 1). When home rule made its passage through Parliament in 1911, unionists took a more active stance and formed an armed militia. Soon the membership of this militia, the Ulster Volunteer Force, surpassed the 100,000 men.

Like Irish nationalism, unionism developed an inclusive ideology and rhetoric toward its own, and like nationalism, exclusive interpretations were adopted toward those who did not belong, namely Catholics. Unionists' opposition was encapsulated in the slogan "Home rule is Rome rule," referring to the possibility of living under the rule of a Catholic majority. While nationalists used tactics that rendered Protestant participation in the nation more and more difficult, unionists retaliated with a growing reluctance to extend their ideas of liberty and freedom of speech to the Roman Catholics (Boyce 1990, 211). The disagreement between nationalists and unionists became a zero-sum game from 1911 onward over issues of national identity and the extent to which the territorial aspects of home rule should reflect each political community (Girvan 1999).

Conclusion

In 1867, Karl Marx wrote to Friedrich Engels, "what the English do not yet know is that since 1846 the economic content and therefore also the political aim of English domination in Ireland have entered into an entirely new phase." On a different occasion, he observed, "I thought that Ireland's separation from England impossible. Now I think it inevitable" (Cronin 1980, 87). The slow pace of political reform, the uneven development of the economy, and the persistent feeling of cultural oppression were the driving forces behind separatist nationalism (Ruane and Todd 1996, 47–48). Resentment and dissatisfaction were translated into the political idiom of the day: territorial separation and exclusive nationalism. World politics contributed to developments by influencing the constraints, incentives, and the means for nationalism. The shift to an exclusive territorial nationalism that occurred during the period described above was influenced by similar trends in Europe and by the development of a Catholic middle class sensitive to these ideas. The power of the Irish diaspora and the growing legitimacy of claims for national independence within Europe were the Irish nationalists' means to achieve independence. Like in the Zionist case, the development of Irish nationalism did not actively engulf the whole Catholic community, but soon, again like in the Zionist case, nationalism gained the momentum to change the course of Irish history.

If Zionism during this period resembles in some respects Irish nationalism, both during this period forming to consolidate a territorial nation-state, after partition in Northern Ireland and Israeli statehood the relations reversed. Catholics in Northern Ireland became a minority struggling against a Protestant majority and a British state, resembling the Palestinians in Israel. Jews in Israel, for their part, formed a Jewish state with a Palestinian minority that grew larger after the war of 1967. Partitions in both cases, rather than putting an end to conflicts, were the starting points for their renewal.

5

Partition as a Solution, Partition as a Problem

A Summary

THE LOGIC OF TERRITORY that dominated the first period of globalization created pressures to demarcate national territories. The difficulties arising in territories inhabited by more than one people (or one potential nation) were to be solved according to the same logic of territory: partition, and the establishment of homogenous, national territorial units. To some, the establishment of homogenous territories, with the new nationalism buttressed by economic separatism and interstate competition, seemed inevitable. Nonexclusive territorial solutions were more complex and difficult, and "the dream of a federated Europe dissolved into the reality of a nationally disparate Europe" (Hayes 1963, 259). Conversely, the idea of partition corresponded to the modern ideology of self-rule, namely, that nations are entitled to territorial sovereignty, and that partition was, therefore, an almost natural solution to the territorial disputes that occurred.

As the two previous chapters illustrate, Zionism and Irish nationalism were both products of the period. Although nonexclusive territorial solutions were debated—home rule for Ireland and cohabitation for Palestine—by the end of the period they were no longer considered the preferred alternative or even a possibility. Both the Zionism of the second aliyah and Sinn Fein nationalism promoted separation and exclusion, and their demands gradually dictated the political results. In 1921 Ireland was partitioned between north and south. Partition plans in Palestine were intensively discussed, but because neither side was able to coerce the other and the British could not implement their own desires, it took another twenty-six years for partition to be implemented.

The concept of partition itself changed during this period of globalization. Before World War I, partition was a tool of empires, which divided territories

102

among themselves or used it to strengthen their rule. After the war, partitions took place as a part of the devolution of authority that granted independence to nations such as Poland and Rumania, or as a solution to ethnic conflicts that were perceived to be irreconcilable. In both cases discussed here, Britain was the power holder that eventually replaced its control by partition. The British Empire has commonly used the policy of "divide and rule" to strengthen its hold on distant territories, and partitions were considered part of that policy, initiated by the British Empire for its own interests. But the partitions carried out in Ireland and Palestine (and India) were essentially different from the earlier policy. These partitions were the result of the changing world order after World War I and were described as "divide and quit," a new policy that enabled Britain to relinquish control over territories it could no longer rule (Kumar 1997).

Despite its victory in the war, Britain found itself facing problems similar to those confronting the fallen Hapsburg empire. The decision to implement partitions in several areas Britain had previously ruled was based on both cost-benefit assessments and a "two-nation theory," involving the identification of an irreconcilable conflict and the conviction that partition could resolve it. British attitudes toward partition were ambivalent, especially with respect to Ireland, where many statesmen denied the existence of two nations. But partition as a solution for divided communities was very much in the air during that period, implemented elsewhere in Europe according to the concept of self-determination, and it gradually came to define British politics.

The empowerment of the two emerging nations in Ireland, the commitment of Britain (especially its conservative politicians) to Ulster's Protestant community, and the growing perception of Britain's inability to rule (or for that matter, create) a united Ireland spelled partition. The logic driving self-determination for Ireland, argued Ulster supporters, should apply equally to Ulster Protestants, who demanded not to be included within an Irish (Catholic-dominated) state. "No one could think," wrote Balfour, "that Ulster ought to join the south and west. . . . no one can think that Ulster should be divorced from Britain who believes in self-determination" (Fraser 1994, 180). An initial attempt was made to soften partition, by creating a "Council of Ireland" that would provide some measure of unity between the north and the south and from which stronger bonds might be forged. However, it failed, as neither side was willing to cooperate. Thus the treaty of 1921 created two separate entities, one independent and the other a part of Britain (Fraser 1994, 180).

The situation in Palestine was somewhat different. There the British, in order to secure their position prior to and during World War I, made conflicting commitments to Jews and Arabs. They had made a commitment to the Zionists in the Balfour Declaration of 1917 but in the Husayn-McMahon correspondence of 1915–16 they had likewise promised the Arabs an "independent Arab state." In neither case were the boundaries defined (Freedman 1972), and throughout the period of the mandate (1922–48), their policy was indecisive and subject to pressures from both sides.

As the numbers of Jewish immigrants to Palestine rose in response to the growing pressure on Jews in Europe to emmigrate, Arab resistance grew, further complicating British rule over Palestine. The Peel Commission of 1937, nominated by the British government after an escalation of violence in Palestine, reached the conclusion that Palestine was inhabited by two nations and, therefore, that partition was inevitable. The committee's decisions received a lukewarm response from the Jews and were passionately rejected by the Arabs, reactions that led the British to the conclusion that partition was unworkable, too. A British cabinet committee on Palestine, established in 1943, again recommended partition. But after a Jewish terrorist group assassinated a British diplomat, the discussions and implementation of the partition were shelved (C. Smith 1992, 119).

The situation changed after World War II with the pressure to find a home for Jewish Holocaust refugees from Europe and the involvement of the United States in the issue. A joint committee of American and British representatives was formed to examine the possibilities. The British members of the Anglo-American Committee objected to partition: they argued that because ethnic groups were so dispersed, partition was impossible, and they recommended continuation of the mandate (Kumar 1997). The great difficulty, however, was to reconcile the demand of Jews for open immigration to Palestine and Arab demands for restriction. The committee decided to allow the immediate immigration of one hundred thousand Jewish refugees but remained vague on the future of Palestine since "any attempt to establish either an independent Palestinian state or independent Palestinian states would result in civil strife such as might threaten the peace of the world" (C. Smith 1992, 130). Consequently, Palestine was to remain under the British mandate "pending the execution of a trusteeship agreement under the United Nations" (C. Smith 1992, 130). The United Nations Special Committee on Palestine (UNSCOP), established in 1947, submitted a report that recommended the partition of Palestine. Britain responded with a decision to end the mandate unilaterally without waiting for the full UN decision. On November 29, 1947, the United Nations voted for the partition of Palestine, and shortly after, the Arabs who opposed the partition plan declared war on the new Jewish state.

The partitioning of Palestine and Ireland conformed to the settled norms of international society and the idea that national community required demarcated territory (Campbell 1998, 13). But in many places, partitions, whether or not they were the lesser of evils, produced new problems and tensions. The attempt to make nations and states coincide has failed again and again, leading to new struggles and demands for independence. In Europe after World War I, some of the new states carved out of the old empires turned out to be multinational and were soon riven by new conflicts. The contemporary debates over the settlement in Bosnia attest that the issues of the morality and political viability of partition remain controversial. In Northern Ireland and in Israel, two entities created out of partition settlements (and war, in the case of Israel),[1] a struggle continues between two competing nations, one dominating the other. These struggles, with high political, social, and economic costs, and their resolution in a "new world" setting, will be the focus of the next part of this work.

1. In Israel, the war of 1967 and the occupation of Palestinian settled territories exacerbated the problem.

PART TWO

Late Globalization and Deterritorialization

6

Globalization, Deterritorialization, and Peace

THE EXPLOSION IN THE GROWTH of networks and flows that transcend national boundaries in the past two decades, commonly known as globalization, created new opportunities and constraints for parties involved in long-term, protracted conflicts. While the growing interconnectedness across the globe toward the end of the twentieth century resembles the period previously discussed, there are also important differences, especially concerning territoriality and political economy. In describing the rise of what he termed as the "virtual state," Richard Rosencrance stated that territory and territorial sovereignty have become "passe." "Countries are not uniting as civilizations and girding for conflict with one another. Instead, they are downsizing—in function if not in geographic form. Today and for the foreseeable future the only international civilization worthy of the name is the governing economic culture of the world market" (Rosencrance 1996, 46).

The widening, deepening, and speeding up of worldwide interconnectedness in all aspects of social life that characterize globalization are evident and to some extent measurable. But beyond the general acknowledgment of the intensification of interconnectedness, there is wide disagreement as to whether significant changes are in fact occurring, especially in regard to the future of the sovereign territorial state, and substantial disagreement on explaining the mechanisms, influences, and consequences of globalization. For some, globalization is a significant historical change, or the end of history altogether; for others it is a myth, or "globalony." Yet, beyond the clichés of the "twenty-four-hour marketplace," "global village," and the like, globalization is real enough to require precise conceptualization and empirical assessment. The current globalization, like its predecessor described in the first part, can also be understood as the manifestation of hegemonic crisis. While in the previous period it was the withering away of the British world order of laissez faire, the contemporary globalization is the decline of the American "embedded liberalism" world order. While the early crisis was characterized by the fusion of state elites and capitalists over the pursuit of territorial expansion and consolidation, the late crisis shows a divergence as capitalist expansion breaks away from territorial constraints.

The debate over the shift of power from the state to economic, nonstate actors began in the 1970s but gained widespread currency under the term globalization some twenty years later. The growth and expansion of multinational corporations was the strongest piece of evidence brought forward by advocates of the globalization thesis, who argued that states have been disempowered by supranational economic forces (Arrighi and Silver 1999, 6–7). The empowerment of nonterritorial actors, supposedly at the expense of the state, led several scholars to conclude that the territorially bounded, sovereign nation-state had become all but obsolete. Kenichi Ohmae pointed to the "outdated vocabulary of political borders" and stated that "traditional nation states have become unnatural, even impossible, business units in a global economy" (1995, 7–8). But given that the death of the nation-state had been declared in the 1970s,[1] and that similar reflections were made on the eve of World War I, it seems that changes in the structure of world politics resist crude generalizations (Wade 1996). Robert Wade, in critique of the thesis of globalization, urged skepticism, and argued that the world economy is more international than global. "In the bigger national economies, more than 80 percent of production is for domestic consumption and more than 80 percent of investment by domestic investors. Companies are rooted in national home bases with national regulatory regimes. Populations are much less mobile across borders than are goods, finance or ideas" (Wade 1996, 61).

The political outcomes of globalization lend even less support for the thesis that states are on the verge of extinction and that a uniform world order and culture is forming. First, while many sovereign states' power seems to be declining, there are states whose power increases (Weiss 1998) and many that never had much power to begin with. Second, states and societies react differently to and are differently affected by flows of people, machinery, money, images, and ideas, hospitable to some and inhospitable to others (Appadurai 1990). And third, while there are significant sectors within most states that cel-

---

1. Charles Kindelberger already in 1969 claimed that the nation-state is "just about through as an economic unit" in the face of transnational corporations (Kindelberger 1969, 297).

ebrate globalization and are geared to take advantage of new opportunities, there are others who, for various reasons, seek to protect and maintain the boundaries.

Benjamin Barber's description of "Jihad vs. McWorld" encapsulates these dialectical tensions of, on the one hand, balkanization and resistance to modernity and any form of its infiltration, and, on the other hand, economic, technological, and cultural forces that push the world toward integration and interdependence. These developments, however, are interdependent rather than contradictory. "Progress moves in steps that sometimes lurch backward in history's twisting maze; Jihad not only revolts against but abets McWorld, while McWorld not only imperils but re-creates and reinforces Jihad. They produce their contraries and need one another" (Barber 1995, 4–5).

The variance and contradictory outcomes imply that globalization is not a uniform (and possibly stateless) political-economic space created by technological innovation or economic necessity but a "structurated" process in which new opportunities, incentives, and constraints unfold and political agency remains significant. In a structurated process, structures establish the range of options available to actors, but, at the same time, these structures depend on an accumulation of actors' decisions for their creation and perpetuation (Scholte 2000, 89). Globalization, therefore, is a "product of both the individual actions of, and the cumulative interaction between countless agencies and institutions across the globe" (Held et al. 1999, 27). Globalization structures the field of politics but is itself shaped (unevenly) by both local and global, intended and unintended actions, interests, and strategies. It is, therefore, a restructuring of politics that can be observed at both the international level and the domestic level in the interaction of various agents and structures.

A self-confident "transnational class," whose members have the interest and the ability to integrate globally and to reap the profits of globalization, has important influence on the process. The members of this class who are at ease operating in a borderless global economy, in which profits rather than citizenship are the driving force, supply by various intended and unintended (or partially intended) decisions and actions momentum and legitimacy to the process. As a result, the focal point of party and governmental politics has shifted from the general maximization of welfare within national societies (full employment, redistributive transfers, and social service provision) to the promotion of enterprise, innovation, and profitability in both private and public sectors (Barber 1995). This empowered class, however, eventually meets with opposition. Pierre Hassner describes the transformations of politics when international order collapses in the emergence of two contrasting phenomena that correspond to Barber's description, the "politics of soil" and the "politics of the satellite," the former grounded in the community, the latter to global issues and to a "transnational class" (Hassner 1993).

The contradictions and tensions described above can be observed in our two case studies, Israel and Northern Ireland, in which despite the incentives associated with globalization, territory and territorial identity seem to remain a major issue of contention. While important advances toward peace, based upon territorial compromise, have been accomplished during the late 1990s between Israelis and Palestinians and between Catholics and Protestants, the processes encountered powerful obstacles and resistance that threatened (and even succeeded in the Israeli-Palestinian case) to reverse the advances made. Thus, while new incentives for the resolution of the conflict influenced the peace process, they have not, in spite of early optimism based on a belief in virtues of liberal economics, made peace inevitable. Globalization, therefore, affects national conflicts less by the elimination of difference or the transformation of identity and more by providing a context in which differences can be more effectively managed (McGarry 2001, 295).

Basic rules of the political game have changed, and the payoff matrix has been altered (Cerny 1990)—by economic opportunities and the declining value of territory associated with globalization—yet territorial conflicts are far from obsolete. Rather, as will be theoretically argued here and empirically demonstrated in the next two chapters, because globalization's opportunities and constraints are distributed unevenly among states, ethnic groups, and classes, it evokes resistance and discontent that negatively affects the resolution of territorial conflicts. This chapter will set the stage for the following two chapters by describing the global transformations within which the two peace processes evolved and will delineate the global matrix of opportunities and constraints created.

Globalizations Compared

The process of globalization of the late twentieth century is a sign of a "hegemonic crisis" analogous to the crises of British hegemony described in the previous part of this work (Arrighi and Silver 1999, 273–75). Globalization occurs in the wake of a declining hegemonic order, previously the British and currently the American, when the leading hegemon loses its capability to maintain order. Intensification of interstate and interenterprise competition and escalation of social conflicts that follow characterize such phases of declining hegemony (30). Periods of globalization are influenced by what Braudel called a "hierarchical compression." In those periods, the world of "capital"—the top level of the economy, dominated by powerful corporations and elites engaged in large-scale, high stakes, and speculative economic activity—comes into closer contact with the lower two levels. The middle level is the market economy that is based on smaller-scale transactions, greater transparency, and regularity. The lowest level is the "material life," all activities outside market and the state controls (Helleiner 1997). As the world becomes more and more interconnected, worldwide high stakes financial operations affect the daily lives of many people, in different ways and extents, across the globe.

Despite the similarities, each hegemonic order was established upon different principles, purposes, and interests. Therefore, different social, political, and economic dynamics operated in its decline, namely globalization. The crises for the Pax Britannica signaled a transformation from a world order based on laissez faire to intensive interstate competition over territory. In the "Pax Americana" established at the end of World War II, the modern nation-state became the principal type of political rule, supported by international, financial, and military institutions. The crises of this hegemonic order entailed a crisis of its related institutions and of the state system itself, essentially the disembedding of the market. This difference underscores the disparate significance of territory in the two globalizations. While in the earlier period discussed territorialization was the dominant political theme, strong deterritorializing dynamics conflicting with ongoing and at times amplified territorial claims influence the current period.

In the earlier globalization, the decline of the hegemonic order and the decline of the hegemon were coterminous as Britain by the end of the period ceased being a first-rate world power. In the current period, it may be useful to make a distinction between the crisis of the American hegemonic order of embedded liberalism and the decline of the United States itself. Arrighi and several other scholars allude to the possibility of a new hegemon arising from Asia. Vogel suggests that the mid-1980s may have marked the emergence of a "Pax Nipponica" as the United States since that period lost its world economic dominance to Japan (Vogel 1986). Others have argued that Japan does not have the capacity to become a hegemonic power (D. Haber 1990).

This argument is overshadowed by a controversy over whether the United States has really lost its hegemony. Unlike the British hegemony whose fate is known and the transition to a new hegemony well documented, the evidence of an American decline is inconclusive and controversial. The question has been debated since the 1970s when several scholars claimed that the decline of the American hegemony replicates the decline of Britain and could again leave the international system without a leader. In the absence of a hegemonic state, it was argued, the risk for another world crisis like the Great Depression is high (Gilpin 1975; Keohane 1984; Kindelberger 1973; Nye 1990). Critics of the "declinist" thesis argue that evidence suggests that American power has actually increased and, therefore, declining hegemony is nothing but a "myth" or an excuse for nonintervention (Strange 1987).

The debate over whether the United States is in decline or is as strong as ever continued in the 1990s over the implications of globalization and, consequently, over the remaining capabilities of the United States (Zuckerman 1998; Krugman 1998). While the United States demonstrated its military capabilities in the war in Iraq in 2003, its political difficulties in forming a coalition demonstrate the difference between power and hegemony. In other words, the United States demonstrated its ability to act and coerce rather than to lead.

Whether the United States itself is in a crisis akin to Britain's fall or whether it still holds sufficient power to outcompete its rivals and retain its hegemony is beyond the scope of this work. What I will elaborate below is not America's relative power (declining or not) but the decline of the American world order known as embedded liberalism. This decline underlies the restructuring of state-society relations, the tensions between territorial and nonterritorial forms of power, and a significant spatial change. The modern system of rule differentiated its subject collectivity into territorially defined, fixed, and mutually exclusive enclaves of legitimate dominion. The rise of nonterritorial forms of power—multinational firms, "offshore" economic spaces, or macroregional blocs—beyond the control of most states challenge the territoriality of the nation-state (Helleiner 1997) and the related world order.

The politics of the late twentieth century have, therefore, been characterized by what Ruggie describes as the "unbundling of territoriality" (Ruggie 1993, 160). The shift of the balance from solely defined territorial politics to nonterritorial forms of organization and identity constitutes a new logic that conjures up the possibilities of new notions of citizenship, democracy, community, and government (Jacobson 1997). These changes, toward the deterritorializing of sovereignty and the corresponding emergence of various global institutions, can offer new incentives and possibilities for the resolution of seemingly intractable ethno-national conflicts by rethinking them in a transnational context (Anderson 1998).

Pax Americana: Rise and Decline

The challenges to British hegemony, which were the setting discussed in the previous part of this work, were concluded by two world wars that marked the end of the Pax Britannica. Writing at the end of World War II, economic historian Karl Polanyi forecast what was about to emerge: "Out of the ruins of the Old World, the cornerstone of the new seems to emerge: economic collaboration of governments and the liberty to organize national life at will" (1957, 253–54). Sure enough, a new world order under a new hegemonic power, the United States, was established at the end of the war, and new principles of hegemony were enshrined, principles that would enable the United States to lead the international system in the following decades.

The United States achieved in the systematic chaos between the two world wars unprecedented financial, industrial, and military power. Like Britain in the nineteenth century, the United States became hegemonic by leading the interstate system toward the restoration of the principles, norms, and rules of the Westphalia system, and, like Britain, it then went on to govern and remake that system according to its own priorities (Arrighi 1994, 69). Politically, World War II convinced American policy makers that the isolationist position of the interwar period was no longer viable. Economically, the crises that led to the war convinced them that laissez faire was no longer viable, and, therefore, the hegemony of the United States discarded laissez-faire principles both between and within states.

President Roosevelt's vision of "one world" drew upon the ideas of the New Deal. If the New Deal brought social security to America, political security for the entire world could be achieved by the same principles applied worldwide. But Roosevelt's one-world ideology was not realistic enough to win the necessary support from the U.S Congress and American business community. It was the cold war and Truman's doctrine of two worlds that made this idea operational—"an aggressively expansionist Communist world on the one side, and a free world which only the United States could organize and empower for self-defense on the other" (Arrighi 1994, 277). This new world order rested upon new economic, military, and political foundations: "At Bretton Woods the foundations of a new world monetary system had been established; at Hiroshima and Nagasaki new means of violence had demonstrated what the new military underpinnings of the new world order would be; and at San Francisco new norms and rules for the legitimization of state-making and war-making had been laid out in the new UN charter" (274–75).

The economic and military supremacy that the United States enjoyed at the end of World War II were translated into a hierarchical interstate system that empowered it to act within the capitalist world as a state above other states (Arrighi 1982). Its leadership role in the monetary system and in the military alliance were two sides of the same imperial coin; nuclear hegemony in NATO matched dollar hegemony in the IMF (Calleo and Rowland 1973, 87). Interstate relations did not rely upon free trade and laissez faire but upon reciprocity and political considerations. Unlike Britain that used its dominance of world trade to act unilaterally to promote free trade,[2] the United States used negative and positive sanctions and its large domestic market to structure the global economy to fit its political goals. "The United States did not unilaterally reduce tariffs, except for the period immediately after the Second World War, but instead linked reductions in, at first, bilateral treaties under the Reciprocal Trade Agreements and, later, in the GATT. The reciprocal trade policy adopted by the United States has brought more countries into the fold, so to speak, by linking access to American markets to participation in the GATT system" (Lake 1995, 128).

American trade policy was strongly linked to the cold war and to political interests. British hegemony operated in an environment that pitted principal capitalist powers against each other in a strategic competition that was both economic and geopolitical. Under the U.S. hegemony, competition was between capitalist powers that were allied politically and militarily against a noncapitalist adversary that posed no serious economic challenge (Mjost 1990, 44). Another aspect of its leadership, critical to postwar stability and contrary to

2. David Lake describes British hegemony as a "second face" type. "Britain effectively restructured the economic incentives facing producers of raw materials and foodstuffs. Over the long term, by altering factor and sector profit rates, and hence investment patterns, Britain augmented and mobilized the political influence of the interests within nonhegemonic countries most amenable to an international division of labor. All this was premised on complementary production and the free exchange of primary goods for British manufacturers" (Lake 1995, 127).

British laissez-faire principles, was the creation of a system that constrained the power of markets on society and states. Policy makers adopted the idea that capitalism was inherently unstable and therefore the capitalist economy must be regulated, strictly limited, and reembedded in the priorities of the domestic economy (Blyth 1999).

Ruggie coined the term *embedded liberalism* to describe this new world order, which compromised the extremes and discarded laissez faire in favor of political and economic stability. "Unlike the economic nationalism of the thirties, it would be multilateral in character; unlike the liberalism of the gold standard and free trade, its multilateralism would be predicated upon domestic intervention" (Ruggie 1982, 393). The postwar institutional reconstruction was designed to allow free trade while ensuring the stability and viability of the welfare state, a framework that "would safeguard and even aid the quest for domestic stability without, at the same time, triggering the mutually destructive external consequences that had plagued the inter-war period" (393).

Embedded liberalism rested, first, upon the principle that money and credit were too important to macroeconomic equilibrium to be left for free-market operation. The Keynesian revolution taught that a stable monetary regime was a public good to be provided by a central bank along with complex regulation enforced on financial institutions. Second, wage formation was also taken out of the free market and replaced by a capital-labor compromise that would guarantee welfare for the workers. Ruggie attributes the establishment of embedded liberalism as a world order to the extraordinary power and perseverance of the United States. The United States that led the Bretton Woods negotiations explicitly opposed a return to the open, liberal financial order, which existed before 1931, and endorsed the use of capital controls to prevent its return. These initiatives were designed to protect the new interventionist welfare state from being undermined by speculative and disequilibrating international capital flows, to facilitate international trade by stabilizing exchange rates, and to support American geopolitical concerns of the early cold war (Helleiner 1994).

Other authors argue that European influence must be taken into account in explanations of the postwar order. The departure from free trade was based upon the experience of the New Deal coalition within the United States but was also influenced by the need of U.S policy makers to accommodate social democratic goals in Europe in the face of a communist challenge. Because of the United States' need to reconcile political and economic goals, Europeans were able to resist and modify the terms of liberal multilateralism and to draw the protection of the United States: "It was the very weakness of the European economies and societies that prevented the United States from translating its array of power resources into bargaining assets. The United States could not push too hard. The Europeans, in turn, could set the terms upon which to pull the United States into economic and security relationships" (Ikenberry 1989, 399).

Toward the end of the 1960s, this American hegemony was perceived to be in decline, manifested in three closely related spheres: the military failure of the United States in Vietnam, the financial difficulty to sustain the Bretton Woods system, and the ideological loss of legitimacy, at home and abroad, for the anti-communist crusade (Arrighi 1994, 300).

The Difficulties of the U.S. Hegemony

Neorealist, "hegemonic stability" accounts of the postwar hegemony focus on the power and the interests of the hegemonic power, the United States, to create a stable international economic (and political) order. Having the most efficient economy, the hegemon has the most to gain from free trade; having the political and military power, it has the resources to induce others to adopt compatible liberal practices (A. Stein 1984). The main public good the hegemon, having the ends and the means, supplies is a stable free-trade economy.[3] Accordingly, the United States created a liberal world order ("embedded liberalism") that surpassed the British hegemony on several counts. First, the United States was superior in productivity to the rest of the world more than Britain was. Second, its trading partners were also its military allies. And third, unlike Britain, the United States used a principal of reciprocity rather than a unilateral free trade, which enabled it to coerce its partners to its economic terms (Keohane 1984, 36–37). But, when in the 1970s the United States seemed to be outcompeted and lost its advantage in the world economy, instability of the international political economy and a return to closed markets was forecasted.

3. Robert Keohane argues that as a hegemon, the United States was willing to assume the cost of maintaining the system: "The United States farsightedly made short-term sacrifices—in growing financial aid, and in permitting discrimination against American exports—in order to accomplish the longer-term objective of creating a stable and prosperous international economic order in which liberal capitalism would prevail and American influence would be predominant" (Keohane 1984, 270).

Robert Gilpin argued that the liberal international order rapidly recedes as the core declines and new cores in the periphery catch up. The most likely outcome is fragmentation and an outbreak of mercantilist economic conflict (Gilpin 1987, 394; Gilpin 1975, 73). In retrospect, neither claim seems to hold ground. While measurements of U.S. commercial and productive superiority from the 1950s to the 1980s show a steady decline and a growing interdependence (Rupert and Rapkin 1985), it is still a leading power economically and its military supremacy is unchallenged. The mercantilist conflict prediction tends to exaggerate the liberalism of the U.S. hegemony[4] and is contradicted by reality. Not only is a mercantilist economic conflict nowhere in sight, but the world economy has become more open and competitive.

The problem, as several authors note, is in the definition of hegemony used by neorealists. Gramsci's concept of hegemony seems to provide a better explanation of American hegemony and even more so of the hegemonic decline. Gramsci's hegemony is defined in terms of structural power (rather than domination or "power over") and consent achieved by the ruling group's ability to define its interests as universal and pertaining to a wider group. Conceptualizing hegemony in terms of leadership refers to a dominant state that becomes a model for other states to emulate, thereby drawing them to its path of development (Arrighi and Silver 1999, 29). This theory of hegemony investigates international power relations, domestic structures, and the interplay between the domestic and the international in order to assess the alignment and realignment that take place within states as a consequence of the structure of incentives and constraints established by the hegemonic power (Cafruny 1990). Hegemonic leadership, therefore, affects in different degrees and measures both international developments and local politics.

A declining hegemony, on the other hand, refers to a system in which contradictions between ruling and subordinate groups become more acute and, therefore, "The ruling group begins to experience difficulty pursuing both its economic corporate interests and the long range needs of the system as a whole" (Cafruny 1990, 105). Three related processes characterize the crisis: intensification of interstate and interenterprise competition, the escalation of so-

---

4. Susan Strange sharply criticizes the description of the postwar order as liberal: "It is hard to see American liberalism in the twenty-five years after World War II as a genuine doctrine rather than an ideology, that is, a doctrine to be used when it was convenient and fitted the current perception of the national interest and one to be overlooked and forgotten when it did not" (Strange 1987, 562).

cial conflicts, and the emergence of new configurations of power (Arrighi and Silver 1999, 30). What the declining hegemony signifies, therefore, is not a decline of power per se but the breakdown of the organizing principles of the system and, consequently, a leadership crisis.

Thus, observing contemporary globalization, what is witnessed is not necessarily a decline of American power, as U.S. military supremacy remains unchallenged, but rather a decline of the hegemonic state system of embedded liberalism established by the United States after World War II. Fred Bergsten described the decline of U.S. hegemony since the 1970s as a result of a "scissors effect," a joint consequence of declining capability and increasing interdependence. "The United States has simultaneously become much more dependent on the world economy and much less able to dictate the course of economic events. The global economic environment is more critical for the United States and is less susceptible to its influence" (Bergsten 1982, 11–12).

Multinational corporations, formerly a tool of U.S. foreign policy, gradually freed themselves from government's influence and developed their own agenda. Rodman found that the decline of the U.S. hegemony and its lessening ability to control multinational corporations had wider political consequences as it negatively affected American ability to apply economic sanctions against its rivals. The global spread of American business placed an increasing proportion of U.S. corporate decision making beyond the commands of public officials (Rodman 1995).

When compared to the previous decline of Britain, the decline of U.S. hegemony requires two explanations. First, why does U.S. power at the international level remain largely unchallenged? (There is no equivalent to the American and German challenge to Britain in the late nineteenth century.) Second, why has this decline not resulted in a withdrawal from free trade into mercantilism? The answer to both questions lies in the concept of hegemony as described above. Hegemonies are differently organized and built on different principles. Similarly, they face different challenges and their decline yields different types of crises. Like the British before them, the United States faced competition with new powers that took advantage of the system it created and enjoyed its protection without bearing the costs. But in contrast to the previous period, a serious challenge to embedded liberalism was presented by nonstate actors that began to undermine the system once they began to feel it was constraining them. Already in 1969 *Fortune* magazine noted the tensions in the world order that stemmed from private interests rather than interstate competition. "The real point is that business everywhere is outgrowing national boundaries and, in so doing, is creating new tensions between the way the world is organized politically and the way in which it will be increasingly organized economically" (quoted in Murray 1971, 73).

The "free trade" slogans of the U.S. government since World War II were in practice a strategy of bilateral and multilateral intergovernmental negotiation of trade liberalization, primarily aimed at opening other states to American commerce and enterprise (Arrighi and Silver 1999). Multinational corporations, a large and important sector of the American economy, were transplanted globally with the help of the government in order to maintain and expand U.S. world power and to reorganize interstate relations. The companies were quick to grasp the prospects of the European market. American tax policies and the insistence that they would be treated as European corporations when doing business in Europe fostered their expansion. Government officials, on their behalf, realized that the growing overseas expansion could serve American interest by helping to create a liberal international economic and political order, by gaining control of scarce resources, especially oil, and by reducing the balance of payments deficit. Essentially, then, corporate expansionism became a powerful support for American hegemony (Gilpin 1975, 108, 139).

But the relationship between the expansion of multinational corporations and the expansion of U.S. state power has been just as much one of contradiction as of reciprocity (Arrighi 2000, 137–39). Eventually these companies developed a dynamic of their own, which at times backfired on American world power for two main reasons. First, these business corporations operated on a strictly business logic and removed much of their liquid assets to "offshore markets" when they encountered crises. Second, European and East Asian corporations emulated American success and became multinational and reduced even more the regulative capacity of the United States or any other state. "The transnational forms of business organization pioneered by U.S. capital. . . . had rapidly ceased to be a 'mystery' for a large and growing number of foreign competitors. By the 1970s Western European capital had discovered all its secrets and had begun out-competing U.S. corporations at home and abroad. By the 1980s, it was the turn of East Asian capital to out-compete both U.S. and Western European capital" (Arrighi and Silver 1999, 146–48).

Companies beyond the control of states were described as more transnational than multinational, footloose, and detached from state control although not completely independent as at times of crisis states, especially the United

States, were often turned to for help. However, they were less dependent upon state power than the nineteenth century's haute finance, which depended on states to back their monopolies and defend their portfolio investment. For the new transnational companies (TNCs), profitability depended less on privileges provided by states and more on structural organization that requires conditions of universal freedom of entry (Arrighi 1982, 92). Therefore, if initially those companies were a tool in the hands of states, once interstate and inter-enterprise competition increased they began to challenge state control. Unlike early joint stock corporations that were highly malleable instruments of state power, transnational companies soon turned into the most fundamental limit of that power. While these corporations could not offer a substitute for the governmental institutions established under U.S. hegemony, the accumulated impact of their actions and decisions contributed to the demise of embedded liberalism (Arrighi 1994, 81).

The new formulation of the world economy was the main reason why the depression of the 1970s, unlike in the late nineteenth century, resulted neither in state protectionism nor in territorial expansion. Because direct investment became the main vehicle of capital, protectionist measures could not protect the weaker sectors of industry or sustain the expansionist tendencies of the stronger sectors of domestic capital. "Protection of the national economy will not restrict, and may actually encourage, its penetration by foreign capital through direct investment; and it will discourage the transnational expansion of domestic capital aimed at producing abroad at a lower cost, commodities destined for the home market" (Arrighi 1994, 93).

The ongoing conflict between east and west and rising tensions in the late 1970s of the so-called second cold war kept those developments that undermined U.S. hegemony in check as economic links were subordinated to the dictates of the cold war (Halliday 1983). The U.S. domination of security, and especially nuclear weapons, as well as its domination of the world's production structure, the ability to control the supply and availability of credit denominated in dollars, and domination of the world knowledge structure, seem to defy any notion of declining power (Strange 1987). Shortly before the collapse of the Soviet Union, one author argued that the reliance of Western Europe and Japan on American military power means that the United States will maintain its powerful position: "Thus, while it may be possible to speak of Western Europe and Japan as economic rivals, their dependency on the United States for their security means that they will necessarily remain in subordinate positions. In the late 1980s there is little sign that this situation would change" (Gill 1990).

The collapse of the Soviet Union and the disappearance of the communist threat left American military power largely unchallenged but made it more difficult for the U.S. government to mobilize the human resources needed to put to effective use its military capabilities (Arrighi 2000). The so-called triumphalist moment after the collapse of the Soviet Union was soon replaced with confusion over power resources and power holders. Economically, the reflation of U.S. financial power in the 1980s and 1990s was very different from its earlier hegemonic power and resembled Britain's reflation of power at the end of the nineteenth century. In both cases, military and finance, U.S. actions demonstrated power rather than hegemony.

> That power rested on the capacity of the United States to rise and raise other states above "the tyranny of small decisions," so as to solve the system level problems that had plagued the world in the systematic chaos of the war and interwar years. The new power that the United States came to enjoy in the 1980s and 1990s, in contrast, rests on the capacity of the United States to outcompete most other states in global financial markets. (Arrighi and Silver 1999, 274)

Despite the slowing growth, the recession, and the relative decline of American hegemony, mercantilist policies of economic closure have not occurred. Rather, an increasing liberalization of the global political economy has been observed since the 1970s. Financial markets, it was quickly realized, had profound effects upon the international system, and transnational corporations became a force that states, including the most powerful ones, had to reckon with. The competitive struggle between transnational companies and states over mobile capital increased the volume and density of the web of exchanges across political jurisdictions and the flows of goods, finance, people, and ideas, which in the 1990s came to be called globalization. In such a chaotic world, even a powerful state such as the United States lacks the material and ideological resources needed to exercise minimal governmental functions, and the diffused authority, in Susan Strange's words, "has left a yawning hole of nonauthority, ungovernance it might be called" (Strange 1996, 14).

The Transnational Class

Carl A. Gerstacker, chairman of the Dow Chemical Company, described in the 1970s the desire of the transnational corporation:

> I have long dreamed of buying an island owned by no nation, and of establishing the world headquarters of the Dow company on the truly neutral ground of such an island, beholden to no nation or society. If we were located on such truly neutral ground we could then really operate in the United States as U.S. citizens, in Japan as Japanese citizens and in Brazil as Brazilians rather than being governed in prime by the laws of the United States. (Barnet and Muller 1974, 16)

The development of a world economy that no longer conformed to geographical boundaries seemed to answer the wishes of transnational (or multinational) corporations, which rapidly freed themselves from state control. Multinational corporations, as outlined in the previous section, were empowered by the United States and its European allies to operate globally, but as they did so in ever increasing numbers they undermined the power of those states themselves (Arrighi and Silver 1999, 279). We will return to the disempowerment of states in the next section. The empowerment of multinational corporations and the increasing mobility of capital, technology, ideas, and people, it is argued, create a wide "transnational class" operating in world politics. This class is both the promoter of the globalization process and its main beneficiary.

The definition of a transnational capitalist class used here (and elsewhere) is different than the traditional Marxist sense of direct ownership or control of the means of production (Sklair 1995, 70–71). What defines this class according to Sklair is that its members perceive their interests and/or their countries of citizenship's interests as best served by identification with the interests of the capitalist global system and hold transnational practices as more valuable than local practices (8). This class, which has been a decisive force in promoting globalization, is wider in scope than the financial community described above. Composed of different elements of society and united by an "outward" perception, it is transnational in three senses. First, its members tend to have outward-oriented global rather than inward-oriented national perspectives on a variety of issues. Second, the members of this class come from many countries and they perceive themselves as "citizens of the world" as well as of their place of birth. Third, they tend to share similar lifestyles, particularly patterns of higher education and consumption of luxury goods (Sklair 1997).

Stephen Gill in detailed research identified an emerging transnational class mobilized by developing its consciousness and solidarity in international organizations, international financial institutions, and the like. The interests of this class, he argues, are bound with the "progressive transnationalization and liberalization of the global political economy" (1990, 50). Its prerogatives are backed by a wide consensus over the ideas they carry and supported by finance and economic ministries who, gaining the upper hand over state agencies linked to industry, employment, and welfare, shape compatible policies (94–95). The result, according to Gill, has been the "transnationalization of the state," a shift in the focus and organization of state action, and the empowerment of transnational capital.

> The growth of such mobility and scale intensifies the need for governments, competing to attract foreign capital under recessionary conditions, to provide an appropriate business climate for overseas investors. A state will be judged in terms of its comparative hospitality to foreign capital. Thus, the policies of the state toward the market, toward labour-capital relations, toward the provision of an appropriate social and economic infrastructure, are incrementally recast in an international framework. (113)

The existence of groups with interests and economic practices that transcend political boundaries is far from novel, and they are well captured in Polanyi's description of nineteenth-century haute finance. What distinguishes the transnational class from the 1970s onward is its ability to transform world politics and to "disembed" liberalism from the postwar world order. James Field describes this as a development of a "new tribe," defined functionally rather than ethnically or geographically (Field 1971). Describing the rise of the multinational corporations in the early 1970s, Barnet and Muller identified a problem the new "world managers" would have to contend with: "America's growing antibusiness mood." To gain hegemony, transnational elites would have to answer the same question that has confronted every new elite aspiring to political leadership and social management: "by what right do a self-selected group of druggists, biscuit makers, and computer designers become the architects of the new world? To establish their political legitimacy, the aspiring world managers must be able to demonstrate that the maximization of global profits is compatible with human survival" (Barnet and Muller 1974, 25).

Class hegemony does not simply "happen" as a result of exogenous changes; rather, it is an outcome of time, energy, and resources expanded by the capitalist class and its supporters (Sklair 1997). The achievement of hegemony, in spite of accumulated power, is uncertain. Since the 1950s, business has worked on restoring its image, damaged after the depression of the 1930s, and its dominant position, constrained by the postwar order. The business community took initiatives to regain its power in the face of what they perceived to be a hostile, antibusiness environment created by the media. American corporate leaders in the 1970s invested in "educating" the media through think tanks, publications, programs at major universities, and so on (Dreier 1982). Similarly, in Britain concerted ideological or ideational efforts by financial institutions and the neoliberal media were able to replace the Keynesian paradigm by a monetarist paradigm (Hall 1993).

In the 1970s, senior businessmen in the United States and elsewhere grasped that globalization, as a process of disembedding markets and encouraging transnational practices, would require persuasion and legitimization on a higher level closer to hegemony that would make globalization a universal rather than a particular interest. The banker David Rockefeller, for example, called for a "crusade for understanding" to explain why global corporations should have freer rein to move goods, capital, and services around the world without government interference (Barnet and Muller 1974, 21). The legitimization of market economy and the campaign to "roll back" the state have been successful, especially after the recession of the 1970s, in influencing not only public opinion but also actual policy making. Globalization, especially of financial markets, therefore, was part of the neoliberal economic agenda and an outcome of political decisions taken by states and shaped by domestic and international coalitions rather than a deterministic outcome of technological developments. The influence of the transnational class on the "globalization of the state" has been significant. Advanced industrial states, as Eric Helleiner's work demonstrates, decided to grant more freedom for market operators through liberalization initiatives, to refrain from imposing more effective control on capital movements, and to prevent major international financial crises (Helleiner 1994, 8–10).

Helleiner (1994) identifies two interrelated reasons for the decision of major states to disembed markets: at the systemic level, "competitive deregulation" by governments attracts mobile capital and, at the cognitive level, a strong "epistemic community" that supported the shift in ideology (see also B. Cohen 1996). Interstate competition encouraged governments to liberalize their economies, but these developments could not have happened without a supportive framework of legitimacy. The neoliberal agenda that rose in the 1970s was supported by a coalition of social groups and especially by central bank officials and large industrial corporations who became frustrated with capital control regimes as their interests became increasingly global (Helleiner 1993).

An advertisement for *Time* magazine describes their member readers in terms that resemble the class described above: "*Time*'s 24 million readers [throughout the world] are apt to have more in common with each other than with many of their own countrymen. High income, good education, responsible positions in business, government and the professions. The readers constitute a community of the affluent and the influential" (Barnet and Muller 1974, 33). This ad may say more about *Time*'s promotion tactics than about the transnational class, but it also suggests that there is a market that crosses borders for those who share common beliefs, practices, and lifestyles.

Those who are part of the transnational class often have more in common with each other than with the mass of the population in their respective societies (Gill 1996). They are attached to the centers in which finance and knowledge production is concentrated for functional but also political and social reasons. They are cosmopolitan in the sense of a readiness for engagement based on feelings of competence and independence. "The cosmopolitan's surrender to the alien culture implies personal autonomy vis-à-vis the culture where he originated. He has his obvious competence with regard to it, but he can choose to disengage from it. He possesses it, it does not posses him" (Hannerz 1996, 104).

Transnational practices have important political effects, discussed below, and therefore need to be mapped and studied. Identifying four main fractions of the transnational class (TNC), Leslie Sklair sets up a framework through which it can be studied "in action," sustaining the process of globalization. Those fractions include TNC executives and their local affiliates, globalizing bureaucrats, globalizing politicians and professionals, and a consumerist elite. Combined, these groups, well-adapted to reap the benefits of globalization, supply the process with rationality, coherence, and legitimacy (Sklair 1999). This class is probably less coherent than Sklair's description in its aims and values, and its internal relations are based as much on tension and competition as on shared commonalties. What unites this class, however, are two major interrelated issues, first, its members are interested in liberalizing the economy of their own state and, second, they are interested in "globalizing" their state, opening its borders to economic and other global flows.

Not only do the qualities described above, it is argued, endow the transnational class with more political opportunities, states and boundaries might interfere with their agenda, especially when they are bogged down in conflicts and/or fail to integrate globally. This has led several scholars to the conclusion that this class is disengaged from local politics and society. Robert Reich has pointed to a "secession" tendency grounded in the economic status of high-income-earners that decide to defect from a social arrangement. This group, labeled "symbolic analysts," no longer depends on the economic performance of other Americans. Gradually, and at times without intent, they secede from the rest of society. "While symbolic analysts pledge national allegiance with as much sincerity and resolve as ever, the new global sources of their economic well being have subtly altered how they understand their economic roles and responsibilities in society" (Reich 1991). Jorge Castenada observes a similar political formation in Mexico of those connected to the American economy: "With time, the interests of the Mexicans in the U.S-connected sphere will displace their traditional affection and concern for Mexico. Because they have a way out of Mexico's misery, they are different from their countrymen" (Castenada 1996).

Generally, this class can be divided between those who are active promoters of globalization and those who, through cultural, ideological, and everyday economic practices, supply the legitimacy to make these developments an essential component of common sense and part of an emerging (attempted) hegemonic order. Many of the latter act as what Gramsci defined as "organic intellectuals": "those able to theorize the conditions of existence of the system as a whole, suggest policies and their justifications, and, if need be, apply them" (Gill 1990). Two qualifications to the concept of the transnational class can be derived from Gramsci's definition, the first regarding its identity and the second regarding its hegemony. The above description of a cosmopolitan transnational class, I argue, may be the exception rather than the rule as it undervalues this class's attachment to its homeland and desire to reshape it rather than simply leave. While some members of this class regard themselves as cosmopolitan and define themselves as tied to a company rather than to a country, many of them, as our two case studies will demonstrate, regard themselves as citizens of a state and loyal members of a nation. Their personal global connections and the liberalization of the country's economy, they argue, benefit all and are an expression of a rational patriotism. Their entrepreneurial and intellectual ability and success should, they also argue, serve an example to follow for their fellow countrymen. As such, this class can be both global-cosmopolitan and local-patriot and, consequently, presents its interests and actions as universal rather than particular.

I use the term *attempted hegemony* to describe this class because its actual position does not amount to hegemony (Ben-Porat 2005). While the economic liberal agenda this class carries is well entrenched, and an extraordinary amount of cooperation between governments of the powerful states, mediated by business interests, has been achieved to manage crises, these achievements fall short of a hegemony. A global hegemony requires not only an entrenched economic paradigm and political effectiveness but also moral legitimacy (Gill and Law 1989) that this class has yet to achieve. Using Albert Hirschman's terms, this class has enhanced its "exit option" as it is able to shift its assets relatively easily and, consequently, influence government decision making. Its "voice option," however, is more limited. "To resort to voice, rather than exit, is for the customer or member to make an attempt at changing the practices, policies and outputs of the firm from which one buys or of the organization to which one belongs. Voice here is defined as any attempt at all to change, rather than to escape from an objectionable state of affairs" (Hirschman 1970, 30).

The "exit option" is a viable option in many situations for this class, making it able to transport its financial or intellectual possessions. But this class may choose to try and exercise hegemony and to use the "voice option" in order to globalize the society and the state in which they live, and to support the resolution of conflicts that interfere with globalization. This attempted hegemony, based upon their expertise and success, would allow members of this class to equate their interests with the general interest and advocate the logic of capital to prevail over that of territory. By participation in different aspects of civil society, this class seeks to transform most spheres into its own image and attempts to exert its political influence and social status to erase the difference between global and local and to internationalize and deterritorialize the state for a supposedly common (local) good. But attempts to globalize and liberalize the state have often encountered the discontent of the local and generate counterattempts to reinforce boundaries.

Sovereignty, Territory, and Discontent

The development of globalization as an increase of flows across state borders places the essential territorial reference of the state under pressure. This "crisis of territoriality" can be observed in the difficulty the state has in performing essential functions, namely, to "monitor competently, and to intervene effectively in, a growing range of aspects of social existence, in spite of the fact that such aspects decisively effect the well-being of its population, the resources available to the state, and its ability to form and carry out policy" (Poggi 1990, 177). The principle of sovereignty, enshrined in the so-called Westphalian system of international relations, established in 1648, was based upon exclusive control over territory. It was premised upon the idea that states were the central actors in international relations, that all member states were to be regarded as equal, and that states would maintain order within their borders and command the necessary resources to conduct relations with peer states. The growing incongruity between economic activity and the territorial sovereignty of states since the 1970s, and the empowerment of nonstate actors, led several authors to conclude that states have become all but irrelevant.

Kenichi Ohmae, one of the leading advocates of the end of the nation-state thesis, argues that the mobility of investments, industry, information technology, and individual consumption (labeled by Ohmae "the four I's") make it possible for viable economic units in any part of the world to pull in whatever is needed for development and makes nation-states, formerly the "middlemen," largely unnecessary. The overall result, accordingly, is that the use of "nation-focused" maps to make sense of economic activity is misleading: "the old cartography no longer works. It has become no more than an illusion" (Ohmae 1995, 4–5, 20).

But the claim that state sovereignty is completely eroded by globalization and that states are irrelevant is exaggerated and requires qualifications. First, from an historical perspective such notions are based on the construction of a "mythical past" in the Westphalian system. While it is true that the effectiveness of state control is challenged by globalization, the authority of states has always been problematic and challenged. Throughout their history, states were influenced by flows of ideas, people, and technology; subjected to external scrutiny; and, when weaker states were concerned, by the power of their neighbors (Krasner 1999). Second, even a shorter historical view points to the fact that prior to globalization, during the cold war, sovereignty was at most partial and limited to few states. While formally more independent states were established during the twentieth century, the Westphalian principles still are not an accurate description. If under the British hegemony a balance of power operating between rather than above states was a fiction, under the U.S. hegemony and the superpower rivalry the idea was even discarded as a fiction when even states such as Japan and Germany were described as being "semisovereign" (Arrighi 2000). Finally, even in the height of the globalization period, not all states have lost their power. Some states have actually gained power and are capable of taking advantage of the changes in the state system (Weiss 1998).

The combined political implications of the declining U.S. hegemony based upon principles of embedded liberalism, on the one hand, and attempted transnational class hegemony, on the other hand, is a transformation of domestic and international politics. Flows across borders, cyberspace, and offshore markets all point to a significant spatial change as the modern system of states may be yielding in some instances to postmodern configurations of political space (Ruggie 1993). Territoriality, part and parcel of embedded liberalism, has been defined as the "attempt by an individual or a group to affect, influence, or control people, phenomena, and relationships by delimiting and asserting control over a geographic area" (Sack 1986, 19). The distinctive feature of the modern system of rule was that it "differentiated its subject collectivity into territorially defined, fixed, and mutually exclusive enclaves of legitimate dominion." Already in the 1970s, Hedley Bull argued that evidence indicated a trend where "the states system may be giving place to a secular reincarnation of the system of overlapping or segmented authority that characterized medieval Christendom" (Bull [1977] 1995, 254).

Several authors adopted the term *new medievalism* to describe the new geopolitical reality. States in this period, they argue, share authority in economy and society with other entities; political power and authority are not necessarily based upon clearly defined, separated and separable domestic markets and politics; and political loyalty is less and less tied to geographic location (Kobrin 1998). The result is a complex international political arena, shared by states and nonstate actors with competing organizing principles. The international system has been geographically transformed by what Ruggie defines as "unbundeled territoriality" (Ruggie 1993). Unbundled, rather than fixed territoriality, while not diminishing sovereignty, has a significant impact upon states' capabilities to govern and upon the dynamics of local-domestic politics.

Politics itself structurally changed as the "playing field" derives less from interstate relations and more from a complex congeries of multilevel games played on multilayered institutional playing fields, above and across, as well as within, state boundaries (Ruggie 1993). What is transformed, therefore, are the "ways that the basic rules of the game work in politics and international relations and . . . the increasingly complex payoff matrices faced by actors in rationally evaluating their politics" (Cerny 1995). Susan Strange, describing states as "defective," argued that state authority has "leaked away, upwards, sideways, and downwards" and, as such, states are increasingly becoming "hollow or defective institutions" (Strange 1995). States, however, are not simply victims of a process entirely beyond their control; many states consciously chose to become a part of the process by adopting a neoliberal and globalizing agenda.

State political elites and bureaucrats develop objectives, structures, policies, and patterns of socialization that are international in scope and ethos in order to adapt the state to what they perceive and describe as "global realities." Domestic politics, therefore, are central for understanding the transformation of the welfare state to a "competition state" (Cerny 1997). The competition state, rather than take certain economic activities out of the market as embedded liberalism prescribed, pursues increasing marketization in order to make economic activities located within the national territory more competitive in international and transnational terms. In this process, the state becomes an agent of its own transformation from a civil association to an enterprise association (Cerny 1997).

The disintegration of the world order of embedded liberalism evinced in the late twentieth century unfolds spatially in various and contradictory expressions and political projects of *deterritorialization* and *reterritorialization*. *Deterritorialization* refers not only to the growing variety of social activities that take place irrespective of the geographical location of the participants but also to political interests, agendas, and decision-making processes that enable these activities. In a world of global production networks, access to capital and technology depends on strategic alliances with those who control global production networks, rather than on control of any particular piece of territory. Furthermore, in a global economy where there is a surplus of labor, control over large amounts of territory can be more of a burden than an asset (Evans 1997). The very nature of interstate competition changed from competition over resources (that are territorially bounded) to a competition over market shares: "In the past states competed for control over territories and the wealth-creating resources within territories, whether national or man-created. Now they are increasingly competing for market shares in the world economy. In this competition, territory is no longer the main basis for wealth-creation . . . industrial policy and trade policy are becoming more important than defense and foreign policy" (Strange 1995, 55–56). Not only has territory lost much of its value but in many cases, as Western powers learned in the Third World, with the growth of resistance and cheapening of arms and technology, the costs of suppressing local population exceeded the benefits of holding on to territories and drawing their resources.

The result of the transformations described above, despite the flows across national boundaries and the rise of transnational networks, is not social homogenization and erasure of national identity but rather a fragmented and contested political arena within and between states and, consequently, various activities that can be described as "reterritorialization" designed to redraw and strengthen national and state boundaries. Because the globalized economy is based on the transnational movement of the mobile factors of production—capital, labor, and technology—states and localities become increasingly vulnerable to economic restructuring, which increases inequalities within and between states (Agnew 1995, 98). A steep rise of inequality occurred during the acceleration of globalization in the second half of the 1980s, first between countries but also within countries. A general tendency toward more inequality can be observed for most of the countries belonging to the Organization for Economic Cooperation and Development (OECD) (Therborn 2000).[5]

The flows across boundaries—of people, technology, finance, images, and ideas—rather than homogenizing are, to use Appadurai's term, "disjunctured" (Appadurai 1990). These disjunctures manifest themselves in, among other sites of political and social interactions, the continuous tension between social demands for states' intervention to ensure minimum levels of welfare, and states' increasing incapability or unwillingness to do so. "The unregulated global economy has greatly reduced the state's capacity for intervention, even though demands for such intervention are becoming increasingly vocal, especially in those quarters that have been seriously disadvantaged by global integration" (Camilleri 1995, 215).

The globalization of the international economy, therefore, is not a smooth process in which differences are erased and a common agenda is formed because the denationalization of national territory is matched by a renationalization: "This denationalization, which to a large extent materializes in global cities, has become legitimate for capital and has indeed been imbued with positive value by many government elites and their economic advisers. It is the opposite when it comes to people, as is perhaps most sharply illustrated in the rise of anti-immigrant feelings and the renationalization of politics" (Sassen 1998, xxviii).

Projects of deterritorialization and reterritorialization are carried by different groups for different ends. From an international economic perspective,

5. It is important to note that for Therborn the growth of inequality is not a necessary consequence; rather, state policies can and do matter.

Robert Cox describes the uneven world structure shaped by globalization as three-part hierarchy. At the top are the people integrated into the global economy, from managers to the relatively privileged workers who serve global production and finance in reasonably stable jobs. The second includes those who serve the global economy in more "precarious" employment. And, at the bottom are those excluded, considered superfluous labor with a potential of disruption of the system's operation (R. Cox 1996). A deep fault line exists between groups who have the skills and mobility to flourish in global markets and those who either don't have these advantages or those who perceive the process as damaging social stability and norms. Workers, especially unskilled workers, have to pay a larger cost of improvements in work conditions and benefits to incur greater instability in earnings and hours worked, and their bargaining power erodes (Rodrik 1997, 5; Tilly 1995). The interests and identities of these groups translate into their concepts of territorial attachment and deterritorializing or reterritorializing strategies. The highly skilled, the educated, and the owners of mobile capital, described above as the transnational class, are set to reap the new advantages globalization affords and, therefore, tend to adopt more flexible identities that are not territorially inscribed or fixed. But fixed territoriality and effective state sovereignty still matter especially for those destined to be on the losing side for which the state supplies either (usually limited) protection from the ravages of the market or a stable source of identity and belonging.

Globalization, therefore, in spite of its powerful thrust, remains politically problematic and unstable (Rupert 2000). Simultaneous integration and disintegration can be observed in the late twentieth century's globalization, which may be approaching a conjuncture in which renewed liberal-economic structures will generate large-scale disruptions and sustained pressure for self-protection (Mittelman 2000). Discontent expresses itself in the rise of ethnic and class tensions, and a reassertion of territoriality can be observed in growing xenophobic nationalism and demands for protection in Europe and the United States (Scholte 1996). Unlike a solidified counterhegemony of the Gramscian sense, with a fixed alternative agenda, the antiglobalization movement is an amalgam of reactions to globalization analogous to the double movement Polanyi identified in earlier historical periods when the liberalization of society was met by a defensive countermovement. Diverse movements such as those given voice by Patrick Buchanan in the United States, Zyuganov in Russia, or Islamists in Turkey may share a common root: a backlash against globalization

(Rodrik 1997). Moreover, discontent is not the sole property of the lower classes. Even some of the middle class feels it is losing ground, as one analyst noted: "While speculators and corporate raiders took home huge sums the average American family wound up fearing for the safety of its bank accounts, insurance coverage, home values and pension coverage" (quoted in Arrighi and Silver 1999, 212).

Thus, while cyberspace, offshore finance, and other developments associated with globalization present serious challenges to territorial sovereignty, they cannot replace it in providing security and welfare to those at the bottom or the middle level of Cox's three-part hierarchy. In addition, globalization does not distribute economic dividends that can compensate for the emotional component of territory and "homeland." The countermovements against the free market, as Polanyi's double movement predicts, can be observed against both the commodifying and deterritorializing effects of globalization. These countermovements are diverse, with different—at times contradictory—purposes, ideologies, and methods alluding to the differential effects of globalization itself. Some of these movements may take advantage of modern technology to promote their message, and others use global networks to pressure governments for their cause. Resistance to globalization, as will be demonstrated in the following chapters, might have wider political ramifications than Polanyi's double movement suggests, as it would promote not only decommodification for social protection but also reterritorialization and renationalization.[6]

Globalization, Peace, and Discontent

If existing state boundaries are the source of many zero-sum conflicts over territorial control, the "unbundling of territoriality" associated with globalization seems to offer both new incentives for ending conflicts as well as new possibilities for resolution. The rise of a transnational class whose interests extend beyond national boundaries and the growth of transnational practices that involve wider circles could potentially change the payoff matrix of conflict and peace. Not only a potentially powerful coalition for peace is formed but also new solutions based on the developments described above may become avail-

6. This may be the reason why the wish at least to slow down globalization comes also from the boosters of this process, now distressed over the instability it generates. See Mittelman 2000, 234–35.

able. The shift of the balance from solely defined territorial politics to nonterritorial forms of organization and identity constitutes a new logic that conjures up the possibilities of new notions of citizenship, democracy, community, and government (Jacobson 1997) and, consequently, may offer new solutions to conflicts hitherto perceived as intractable by rethinking them in a transnational context (Anderson 1998).

The development of new opportunities for the resolution and management of conflicts explains the proliferation of peace studies at the end of the cold war and the attention to the potential of economic incentives to promote peace (Cortright 1997; Crumm 1995; Solingen 1995). The linkage established between peace and economic growth or prosperity suggested that potential or real peace dividends in the form of global integration could motivate the business community and its allies to actively support peace (O'Hearn 2000; Shafir 1998; Shafir and Peled 2000). The pacifying potential of dividends related to globalization portrays a virtuous cycle in which peace and economic development cross-pollinate each other. Initial advances in resolution of the conflict enhance business confidence, enable global integration, and generate economic growth. Economic betterment, or peace dividends, on their behalf, widen support for peace and make territorial compromises easier. Thus, according to this logic, globalization creates new external conditions and new opportunities that local actors may draw upon in order to promote their agenda of peace and global integration.

The impact of external conditions on domestic politics has been studied by several authors. In a historical study using the Stolper-Samuelson Theorem,[7] Ronald Rogowski examined how changing exposures to trade affect political cleavages. Landowners, workers, and capitalists, according to the study, respond to external change and form coalitions to protect or promote their interests. Those expecting to benefit from cheaper trade will demand greater openness, they will be strengthened politically by any such exogenous change, and those changes will be brought to bear in the political arena (Rogowski 1989). Focusing on international capital mobility, Jeffrey Frieden argues that in the developed world, financial integration favors capitalists with mobile or diversified assets and disfavors those with assets tied to specific locations

7. The theorem predicts that protection benefits (and liberalization harms) owners of factors in which, compared with the rest of the world, that society is poorly endowed, as well as producers who use that scarce resource intensively.

(Frieden 1991). But while the interests of certain classes in peace is obvious, the question remains whether they have the capacity to co-opt wider circles for support. Unlike the more specific economic issues described above, often lost for "experts," peace processes pertain to questions of national security, identity, and sentiments and therefore involve wider political involvement and require the exercise of hegemony.

Global integration can be an incentive for the business community and other groups to support territorial compromise, but it can leave some groups indifferent or even hostile, especially if benefits of peace are uncertain or unevenly divided. Contrary to those who believe that integrating globally would improve their life, those who either have less to gain from global integration or prefer to remain attached to local identities may view the process as negative. In the more extreme cases, "spoilers," leaders and parties who believe that peace threatens their power, worldviews, or interests, may favor a separatist agenda regardless of the economic consequences and might have the power to derail the peace process by extreme actions (Stedman 1997). The power of spoilers and their legitimacy can negatively influence not only the ability to reach an agreement but also its implementation. Peace processes are a complex succession of transformations punctuated by long periods of inertia, sticking points, and setbacks. Even when settlements are reached, they are in danger of collapsing if new life is not breathed in to them by the will of the parties, their constituencies, and external supporters to make them work. This is especially true if the euphoria that often accompanies the early stages of settlement, with promises of material betterment, turns to disillusionment when hopes, realistic or not, evaporate (Crocker and Hampson 1996; Miall, Ramsbotham, and Woodhouse 1999, 183–84).

Globalization, in conclusion, offers new incentives and opportunities for the resolution of long-standing territorial conflicts or, at least, for their management. But these incentives, due to various sources of discontent and spoilers, are not easily translated into stable long-term peace agreements. The transformation of world politics according to a liberal economic logic, if globalization would follow the course of its enthusiast adherents, could lead to peace. In a world set free for business to serve consumers, states and military power cease to matter and war ceases to have any connection with economic rationality and becomes the recourse of failed and economically backward societies. But in reality globalization is an asymmetrical process whose benefits are unequally distributed, so that territory matters and retains value, even in developed societies. Populations, despite globalization, remain territorial, subjected to the citizenship of a national state and dependent upon the state for protection from the vagaries of the market and for providing them with secure identities. Deterritorialization has been the defining logic of this period of globalization, but reterritorialization and renationalization have been quick to follow and present new challenges for those seeking peace. Globalization, by itself, does not transform conflicts by eliminating identity but can provide a context in which differences can be more effectively managed (McGarry 2001, 295). The success or failure of the management of conflicts and peace processes depends on the ability of the propeace leadership to exploit new opportunities, make incentives and gains universal, and marginalize spoilers.

The following general hypotheses underlay the research work of the next two chapters. Those expecting to reap the benefits of globalization—highly skilled, educated, owners of mobile capital—adopt flexible identities that are not territorially inscribed and value international integration, both cultural and economic, over domestic politics. Insofar as it is perceived that conflict resolution is a precondition for successful global integration, those constituencies support or even actively promote the peace process. But for those who perceive the process as deleterious—the immobile, those protected by closed markets, the unskilled, and those committed to territorial nationalism—territorial identity becomes ever more important, and their insecurity produces a domestic reassertion against globalizing that exacerbates both real and imagined intergroup conflicts and reinforces rather than diminishes domestic struggles.

7

Israel, Globalization, and Peace

DEVELOPMENTS IN ISRAEL in the early 1990s appeared to support the argument that globalization creates new opportunities to transform seemingly intractable conflicts. Because of its longevity and complexity, the Israeli-Palestinian conflict was considered intractable for a long time. In late 1993, with the August announcement of secret talks between Israel and the Palestine Liberation Organization (PLO) and the signing in September of a declaration of principles in Washington, D.C., resolution of the conflict briefly seemed possible. The breakthrough and ensuing optimism were short-lived, however. Relations between Israel and the Palestinians oscillated between hesitant political developments, deadlocks, and sporadic violence. With the collapse of the talks at Camp David in the summer of 2000 and the escalation of violence to an unprecedented scale, the conflict seemed to have returned to a point of intractability that even Israel's withdrawal from Gaza in August 2005 did not change. Chapter 6 elicited a framework in which the incentives and opportunities associated with globalization both promote the resolution of territorial conflicts and provoke a double movement of resistance; in this chapter, this framework will be used to explain the dynamics of the Israeli-Palestinian conflict and the rise and fall of the so-called New Middle East.

Embedded in a wider Israeli-Arab conflict and in the dynamics of the cold war, and containing intercommunal, interstate, and even interreligious elements, the Israeli-Palestinian conflict may be described as multidimensional and complex. For decades, scholars, policy makers, and the general public have tended to treat the Arab-Israeli conflict in general and the Israeli-Palestinian conflict in particular as inherent, believing it can be restrained but not resolved (Evron 1973, 207). Azar and Cohen described the Israeli-Arab conflict as "protracted" in nature. Conflicts of this type tend to deepen, as they do not permit the parties to take decisive steps toward peace or even deter them from attempting such steps: "Any such steps actually prove disruptive. Since peace would so profoundly modify the nature of inter-state and inter-personal relations in the area, peace in this situation would constitute a breakpoint. Moves towards peace are thus tentative and hesitant, and protracted war is a powerful temptation because it offers a way to avoid the anxieties entailed in attempts at negotiating and direct communication" (1979, 164).

For many Israelis conflict (or even war) became inevitable. For some this was a result of what they perceived as Israel's position between hostile states. For others it was a continuation of a typical pattern of Jewish survival in a hostile world. Many Israeli policy makers and scholars of the conflict have tended to perceive it as forced upon Israel, viewing its sources as exogenous to Israel's policy. Israel has been described as responding to a regional (or world) anarchy that generates objectively defined security interests and, consequently, as reacting to an external reality that constrains its behavior (Y. Levy 1997, 19–20; Telhami 1996). Critics of this type of scholarship argue that it overlooks those instances in which Arab leaders displayed pragmatism, does not force the reality of the conflict upon Israel, and ignores the internal dynamics of Israel's politics and social structure (Y. Levy 1997, 19–20). The Israeli/Jewish-Palestinian conflict, these scholars argue, must be incorporated into the analysis as a constituent element of Israeli society rather than an exogenous force autonomous to Israeli policy and actions (Peled and Shafir 1996).

The peace agreement between Israel and Egypt in 1978 and the dramatic developments of the 1990s—from the Madrid conference to the Labor Party's victory in the 1992 elections and the agreement between Israel and the PLO—attest to major changes in the dynamics and perceptions of the conflict. Those changes not only call into question previous assumptions of the conflict's inevitability but indicate the need to study the dynamics of the conflict as an interaction between domestic politics and foreign relations, between global and local developments, and between global (economic and other) incentives and disincentives for peace.

An international business journal declared in 1989 that Israel, from an economic perspective, has everything it needs to become a first-rate economy except peace. In the midst of a low-intensity civil war, the journal explained, Israel is in process of a multi-billion-dollar transformation. With a sweeping program of privatization and deregulation starting to attract huge amounts of foreign capital and growth of high-technology start-ups, the country is emerging from a two-decade-long recession. The only problem, the journal concluded, was geopolitics, which soon may be resolved. "The Israeli economy is very fragile and will continue to be so until the outlines of a peace settlement become much clearer. Israeli business people understand that there is little chance of the country building a stable civilian economy without peace with the Arabs. The pragmatic business community is pressuring the Shamir government to negotiate with the Palestinians" (Rossant 1989).

David Trimble, leader of the Northern Ireland Protestant majority and later on the elected prime minister, argued in a visit to Israel two years after the signing of the Good Friday Agreement that the Israeli-Palestinian conflict is more complex than the Irish, but he recommended a familiar formula for the progress of peace. Promotion of economic growth and an improved standard of living for the people, he suggested, would make them realize that peace is desirable *(Haaretz,* June 27, 2000, A12). Trimble's suggestion and the business journal's observation were no news to Israeli politicians, businesspeople, and scholars who since the 1990s made the linkage between peace, global integration, and economic prosperity.

The relations between economic development and peace and the vested interest and involvement of the Israeli business community in the peace process have been studied by several scholars. In a comparative study of Israel and South Africa, Shafir argues that business communities emerge as major players resolving conflicts (1998, 102–19). Similarly, Shafir and Peled (2000) examine the work of the outward-looking sectors of the business community in league with the professional and technical elites of the civil service to replace the zero-sum configuration of the conflict with a more open-ended game in which both sides could be winners. Nitzan and Bichler (1996), using a political economy framework, describe a transformation of Israel from a militarized economy characterized by large government deficits, heavy dependency on the United States, and intense stagflation to an economy geared toward peace and regional integration, economic growth, and declining military spending. There is no denying that the business community as well as the wider transnational class has a vested interest in making peace. Yet, as I will argue below, the ability of the business and the wider transnational class to influence the peace process has been limited, as the elections of 1996 results discussed below clearly indicated.

Uri Ram (2000) describes the tensions between globalization and localization as *glocalization.* In Israel, according to Ram, glocalization includes the decline of nationalism and the welfare state, the globalization of Israeli capital, and, conversely, the localization of the Israeli lower classes and their adherence to ethno-nationalism. Translated into support for the Oslo process, a spirit of rapprochement, related to the decline of nationalism and globalization, developed at the elites' level. But this spirit did not diffuse down into the grass roots, leaving the process with a limited amount of support (Hermann and Newman 2000).

The selection of Yitzhak Rabin and Shimon Peres as winners of the Nobel Peace Prize was supposedly one of the high points of the process, yet Yossi Beilin, Peres's deputy at the time, recalls little euphoria, as opinion polls in Israel at the time showed a slight advantage to the opposition. The biggest mistake, he reflected in retrospect, was the belief that peace would speak for itself and support would be forthcoming. "We thought that people would automatically make the link between the diplomatic process and the end of the Arab boycott, the enormous growth of investment in Israel, the drastic decline in unemployment, the quick rise of living standards, the end of the threat of war, the rise in tourism, and the transformation of Israel from an ostracized state to a welcome and important partner" (Beilin 1997, 308).

What was missing from the peace process, as several of those involved were aware, was "cognitive legitimacy" at the grassroots level, a real culture of change that takes place as populations are prepared to think in terms of peace rather than conflict and to view the "Other" as a potential partner rather than an enemy (Hermann and Newman 2000). Decision makers in Israel have had to face the fact that the formal signing of the agreement was not the end of the domestic debate but its beginning (Bar-Siman-Tov 2001).

Globalization, therefore, created new opportunities and incentives for peace, but also winners and losers, promoters of peace and spoilers and, consequently, pendulum swings between steps toward peace and regressions to violence. The purpose of this chapter is twofold: first, to identify the changes associated with globalization that helped to launch the peace process and, second, to explain why, despite the initial success, the Israeli-Palestinian process turned out to be fragile and lacking the required legitimacy.

Partition, Conflict, and Perceptions

By the mid-1930s, under the British mandate, the Palestinian and the Jewish populations in Palestine developed into cohesive and self-sustaining communities that were moving toward confrontation. The Jewish settlement in Palestine expanded and matured in the period between the two world wars, in population size and in economic measures. Between 1924 and 1931, about

75,000 Jewish immigrants arrived and almost doubled the size of the *yishuv* (the Jewish settlement in Palestine) to about 175,000 Jews compared to 860,000 Palestinians. The large amounts of Jewish capital channeled to Palestine between 1919 and 1936 were used to purchase more land and to create new agricultural settlements. Finally, many Jewish institutions were established during this period, including a defense force (the *Hagana*), the general union of Jewish workers (the *Histadrut*), and an educational system (Tessler 1994, 185–90).

Palestinians, if to a lesser degree, developed their own infrastructure and political agenda that turned them into a coherent national community. For the Palestinians, the Jewish settlement was perceived to be a foreign element, dependent upon the British mandate and therefore bound to disappear once Britain was ousted. But the continuing growth of the *yishuv* through immigration and land purchases, forced the Palestinians to realize that Jewish presence was not temporary. Clashes between Arabs and Jews erupted several times during the years between the world wars, and in 1929 Arab riots ended with 133 Jews and 116 Arabs killed, most Arabs killed by the British police. In 1936 under the leadership of the newly formed Higher Arab Committee, an organized Arab rebellion was initiated that included a general strike and numerous attacks on Jewish settlements.

After the rebellion of 1936, both sides came to perceive the conflict as a zero-sum game as Palestinian Arabs recognized the threat of Jewish settlement and Zionists abandoned their earlier hopes that the Arab natives of the land would learn to accept their presence. But while recognizing they were facing a national movement, Zionists refused to grant the Palestinian movement legitimacy and treat it as their equal (Benvenisti 1990, 118–19). Both sides invested efforts to influence British immigration policy to Palestine—Jews demanded unlimited immigration and Palestinians demanded a halt to all immigration and Jewish land purchases—but the British had their own interests to consider. The Peel Commission appointed to investigate the motives for the Arab rebellion of 1936 concluded that the British mandate was impossible to sustain and recommended the partition of Palestine. Strategic concerns on the eve of World War II and the Arabs' violent rejection of the partition plan led the British to issue the 1939 White Paper, which, in a dramatic reversal of policy, called for severe restrictions on Jewish immigration and a postponement of partition (C. Smith 1992).

In September 1947, Britain declared its intention to withdraw from Palestine, ended the mandate unilaterally, and handed the matter over to the United

Nations, which decided two months later to partition Palestine. The partition decision and the establishment of the Jewish state initiated a new stage in the Israeli-Arab conflict. The UN decision was followed by Palestinian attempts to stifle its implementation by an offensive guerilla campaign that failed to prevent the establishment of the state of Israel. Israel's declaration of independence on May 15, 1948, was followed by the invasion of five Arab states' armies and a full-scale war between Israel and its Arab neighbors. The war ended in early 1949, in an armistice agreement between Israel and its neighbors, with Israel gaining an additional 2,500 square miles to the 5,600 allocated to it by the UN partition resolution. The state of Israel became an established fact, militarily secured and recognized by the international community (Tessler 1994, 264).

The complex reality of the conflict was revealed after the war. On the one hand, the Arabs viewed the establishment of Israel as a blatant historical injustice and refused to recognize its legitimacy. On the other hand, Israel refused either to give up significant portions of the territories it gained in the war, or to allow a significant number of Palestinian refugees to return to their homes in Israel (Bar-On 1996). About three hundred thousand Palestinians were displaced during the war and became refugees in neighbor Arab states. Some were deported by the Israeli defense forces; others fled in fear of the invading Israelis, driven by Israeli scare tactics, Arab propaganda and evacuation appeals, or both.[1] The Palestinians who remained in Israel as a large minority were officially recognized as full citizens of the state; in practice, however, they were placed under military rule lasting until 1966 that restricted their movements and prevented them from entering the crowded labor market.

The war of 1948 transformed the dimensions of the conflict from an intercommunal to an interstate conflict (Benvenisti 1990, 118). From 1948, the Arab-Israeli conflict was perceived by Israeli scholars as embedded in the Arab world's perceptions of Israel. Yehoshafat Harkabi, former director of Israeli military intelligence, described in a 1965 article the general Arab ideology as "politicide," a desire to annihilate Israel. Accordingly, at this stage of the conflict, the Arabs' position was perceived as the major factor preventing its resolution and Israel as having little if any influence on terminating the conflict

---

1. For a review of the literature, see Tessler 1994, 284–306. Benny Morris, in a detailed report on the Palestinian exodus and Israeli policy, provides several accounts of forced deportations but concludes that these were ad-hoc decisions and that there was no "master plan" of deportation. See Morris 1987.

(Harkavi 1969). The conflict with the Palestinians was perceived to be part of the wider Arab-Israeli conflict and not necessarily the most important part.

After the war of 1967, the Israeli-Palestinian conflict retained its centrality. The war ended with a decisive military victory for Israel, which now occupied new territories won from Egypt, Jordan, and Syria. The occupation of the West Bank and Gaza added a Palestinian population greater than that within Israel, about 750,000 people in the West Bank and 400,000 in Gaza. The issue of the occupied territories became not only a major factor of the Israeli-Arab conflict but has become since the late 1970s the most contentious and divisive issue of Israeli politics.

Convening in Khartoum shortly after the war, Arab states declared their refusal to negotiate with Israel or to recognize its right to exist. Israel, on its behalf, declared its wish to negotiate and willingness to return territories for peace, but refused to withdraw without a comprehensive peace agreement. The Israeli government, for its part, had no clear policy regarding the future of the newly acquired territories. A week after the end of the war, the cabinet communicated a secret message to the U.S. state department for transmission to the Arab governments that indicated Israel's willingness to sign peace treaties in return for territories with some border adjustments. But in August the decision was annulled, possibly as a result of the Arabs' insistence on unconditional withdrawal and the "three No's" (no peace with Israel, no recognition of Israel, no negotiations with Israel) pronounced at the Khartoum summit conference, or because of internal opposition (Shlaim and Yaniv 1994). Five weeks after the war, Israel's deputy prime minister, Yigal Allon, submitted to the cabinet a plan that Israel maintain control over strategically important areas and return the populated areas to Jordan. The cabinet chose not to decide and to keep all options open.

Shlaim and Yaniv (1994) attribute the deadlock and immobility of Israeli policy to the breakdown of domestic consensus after the 1967 war and the development of deep cleavages on the issues raised by the war. The variety of viewpoints between and within the parties and the creation of extraparliamentary pressure groups resulted in government coalitions based on vaguely defined programs that had difficulties reaching decisions on the future of the territories. Some Israeli statesmen treated the Palestinian problem as a refugee problem, in the solution of which Israel was ready to play a part, with international assistance. Golda Meir, Israel's prime minister, refused to recognize the issue as a national problem and argued that recognizing the Palestinian people as a nation cast doubt on the very existence of Israel (Sella 1994).

Despite the declaration of the Israeli government after the war that Israel had no intention of expanding its territorial boundaries, the temporary occupation was gradually entrenched. Not only were the newly occupied territories valued strategically, but their religious and sentimental value was popularized, and several government policies de facto annexed the territories. First, the decision to open the Israeli market to Palestinian laborers from the occupied territories and to make the Israeli currency a legal tender in the West Bank, alongside the Jordanian, made the two economies intertwined. Second, the gradual settlement of Israelis in the occupied territories continuously blurred the boundaries between the territories and the rest of Israel.

Between 1967 and 1977 the settlement of the territories was gradual with the Israeli government reluctant to allow settlement in heavily populated areas. Settlement policy was limited to small communities in the Jordan valley whose construction was motivated by security considerations. But new extraparliamentary movements tried to force the government to allow them to settle in the occupied territories and make them a part of Israel. For some Israelis, the occupation of the old city of Jerusalem, the West Bank, and the rest of the territories were seen as the fulfillment of a divine promise and the establishment of Israel in its "natural" borders. Initially, "the movement for the greater land of Israel," established shortly after the war to influence the government to annex the territories, was made of Labor Party hawks that called for Jewish settlement of the new territories, but soon young orthodox religious Jews came to dominate the movement.

Early attempts of settlement of the territories by religious-nationalist Jews were sporadic and included the act of a small group of orthodox Jews who in 1968 squatted in the midst of the Arab town of Hebron. The movement gained real momentum with formation of *Gush Emunim* (bloc of the faithful) in 1974. This movement, made of young members of the National Religious Party (NRP), took it upon itself to establish Israel's control over the territories and perceived itself as a leader of a national revival that secular Zionism could no longer carry. Between 1974 and 1977 Gush Emunim launched a settlement drive and pressured the government to authorize settlements, even those established without permission. In demographic terms, this drive did not amount to much as by the beginning of 1977 fewer than four thousand Jews lived in the West Bank in four settlements (Bar-On 1996) but an important precedent was set.

In 1977, for the first time in Israel's history, the Labor Party lost the elections to the Likud, a party favoring territorial maximalism and the retention of the West Bank and Gaza. Menachem Begin, Israel's new prime minister, was quick to declare his commitment to the territories and stated that "Samaria and Judea [the Jewish name for the West Bank] are an inalienable part of Israel." The Likud embarked on a wide-ranging initiative to institutionalize beliefs in the legitimacy of the new boundaries. Its pattern of Jewish settlement in the territories carved the territories up in such a way that any future partition agreement would require the removal of established settlements (Sandler and Frisch 1984, 140–41). Between 1978 and 1983, the drastic increase in expenditures on settlements was accompanied by policies in the educational, broadcasting, judicial, and administrative spheres designed to accelerate the disappearance of the "Green Line," Israel's pre-1967 border, separating Israel from the occupied territories, from the practical life and ordinary language of all Israelis. The settlement pace increased to the point that in the mid-1980s leading Israeli scholars came to the conclusion that settlement expansion created irreversible facts that made Israeli disengagement from the territories impossible.

The elections of 1981 and the Likud's victory proved that the 1977 elections were not a fluke and proved the depth of the divide between right and left, which signified in the Israeli political discourse not socioeconomic perceptions but a division between, respectively, hawks and doves. Despite the efforts to blur the border between the occupied territories and Israel either by Jewish settlements, roads and other infrastructure, or the establishment of an ideological hegemonic position regarding "Greater Israel," the territories remained a deeply divisive issue (Lustik 1993, 358). Against the right-wing settlement initiatives, extraparliamentary propeace movements were formed, advocating territorial compromise or "land for peace."

It was the Likud government that in 1979 signed a peace treaty with Egypt. The peace treaty, which followed a dramatic visit by Egyptian president Anwar Sadat to Israel, was based on a withdrawal of Israel from the Sinai Peninsula, occupied in 1967, including Israeli settlements whose residents were relocated to Israel. The exchange of territory for peace was in many respects a precedent and involved debate between left and right, but its implication for the Israeli-Palestinian conflict was limited. The Egyptian-Israeli conflict was a territorial and strategic dispute much more than an ideological struggle. Israel attributed strategic value for Sinai only as a buffer zone for which a peace treaty was an acceptable substitute. In return for the Sinai, Israel received full recognition, formal peace, diplomatic relations, normalization, and freedom of navigation for

Israeli vessels in the Red Sea and the Suez Canal (Kacowicz 1996). In a wider, regional, perspective, after the treaty with Egypt and the lack of support by other Arab regimes for the Palestinian cause, a conflict that had been a region-wide interstate conflict shrank to its original core, namely Israeli-Palestinian intercommunal strife (Benvenisti 1990, 118).

Despite the breakthrough of the peace process with Egypt, there was no sign of similar development with the Palestinians. The Camp David framework was vague and characterized by broad guidelines in regard to the West Bank and Gaza, amenable to different interpretations. While Egypt claimed the accords implied an Israeli withdrawal from the West Bank and Gaza strip, Israel argued it only promised to participate in talks over the future of the territories and not to any particular outcome of the so-called autonomy talks (Tessler 1994, 514–17). The Israeli government under Begin was willing to grant only limited autonomy to the Palestinians, neither sovereignty nor self-determination. It set out almost immediately to increase substantially the number of settlers and settlements in the West Bank and elsewhere, taking control of large tracts of land for that purpose. In addition to the ideological settlement drive of Gush Emunim, ordinary Israelis were encouraged by the government to settle in the West Bank, tempted with subsidized housing and a suburban lifestyle. With these subsidies, a small apartment in Tel-Aviv could be traded for a villa and a spacious lot of land in the West Bank.

The government also attempted, by a stick-and-carrot policy, to make Palestinians realize Israel's stay was permanent. It sought to suppress Palestinian national activities and, at the same time, to create a new and cooperative Palestinian leadership. Israel used the military to close or monitor universities and censor newspapers or ban their publishing. The "carrot" policies included offers to finance projects and government jobs for those who joined the "village leagues" that cooperated with Israel's occupation administration. In 1984, when it was clear that the leagues had failed to attract legitimacy and become an alternative leadership, they were officially disbanded (Tessler 1994, 548–53).

The larger and direct clash between Israel and the PLO happened in 1982 in Israel's invasion of Lebanon. The PLO established a strong base in Lebanon in the large Palestinian refugee camps amid a civil war that allowed it to operate with little interference. From southern Lebanon, the PLO carried out mortar attacks against the Galilee region of Israel. In 1981 the United States brokered a cease-fire between Israel and the PLO, but in 1982, after the cease-fire broke down, Israel invaded Lebanon. What had been declared a short-term operation with a precise military objective against PLO bases in southern Lebanon turned into a long and costly war. The Israeli army occupied part of Beirut, fought against the Syrian army, and did not completely withdrew from Lebanon until eighteen years later. The secret agenda of the war, that later became exposed, was to crush the PLO in Lebanon in order to impose Israel's control over the occupied territories. The war had important implications for Israel's political divide. Until that war, a large majority believed that for Israel, war was not an instrument of policy but a necessity forced upon it by outside factors. This position of "no choice" carried a moral-normative argument that Israel fights only when forced by its opponents. The war in Lebanon raised a fierce public debate regarding its necessity and it justness that deeply divided Israeli society. Despite the government's claim that this war was imposed upon Israel, the opposition argued that because Israel was under no existential threat, all options had to be exhausted before war (Inbar 1994). For the first time, Israelis in large numbers were protesting against a war, some even advocating refusal to serve in Lebanon.

The Palestinian uprising that began in 1987 (the intifada) shattered another embedded belief among Israelis that the occupation of the territories had relatively low economic, political, and moral costs. The harsh measures the Israeli Defense Forces (IDF) used to quell the uprising brought world attention to the conflict and deepened the political rift within Israel between those who demanded a firm hand to put down the uprising and those who argued that advances toward territorial compromise, including negotiations with the PLO, must be made (A. Shalev 1990, 142–44). Israel's chief of staff, Dan Shomron, in 1989 openly acknowledged that the intifada was a genuine popular resistance movement and doubted that it could be resolved militarily (Tessler 1994, 70). The Green Line was resurrected as most Israelis began to see the territories as insecure zones that needed to be avoided, and many realized the rising costs of occupation. In 1988 Jordan drew away from the dispute by declaring it had no claims over the West Bank it lost in the 1967 war and that the land belonged to the Palestinians. The fate of the West Bank, therefore, was to be determined directly between Israelis and Palestinians.

Israel: Left, Right, and Other Cleavages

In the 1980s, Israeli scholars began describing the Israeli polity as overburdened and Israeli society as deeply fragmented or cleavaged. The crisis was related to the aftermath of the 1967 war and the occupation of the territories, which required an impossible balancing between a democratic regime, military occupation of the territories and their inhabitants, and maintenance of social solidarity in face of growing internal conflicts. Social conflicts and the frustrations of marginal groups, argued Lissak and Horowitz, two of Israel's leading sociologists, impeded the functioning of Israeli democracy to the point of making it ungovernable (Lissak and Horowitz 1989, 16). Critics of this description disputed the claim that the 1967 war was a watershed event that disrupted the "normal" process of nation and state building. While they accepted the description of the crisis, they argued that it is inherent to the very foundations of Israel's social order (Levy and Peled 1994).

The future of the occupied territories—that had became since the 1970s the major divisive issue in Israeli society—correlated with other cleavages that divide Israeli society—a Jewish-Arab cleavage, a religious-secular cleavage, an ethnic/cultural cleavage, and a class cleavage. The religious-secular cleavage can be examined in three different contexts. First, there is a social and political context that refers to the extent of distinctiveness and separation between the religious and the secular. Second, the legal context refers to the formal status of religious institutions and their jurisdiction over the wider society. And third, the ideological context focuses on the meaning of the state of Israel as a Jewish state (Lissak and Horowitz 1989, 52). This cleavage is far from dichotomous, as the majority of Israeli Jews are located in between the extremes. Surveys indicate that only a minority of Israelis define themselves as secular or religious and a majority defines itself as "traditional" (Levy, Levinson, and Katz 1997). After 1967 the religious-secular divide became linked to the debate over the future of the territories as the settlement movement is dominated by national-religious Jews and the peace movements by secular Jews.

The ethnic cleavage divides between *Ashkenazim* (Jews of European descent) and *Mizrachim* (Middle Eastern and North African Jews, sometimes referred to as *Sepharadim* or Oriental). The vast majority of Mizrachim immigrated to Israel after statehood. With few connections in the new land, on the average lower skilled, and suffering from discrimination from the Ashkenazi elite of the Labor Party (then called MAPAI), they were relegated to the periphery, geographically and economically. As a result, ethnicity became correlated with patterns of residency, labor, occupational status, and class (Cohen and Haberfeld 1998). The political salience of this cleavage is expressed in Mizrachim support of the Likud, or later the religious Shas party, in both cases showing a rejection of Labor-Zionist ideology (Peled 1998).

The class cleavage in Israel is, relative to the other cleavages, muted and is expressed through other cleavages. Lissak and Horowitz found that since the establishment of the state inequality in the distribution of income and property has increased considerably while the consciousness of class differences has decreased (1989, 83). From being one of the most egalitarian countries of the world, Israel has become since the 1980s a country with high levels of inequality. This cleavage, as mentioned before, is embedded in other cleavages and therefore has little political salience on its own. When class tensions and disturbances occurred in the 1950s and 1970s, they were overshadowed by ethnic protest. Economic debate in general receded as both major parties since the 1970s are committed to market economics and the left-right division in Israel describes doves and hawks rather than political economy.

The Jewish-Arab cleavage is the most entrenched cleavage. Unlike the other cleavages, it is dichotomous and unchangeable. The definition of Israel as a Jewish state limits or totally excludes non-Jewish participation in determining the common good. Peled and Shafir describe a citizenship regime that sets a hierarchy with Arabs at the bottom. Smooha defines Israel as an "ethnic democracy" that favors Jews over non-Jews. Yiftachel defines the Israeli regime as an "ethnocracy," a regime in which the interests of the dominant ethnic group shape most public policies (Peled and Shafir 1996; Yiftachel 1997). The Jewish definition of the state is almost a consensus among Israeli Jews, religious and secular alike (Ben-Porat 2000).

The cleavages described above overlap in various degrees and are reflected in political affiliations and voting patterns. A commitment to democracy, a favorable attitude to peace, and a feeling of security are associated with the upper and middle classes, while intolerance, national sentiments (and at times xenophobia), and a feeling of insecurity are more common among the relatively poor sectors. Secularism is strongly correlated with tolerance and a preference for democratic over nationalist values (Peres and Ya'ar-Yuchtman 1999, 74–75). Ashkenazim tend to be more secular, are proportionally overrepresented in the middle and higher classes, and support the left-wing parties. Mizrachim tend to be more traditional and are overrepresented in the lower classes. Because ethnicity is related to religiosity and class, it is also related to ideological preferences. Since the 1970s, ethnicity has become identified with voting patterns (Shamir and Arian 1982). The Likud, the large and moderate right-wing party, enjoys strong support from Mizrachim who carry deep animosity toward the Labor Party they perceive as responsible for their absorption and their peripheral status. Both of the extraparliamentary movements, Gush

Emunim and Peace Now, are dominated by middle-class Ashkenazim. While the right tends to benefit from the support of Mizrachim, who associate with the Likud, the peace camp is predominantly Ashkenazi and middle-class.

Political Economy: The Disembedding of the Market and Peace

Since the 1980s, the Israeli economy has been in a process of rapid liberalization, away from being state-led and toward becoming a western-type liberal economy, well integrated in the global economy. These developments created new incentives for conflict resolution but deepened the cleavages in Israeli society. The global economic and political developments described in the previous chapter have not escaped Israel as its welfare-state structure gave way to an expanding market economy. Specifically, the liberalization of the economy can be traced to the period between 1974 and 1985 during which Israel experienced its worst economic period, described by economists as the "lost years" (Razin and Sadka 1993, 175). Inflation spiraled (reaching in 1984 a monthly rate of 10 to 25 percent) and tax receipts fell drastically and increased the budget deficit (12 percent of GNP between 1980 and 1984). Fears that the government would fail to honor its liabilities caused an outflow of capital abroad, and stock market speculation and government inattention produced an unprecedented crisis in the banking system (Keren 1993). In 1985 the economic crisis came to pose a real threat to the state's legitimacy and viability. The emergency economic stabilization plan initiated during that year not only brought the economy back from the brink of hyperinflation but also inaugurated a structural shift of liberalizing Israel's political-economic regime (M. Shalev 2000).

The government's stabilization program included balancing the budget by drastic cuts in subsidies and a gradual reduction in domestic defense spending. It also devalued the shekel, stabilized the nominal rate of exchange, and cut wages through a reform of the wage indexation system. These measures led to a dramatic reduction in inflation and in the public sector's budgetary deficit. Productivity began to increase, exports surged, imports shrank, and confidence in the shekel gradually returned (Keren 1993). The significance of the economic plan lies beyond its successful reduction of inflation in recasting the Israeli economic structure away from its protectionist and state-centered formation into a more neoliberal type of economy with wider social gaps. Important also was the development of an autonomous business community that had the desire and a growing ability to integrate globally. With the liberalization of the capital market, the private sector was able, for the first time, to raise capital through the stock exchange free from government control. Moreover, Israeli corporations began offering their securities on the New York Stock Exchange (Shafir and Peled 2000). In the 1990s, the economy experienced a wave of growth resembling that of the East Asian "Tigers," and living standards were within the reach of the rich OECD democracies. At the same time, social gaps also grew. The fruits of the 1985–95 cycle of prosperity have been unevenly and regressively distributed with relatively few benefits for Palestinians outside and inside the green line (M. Shalev 2000).

Shalev delineates three trends during the 1980s and 1990s that facilitated the emergence of the new political economic regime. First, the decomposition of Histadrut greatly decreased the multifaceted political exchange between the union, also an employer and a significant economic actor, and the state. Second, several key centers of the "big economy" were weakened by serious crises. And third, globalization offered new opportunities for business that were further enhanced by free-trade agreements and the peace process (M. Shalev 2000). An additional factor was ideational, or an epistemic change that can be attributed to the work of a group of professional economists trained in the Chicago school tradition who in 1985 took part in the reforms and reasserted what they perceived as their professional status and authority within society. Prime Minister Shimon Peres's office became the center of an informal yet rather structured advisory system with economists supplying information and consultation (Keren 1993).

By the 1990s, the Israeli economy was both liberalized, in terms of a shift to market economics, and on the course of becoming globalized, integrated in the world economy. With the shrinking of state control over capitalist markets, the decline of the Histadrut, the reduction of monopolies, and the convergence of the two main parties toward a neoliberal economic agenda, Israel's economic policies resembled those of many other western states. But despite these developments, the economic changes of the 1980s were not matched by the political developments. The Palestinian uprising that began in 1987 not only raised the costs of occupation but also impeded the country's integration in the world economy. The economic developments described above did not begin to bear fruit, even if unevenly distributed, until the 1990s. This success was due to three main factors, a wave of immigration from the former Soviet Union, the growing high-tech sector, and the peace process.

After 1990 more than 700,000 Soviet immigrants arrived in Israel. Their relatively quick absorption in the economy and the negative pressure it exerted on wages led to an expansion in aggregate supply that was reflected in a high growth rate. From 1992 onward, the peace process became the dominant factor determining investment, making the business community more optimistic and more willing to invest (Zilberfarb 1996). Liberalization and globalization were accompanied by growing social disparities in Israel. Israel experienced considerable growth with GDP per capita moving from $5,600 in 1980 to $15,100 in 1998 but the rewards of the 1985–1995 cycle of prosperity have been unevenly distributed. The obvious winners were capitalists, business executives, high-tech workers, and members of the "professional," "service" or "new" class. The losers were unskilled laborers whose jobs were cut due to imports or relocation of the production process elsewhere. Like other countries, Israel in the process of globalization was moving away from being a welfare state to becoming a "competition state." The growing gaps have important political implications with different sectors of society developing different perceptions on the benefits of globalization and peace.

Transnational Class and Transnational Practices

Liberalization, globalization, and peace, as argued in the previous chapter, have not happened by themselves. In Israel since the 1970s, a growing transnational class has been working to liberalize the economy and society, deregulate government, and integrate globally. The business class, discussed separately below, has been an important component of Israel's globalization, but the transnational class is a wider phenomenon whose boundaries tend to be fuzzy. It includes, in the Israeli case, large parts of academia, the media, and others who share lifestyles and political views. The globalization of Israel was led and supported by those elites who were constrained by the confines of the earlier phase of development and lost interest in maintaining the primacy of republican citizenship, a strong state, and communal public-spiritedness (Peled and Shafir 1996). This elite saw itself as a part of wider world developments—economic and cultural—but its desire to be part of the globalizing world was held back by the continuation of the conflict that left Israel on the margins of globalization. Their aim to "normalize" Israel and make it a "nation like all nations" was translated into a three-part agenda that included economic and political liberalization, termination of the conflict with the Palestinians, and global integration. The deterritorialization this class pursued was rather limited: in no way was this meant to be the end of Zionism and Jewish territoriality but only the decline of value attributed to the territories taken in the 1967 war in favor of conflict resolution and global integration.

The open desire to integrate globally indicates a change in Israeli society that earlier in its history sought to seal itself from outside cultural influence. The young state was committed to assimilation through a melting-pot approach and to the creation of a unifying Israeli culture. Outside cultural influences were rejected either because they were identified with Jewish life in the diaspora, the sort of life Zionism sought to negate, or because they were considered decadent and therefore potentially weakening to society. David Ben-Gurion, Israel's first prime minister, opposed the entry of television in fear it would have a negative influence on the efforts to create a unique Israeli culture. When introduced in 1967, its function was educational rather than entertainment or commercial (Katz and Haz 1995). Cultural icons were also suspiciously viewed. In a famous incident in the 1960s, the ministry of education refused to allow the Beatles to perform in Israel and argued the performance would corrupt Israeli youth.

Significant changes occurred in patterns of consumption and culture since the 1970s as Israelis were more and more exposed to foreign influence, either through travel or the electronic media. Several scholars referred to the process as an "Americanization" of Israeli society that included the introduction of consumerist behavior and values, leisure activities and entertainment patterns, and lifestyles into the previously relatively closed Israeli society (Nagid 1993). From a society of austerity in the 1950s, Israel was turning into an affluent society with more hedonistic values, open to foreign cultural influences and deeply engaged in consumption, evident by the gradual increase in the number of motor vehicles, electric appliances, and later mobile phones and Internet access (Azaryahu 2000; Ram 2000). Until the 1980s, government and industrialists encouraged the public to buy locally made products (so-called blue and white). But in a decade of liberalization on imports, the market was exposed to competition and Israeli consumers were offered a growing variety of products in lower prices later accelerated by electronic commerce. The desire to "normalize" Israel that included a privatization ethos, rationalism, and professionalism received its first political expression in the formation of the Democratic Party for Change (DMC) that competed in the 1977 election. The DMC's platform emphasized the need to get corruption out of politics, the liberalization of the economy, and the relaxation of the state's control over public issues such as culture and mass communication. The DMC in its first election won fifteen Knesset seats, mostly at the expense of the Labor Party. Though the DMC did not survive politically, its platform did, as liberalization and deregulation became almost a consensus among parties and senior bureaucrats.

The "new Israel" that was replacing a pioneering society was the making of the Israeli middle class and upper class. Israel's secular elite, formerly identified with the ethos of nation building, was now eager to transform Israel into what they perceived as an advanced, sophisticated, and more tolerant society. By the 1990s, the cultural changes in Israeli society were striking. American fast food and retail chains were established across Israel, a new language imbued with English words and slang was used, rock music and other (mostly) American musical influences could be heard, and reading material included journalism that imitated American style and literature concerned with the individual and departing from the collectivist spirit. The introduction of commercial television in the 1990s, dependent on advertising, changed the patterns of broadcasting that now had to appeal to popular ratings. Like in other places, the advertising sector plays a leading role in economic and cultural globalization. In 1997 the annual domestic outlay on advertising reached almost 1 percent of the GDP, and some fifteen global advertising firms were represented in Israel by local offices (Ram 2000).

A major and relatively new component of this transnational class was the high-tech industry, responsible for a large share of Israel's economic growth. Between 2,000 and 10,000 new rich emerged who accumulated wealth on levels previously achieved only by inheritance and introduced a new lifestyle and culture. One economic columnist described this as a different country emerging within Israel.

> Take all the values upon which the Israeli economy was built: the collective, institutions, social security, political support—turn them over and you get the new high-tech industry's values. Risk taking is fashionable, individual entrepreneurship is most valued, detachment from every Israeli character and obedience to market forces, usually the American, is necessary. The high-tech industry is the "mixing" of the Israeli market: it is done by Israelis, in Israel, but it obeys, lives and breathes only the Western "religion"—the forces of western market economy. (Rolnik 1999)

The ethos of rationality and professionalism carried by the emerging transnational class has also shaped its optimism in regard to the possibilities for resolution of the conflict with the Palestinians. Since the 1970s, the Israeli transnational class was seeking to integrate itself globally, on both economic and cultural terms. Liberalization of the economy and putting an end to the conflict were two sides of the same coin, namely the "normalization" of life. The military rule over a million Palestinians, a settlement policy bound to prolong the conflict, and the messianic terminology justifying the settlements all seemed to belong to an irrational world. The linkage between a global outlook, liberalism, and peace can be observed in the formation and development of the "Peace Now" movement that emerged in the late 1970s. Bar-On describes the movement as made of three concentric circles. The inner circle was comprised of some 500 activists, mostly well-educated middle—and upper-middle-class Ashkenazim in their mid—to late twenties. The second circle, of loyal participants, and the third, made of sympathizers, were somewhat more heterogeneous but only to a limited extent. "Early in Peace Now's development it became evident that a large measure of ethnic, social, and economic homogeneity existed throughout the movement. Most members were well-educated, well-off Ashkenazim—and their personal closeness was cemented by their similar life histories" (Bar-On 1996, 103).

Peace Now attempted to incorporate Mizrachim from poor neighborhoods in a joint struggle against the government's allocation of resources to the settlements instead of poor neighborhoods within Israel, but its success was at best limited. Several neighborhood activists suggested cooperation under the title "Peace Now—Welfare Now," but this was rejected by the members of Peace Now. Some of the leaders of Peace Now were reluctant to commit the movement to other goals besides peace. The activists of Peace Now complained that the neighborhood activist groups were suspicious and reluctant to cooperate while the latter complained that they were only used by Peace Now, whose members had little commitment to social issues (Reshef 1996; Palgi 1979).

The Business Community

A web of personal and working relationships connect the Israeli business community to the political arena. Recent research has found that the closest personal friends of Israeli politicians are either businesspeople or lawyers (Etzioni-Halevy 1997). Many of the members of the business and the political elite either cooperated in earlier periods when government was more involved in economics, in more recent times when government worked to direct investments and granted favored status to chosen enterprises, or became acquainted in other social settings like the army. Studies of the Israeli business elite show that almost two-thirds of its members are Ashkenazim and only 8 percent are Mizrachim. Similar lifestyles, cross-memberships in boards, and shared economic interests and institutional settings keep the business elite not only interconnected but also closely related to the political, academic, and bureaucratic elite. The relation between elites is supported by the relative ease in which members move between them in different roles and the policy forums where business elites interact with politicians and bureaucrats that enable them to exert their political influence (Etzioni-Halevy 1997; Maman 1997).

Israel's six major business groups developed around the defense industry that was the engine of growth of the Israeli economy between 1967 and the mid 1970s. The self-sufficiency doctrine Israel held regarding military equipment provided these groups with a protected and high-demand internal market. In the late 1970s, however, the economic stagnation followed by the 1985 stabilization plan with its drastic budget cuts forced Israeli business groups to change their strategies in order to regain dominance (Maman 1999). Having realized that the old economic order had run its course, the business elite has "gone global" and taken advantage of the new opportunities globalization and the peace process provided. Not only the six business groups but also other Israeli companies have become, since the 1980s, global companies through partnerships, registration in the U.S. stock market, relocation of production according to economic considerations, or by partial or full foreign ownership. To note a few examples, Teva, a pharmaceutical company, has been registered in the U.S. stock market since 1982. Delta, a textile manufacturer, opened a factory in Scotland in 1983 in order to remain close to the European market. It also manufactures in Egypt and Jordan, taking advantage of the low costs of labor. Finally, Osem, a food manufacturer, entered a partnership with the Swiss company Nestle.

The CEOs of the three companies mentioned above were active supporters of the peace process, like many other prominent members of the business community. Members of the business community interviewed for this work and elsewhere[2] stressed their interest in developing their companies globally and finding new markets, new investment opportunities, or new production sites. Peace, they argued, was required to achieve these economic goals and was, therefore, a significant interest of the business community. The global percep-

2. Joshua Stauber recently published a series of interviews (Stauber 2001).

tions of the Israeli business community, however, combined with a "local" Zionist ideological commitment and an attempt to position itself in a leader position. In supporting the peace process and globalization, Israeli business-people, much like their Irish counterparts, saw themselves as leading Israel toward a better future as well as promoting their own business. "My generation who was raised on the essential values of Zionism was concerned that we are not passing this legacy to the next generation," explained one businessperson. "Is Zionism still relevant? My Zionism is peace. This is a new Zionist goal" (Gaoṅ 2000). Economic liberalization and territorial compromise were described by businesspeople as two faces of a new Zionism based upon rationality and open-mindedness and the application of business pragmatism to solve politically charged dilemmas.

> The business community was able to transcend the political questions. I think the gaps between left and right are not very big. We, as business people tend to be practical. We saw in this breakthrough [the peace process] an important opportunity for Israel's economic development. You might say we are opportunistic, but here was a rare combination of a group of business people and economists who saw this breakthrough as a solution or a beginning of a solution for a significant problem. (Groffman 2000)[3]

The political position the business community gradually adopted aligned it with the Labor Party in spite of Likud's greater commitment to market economy. While Likud's foreign policy deterred many businesspeople, the Labor Party rapidly detached itself from its social-democratic roots and adopted a neoliberal agenda little different from Likud's. If anything, Rabin's government was probably Israel's most liberal government and received high praise from the business community. Rabin and his ministers committed themselves to market reforms and maintained close ties with the business community. In one instance, in front of American CEOs, Rabin declared that he intended to continue with privatization despite objections and that he was not concerned by the protest of the trade unions wishing to obstruct privatization just as he was not worried about Islamic fundamentalist groups that wish to obstruct the peace process (*Haaretz,* November 21, 1993, A1).

The relations of Rabin with the business community were beyond a shared

---

3. Similar descriptions were given by other interviewees.

economic perspective. Some were personal friends; others were invited to informal dinners, formal events, or to join the prime minister on his visits abroad. During his tenure and in retrospect, Rabin was perceived as extraordinarily attentive to economic issues and involved in the details of economic developments. He often consulted with senior businesspeople and economists, and sometimes, at their request, he met with interested foreign investors to help convince them to establish their businesses in Israel. For example, after a meeting between Rabin, an Israeli entrepreneur, and the president of Holiday Inn International, the latter decided on making Israel the Middle Eastern center of Holiday Inn (Plotzker 1995; Sharony 1995; Groffman 2000). Rabin, wrote one liberal commentator in a eulogy shortly after the assassination, learned to trust market forces and even to love them. "Rabin began [his political life] as a socialist, continued as a social democrat, and in his last year in office was a pure economic liberal" (Plotzker 1995). The transnational class in general and the business community in particular were the powers behind the limited deterritorialization that began with a peace process that emphasized the benefits of global integration over territorial possession. But in order to make that vision of globalization and peace universally acceptable, other sectors across both societies had to be convinced.

The Palestinians

Like in Israel, political and economic changes made the Palestinians in the early 1990s more ready for negotiations and compromise. Moderate voices from the Palestinian leadership were heard already in 1974, following the War of 1973 when the PLO accepted the liberation of parts of Palestine, a step toward the acceptance of a two-state solution, although armed struggle and terrorism remained a part of the agenda (Schultz 1999, 45–49). The armed struggle, however, especially after the Lebanon War in 1982, seemed increasingly futile. With the PLO leadership deported to Tunisia, developments in the West Bank and Gaza shifted the balance to resistance activities against the Israeli occupation. The Palestinian struggle essentially shifted from "outside," led by the PLO, to "inside" where a new local leadership, loyal to Arafat, replaced the elder notables to lead the intifada, a struggle to end the occupation of the West Bank and Gaza. The uprising was a mass movement that combined a strategy of limited violence (most notably stone-throwing youth), large-scale confrontation with the Israeli armed forces, civil disobedience, and the use of world media to expose the realties of the occupation and to apply pressure on Israel. During the period that followed the war in Lebanon, Arafat was confirmed as the single most important national symbol and arbiter of Palestinian politics, a position that enabled him to take diplomatic initiative (Sayigh 1989).

The intifada that erupted in December 1987 brought also important changes to the political organization and goals of the Palestinians, including within the PLO leadership in Tunisia. The PLO declaration in 1988 of the establishment of a Palestinian state based on the partition of Mandatory Palestine (according to UN resolution 181) indicated a new pragmatism. After the withdrawal of Jordan from the conflict, in its declaration that it had no claims on the West Bank, the PLO was forced to adopt a more moderate position in order achieve international legitimacy, especially from the United States, as a partner for negotiation. In 1988 a senior member of the PLO, Bassam Abusharif, published an article in which he recognized Israel's needs and called for bilateral negotiations between the two sides. In the West Bank, local intellectuals drafted their own document with similar ideas.

In November 1988, the Nineteenth Palestinian National Council, meeting in Algiers, decided to work via political measures to reach an agreement in which Israel would withdraw from all territories captured in 1967. Israel responded with an initiative that included a willingness to negotiate with elected Palestinian leaders from the territories but not with the PLO and also reiterated its objection to a Palestinian sovereign state. The Palestinians rejected both conditions (Shalev 1990, 150–59). Yet after accepting the American conditions (the acknowledgment of Israel's right to exist, acceptance of UN resolution 242, and renouncement of terrorism), a dialogue with the United States was opened. More important, the decisions made at the nineteenth council strengthened the international position of the PLO and the legitimacy of the Palestinian struggle (Sayigh 1989).

In 1990, however, the tables turned on some of the political achievements the Palestinians made. First, the intifada seemed at an impasse as the economic and political costs of the struggle exhausted Palestinian society. Especially significant was the gradual closing of the Israeli labor market the Palestinians depended upon. The mass-based, limited-violence struggle was replaced by escalating involvement of gangs using larger scale and more intensive violence and the local leadership was gradually replaced by PLO appointees (Schultz 1999, 72). But the most important change was the decision of the PLO to align with Iraq in the Gulf War. The Gulf states retaliated by expelling Palestinian

workers and canceling financial assistance to the PLO, adding to the dire economic situation in the West Bank and Gaza. Politically, the PLO's support of
Iraq eroded their diplomatic achievements in Western states in general and the
United States in particular. Finally, while the PLO retained control of the intifada, a growing Islamic opposition presented a new political challenge from
within.

In the aftermath of the Gulf War, the PLO in Tunis was fiscally bankrupt
and politically dying. Without its major sponsors, the PLO was unable to pay its
own personnel and had to cut down on many of its activities, including financial assistance to families of "martyrs" or prisoners in the occupied territories.
Politically, the demise of the Soviet Union left the PLO without a superpower
patron and the position it took during the Gulf War evoked hostility not only
from the United States but also from many Arab states who supported the U.S.
effort to reverse Iraq's occupation of Kuwait (Robinson 1997, 175–76). Under
these circumstances, the PLO had to work its way back to a political position it
had once held, even by accepting terms it previously rejected. Thus the PLO
was ready to agree to a United States-initiated peace conference in Madrid despite the fact that Israel refused to allow its official participation and agreed to
talk only with Palestinians not related to the PLO, hoping to create a wedge between the Palestinians in the territories and the PLO in Tunisia (Bentsur 1997).

The Madrid Conference and the Business Community

Although the Madrid conference had no real results, it set a precedent of Israeli-Palestinian negotiations and created new hopes and fears. For the Israeli
business community, it was not only the lingering intifada but also loan guarantees from the United States that were conditioned upon Israel's participation
in the peace process that made the conference important. The daily *Haaretz*, a
newspaper read by Israeli business and other elites and reflecting their general
attitude, warned the government before the conference on the need to promote
peace. Without advancing the peace process, it argued, Israel would not receive
the loan guarantees from the United States amounting to $10 billion that were
required to absorb the mass immigration of Jews from the crumbling Soviet
Union. "This is how Israel can miss its chance to become a bigger and stronger
state with greater human capital," the paper scolded Prime Minister Shamir in
an editorial on October 11, 1991. "But what interests Shamir is another road
and another settlement in the West Bank—and to hell with immigration."

Shortly after the conference, Israeli businesspeople expressed enthusiasm about economic prospects. Fifty entrepreneurs interviewed from various businesses—real estate, tourism, manufacturing, and others—all expressed belief in the new possibilities in the Arab world: exporting, importing, building hotels and highways, and joint tourist ventures were all mentioned as potential investments (*Maariv* editorial, October 29, 1991). But whatever hopes the conference raised, they were short lived. Shamir and Likud were ideologically too committed to a "Great Israel" to make real strides toward peace. According to *Haaretz*, Shamir was oblivious to the relationship between the lack of peace and the growing problem of unemployment. Without regional stability, the paper argued, there is little hope for investment, foreign or local, and growth. For an economic plan to succeed, it must receive a stable political backing, a background of peace, stated the paper's economic section, and an editorial sarcastically asked, "Is Shamir aware of this?" (*Haaretz,* November 1, 1991, C1).

The business community drew the same conclusion, and a growing number of high profile businesspeople began to make their voices heard, encouraging the government to make peace. Just before the elections of 1992, Dov Lautman, president of the Israeli Manufacturers Association, stated that the major obstacle to foreign investment was political instability and that progress in the peace talks was a necessary measure to stimulate investment. The business community was not alone in its perception that Likud's policy had reached a dead end. Seven months later, in the elections of 1992, the Labor Party returned to power after fifteen years.

The 1992 Elections

The dilemmas relating to the Israel-Arab conflict, the territories, and the intifada were a major factor in the electoral change in the 1992 elections. The Labor Party led by Rabin successfully introduced wedge issues in its campaign and highlighted Likud's settlement policy and the ongoing intifada (Arian and Shamir 1995). The elections counterposed the two major parties, which introduced supposedly diametrically opposed "operational codes." While Likud's campaign emphasized the continuous threat to Israel and the commitment to the territories, Labor argued that a better political and economic future was possible. Likud's hard-line policy and refusal to compromise on territory, stressed the Labor campaign, not only harmed Israel's foreign relations but also undermined its economic regeneration due to the withholding of the necessary loan guarantees by the United States and the distorted priorities of investments in settlements that do not contribute to security and are an impediment to negotiations (Steinberg 1993). Labor's campaign appealed to the desires of more and more Israelis of the growing middle class who were concerned with their personal economic betterment. It did not mention swapping land for peace but emphasized the need to "change priorities" by shifting resources from settlements to infrastructure, education, and better immigrant absorption and argued that Israel's security depended upon separation from the Palestinians (Makovsky 1996). Labor's platform emphasizing economic reforms, promotion of growth, and privatization (Klein 1993) was not very different from Likud's, but as the Labor campaign successfully argued, Likud's political commitments stood in stark contrast to "economic rationality."

The linkage between peace and prosperity was explicit in the election campaign platform of Meretz, the propeace liberal party and an ally of Labor whose voters resemble the group that constitutes Peace Now described above. One of the Meretz campaign pamphlets explained, "Peace agreement with our neighbors and a policy consistent with the values and interests of the democratic world will enable Israel to integrate into the world economy and into a stronger and expanding European Community, to become the recipient of investments and credit and to possess a progressive and exporting economy" (quoted in Shafir 1998). Within the Labor Party, some younger members of the Mashov group advocated economic and social reforms similar to those advanced by Meretz. While the party has not adopted the reforms, the debates were covered in the media and helped portray the party as actively coming to grips with reform issues.

The growing affiliation of the business community with the Labor Party was also indicated in the stock market's fluctuations. Since the Madrid conference, the stock market has been sensitive to the issue of peace, and prior to the elections, sensing that Labor would win, it was on the rise. Two days before the election, a 3.5 percent rise was registered; after the elections, the stock market responded with a 7 percent rise. "Whereas in the ballot box investors vary in their political views," explained one analyst, "in the stock market there was largely a consensus. For most investors the return of the left (the Labor) means higher chances for conflict resolution" (Rolnik 1993, B3).

The victory of the Labor Party was impressive, but, as it was soon revealed, insufficient in terms of support for the peace process. Labor increased its number of seats in the Knesset from thirty-nine to forty-four, while Likud dropped from forty to thirty-two. Voters for the left wing totaled 1,284,992 votes compared to the right's 928,380, but combined with the voters of the religious party, the right/religious bloc reached 1,273,557 votes, leaving only a small advantage to the left bloc. In terms of seats in the parliament, the left parties had only a slight edge of sixty-one to fifty-nine (Arian and Shamir 1995). Nevertheless, the left bloc, secular, more Ashkenazi than Mizrachi, and more middle-upper than lower class perceived itself as the rightful winner of the elections. Already in his first speech as prime minister, Rabin indicated the change of policy direction, expressed his commitment to peace, and appealed to the Palestinians to join in the effort. Israel, he stated, must move forward with peace or risk staying behind the rest of the world. "We are no longer a nation that dwells alone and it is not true that the whole world is against us. We must release ourselves from the feeling of solitude that's been holding us for almost fifty years. We must join the voyage of peace, reconciliation and international cooperation that rapidly moves across the globe. Because if not we will be left behind alone" (Ben-Simon 1997, 98).

The business community was comfortable with the new government and especially with Rabin, who had maintained close relations with many business-people before becoming prime minister possibly because he realized that in his previous term as prime minister (1974–77), he overemphasized the military-security agenda and underemphasized the economic. Throughout this second term, close relationships were maintained with the business community in formal and nonformal settings. These close relations at times received negative public reactions. One "black spot" was the overturning of a decision to tax profits made in the stock market. Businesspeople close to Rabin used their proximity to pressure him to change the decision (E. Haber 2000). In other cases, despite the government's investments in education and infrastructure, he was criticized for not paying enough attention to social issues. In an internal party discussion, Rabin strongly opposed an initiative by some of his party members for extra school funding in poor neighborhoods: "It is time we stop this social demagogy, the Americans are tired from our channeling of money to social projects . . . you must remember that we as a party must take care of our constituencies. We can't take their money and divide it among the poor" (Ben-Simon 1997, 107).

The business community, for its part, felt that the government was heading in the right direction. Benny Gaon, a senior businessman, expressed great optimism in Israel's economic future in a *Haaretz* editorial: "We presently have a government that places the economy in the highest priority. It gives the business community 'the sky' to work in. If we show entrepreneurship there is no reason why we should not succeed" *(Haaretz,* November 24, 1993, C1).

The business community's wish to see developments in the peace process was conveyed to the government and Rabin in private discussions but also in public statements. In June 1992, shortly after the election, the Caesarea conference was established. This conference, held annually since, is an economic summit in which Israeli government representatives, academics, businesspeople, bureaucrats, and politicians discuss economic policy, with a strong neoliberal bias. Peace was a major issue in the 1992 summit. Dov Lautman, the president of Israeli Industrialists Association (IIA) and a long-time peace activist, explained that the peace process has already opened new markets for export, and that there is a potential for more benefits (Israel Democracy Institute 1993). The idea of the "New Middle East," coined by Peres, was now reiterated by Israeli businesspeople who saw a role for themselves in the peace process and the New Middle East, especially after the details of the Oslo negotiations were disclosed. Danny Gillerman, president of the Chambers of Commerce, highlighted the economic benefits that peace would bring to Israel and the region and suggested measures to promote peace that resembled Peres's ideas: a joint Israeli-Palestinian economic council, a Middle East investment fund, and international projects. These projects and institutions, he argued, would be the catalyst of peace and would transform the region: "Israel could become just another state . . . or, it could become the strategic, logistic and marketing center of the whole region like a Middle Eastern Singapore or Hong Kong where multinational companies base their head offices . . . we are talking about an utterly different economy . . . Israel must act and fast to adjust or this once in a lifetime economic opportunity will be missed only for us to say: 'We could have' " (Chambers of Commerce press statements, August 31 and September 6, 1993).

An example of the growing optimism was a new trust fund called "Heights of Peace" that published a brochure in July 1993, just before the talks in Oslo were revealed. The trust was designed to invest in sectors and companies it believed peace would benefit. Peace, the brochures explained, would bring investments, link Israel regionally and globally, and would allow Israel to exploit its advantages. Because investors would require information and analysis both on the development of the peace process and the specific economic opportunities, the trust would help to "pick the winners."

The New Middle East

The New Middle East, written by Shimon Peres shortly before the Oslo agreements, intended to provide a blueprint for the future of the region based on economic rationality, peace, democracy, cooperation, mutual gain, and general prosperity. What started as an "intellectual exercise" or a utopian vision became part of the political discourse when the peace process began. Peres's blueprint was quickly embraced, even if with a grain of cynicism, by the liberal press, the business class, and the liberal elite. The "New Middle East" quickly became the buzz phrase of the period and encapsulated the vision of the political elite and the emerging transnational class. It indicated a paradigm shift among policy makers and bureaucrats away from the conceptualization of the conflict as inevitable, permanent, or intractable and outlined the choice between peace, global integration, and progress or continuing conflicts and backwardness.

> Peace between Israel and the Arab states and the Palestinians will eliminate an important source of tension, if not the most dangerous. Instead of visions of blood and tears there will rise visions of happiness and beauty, life and peace. We are at a historic crossroads. Do we choose the path of the tongues of fire, billowing smoke, and rivers of blood, or of blooming deserts, restored wastelands, progress, growth, justice and freedom? The higher the standard of living rises, the lower the level of violence will fall. (Peres 1993, 46)

Globalization provided Peres with a powerful rational for peace that converged with business and professional perceptions developed earlier. The New Middle East concept largely embraced the fait accompli thesis of globalization and its related virtues, the democratization of the world and the rationalization of governments. It shared with the liberal accounts of globalization not only their optimism but also the faith in market economics as forces of rationality and progress and the recognition of a new world order.

> In the past, national relations were contingent on quantitative factors: size of an area, natural resources, population density, locations. Countries competed to own or control these resources. . . . Toward the end of the twentieth century, relations began to take on a new, qualitative dimension. There was increasing significance in scientific progress, rapid communication, methods of data collection, higher education, artificial intelligence, high technology, and fostering a peaceful environment that creates wealth and goodwill. These are

the elements of contemporary power. The scale has tipped in the direction of economics rather than military might. Armies might conquer physical entities, but they cannot conquer qualitative ones. At this stage of the game objects that may be subjected to a military takeover are no longer of value. (Peres 1993, 35)

In the Middle East, like elsewhere across the globe, according to *The New Middle East,* borders have lost much of their significance even for the purpose of national defense, which now requires wide-ranging regional arrangements. Moreover, a common enemy, poverty, changes the priorities of the states of the region and requires cooperation and redirection of its resources.

> The tremendous arms budget swallows any profits ... the tremendous investment in weaponry and the concentration of knowledge and talent in the area of security come at the expense of social considerations and lead to poverty and distress, which in turn give rise to fanaticism, fundamentalism, and false messianism. The solution to breaking this vicious cycle is clear: crush the barriers of hatred. (45–46)

> If war is the source of regional distress, the one and only solution is peace. In addition to the direct economic advantages of peace, a wide spectrum of fantastic opportunities will open up, with backing from local and foreign sources as well as government and international aid. (93)

Peace, therefore, was the way out of the web of poverty, backwardness, hatred, and authoritarianism in which the region is trapped. The barriers of hatred can be crushed by the rational world of business, creating a common interest overriding the conflict, and by the realization of all parties to the conflict of the stakes involved, an obvious choice between the "hatred of the Balkans" and "the road paved by Western Europe" (75). As regional common markets, reflecting the "new zeitgeist," form across the world, it is both inevitable and desirable that the Middle East should follow that course: "With the establishment of these new world trade organizations, can the Middle East afford to remain on the sidelines? The transition from an economy of strife to an economy of peace has set the stage for the Middle East. We have a real interest in using the peace opportunities at hand to raise the standard of living for our region, our countries, and our citizens" (96).

If in the period that followed the Oslo Declaration of Principles the New Middle East seemed a reality, with the collapse of the peace process it became the object of ridicule and an example of a pipedream. As will be demonstrated below, while the New Middle East changed the business atmosphere and initiated economic growth, significant sectors across the region remained indifferent or hostile to the peace process and its future promises. As a result, the process itself turned into a zero-sum territorial game.

Declaration of Principles

After his election, Rabin expressed several times his belief that there was a real opportunity to resolve the conflict with the Arab world and that Israel must take advantage of the changes in the region and concentrate on new dangers. The Gulf War, Rabin perceived, strengthened the moderate elements in the Arab world and weakened the PLO so the Palestinians might be prepared to negotiate a settlement on terms Israel could agree with. For Israel, the resolution of the core conflict with its neighbors would allow it to concentrate on the primary long-term strategic threats from Iran and Iraq. But negotiations in Washington between official Israeli representatives and non-PLO-affiliated Palestinians, a continuation of the Madrid Conference, were going nowhere. Several of the frustrated Israeli delegates advised the newly elected Labor government to initiate direct negotiations with the PLO. While the talks in Washington continued, and without the knowledge of those participating delegates, secret negotiations were held in Norway between Israeli academics (supported by the deputy foreign minister, Yossi Beilin) and senior members of the PLO.

Informed about the secret channel established, Rabin agreed to allow the two academics, Ron Pundik and Yair Hirschfeld, to continue their discussions in Oslo, skeptical that the talks would amount to anything. In February and March 1993, however, the Israelis and Palestinians in Oslo produced a draft of an interim period of self-rule, many of its elements contravening long-standing Israeli policy. In May 1993 Rabin and Peres decided to "upgrade" the Oslo talks and sent Uri Savir, the director-general of the foreign ministry, to head the talks, thus changing them from academic, exploratory discussions to genuine official negotiations. On August 19, the Palestinian and Israeli representatives agreed on a Declaration of Principles (DOP) and soon after the agreement became public (Makovsky 1996).

The DOP was the work of professionals done behind closed doors that reflected a "technocratic predilection combining political caution with technological fantasy," corresponding to its makers' cultural predispositions and economic perceptions (Keren 1994). The thorny issues of sovereignty, final borders, refugees, Jewish settlements, and the status of Jerusalem were side-stepped and deferred to a later stage in the negotiations. Keren describes this as "escapism," arguing that "ascending to the heights of technological vision, it is all too easy to evade the political hardships of a situation" (Keren 1994, 159). But the decision to postpone these issues can be explained by the intentions of the agreement's architects to rely on confidence-building measures that would soften the parties' starting positions. This logic corresponded with the general belief of the professionals and politicians behind the agreement in economic rationality and the power of markets to diminish the importance of territoriality. Holding off on discussions of issues that seemed at this stage impossible to resolve until after peace began to pay off materially and trust became more entrenched would make both sides more susceptible to compromises.

The DOP, whose details were finalized in the Cairo accords of May 1994, set forth a gradual process whose first step transferred two cities, Jericho and Gaza, to Palestinian control. The interim period during which gradual control of cities was transferred to Palestinians was to last a maximum of five years and was to be followed by permanent status negotiations that would include all issues deferred, based on UN resolutions 242 and 338. The interim agreement of September 1995 expanded the self-government to six major cities in the West Bank, excluding Hebron, and divided the West Bank into "A areas" of self-government (the major cities, about 3 percent of the total West Bank area), "B areas" of joint Israeli-Palestinian responsibility (about 27 percent of Palestinian villages), and "C areas" of exclusive Israeli control.

Shortly after the drafting of the DOP, Israeli foreign affairs minister Peres met with U.S. foreign secretary Warren Christopher and raised two issues he believed vital to the success of the process. First, the new Palestinian entity needed funding in order to make it viable and, second, public support for the DOP within Israel, he argued, would be contingent upon a "peace dividend." In order to create such dividends, Peres urged the United States to persuade pro-Western Arab states to break the Arab boycott, recognize Israel's right to exist, and establish diplomatic and economic relations with Israel (Makovsky 1996, 75). The linkage made between economic development and peace provided a central role for the business community. In launching the peace, the government set new conditions for business to take advantage of, and by exploiting the new opportunities and creating economic growth, business would make peace a reality and the difficult issues resolvable. The Israeli government conveyed a simple message to the business community, explained Benny Gaon, Koor's CEO at the time: "We (the government) are making the breakthrough in

the peace process, and you (the business community) have to consolidate it."
(Gaon 2000)

Peace Festival

The "peace festival" (Wolfsfeld 1997) began shortly after the disclosure of the
Oslo talks and reached its peak after the signing ceremony on the White House
lawn. The DOP, despite being an important breakthrough, was only a framework for further negotiations, but the Israeli government, in need of bolstering
support, chose to ride the waves of optimism for as long as they lasted, an effort
in which they were helped by the business community and the media (Wolfsfeld 1997). The Israeli transnational class in this period pushed forward the
message that peace and globalization entailed a new future for Israeli society.
Not only were business organizations and private businesspeople quick to con-
gratulate the government and express their support, they took an active part
together with the media and political elites to highlight the benefits of peace.
This was especially true of two large business organizations. Dov Lautman,
chairman of the Manufacturers Association, who was nominated by Rabin before the DOP as a special envoy for the government, was a long-time supporter
of peace. Danny Gillerman, president of the Chambers of Commerce, also became an enthusiastic supporter of the peace process; ten years later he was appointed Israel's representative to the United Nations. Michael Bruno, a senior
Israeli economist in the World Bank, was quoted in an editorial in *Yediot
Acharonot,* Israel's largest daily newspaper, on September 26, 1993, that the
agreement with the PLO was the best thing that ever happened to Israel. Dan
Proper, the new president of the Manufacturers Association, in an interview titled "Peace Is Good Business," predicted "a brilliant economic future for Israel
due to the agreement with the Palestinians. Everything will change. A regional
economic block of 200 million consumers will form, that Israel will be its natural business center" (*Yediot Achronot,* September 3, 1993). A day before the interview ran, Proper and seventeen other leading businesspeople and other
public figures published an ad in *Yediot Achronot* supporting the peace process.
  The daily papers were filled with enthusiastic press headlines, positive sto-
ries, and optimistic forecasts of Israel's forthcoming global integration and
prosperity. *Yediot Acharonot* reported on September 5 that foreign investors—
Japanese, European, and American—were already showing an interest in Israel.
The stock market was another indicator of the positive business mood. On
September 2, shortly after the announcement of the agreement, the market was

rising due to what one paper described as "investors betting on peace." Three days later the stock exchange reached an unprecedented peak, breaking all records. "Arafat is the hero of the stock exchange," declared a *Yediot Acharonot* editorial on September 6, 1993. A *Haaretz* editorial argued on September 7 that the stock exchange was an indication of the upcoming economic boom and that the peace accords were one of the best things that ever happened to the Israeli economy.

In mid-September after the ceremony on the White House lawn, the media frenzy reached its peak. A week before the ceremony *Yediot Acharonot* and *Maariv* ran headlines such as "On the Road to Economic Prosperity" and mentioned again and again the emerging interest of investors from around the globe and the "peace madness" in the local stock exchange. The closer it got to the agreement, the more enthusiastic the headlines became. "In the air, the land and the sea—Israel is on the map," exclaimed a major daily on September 12, 1993. It then outlined Israel's new goals that included a "Mediterranean highway" linking Israel to Europe, tourist packages that would include Israel and its neighbors, unification of the electricity networks of Israel, Syria, and Jordan, and other joint projects *(Yediot Acharonot,* A6). The papers drew a new map of the world with countries like Tunisia, Malaysia, Cambodia, Oman, and others opening up to Israel, and made estimates of potential gains that would accrue to Israel *(Maariv,* September 9, 1993, A8). Senior bankers announced that Israel could now become an international financial center *(Haaretz,* September 14, 1993, C1). Israel, according to these scenarios, would gain a prominent role in the region and worldwide.

> After all signatures, reality will come. The quickest way to establish connections in the Arab world is through business. There is no reason why petrol and petrol money will not flow here. But the greatest gains will come from the West. All the multinational companies previously afraid to take a risk with us will come to the region. If Lebanon was the "Switzerland of the Middle East" there is no reason that we should not be Hong Kong. (Lipkin 1993)

Koor, one of Israel's largest conglomerates, revealed a day before the ceremony in Washington an ambitious peace project secretly launched a year earlier. The project, titled "Salaam 2000," was a $100 million investment firm in which Koor had joined forces with a Spanish bank (Banesto), a large Spanish banking company (ONA), and a group of Palestinians. Gaon, Koor's CEO, explained that the company reached the conclusion that the war industry had run its course and peace, therefore, is a better investment. "We were examining what to invest in and saw that in many things the market was saturated. How many food factories or shopping malls can you build? We focused on peace" (Plotzker 1993a). Other large firms took their own expansion initiatives. Dan Proper, president of the Manufacturers Association and CEO of Osem, explained that Osem would be transformed from an Israeli company to a Middle Eastern one. Shortly after, Osem formed a partnership with the large multinational Nestle.

In sum, four major factors would account for Israel's forecasted economic leap. First, the end of the Arab boycott would open to Israel markets in central Asia and the Far East. Second, multinational corporations, which hitherto had been reluctant to invest in Israel, would take advantage of the new opportunities the peace process would create. Third, direct trade between Israel and the Arab world would be established. And, fourth, provided that genuine peace prevailed, military expenditures could be reduced. One study estimated that Israel would gain about $35 billion in additional output over a ten-year period as a result of decreasing military expenditures (Zilberfarb 1994).

Business Backs Peace

The business community was quick to express support for the peace process through public statements, private disclosures, and economic initiatives. Business became an active participant in the peace process by taking advantage of the new opportunities that became available and by cooperating with the political elite to solidify and legitimize the peace process. "On the one hand, I was operating as a businessman and my company was building factories and partnerships. On the other hand, there was a public involvement in lectures, contacts, delegations, and various attempts to convince the public that peace is good for the economy and for the general quality of life" (Lautman 2000). While some businesspeople believed their support was helpful in the "marketing" of the peace process (Rozen 2000),[4] others believed that their role should be expanded so that the business community would be a leader rather than a supporter. Peace, according to the latter, should be "privatized" and the process submitted to business logic. "I strongly believe in the peace process, I don't believe a country can exist without a strong economy and peace is part of it. We

---

4. "The Oslo Agreement was like a chocolate that needed a nice wrap to be sold; the economy was a part of this" (Rozen 2000).

cannot continue living on support and we can become independent. A strong state will not make the economy . . . [Rather] the economy should make the state strong and the peace real" (Strauss 2000).

Businesspeople interviewed for this work described their support of the peace process as based on "pragmatism" or "realism," explaining their support as a combination of business logic and a civic duty. Pragmatism was evident in that even businesspeople identified with Likud acknowledged the economic significance of peace. For example, Moshe Verthaim, Coca-Cola Israel's CEO, stated in a rare interview (*Haaretz*, Oct. 1, 1993) shortly after the DOP signing that despite his personal political dislike of the peace process, as an industrialist he prefers a Palestinian state. Moreover, he also disclosed that since 1991, anticipating the future events, he had established business contacts with Palestinian industrialists planning various joint ventures. Statements made by the business organizations in support of the peace process raised little if any objections among businesspeople. The statements themselves attempted to avoid being explicitly political and focused on the importance of stability for economic growth and investments. The Manufacturers Association, for example, explained to its members that its support is for the peace process because of its economic importance and not for Rabin's (or any other) government (Proper 2000).

Civic duty was no less important than pragmatism as the Israeli business community began to perceive itself, like other examples of the transnational class described above, as a potential leader or a new hegemony. In the promotion of liberalization, peace, and globalization, the business community and its supporters saw themselves as leading Israeli state and society in the right direction. Accordingly, businesspeople interviewed for this work stressed that their support for peace was beyond personal economic gains and was part of a wider societal agenda (Horowitz 2000). The support of peace, therefore, was based on value judgments just as much as on economic considerations. As the owner of a large hotel chain explained, "We have used the language of profits to convince others personally. I would support peace even if it would not be profitable to my business because I think it is best for Israel" (Federman 2000).

Peace and Globalization

Israeli entrepreneurs described Israel's geographic position between Europe and the Far East as an important advantage that endows it with a potential, with the advancement of the peace process, to become a new Singapore, an entrepot in the Middle East. In 1995 a Manufacturers Association brochure declared that Israel was now working with a "new paradigm" within which "Old enemies have become new friends; opportunities beckon from across our borders." Israel, the brochure declared, is "the dynamo of the Middle East" and a logical point of entry into the region. The new economic contacts made with the Arab world received special attention in the media,[5] but many businesspeople, despite the media hype, remained skeptical about the economic potential of the region and saw the greater advantages beyond the Middle East. Eli Horowitz, Teva Pharmaceutical's CEO, argued that the Arab market is not a client for Israel's industry. According to Horowitz, for Israel, with its high wages and expensive services, its type of products and their quality, almost all new markets must be sought in the affluent western world (Horowitz 2000). The general public also shared this view that peace should bring Israel closer to the West than the East. In an opinion poll conducted in February 1995, only 23 percent of the respondents wanted to integrate economically in the Middle East and only 14 percent culturally; the numbers for the West were, respectively, 50 and 64 percent (Ya'ar, Hermann, and Nadler 1996).

Globalization of the Israeli economy occurred rapidly after the signing of the DOP, as international credit rating agencies and multinational companies expressed growing confidence in Israel. The International Country Risk Guide (ICRG) raised Israel's rating from 79th out of 130 countries in 1991 to 43rd in August 1994. Merrill Lynch predicted in 1994 that Israel was expected to post high growth rates, and the IMF in the spring of 1994 stated that "Israel presently enjoys the basic preconditions for high and sustainable medium-term economic growth" (Ministry of Economic Planning 1995). The list of foreign companies that entered the Israeli market included major American businesses such as Pepsi-Cola, McDonalds, Burger King, Tower Records, Office Depot, and Ace Hardware. European, East Asian, and other companies also began operating in Israel. Daimler-Benz opened a representative office in 1994, Heineken commissioned a plant to manufacture and distribute Amstel beer in Israel, Hyundai began marketing its cars and Taiwan-based Acer decided to begin manufacturing in Israel. Its president explained, "When the peace

5. Right after the signing of the DOP in Washington, for example, the prime minister's plane, with a delegation of senior Israeli entrepreneurs, headed to Morocco to discuss joint investments (*Maariv*, September 13, 1993, business supplement, 1).

process advances, we will upgrade our Israeli assembly plant to become the distribution center for neighboring states." Other companies were buying shares in Israeli companies: Cable and Wireless purchased shares in Bezeq, the Israeli telephone company, Swiss giant Nestle bought 10 percent of Osem, the country's second largest food company, and Canada's Northern Telecom purchased 20 percent of Telrad, an electronics company (Salfiti 1997). Israeli advertising agencies began making affiliation agreements with foreign advertising firms including a sale of shares to the foreign partner (Haaretz, December 28, 1999, C4).

Israeli businesspeople, in general, began to feel part of the global economy, more able to establish contacts and to conduct business abroad. One interviewee described the psychological effect of the peace process on foreign businesspeople as "amazing," as businesspeople that previously did not consider doing business or even visiting Israel began to express great interest in the region (Groffman 2000). Tourism recovered from the difficult period of the Gulf War and enjoyed between 1992 and 1995 unprecedented revenues with a peak in 1995 of 2.5 million visitors (Israel's Hotels Association). Finally, for the first time Israel received significant inward investments. At the Caesarea conference in the summer of 1994, beside arguments over fiscal policy, a growing business self-confidence and satisfaction was expressed. The general director of the ministry of finance described the economic changes as astonishing in terms of 6 to 7 percent yearly growth and a decline in unemployment from 11 to 8 percent. Businesspeople at the conference highlighted the great opportunities peace created that changed Israel's outward perception.[6] In his personal contacts, Rabin received even more positive feedback from businesspeople who reported new contacts, investments, and opportunities and about a world that was opening up to Israeli business (E. Haber 2000).

Overall, the government and the business community saw eye to eye on the relationship between peace and economic development. Businesspeople at times quoted Peres's phrases of "the economy as the glue for peace" or "the smell of peace is the perfume of the economy" (Lory 1994). In the closing keynote lecture of the Caesarea conference, Rabin reiterated the government's commitment for both peace and economic development, each dependent upon the other. Benny Gaon offered the business community's perception of

6. See, for example, the lecture of Dov Fruman, CEO of Intel Israel (Israel Democracy Institute 1994).

the developments: "There is no doubt that the business sector fulfilled a major role in the peace process. The government has opened the gate to peace and the business sector paved the road to the world. The peace process produced economic benefits, raised the standard of living and gave hope for a better future" (Gaon 1997).

But amid the general optimism, several speakers at the Caesarea conference raised concerns over the disparity between business mood and general public support for the peace process. Rabin noted that the government must continue public investments that would improve the public's view of the government. Danny Gillerman, president of the Chambers of Commerce, expressed concern over the gap between reality and perception, between positive economic indicators and a general feeling of gloom, and he called for positive measures that would create a better atmosphere (Israel Democracy Institute 1994). In a letter he sent to Rabin, Gillerman noted that in both the economy and the peace process the government and the business organizations had done better in exporting the image to the world outside than in marketing it locally (Chambers of Commerce memorandum). A more strongly dissenting voice was that of MK (Member of the Knesset) Haim Oron of the socialist faction of Meretz, who openly challenged some of the optimism: "I agree with the estimates that the Israeli economy has gone through three positive years on many parameters, but Israeli society has gone through three difficult years. There must be some connection between the two. . . . I think that this discussion, like the one last year, has a general feeling of self-satisfaction or at least some comfort . . . it is about time that somebody would say that he is concerned with high income differentials" (Israel Democracy Institute 1994).

The concerns raised at the Caesarea conference were not unfounded; the positive mood of the business community did not reflect general public opinion. In a Gallop poll published in *Yediot Acharonot* on September 15, 1993, shortly after the ceremony in Washington and at the peak of the "peace festival," only 33 percent of the respondents believed that the agreement with the PLO would improve their economic well-being while 51 percent foresaw no change. Polls conducted by a research center at Tel-Aviv in the summer of 1994, after a celebrated economic year, found the general support for the agreement quite moderate. Less than 52 percent of Jewish Israelis expressed support for the peace process; almost half perceived the territorial and political "price" of the agreement to be too high (Ya'ar, Hermann, and Nadler 1996).

"Peace Dividends" and Regional Relations

In the process of "going global," Israeli businesspeople were encouraged by the government to seek and exploit the new opportunities in the region. Economic opportunities, however, were rather limited. The total export of all Arab countries in 1993, wrote one skeptic, equaled about $130 billion per year, less than Italy or France, and Arab imports were mainly cheap consumer products or arms. Israel's exports, conversely, tended to be expensive products that had limited markets in the region (Caspi 1993). In addition, there were political difficulties for regional economic cooperation. While Israeli policy makers perceived economic cooperation to be an essential component of any peace plan and the normalization of Arab-Israeli relations, Arab states remained reluctant. Arab states were suspicious of Israel's intentions and feared that, because of Israel's economic superiority, cooperation would translate into Israel's advantage and their own exploitation. The "New Middle East," for example, was perceived as arranged by Israel so that all political and economic roads would run through Tel Aviv and Haifa (Drake 1999).

The *Saudi Gazette,* quoting Arab economists and bankers who met at a conference in Beirut, argued in 1994 that Israel, with its advanced industry and commerce, would use the peace process to control the Arab economies. Economic cooperation, therefore, whether initiated by the government or by Israeli businesspeople, was perceived by the Arab world as primarily a political rather than an economic issue. Even Egypt, in spite of a fifteen-year-old peace treaty with Israel, showed concern. "What is a new Middle East?" asked Egyptian president Mubarak. "If it means peace and cooperation that's OK. But people say Israel wants to be the strongest state in the region and control the economy. Talk like this makes all the countries in the region afraid" (Drake 1999).

Regional projects initiated by Israeli businesspeople or the government aroused suspicion among Arab states. Even in tourism, a sector perceived as certain to benefit from peace and an area in which Arab states and Israel are relatively on economic par, most regional plans did not materialize. Israel's Hotels Association suggested joint projects with Arab neighbor states and predicted that with the continuation of the peace process the revenues from tourism could double from $2.5 to $5 billion per year. But, again, Arab states feared that Israel, because of its infrastructural advantage, would reap the large share of the tourism industry's benefits gained from service and management aspects (Drake 1999).

The Casablanca business summit in November 1994 is exemplary of the different perceptions described above. For Israeli policy makers, the summit that included the major Arab states and senior Arab businesspeople as well as businesspeople from across the world was proof that economics could be the driving force behind the peace process. Uri Savir, former general director of the Israeli foreign office, describes the business summit as a successful event that released the forces of economic change in the region. Structural changes included initiation of reforms in Arab economies, the rise of new educated economic elites, cooperation between Israeli and Palestinian businesspeople, and the decision to establish a regional development bank (Savir 1998, 179). Many of the summit's ideas and initiatives, however, never materialized. The idea of creating a Middle East development bank, for example, lacked specific funding details and its actual creation remained questionable *(International Trade Finance,* November 18, 1994, editorial). But the major problem of the summit was the alarm bells it set off all over the Arab world in response to the overbearing presence and determination of Israeli businesspeople. In the follow-up summit in Amman, a year later, the Israeli foreign office advised attendees to learn the lessons of Casablanca and tone down their message (Drake 1999).

Economic relations between Israel and Jordan, after a formal peace agreement was signed in 1995, suffered from similar problems. Farida Salfiti, a Palestinian economist, argues that Israel has been the main beneficiary of the peace agreements while Jordanians have seen little if any benefits. "The Israeli approach to business dealing with Jordan indicates that Israel wants to exploit the peace treaty in a manner that Jordanian businesspeople believe will not best serve their interests. That in return, has consolidated deeply rooted suspicions about Israel and its willingness to be a partner in the joint, and regional, development process" (Salfiti 1997).

Most Israeli-Jordanian joint ventures were in the form of subcontracting in which Israeli producers bought cheap Jordanian labor and, in so doing, contributed to the worries of Israel's economic takeover. Other Israeli ventures in Jordan were designated as a "launch pad" for the infiltration of still-closed Arab markets, which also added little to Jordanian confidence (Salfiti 1997). Beside the fear of Israeli takeover, there was also some disappointment and unfulfilled expectations. One Jordanian observer noted, "People thought the peace process meant a new house, a new car, a better living standard. But now they see only that their lives are the same and in many cases worse" (Drake 1999).

In sum, in spite of the great enthusiasm the Israeli government and some businesspeople showed, the Arab markets were either too small or too impoverished for strong and diversified trade patterns with Israel (Drake 1999). Also, political factors impeded regional economic development as Arab countries often conditioned their cooperation upon developments in the Israeli-Palestinian peace process. "It's all talk," complained one Israeli businessman, "we meet, we discuss, delegations arrive, but nothing really happens" (Lory 1994).

Israel, the Palestinians, and the New Middle East

In 1993, the Palestinian economy was in shambles as a result of three political events. First, the intifada had exacted a heavy economic cost from an economy dependent on Israel's in the form of declines in productivity, trade with Israel, and employment in Israel. Second, Palestinian support of Iraq during the Gulf War resulted in termination of aid from Kuwait and Saudi Arabia and terminated remittance income from Palestinians working in the Gulf, who were deported. And third, after terrorist attacks within Israel, the government closed the borders with the territories, preventing Palestinian workers from entering Israel and handing another severe blow to the Palestinian economy (Roy 1998).

Not only the Israeli government but also third parties involved in the process and global institutions like the World Bank recognized the need to drastically improve the lives of Palestinians. A World Bank Emergency Assistance Programs for the Palestinian Authority (PA) central aim was to stimulate private investment. But with the dire situation of the Palestinian economy free-market economics seemed a doubtful solution, despite the Palestinian elite's adoption of liberal rhetoric. Israeli businesspeople that invested in the PA maintained their cautious optimism. Senior Israeli businesspeople began meeting Palestinian counterparts soon after the DOP signing to discuss economic development in the territories but emphasized that the Israeli government and the PLO had first to determine their policies. Benny Gaon explained that Koor was investing with long-term expectations and warned others not to take a patronizing attitude toward Palestinians (editorials in *Yediot Acharonot,* September 9, 1993; *Haaretz,* November 24, 1993). Other businesspeople and economists were skeptical that cooperation could succeed, and argued that Palestinians would give higher priority to political issues and warned that creating high expectations among Palestinians might backfire if those expectations did not materialize.

While the political and economic elites in Israel recognized the need to bolster the Palestinian economy, they were also concerned with Israeli economic interests. The economic organizations, the Manufacturers Association of Israel and the Chambers of Commerce, debated the possible adverse economic consequences of an autonomous Palestinian entity. Eli Horowitz, CEO of Teva Pharmaceuticals, argued that there was nothing to fear since the territories' industry is less than 2 percent the size of the Israeli. Dan Proper, president of the Manufacturers Association and CEO of Osem food industries, warned that measures must be taken to protect the Israeli economy from competition from cheap labor and production in the new Palestinian entity (*Haaretz,* September 15, 1993; *Haaretz,* October 1 1993, C1).

The government, in an attempt to balance its interests, was essentially in favor of open borders as were many senior economists and businesspeople. A professional committee nominated by the minister of the economy that included thirty academics and senior businesspeople recommended opening the borders between the two economies. The recommendation included not only industrial products but also the entry of agricultural products into the previously protected Israeli market. Professor Haim Ben-Shachar, chairman of the committee, recommended that the peace process be designed to benefit both sides. "The Palestinians and us are not engaged in a zero-sum game . . . as a result of peace the unemployment will decline. New markets we haven't dreamed of will open. Instead of insisting on some silly taxation of a pair of shoes or a T-shirt, let's open the borders and concentrate on the major issue, the transformation to a joint peace economy" (Plotzker 1993b, 16–17).

Not all were convinced, however. A week after the euphoria in the stock exchange in early September, industrialists, farmers, and the labor unions warned about the adverse consequences the peace process might have. The economic department of the Chambers of Commerce produced a working paper on the "benefits and difficulties of the agreement" that raised several concerns. First, the agreement did not guarantee tax parity and a difference in tax levels could draw business away from Israel. Second, the agreement did not address the status of the territories in regard to Israel's trade agreements. Third, the exclusive status of Israeli representatives of foreign companies and of licensed importers was not guaranteed. Fourth, health and safety standards were not made clear and the lack of enforcement might create unfair competition for Israeli producers who have to abide to higher standards. And, fifth, the agreement did not specify whether agricultural produce from the territories would be allowed to compete with Israeli produce and under what terms. The Chamber of Commerce established a new department for the peace process in order to collect and analyze data, establish connections with Palestinian and other Arab counterparts, and to monitor difficulties that arose and suggest solutions (Chambers of Commerce 1993b).

Both the Chambers of Commerce and the Manufacturers Association were overall in favor of open borders between Israel and the Palestinian Authority, but they insisted that customs regulations be unified and controlled by Israel, something many Palestinians rejected *(Haaretz,* November 3, 1993, C1). At the end of September 1993, the Chambers distributed a letter to members that highlighted the economic benefits of the agreement and expressed confidence that the peace process would make Israel an economic entrepot and enhance the position of importers, agents, and representatives of foreign companies in Israel (Chambers of Commerce 1993b). The position the Israeli minister of the economy adopted, based upon the recommendations of two professional committees, was similar to that of the business organizations. Those included free trade, Palestinian fiscal autonomy, and a demand for customs unity *(Haaretz,* September 22, 1993, A4). The latter not only protected Israeli businesspeople from "unfair competition" but also had a political motive: Israel's control of borders would prevent the PA from becoming a sovereign state prior to an agreement with Israel. The understanding between the government and the business organizations was maintained during the negotiations with the Palestinians on the economic agreement as business organizations were kept informed and were often consulted (Proper 2000).

The economic protocol between Israel and the Palestinian Authority, known also as the Paris Agreement, was signed in April 1994. In the agreement, the two sides agreed on coordinated import taxes, customs duties, monetary policy, direct taxation, flows of labor, and open borders for industrial and agricultural produce, with a limit on quantities of six agricultural products. Despite the reciprocal language of the agreement, according to critics, it was structurally favorable to Israel. The agreement allowed the Palestinians some freedom at the micro level—the level of individual economic sectors—but not on the macro level, where the structural terms of Israel's economic relationship with the West Bank and Gaza were employed (Roy 1998). The economic agreements between Israel and the Palestinians, whatever their merits, were short lived. Since March 1993, Israel responded to terrorist attacks by closures on the territories. Gradually, these measures turned the free movement of labor and goods inscribed in the agreement into a dead letter. Israeli industrialists, farmers, and developers, with the government's permission, replaced Palestinian laborers with foreign laborers (Arnon et al. 1997). Since Israel retained authority over all borders, the closure of the territories, and especially the limits on labor movement, was a hard blow to Palestinian economy. As will be discussed later, economic conditions on the West Bank not only have not improved but have worsened since the Oslo agreements.

Peace Dividends: Israel's Balance Sheet

A combination of massive immigration, a highly successful high-tech industry, and the peace process undergird what was described as Israel's decade of growth in the 1990s. A document produced by one of the largest banking groups, published in 1996, concluded that the peace process was essential for employment, welfare, and economic growth (Gabai 1996). Overall economic growth measured in GDP reached 6.8 percent in 1994 and 7.1 percent in 1995 after a long period of slow growth. GDP per capita has grown from $12,610 in 1992 to over $16,000 by the end of the decade. The Israeli economy of the period was also attractive to foreign investors. In the early 1990s, foreign direct investment averaged $240 million annually; in the last four years of the decade it averaged $2.4 billion, a tenfold increase. Israel's international risk rating has also markedly improved. *Euromoney* ranked Israel in fiftieth place among states surveyed in the early 1990s and in twenty-ninth place by the end of the decade; *Institutional Investor*'s ranking went from fifty-one to forty-one. Standard and Poor's rated Israel AA—and Moody's, A2, interpreted as "high quality" and "strong payment capacity." Israel's economic growth, its fiscal policy, and the peace process were the explanations for the favorable rating (Bank of Israel 1998). Beside the booming high-tech industry, the tourism industry, most sensitive to geopolitical developments, almost doubled itself, from an average of 1.4 million to 2.5 million visits and the total revenue growing from $1.8 billion to $3.5 billion (Israel's Hotels Association 1999).

With the continuation of the peace process, economic forecasts were positive predicting continuing growth of Israel's economy (Sagi 1996). The globalization of the economy in terms of consumption, investment, and growth patterns amounted to what was termed an "unstoppable roll" (Retzky 1995). But as will be discussed below, the positive macroeconomic changes of the decade had limited political effects, especially regarding the peace process. In Israel, like elsewhere, globalization, in spite of its powerful thrust, was politically problematic and unstable, generating simultaneous integration and disintegration and disruptions from various sources of resistance or rejection. The attempted deterritorialization promoted by business, political, and other elites that performed the role of the transnational class was challenged by groups that sought to "reterritorialize," redraw and strengthen national and state boundaries.

Spoilers

The ethos of globalization, liberalization, and peace promoted by the Israeli transnational class remained foreign to many parts of Israeli society. Like in other countries, the disjunctured flows of globalization have had different effects on different sectors of Israeli society. Consequently, the peace process, in spite of the impressive balance sheet described above, remained problematic, unstable, and vulnerable. The opposition of the ideological right—Gush Emunim, the settlers, and religious right parties—was expected, though it may have surprised some in its extremism. But the peace process also failed to gain the support of the more moderate right, Mizrachim, traditional Likud voters, whose attachment to the territories was mild. The economic developments discussed above, contrary to the expectations of the Labor political elite, failed to acquire the required legitimacy and to provide the "glue" that would hold the peace through difficult negotiations. While the members of the ideological and mostly religious right have been "active spoilers" engaged in various acts of opposition, it was the moderates' relatively quiet resentment that was detrimental to the Oslo process and, consequently, the Labor government.

For the ideological right wing, the peace process and the general desire to "normalize" Israel through global integration was an anathema. Against the deterritorialization drive of the transnational class, spoilers advocated reterritorialization. They attributed a high value to the territory and the entrenchment of citizenship, solidarity, and destiny within the bounded space of the homeland and downplayed the significance of peace dividends. Gush Emunim, who fought against the withdrawal from Sinai in 1982 and lost, led mass demonstrations against the Labor government, determined to prevent any territorial compromise in the West Bank and Gaza. Territorial compromise was perceived by the members of the ideological right as a betrayal of the essence of Zionism and Jewish values. Accordingly, the language used in the anti-Oslo campaign described the government in harsh terms such as "traitors," and some of their demonstrations have turned violent. One right-wing journal, for example, described the peace process as a humiliating return to Jewish life in the diaspora, being again at the mercy of gentiles. The editorial, entitled "How to Buy Peace with Money" (1994), scorned Peres's vision of peace as "a pathetic attempt to buy your enemy with money that carries a historic stench of buying the mercy of the landlord." Another article by a secular writer criticized the "making territorial concessions a national ideology," arguing that since the mid-1970s, Israel has turned its back on a past marked as "The period of territory for peace, territory for votes at the polling booth, over-generous giving away of national resources, and increasing disdain for the connection between territory and the past: a period of 'one dunam and then one less' " (Sofer 1998).

The peace agreement and promised dividends failed to convince wide parts of society who perceived the peace desired by the political, business, and other elites to be self-serving. The peace festival described above, in which government and business cooperated to promote the peace process, added to this image of the peace that was difficult to erase in spite of the government's attempts. "Businesspeople came along to all the events, they were always seen, always interviewed on their achievements. This created a totally unbalanced image. When I understood this I began inviting other people to travel with us, mainly mayors of development towns. But unfortunately they were not as noticeable as the businesspeople were" (E. Haber 2000).

A hint to the general lack of enthusiasm toward peace can be found in the words of two residents of Kiryat Shmone, a town on the Lebanese border, about the prospects of peace with Lebanon and Syria.

> I don't believe that this peace will do any good for the residents of the town. We will become another peripheral poor town and then who would care about us? . . . If there was no security threat nobody would even come close to this place.

> In a situation of peace Kiryat Shmone has no justification because the city has no base that would allow it to exist on its own. (Ben-Simon 2000, B5)

Some eighteen years earlier, a resident of another peripheral town, Beit Shemesh, gave a strikingly similar argument to the famous novelist Amos Oz, a former kibbutz member and a Peace Now supporter, who published a book based on a series of meetings with Israelis across the country.

All my life I have been on the bottom and you [ashkenazim] have been on top
... Why did you bring my parents to Israel? Wasn't it to do your dirty work?
You didn't have Arabs then, so you needed our parents to do your cleaning
and be your servants and laborers. You brought our parents to be your Arabs.
But now I am a supervisor and my friend over here is a self-employed con-
tractor. And that guy over there has a transport business. If they give back the
territories the Arabs will stop coming to work, and then and there you will put
us back into dead-end jobs like before. If for no other reason we won't let you
give back those territories. (Oz 1983, 35–36)

Leading Israeli sociologists' evaluations of the social effects of the peace
process and liberalization raised the possibility that peace might have adverse
economic effects upon the weaker sectors of society. Smooha (1994) estimated
that the normalization of Israel's relations with the Arab world would affect Israel considerably, and differentially. With fewer material and mental resources
allocated to the external conflict, Israeli society would become increasingly
bourgeois in values and standard of living and consequently class, ethnic, and
national cleavages will deepen. Based on data about Israel's socioeconomic
schisms between ethnic groups and disparities in employment and income, Semyonov (1996) forecast a pessimistic scenario in which the peace process and
the opening of borders would intensify the preexisting social divisions.

Peace dividends were supposedly an incentive to support the peace
process, but, unevenly distributed, they failed to generate the needed support.
The period of 1990–96 was a period of economic growth in the country overall, but income gaps not only have not closed but actually widened (Central Bureau of Statistics 2001). Between 1990 and 1994, the general level of poverty
grew, then decreased, returning in 1997 to its previous levels of about one-sixth
of the population, hardly a cause to celebrate. The data provided by Adva, an
independent research center, shows an even grimmer picture of social gaps. In
1988, families in the top income decile received 8.4 times the share of the bottom decile; in 1997 the share of the uppermost decile increased to 10.6 times
that of the lowest. The proportion of individuals earning poverty-level wages,
before income support payments, increased between 1979 and 1997 from 23.8
percent to 31.5 percent. Ethnic inequality also remained deeply entrenched
with Israeli-born Ashkenazi salaried employees earning 1.6 times more than Israeli-born Mizrachi employees and 1.9 times more than Arab employees.

Israeli society in the period discussed was gradually characterized by large gaps even in comparison with other high GDP per capita states. This was facilitated by two additional intersecting factors: relatively low social expenditures and low tax burden. With the rollback of the welfare state that began in the 1980s, Israel lagged behind fifteen industrialized states in the levels of social services it provided. Tax burden decreased in Israel, especially for employers (see below), and indirect taxes, which are not proportional to income, relatively increased (Ram 2000).[7] Labor was negatively affected during this period by several trends. First, downsizing, subcontracting, or "flexibilization" of labor relations, especially in the traditionally labor-intensive industries, accompanied integration in the global economy and privatization. Second, some labor-intensive activity was exported from Israel to locations where costs of labor were cheaper. The peace process, for example, enabled some twenty-five Israeli textile manufacturers to relocate to Jordan, Egypt, and the Palestinian authority. And third, cheap labor was also exported to Israel. In the 1980s, almost half the construction and agriculture laborers were Palestinians. In the 1990s, as a result of security constraints, the state authorized massive import of laborers mostly from Eastern Europe and East Asia (Ram 2000).

While most salaried Israelis earn less than the average wage and less than their European counterparts, Israeli senior managers and officials earn salaries that are on par with those in Europe (Swirski, Konur, and Yecheskel 1999). The average monthly salary in Israel in 1998 was the equivalent of $1,500, but high-ranking officials in the public sector earned five-digit salaries and in the private sector salaries were considerably higher. In 1994 senior managers earned thirteen times the average wage and by 1998 nineteen times the average wage (Swirski, Konur, and Yecheskel 1999). With high salaries came the elite prestige, previously reserved for army officers, for business executives whose success and lifestyles began filling stories in popular magazines (Ram 2000).

The resentment toward the Oslo process cannot be attributed solely to economic calculations and resentment of the growing gaps described above. For large segments of Israeli society, and particularly lower-class Mizrachim,

---

7. Relative to those of other industrialized states, Israel's tax burden (which averages 39.3 percent) is high compared with Japan's, Britain's, and the United States' (average 30.5 percent) but low compared with those of European countries like Germany or France (average 42.6 percent). The indirect tax in Israel (20.7 percent) is high compared to the average of fourteen other high GDP per capita states. Finally, since 1994 the marginal rate of taxation, paid on high income, is 50 percent, ranking Israel in twelfth place among nineteen states whose average rate is 56.7 percent.

the bundling of peace with secularization, deterritorialization, and liberalization of the state seemed to conflict with not only their more traditional values, but also their status as Jewish citizens of the state. These groups sought in the state not only protection from the adverse effects of liberalization but also an affirmation for their status as Jews in society (Peled 1998). Peace coupled with liberalism, secularism, and globalization, designed to "normalize" the state and make it "a nation like all nations," threatened to undermine all status advancements made by incorporation through republican duties such as army service. A vision of peace that was detached from local symbols in favor of a more cosmopolitan or global stance failed to appeal to large parts of society that remained attached to local-territorial identity.

The rise of Shas, a religious Mizrachi party, during this period is a good example of this accumulated resentment. Shas entered the political arena in the 1984 election and gained four Knesset seats, six in 1988 and 1992, and ten seats in the 1996 election that made it the third largest party in the fourteenth Knesset. The majority of Shas's electoral power is drawn from poor neighborhoods and peripheral development towns. Its electoral success was attributed to grassroots organization work, offering day care and other social services that replace the "rolled back" welfare state. No less important was the party's ability to formulate its political message in religious instead of ethnic terms, the latter being somewhat "illegitimate" in Israeli politics. Shas was able to direct the resentment of its constituency not against Ashkenazim or the state but against the secularizing and modernizing component of the elite's culture. As Yoav Peled convincingly argues, rather than negate Jewish nationalism as defined by the Zionist-Ashkenazi establishment, Shas sought to redefine it and by so doing, it reaffirmed the status of its constituency (Peled 1998). While Shas began its way with moderate views on the Israeli-Palestinian conflict, its positions, influenced by its voters' views and resentment of the secular left, gradually shifted to the right.

The "New Middle East" was supposedly becoming a part of the global world where relations between nations take a new, qualitative dimension and foster a peaceful environment that creates wealth and goodwill (Peres 1993). But such "peace dividends," to large segments of Israeli (Jewish) society were at best a myth and at worst a threat to their social status. The belief that globalization and the peace process would generate material benefits and economic rationality that would override the territorial conflict failed not only in underestimating national sentiments but also in overestimating the impact of peace dividends.

Palestinians, Peace Dividends, and Spoilers

If peace dividends were unevenly distributed in Israel, they were practically nonexistent for Palestinians. Uri Savir, the director general of the Israeli foreign office, acknowledged in retrospect that the economic issues between Israel and the Palestinians were ill planned. To start with, much emphasis was placed upon inward investments, but the private sector was hesitant to invest in the territories before stability was secured. As a result, the donations from foreign governments were only enough to keep the Palestinian economy afloat. Second, the Palestinian Authority itself failed to promote economic development. And third, Israel was looking to maintain its own economic interests and overlooked those of the Palestinians. A document written by the Israeli foreign office warned of Israeli military rule being replaced by economic rule and recommended that Israel be more generous toward the Palestinians. "We principally agreed with this recommendation but did not do much beyond agreeing because the general notion was that Israel's economic interests must be kept rather than taking account of the economic stability and cooperation. . . . both sides would pay dearly for this lack of foresight" (Savir 1998, 179).

The DOP, despite its limitations, created "facts on the ground" that seemed hard to reverse, especially Israel's recognition of the Palestinian people and the PLO as their representative (Shikaki 1996a). It also enabled the Palestinians to begin a project of state building that included building a variety of institutions and election of a Palestinian council. The establishment of the Palestinian Authority also sharpened the political debate over various issues of internal and external politics and economic development. While Arafat and the Fateh faction of the PLO dominated the political sphere, an active opposition who boycotted the elections and criticized the Oslo agreements was highly noticeable. The commercial class was one of the three groups Arafat sought to base his authority upon (the other two being PLO senior officials and bureaucrats from abroad and the local PLO leadership) but, in spite of their importance for the reconstruction of the economy, Palestinian businesspeople had minor political influence (Shikaki 1996b).

Palestinian economic priorities were employment generation, the improvement of productive capacity (especially in agriculture and industry), investments, private sector growth, improved education and health care, and ending dependency on Israel. But after September 1993, the peace process worsened rather than mitigated economic hardship for the majority of Palestinians. Measured against the advances made by other states in the region, argues Sara Roy, the Palestinian economy became weaker than it was in 1967 (Roy 1999). "Not a week passes in Israel without receiving a foreign delegation interested in initiating economic links," noted one Palestinian observer with envy, as little of that fortune was shed on the Palestinians (Salfiti 1997). The closure policy imposed by the Israeli government between 1993 and 1996 in retaliation for terrorist attacks within Israel almost tripled the unemployment rate in the West Bank and Gaza, from 11 to 28 percent. Following the total closure of March-April 1996, 66 percent of the Palestinian labor force was either unemployed or severely underemployed. This forced the PA to increase public-sector employment and donor countries to redirect as much as 40 percent of their disbursements from long-term investments to emergency budget support and employment generation. Trade was also adversely affected by the closure both because the Israeli market was closed to Palestinian exports and because the ties between Gaza and the West Bank were severed. The overall result has been a significant decline of per capita GNP by approximately 30 percent since 1993. Real wage rates declined by 38 percent between 1992 and 1994 and by an additional 15 percent between the end of 1995 and the end of 1997 (Roy 1999).

For Israelis the closures imposed on the Palestinians were the outcome of security concerns, but Palestinians saw them as a form of collective punishment (Arnon et al. 1997). The overall result was that among Palestinians, like among Israelis, the support for the peace process declined. Relations between Israel and the Palestinians entered a vicious cycle in which terrorist attacks led to closures and closures to growing discontent among Palestinians and waning support for the peace, or in more extreme cases growing support for terrorism. In a survey held in the PA in September 1993, about 65 percent expressed support of the DOP. A little more than a year later, in December 1994, only 41.5 percent expressed support. In 1995 a majority of Palestinians (59.5 percent) said they do not expect a lasting peace with Israel and only 23 percent did expect a lasting peace (CPRS 1996). In general, when the progress of the negotiations created optimism, support for the peace process grew although support for specific agreements was less stable (Shikaki 1996b).

With the difficulties of the peace process, just like in Israel, the Palestinian anti-Oslo opposition grew in size and political influence. Islamic movements began to make their mark on Palestinian politics, noticeably in university student body elections in the 1980s (Robinson 1997, 136–38). The Hamas movement established during the intifada constituted an internal coup that brought middle-stratum cadres to the fore of the Palestinian Islamist movement, adopted a nationalist ideology, and reiterated the claims made earlier by Muslim activists that not an inch of Palestine can be ceded to Israel or any other non-Muslim entity (Robinson 1997, 136–38; Schultz 1999, 79). Hamas discourse, therefore, denoted a clear territorialization of Islamism with "Palestine" becoming a nonnegotiable value (Schultz 1999, 80). Hamas built its power base through the establishment of social-welfare structures—schools, mosques, youth clubs, and charity organizations—that widened its support from the educated middle class to the dwellers in the refugee camps that enabled it to challenge to the PLO. The Oslo accords and the elections for the Palestinian Council that it boycotted positioned Hamas, who ruled out the possibility of participation in the PA under Oslo terms, as the main opposition to Arafat and the Fateh. The Hamas (together with the smaller Islamic Jihad) terrorist campaign of suicide bombers against civilian targets in Israel undermined the attempts of the PA to co-opt the Hamas and diminished its support among the Palestinian population. After a series of attacks in February and March 1996 that killed more than sixty Israelis, for example, the support for Hamas, according to polls conducted by the CPRS, dropped to a low of 8 percent ("The peace process" 1996). But with its rejection of the Oslo accords and the DOP, Hamas was not only able to derail the peace process but was able to garner popular support when the peace process failed to deliver the promised results.

Dynamics of Peace

The negotiations between Israel and the Palestinian Authority attempted to combine partition with cooperation but in a short time partition has overshadowed cooperation. The negotiations, from the Israeli point of view, were based on six strategic elements: gradual implementation and evolving negotiations, a shift from unilateral security to security cooperation, advancement of political separation through support of the Palestinian entity, making peace with Jordan, establishment of relations with the countries of the region and the mobilization of global support (Hirschfeld, 2000). The issues that could not be resolved were deferred to a later stage, in hope that trust and cooperation built in the interim agreements would facilitate their resolution.

Economic cooperation, as mentioned above, suffered from the lack of a supportive regional framework and the deep structural inequalities between Israelis and Palestinians. Security cooperation fared even worse than economic level, as even common goals were difficult to agree upon. Israel's demand that the Palestinians take measures against the Islamic fundamentalist groups clashed with the Palestinian reluctance to cooperate without advancement in the peace process. Israel, on its behalf, refused the advancement of the peace process without its security demands fulfilled. As the settlements were to remain in place until the final agreement the security demands of Israel were high and unacceptable to Palestinians. The inability to curb violence and Israel's resort to unilateral measures of closures have added to Palestinians frustrations and further diminished their motivation to cooperate on security issues.

The core of the peace process was a series of agreements, based on Israeli redeployments the extent of which has been a constant source of tension between Palestinian demands for sovereignty and Israel's security demands. With the deferral of contentious issues to the final status negotiations both sides were concerned with expanding their gains and were frustrated with the tactics of the other side. The Palestinians were expecting to reach the final status negotiations after most of the West Bank and the Gaza Strip territories had been transferred to their control, while Israel was aiming to retain more territories as negotiation cards for the final status agreement and declared its intention to keep parts of the territories after the agreement.

The interim agreements came short of the Palestinian expectations for territorial control. The first agreement signed in Cairo in May 1994 transferred Jericho and large parts of Gaza to the Palestinians and facilitated the return of Arafat from Tunisia and the initial establishment of the Palestinian Authority. The second major agreement signed in September 1995 transferred more cities to the Palestinian Authority. The decision to leave all settlements intact until the future final phase negotiations implied extensive Israeli security demands that included the control of all the major roads of the West Bank. Under the interim agreements the West Bank and Gaza became a patchwork of small and unconnected areas under full Palestinian control, falling far short of Palestinian expectations. The other areas, under Israeli or joint Israeli-Palestinian control, proved difficult to manage and created more frustrations and dilemmas.

The frustrations of Palestinians and Israelis with the process have made the implementation of the agreements difficult. Each side blamed the other for breaching the agreement and refused to cooperate before the other party fulfils its obligations. Israel was concerned with the Palestinian Authority's lack of commitment to combat fundamentalist terrorism and the continuation of inflammatory anti-Israeli propaganda in the Palestinian media and schools. Palestinians were frustrated by Israeli military checkpoints across the West Bank and Gaza and perceived the continuation of building in the settlements as an Israeli attempt to determine unilaterally the borders of the final agreement. The years that followed the signing not only left Israelis and Palestinians with little confidence in each other but also with difficult domestic settings that made compromise evermore difficult and the incentives associated with globalization less influential.

Interlude: Enter McDonald's

In December 1993, when McDonald's opened its first restaurant in Israel, it drew large crowds and its sales reached $1.3 million. In the next seven years, the company opened over eighty new restaurants all over Israel to mark another successful entry to a new market. Between McDonald's entry and the year 2000, sales in the hamburger industry in Israel grew by 600 percent and reached an annual revenue of approximately $200 million, with McDonalds, the leading chain, responsible for 50 percent of the sales (Ram 2004). The story of McDonalds in Israel, like elsewhere, is beyond economic success as it encompasses the tensions of globalization described above and has become a symbol of the process. To start with, the personal biography of Omri Padan, the owner of McDonald's Israel's license, is representative of the emerging Israeli transnational class. Padan, a veteran of an elite army unit, was also one of the founders of Peace Now. After he completed his academic studies (he holds a Ph.D. in economics), he pursued a business career first as a manager of an Israeli textile company and then as the joint owner and manager of McDonald's Israel.

Despite McDonald's declaration that it "respects Israel's local culture,"[8] the company's entry and establishment in Israel was far from smooth. While it was received enthusiastically by many who saw its entry as a symbol and affirmation of Israel's globalization, there were those who did not share the enthusiasm. The global company encountered the resistance of two "localizing" forces: farmers who demanded economic protection and the religious establishment who defended what it regarded as the state's Jewish character. The company decided to import potatoes rather than use local produce because, it argued, the latter did not meet McDonald's required standards. Israeli farmers protested

8. See, for example, the company's Web site, www.mcdonalds.com.

the decision and demanded that the company not be allowed to import potatoes. They were supported by the ministry of agriculture who refused to allow
the imports. After a heated public debate among government ministers and in
the press, a compromise was reached by which McDonald's will be allowed to
import until Israeli farmers begin to produce potatoes that meet its standards.

With the religious establishment, things were more difficult. This struggle
was quickly identified in the press as a "cultural war" between modernizing and
antimodern forces in Israeli society. The company attempted to employ economic logic and opened several kosher branches where there was a demand,
but it pursued a liberal agenda in most sites, serving nonkosher food and operating on Saturdays. The first clash occurred when McDonalds aired a television
commercial that featured cheeseburgers and angered the religious establishment, who demanded the commercial be stopped (Jewish religion forbids the
mixing of milk and meat). Padan, however, decided for what he described as a
matter of principle to continue running the commercial (Meidan 1997). The
second clash occurred when in 1997 the minister of labor, Eli Ishay of the Shas
religious party, invoked a rarely used law regarding work on the Jewish Sabbath
to try and force McDonald's to close its branches on Saturdays. Padan declared
he would fight against the ministry of labor's actions and explained that this
was a war for two causes, economics and culture.

> Economically, Saturday matters for us greatly. Our branch in the Bilu Junc-
> tion [the Labor Ministry's officials visited] sells on the Saturday eight times
> more than in the rest of the week . . . closing it on Saturday would be a severe
> financial loss. The other side of my war is the quality of my life as a citizen of
> this country. It is unacceptable that officers of the labor ministry will dictate
> to the secular public, who is a majority in this country, how to live and what to
> do on a Saturday . . . I did not serve in the army and fight in wars for this
> country in order for it to become Iran . . . these demands of the religious lead
> us to the Middle Ages. (Meidan 1997)

Several charges were filed against the company, but Padan declared he would
appeal to the Supreme Court. If the legal battle failed, he promised to involve
McDonald's International and the American government to apply pressure on
Israel. In the first ruling in a series of trials in June 2000, McDonald's and Padan
were fined 80,000 IS (about $20,000). Prior to the trial, Padan ran a campaign in
the newspapers warning that "Israel would turn into Iran," but he failed to organize a lobby to change the law used by the labor ministry against McDonald's.

The struggle between Padan and Ishay was described by one writer as a struggle between the two poles of Israeli society. "Religious against secular, Sepharadic [Mizrachi] against Ashkenazi, symbol of the deprived against a symbol of the elite, symbol of entrenchment in Jewish culture against symbol of Americanization. In other words: Ishay represents everyone who is not Padan's customer" (Kadosh 2000). This is probably an exaggeration as it is safe to assume that McDonald's attracts a fair number of consumers who are not members of the elite. Yet the struggle between an international company that has become a symbol of globalization and a local Israeli religious party that involved economics, culture, and politics attests to the nonlinear character of globalization and resembles the difficulties of "marketing" the peace process. With an international brand name, economic power, and successful marketing strategy, McDonald's in Israel seemed to overpower local resistance and continuously grow, demonstrating the power of globalization. Local resistance matters, however, as the struggle with Shas demonstrates that economic power does not easily translate into political power.

The End of Euphoria and the 1996 Elections

The peace festival of September 1993, regardless of the impressive economic balance sheet, was short lived. The vision of peace associated with the New Middle East portrayed a virtuous cycle in which peace and economic development cross-pollinate each other as steps toward resolution of the conflict generate economic growth and economic growth, or "peace dividends," widens support for peace and makes territorial compromises easier. But this optimistic scenario rests on the assumptions that global integration is universally open and universally desirable. The first assumption neglects the fact that globalization creates winners and losers and therefore peace dividends may be paid out unevenly, alienating those who are on the losing side and leaving the process vulnerable to its opposition. Spoilers can derail the process and offset the virtuous cycle by undermining both economic growth and political support and, consequently, create a vicious cycle in which a setback in the peace process can hold back economic progress and vice versa.

The existence of spoilers (or would-be spoilers) in a peace process that involves significant compromises is almost inevitable. The question, however, is how wide and stable the support for peace is and, consequently, whether spoilers will remain marginalized or will be able to set the agenda. The power of spoilers to derail the Israeli-Palestinian peace process, and the fragility of the agreements, became evident very soon. Already in 1994 Israel faced a series of terrorist attacks, the worst being suicide bus bombings in the cities of Hadera and Afula and then in Tel-Aviv and Jerusalem. The attacks hurt the Israeli public's sense of security and further eroded support for the peace process. The government's reaction of closures in the territories not only helped little to restore confidence but also severely damaged the Palestinian economy and caused much resentment among Palestinians.

The Tami Steinmetz Research Center at Tel-Aviv University began in the summer of 1994 to conduct a series of opinion polls about the peace process. Terrorism and terrorist attacks, according to survey findings, initially had overall small effects of the level of support for the peace process, which remained limited but stable. But in January 1995 following another suicide attack, a noticeable decline in support was measured. The authors concluded that the peace process was in danger, having only limited credibility left with the Israeli public, who perceived the Palestinian Authority as indifferent or supportive of terrorist attacks and doubted their sincerity as partners in a peace process. The government attempted to differentiate between the radical Hamas and the moderate Palestinian Authority but often failed to persuade the Israeli public. Conversely, the imposition of closures or withdrawals from the peace negotiations had adverse effects on the Palestinian public and undermined the position of the Palestinian Authority.

Spoilers also operated on the Israeli side with the settlers and the religious right's campaign against the government. Made up of a fragile coalition, the government seemed unable to make any moves that would include removal of settlements. Even when twenty-nine Palestinians in Hebron were gunned down by a settler in February 1994, the government avoided the removal of the settlers from the city. Moreover, despite the agreements, the settlements in the West Bank and Gaza continued to grow and large sums were invested in the construction of new roads that bypassed the Arab cities. While antiagreement demonstrations grew more and more violent in their language, it was an act of a lone extremist that shocked the Israeli public when in November 1995 Prime Minister Rabin was assassinated. The assassin, a young Israeli religious Jew, explained his act as an attempt to stop the peace process and save Israel.

Initially, the assassination created a shock wave that put the blame on the opposition and gave renewed legitimacy to the peace process, perceived as fulfilling the legacy of Rabin. But as the structural difficulties remained intact, the change was temporary. Two months later, after another Hamas-led terrorist campaign, the levels of support/opposition returned to where they had been prior to the assassination. Surveys since August 1994 indicate that the peace festival of September 1993 was either short lived or was more about the media frenzy than a deeper level support. The media itself has changed its course following the terrorist attacks from the uncritical promotion of the "peace festival" to a "hysterical" reporting of terrorist attacks (Wolfsfeld 1997). The media change coincided with the public mood and broadcasted continuous coverage of carnage, fears, and grief. Opinion polls in Israel demonstrated that the public's sense of security had diminished as well as its belief in the economic benefits of peace. In July 1995, only a small minority (21 percent) felt an improvement in their personal security against 48 percent who felt less secure. In May 1996, only 46 percent of the respondents said that the peace process had positive effects on their economic well-being (Hermann and Newman 2000). The peace dividends and the New Middle East had crumbled under the spoilers' derailment of the peace process.

What has become evident is that the business community and the wider transnational class, in spite of their perceived political empowerment, have had little if any effects on wider public opinion and, consequently, a limited ability to set the political agenda. The business community's power, demonstrated in the past three years, was the result of their close association to the political elite of the Labor Party. The business community was able not only to convey its desires and perceptions directly to the government but also to take an active part in the peace process by doing business and exploiting new opportunities that would supposedly make peace a reality. The business-government nexus, however, kept civil society and nonbusiness economic sectors in the shadows. In the heights of the process, this nexus seemed sufficient as it was believed the incorporation of the rest of society would follow the trickle down of prosperity. But when the peace process lost momentum and public support was needed, the government-business nexus was proven insufficient to generate it.

The 1996 election was in many respects a repeat of 1992, a competition between two conflicting identities, "primordial" and "civic" and, respectively, two perceptions of Israel's place in the world (Kimmerling 1999). What made the 1996 elections different was that they took place after three years in which the "civic" agenda was at least partially or relatively implemented by the Labor government. The period between the signing of the DOP and Rabin's assassination was perceived by the transnational class as one during which Israel made important strides toward normalization, including the attempt to resolve the conflict, liberalization of the state through various constitutional reforms, and global integration. But for others this period seemed to show that Israel had lost its direction and compromised its core values. From the primordialist viewpoint, Israel during these years had gone through a process of de-Judaization and de-Zionization that implied a loss of its founding ethos and, more worrisome, of its spirit and will to fight (Kimmerling 1999). The elections, in other words, were a public reassessment of Israel's attempted peace making and globalization of the previous three years.

In the early stage of the election campaign, the Labor Party seemed to have a comfortable lead. With the memory of Rabin's assassination still fresh in the public's mind, Labor enjoyed wide sympathy while Likud and the other parties of the right were blamed for instigating the anti-Oslo campaign and the atmosphere that made the assassination possible. But after a series of terrorist attacks, a poorly run Labor campaign,[9] and voters "returning home" to the Likud, the gap between the parties gradually closed. The change in public opinion evoked deep concerns in the business community over the future of the Labor government and the peace process. On May 3, two weeks before the elections, the business community for the first time made its position explicit, publicly supporting not only the peace process but also the Labor Party itself.

The event, organized by Lautman, drew an impressive number of 350 senior businesspeople, even some previously identified with Likud. The participants wanted to deliver their concerns about the economic future of Israel after the elections and their support of the Labor Party. Michael Strauss, a senior businessman who until then had shied away from political gatherings, described this event as a "coming out" and explained his reasons for speaking: "Board directors of multinational corporations I am in touch with expressed grave worries about the elections. If they are worried, I should be worried as well" (Strauss 2000). Gillerman, president of the Chamber of Commerce, described what could happen to the Israeli economy if the Labor Party lost the elections in apocalyptic terms in a May 5, 1996, *Haaretz* story. "We will find ourselves in the midst of an apocalyptic scenario. End of investments, flight of investors and foreign capital, and unemployment among young people and immigrants. This is a frightening scenario that should not happen."

The business community, as one writer explained, came out to support not only the peace process but also the most liberal government Israel had ever had.

9. For an internal report of the Labor Party, see Weiss 1997.

The danger, he noted, was that the Labor Party become identified as the party of big business (Tal 1996). The real problem, however, was quite different. If the gathering of an overwhelming majority of the business community in support of Peres was indicative of their support of the peace process, the result of their effort was indicative of their limited influence. The event described above, in spite of the impressive turnout of Israel's business community, received limited press coverage and had little public appeal. For the general public (and now the press), the opinions of senior businesspeople were already well known and, more importantly, mattered little in the election ballots.

The Labor Party was defeated by what some described as a "rainbow coalition" that Benjamin Netanyahu and Likud managed to mobilize against the peace process. Likud's campaign captured the support of those leaning toward the primordial identity as it managed to portray the Labor Party and Peres as less patriotic and unconcerned with the Jewish essence of the state. Two campaign slogans encapsulated this message: "Peres will divide Jerusalem" and "Netanyahu is good for the Jews." The first threatened that Peres would be willing to compromise over the future of Jerusalem, supposedly the heart of Jewish nationalism; the second implied that the future of the Jewish people is safer with Likud. Thus the Labor-Meretz alliance, with its liberal propeace agenda, united an opposition of the sectarian parties of Orthodox religious, Mizrachim, and new immigrants who resented an agenda they perceived as elitist and self-serving. In an editorial in the May 31, 1996, issue of *Yediot Achronot,* Nachum Barnea, a senior columnist, described the roots of hostility and alienation toward the Labor Party displayed in the election outcomes: "It was a coalition of communities and individuals that believed he [Peres] is not loyal enough to the national, Jewish interest. . . . It was a coalition of the hungry. Many of them feel neglected, treated unfairly and marginalized in Israeli society. They identify, not without justice, the left with the political, economic and cultural establishment, in which they have no share."

After the elections, senior members of the Labor Party expressed regret over the alliance with Meretz, an alliance that identified the party as secular and leftist and pushed potential religious or Mizrachi traditional voters away from the party. The liberal ethos of Meretz, that includes secularism, individual rights, universal identity, a modern Israel, rationality, and capitalism, was in line with (and representative of) the belief system of the transnational class, but it stood in opposition to that of the majority of Israelis (Weiss 1997, 89–97; Ben-Simon 1997, 34–35). The elections of 1996, summarized Weiss, a former

Labor MK and a professor of political science who wrote an analysis of Labor's campaign, proved that sometimes the sum of the minorities can become a majority. Despite its market-economic orientation, Likud managed to gain the support of a rainbow coalition, including many disadvantaged groups. Not only did the Labor-Meretz coalition represent to these minorities a closed elite, the peace process itself was identified as a self-serving elite interest. One writer explained bluntly the results:

> Oslo and the New Middle East are in our eyes a conspiracy of the rich for the rich. A window of opportunities to the wealthy who are always at the table of the Laborite prime ministers. A window that is still closed to us, the "irrational" . . . for us your peace ceremonies are a mockery. A celebration that white elite organizes for itself. An academic experiment in the price of our blood . . . the rich and the bourgeoisie open new markets and make money while we are blown apart in buses. (quoted in Weiss 1997)

While the statement above might not be representative, the results of the elections indicate that the divide between the so-called right and left was unaltered between 1992 and 1996. Support for peace, in spite of the impressive economic advancements and global integration associated with the peace process, remained limited.

Conclusions

The dynamics of the Israeli-Palestinian peace process established limited trust between the sides, limited domestic support and, consequently, pendulum swings between negotiations and violence that continued to haunt the process. Both the violent collapse of the Camp David negotiations in 2000 and Israel's unilateral measures of the fence and the 2005 withdrawal from Gaza were the outcomes of the zero-sum dynamic established earlier and indicated the limited impact of globalization and the related peace dividends. A year after losing the elections Peres' reflections on the peace seemed different from the New Middle East scenario, somber and less confident. "People think that a peace process is a poetic event. Songs are sung, festivities are held, photographs are taken, and charismatic speeches are delivered. I saw this process as it really was, as it emerged behind the scenes: a process fraught with blood, tears, and frustration" (Peres, 1997).

The government-business nexus in Israel that ignited the peace process was not enough to carry the process beyond its initial momentum. The asymmetries and unequal distribution of the benefits of globalization were difficult to translate into stable long-term peace agreements. As such, the double movement of globalization was the framework in which the idea of the New Middle East developed but also the context for its opposition and the source of its collapse. While active and violent opposition to the peace process offset the virtuous cycle envisioned by architects of Oslo it was the failure to incorporate wider parts of society that was detrimental to the peace process. The continuing reality of, on the one hand, settlement building, checkpoints and economic instability, and, on the other hand, anti-Israeli propaganda, terrorism, and lack of action against Palestinian fundamentalists groups left both publics skeptical of the other's commitment to the process and disillusioned with the prospects of globalization and peace and, consequently, left the peace process vulnerable to its determined opposition.

8

Northern Ireland and the Good Friday Agreement

THE CONTINUOUS AND BITTER STRUGGLE between Protestants and Catholics demonstrated that the partition of Ireland in the 1920s was a short-term and tenuous solution at best. The partition of the island allowed the northern Protestant minority, 30 percent of the island's population, to remain part of the UK but turned the Catholics in the new Northern Ireland entity into what they defined as an oppressed minority. The discord between the Catholic minority who wanted to integrate with the Republic in the south and the Protestant majority who refused to compromise the status of the province and did little to incorporate the minority escalated into open conflict in the late 1960s, demonstrating that Northern Ireland was a textbook example of what scholars described as "state and nation building failure" (O'Leary and McGarry 1999).

The conflict in Northern Ireland, somewhat like the Israeli-Palestinian conflict, has religious, cultural, and economic dimensions that are difficult to separate from each other. In a detailed study of the conflict, O'Leary and McGarry describe the relationship between Protestants and Catholics in the province as an ethno-national conflict characterized by "a systematic quarrel between the organizations of two communities who want their state to be ruled by their nation, or who want what they perceive as 'their' state to protect their nation" (McGarry and O'Leary 1995, 344). The root cause of the conflict, therefore, is the existence of two competitive communities in the same territory whose differing views concern the legitimacy of the state and its boundaries (Hayes and McAllister 1999).

For a long time, the conflict was perceived to be intractable. As long as each community believed that its vital interests were at stake, there seemed to be little room for compromise, and the two sides remained deeply entrenched in a zero-sum struggle. The Protestants hoped to ensure their economic, political, and cultural position within Northern Ireland, which was guaranteed, they believed, by their second important interest, continued membership in the UK. Catholics, on the other hand, demanded equality in all aspects of life and perceived that this could only be achieved through their second important interest, making Northern Ireland a part of a united Ireland separate from the UK. From the 1960s on, these conflicting national interests led to armed struggle as both respective communities attempted to advance their interests and impose their territorial sovereignty.

In the 1990s, however, due to global, regional, and local changes discussed below, the conflict no longer seemed intractable. Although peace was far from guaranteed, its tenets were formalized in the Good Friday Agreement of 1998 that reflected the new perceptions among a majority of Protestants and Catholics. The possibility for the resolution of the conflict, as several scholars have convincingly argued, was the result of the ability to consider solutions not based upon territorial exclusiveness and, consequently, a move away from zero-sum nationalistic approaches to the conflict. The changed context is all the more striking when the Good Friday Agreement of 1998 is compared to the unsuccessful Sunningdale Agreement of 1973. Seamus Mallon, the SDLP deputy leader, described the Good Friday Agreement as "Sunningdale for slow learners" (Mitchell 2003). Both agreements were based upon the idea of a combined governmental structure that would involve the British government, the Irish government, and a Northern Ireland assembly. This structure, it was argued, was a compromise leading out of the zero-sum struggle by redefining the concept of territoriality from an exclusive type to a shared one. The difference between the Sunningdale Agreement that quickly collapsed and the relatively successful Good Friday Agreement lies not in constitutional and institutional details, but in the context, wider social changes both internal and external. Like in the Israeli case, this chapter will argue, it was the changing context of world politics and related developments in domestic politics that changed attitudes and encouraged influential sectors within Northern Ireland to promote and later back the agreement.

While decisions in the peace process, like in the conflict, are not made simply upon expected material peace dividends, it is reasonable to assume that socioeconomic issues and perceptions concerning economic well-being are part of the fabric of the political debate (Shirlow 1997). Ruane and Todd note several changes in Northern Ireland that facilitated the formation and acceptance of the Good Friday Agreement (1996, 119–22). First, the changed demographic balance between Protestant and Catholic from 63:37 in 1971 to 58:42 in 1991 forced many Protestants to acknowledge the need for compromise. Second, the deindustrialized economy of the region was in dire need of investment that the conflict deterred. Third, perceptions have changed within the Catholic community, specifically, toward the belief that the armed struggle has reached a dead end. Fourth, a change in perceptions in the Irish Republic expressed in the elections of moderate nationalists. Fifth, the victory of the Labour Party in Britain brought new participants to the table who were both able and determined to resolve the conflict. And sixth, the development of the EU, the end of the cold war, and globalization meant a changed international context. While rejecting economic explanations of the conflict as "reductionist and unpersuasive," McGarry and O'Leary (1995) acknowledge that the conflict in Northern Ireland, like any other conflict, has its economic context. Unionists and nationalists have different measurements of the success/failure of the region, the conflict is embedded in the sensitive issue of labor market discrimination, and the economic utility of cross-border cooperation has political consequences.

Considering the high cost of the conflict, the state of the Northern Irish economy in the early 1990s, and the opportunities provided by globalization, it is reasonable to assume that global changes, economic and social, played a significant part of the peace process. Globalization and the developments of the EU, this chapter argues, were significant incentives for ending the conflict that were picked up by the local transnational class, the business community, and other sectors of civil society who sought to promote peace and back compromising initiatives of politicians. During the 1990s, this group's self-confidence has grown and its members were able to publicly articulate their ideas and demands. But, like in the previous case study, globalization's effects in Northern Ireland were differential and the opportunities and incentives afforded by the process were unevenly spread. While proposed political structures and nonterritorial solutions that previously seemed "unrealistic" became a legitimate part of the political debate, they were not universally acceptable and faced opposition from both sides of the conflict. Again, in a manner that both resembles and is different from the Israeli case described in the previous chapter, a "double movement" was formed as, against the coalition for peace and globalization, an opposition with its various spoilers arose to protect what it considered vital interests being compromised.

Protestants, Catholics, and Conflict

From the late 1960s until the early 1990s, identity became a zero-sum game as unionists and nationalists were split over the fate of Northern Ireland. Political affiliation reflects the deep division between the two communities: over 80 percent of the population votes for parties that are identified with their own community. By itself, nationalism, like economics, tends to be a reductionist explanation for the development of the conflict in Northern Ireland. Several research surveys conducted in Northern Ireland demonstrated that there are significant issues other than "self-determination" that concern both communities and that there is variance within both communities regarding the significance of their identity. The evident polarization of the two communities, therefore, is not simply a function of national identity (Ruane and Todd 1998). It is this variance and dynamism that explains the developments in the changing perceptions of identity as even during the peaks of the conflict both communities were divided between moderates and extremists. While there was a relative consensus among the communities over their desired goal, becoming a part of a united Ireland or remaining a part of Britain, there were differences over how these goals were to be achieved and, specifically, in regard to the use of violence and the ability to compromise for something that fell short of the desired goals.

As a minority in Northern Ireland, Catholics have suffered from various discriminations in employment, housing, education, and politics. In the job market, Catholics were underrepresented in the public sector, even in those areas where the majority of the population was Catholic. In the private sector, discrimination was also pervasive. Most industry was located in places that were difficult or dangerous for Catholics to reach. In addition, Protestant employers preferred employing Protestants, and several trade unions for a long time were also effective in blocking Catholic entry into preferred jobs. The unionist control of local government facilitated the continuing discrimination. Among other issues, local authority housing and jobs were divided unevenly in favor of Protestants and gerrymandering ensured that very few local elections were contested. The government also gave itself security powers that were remarkably coercive by liberal standards (Ruane and Todd 1996, 119–22). According to the 1971 census Catholics were underrepresented in key occupational sectors: administration and management, engineering and allied trades, clerical and professional. They were also likely to be less skilled, hold lower status jobs, and be unemployed (156).

Catholics, under these circumstances, reached the conclusion they had no hope of improving their situation through constitutional politics, and that only a change in the status of Northern Ireland would solve their problems. Their frustration with ongoing discrimination combined with national aspirations and resentment toward the partition to the demand that British presence be ended and the island be united under one government. The debate over how this was to be achieved divided the Catholic community into two main factions, republicans and nationalists, each with its own agenda and representative organizations. Republicans, represented by Sinn Fein, adopted a hard-line attitude and a strong commitment to Irish unity. They demanded the immediate withdrawal of Britain, and some, through the IRA and various splinter groups, were engaged since the late 1960s in an armed struggle against British rule and the Protestant paramilitaries.

Nationalists, represented by the Social Democratic and Labor Party (SDLP), adopted a moderate and pragmatic attitude toward the conflict and its resolution. The nationalist agenda included ideas like power sharing within Northern Ireland, cooperation with the Republic of Ireland, and some aspiration for a future consensual Irish unity. Unlike republicans, who held that the British presence in Ireland is a result of its imperialist ambitions, nationalists believed that three factors account for British presence in and policy toward Northern Ireland: inertia, commitment to Ulster unionists, and specific strategic interests. In the 1990s, with the end of the cold war, most nationalists came to believe that the factor of Britain's strategic interests, of maintaining control over Northern Ireland as part of the NATO alliance, had become redundant,[1] and, consequently, that real possibilities for negotiating the status of Northern Ireland had emerged.

Protestants overall associated themselves with Britain and perceived Northern Ireland to be an integral part of the United Kingdom. Their positive British identity and the material benefits of British citizenship combined in some cases with a feeling of supremacy toward Catholics. Protestants, who overall held a privileged position in the region, objected to the idea of a self-governing Ireland both because of a desire to protect their position and a general objection to becoming a minority among Catholics. Thus, the idea of "home rule" raised now and again was rejected on national grounds encapsulated in the often used slogan "home rule is Rome rule." Practically, the unification was rejected because industrial output was exported to Britain and the rest

---

1. These strategic interests were the interpretation of nationalists and more so of republicans, especially Sinn Fein. It is plausible that Britain's interests in Northern Ireland were different and based on the commitment to the Protestant community (McGarry and O'Leary 1995, 30–31; see also M. Cox 2000).

of the empire. Many Protestants were concerned that an Irish entity would attempt to strengthen the economy by protection against British imports and, by so doing, would undermine their position (Rowthorn and Wayne 1988, 22–23).

In general, Protestants favored the present status of the region and sought to preserve the relation with Britain, but, like Catholics, they were divided over how to accomplish these goals and whether compromise should be sought. The loyalists, mostly represented by the Democratic Unionist Party (DUP), tend toward fundamentalist Protestantism and adopted an uncompromising position over the British/Protestant identity of the region. Since the 1960s, the extreme loyalists, who formed several paramilitary organizations, became engaged in a violent struggle against Catholic attempts to alter the status of Northern Ireland. Unionists, the more moderate and pragmatic, are represented by the Ulster Unionist Party (UUP), traditionally the largest political party in Northern Ireland, and tend toward mainstream Protestantism and a relatively flexible British identity. These political divisions have a class basis especially after the industrial decline of the 1980s hit many working-class Protestant communities. Rising unemployment and a sense of pressure from neighboring Catholic areas have led many young males to a "street culture of loyalism." Middle-class unionists, on the other hand, sought to secure their position through systematic assimilation to wider British norms (Ruane and Todd 1996, 60–62).

The pressures that emanated from issues of identity, equality, and sovereignty turned into armed conflict in the late 1960s with Catholics' demand for equal rights and the Protestants' refusal to reform the political system, despite pressure from the British government to do so. Catholics' civil rights demonstrations were met by loyalist responses and the crisis escalated in August 1969 when rioters clashed with each other and with the police. British troops, requested by the Stormont government (the Northern Ireland devolved government), were sent to restore order, but the conflict escalated and seemed out of control. The IRA itself split and the Provisionals, the extreme splinter, emerged as defenders of Catholic neighborhoods against loyalist attacks. In 1970 they went on the offensive, bombed public targets and staged attacks against the security forces. While both sides took part in the violence, the internment introduced by the British government in August 1971, to restore order, was directed against Catholics. The resentment of Catholics increased when in an anti-internment demonstration in January 1972, British troops shot dead thirteen unarmed Catholics. The British government, who abandoned hope that the

Stormont government could be reformed and a legitimate and stable political system created, instituted direct rule of Northern Ireland from Westminster.

The abolition of Stormont resulted in a power vacuum in which violence became endemic and claimed more than three thousand lives in the following decades. All efforts to end the violence either by more effective security measures or by new constitutional and institutional structures had limited success (Ruane and Todd 1998). In 1974, the British government attempted to restore the Stormont government and initiate a peace process. The Sunningdale Agreement, mentioned above, included an eighty-seat assembly and a vaguely expressed willingness to consider the establishment of institutional forms of cooperation between Northern Ireland and the Republic. The agreement lasted only several months as unionists argued that the agreement overcompromised their vital interests. The Ulster Workers Council orchestrated a strike to protest the agreement on May 1973 that led to the collapse of the agreement. This failure signaled to the nationalists and especially to republicans that constitutional nationalism had failed and that compromise in the near future was unlikely (Loughlin 1998, 78).

A major step toward peace was taken in 1985 when the British and Irish governments began to cooperate to restore order in Northern Ireland. The Anglo-Irish Agreement of November 1985 reiterated the guarantee of constitutional status to Northern Ireland but also recognized the island-wide identity of nationalists and gave the Irish government a role in policy making. Unionists were outraged by this agreement. On November 23, 1985, more than one hundred thousand unionists attended a demonstration against the agreement at Belfast City Hall, all fifteen unionist MPs resigned their seats in protest, and violent demonstrations took place all over the province (Hennessey 1997). The protests of unionists and loyalists succeeded in slowing down or preventing some of the reforms, but the agreement and cooperation between the two governments remained intact and an important precedent was set as the Irish government became a partner to any future agreement. The agreement also changed some perceptions among Catholics, as it confirmed nationalists' perceptions that Britain had little interest in Northern Ireland other than its obligations to the Protestant community, and that the armed struggle was preventing rather than forcing them to withdraw and was therefore counterproductive.

These perceptions of British motives and interests received strong affirmation when in 1990, the secretary of state for Northern Ireland, Peter Brooke, declared that the British government was not an obstacle for peace in the region since it "has no selfish strategic or economic interest in Northern Ireland." This speech, repeated in a declaration in 1993, convinced John Hume and the SDLP that there was a potential for ending the conflict through negotiation after Britain assumed a neutral position. It turned out that Britain was more than a neutral facilitator in the process but an active persuader as the government of John Major had already decided it was time for a decisive break with the past. There were several reasons that compelled Britain to reconsider its relationship to Northern Ireland. The escalating costs of maintaining the province and its security together with the increased export of IRA violence to Britain since the early 1980s led to growing support within Britain for withdrawal. In addition, the perception of the Irish Republic as a partner for peace process, and the growing American intervention in the conflict also led British statesmen to revise their policies (McSweeny 1998). But the real important strides toward peace were made only when moderate elements within the communities in Northern Ireland began to take initiative on their own and attempt to translate new regional and global incentives into an agenda of conflict resolution.

The Political Economy of the Conflict

Back in 1989 when the peace process was nowhere in sight, political economists Bob Rowthorn and Naomi Wayne concluded that the only workable economic solution for the region's difficulties would be a united Ireland. Yet, they argued, this solution may be impractical when many of those who are in favor of a united Ireland are unwilling to call for British withdrawal because they believe it could lead to civil war and a blood bath. On the other hand, they noted, economic incentives could serve to ameliorate Protestant fears and discontent, make Ireland as a whole more competitive and allow an economic recovery from "the Troubles" (Rowthorn and Wayne 1988, 140). Like many other conflicts, the conflict in Northern Ireland has its economic context that influenced the dynamics of the conflict and its attempted resolution. First, the Northern Ireland conflict was (and some would argue still is) embedded in the sensitive issue of labor market discrimination toward the Catholic minority. Second, questions like economic cross-border cooperation with the Irish Republic are measured not only according to their economic utility, but by their political implications. And third, the conflict had a heavy economic cost on the province while its resolution, it was believed by many, could turn around the economic fortunes of Northern Ireland.

The economy of Northern Ireland after the peak years of the conflict was described by political economists as a "workhouse economy," one in which "most of the inmates are engaged in servicing or controlling each other" (Rowthorn 1987, 117). Since the 1970s the economy of the province was in steep decline, with a growth of unemployment and dependency upon British subventions. The economic crisis of Northern Ireland was not entirely a consequence of the conflict as a world recession and dying traditional industries played their own part in the process. Yet resolution of the conflict was more and more perceived as a precondition for economic recovery. In 1987 Rowthorn explained that the lack of foreign investments was not simply a problem of misperceptions of the region by would-be investors but a result of "real" issues. "There is armed conflict in the province, sectarian strife is rife and the political situation is unstable, and until a lasting political settlement is achieved, it is unlikely that Northern Ireland will ever attract new investment from outside on a significant scale" (Rowthorn 1987, 117).

Prior to the conflict and even after it began, in the period between 1958 and 1975, the Northern Ireland economy experienced a positive cycle whose benefits mostly accrued to the Protestant community. The province was able to attract inward investments and a relatively large number of multinational companies, which by the early 1970s became the central dynamic force in the province, especially in the manufacturing sector (Teague 1987). The estimated 65,000 new jobs created during the period were unevenly distributed with the majority of new investment directed to the Protestant areas around Belfast. Private investment preferred the Protestant areas, which were more conveniently situated and usually possessed larger supplies of skilled labor than Catholic areas. As a result, despite improvement in Catholic education and some catching up, the rate of unemployment remained significantly higher among Catholics (Rowthorn and Wayne 1988, 74–76).

By the 1970s, the fortunes of Northern Ireland had changed as the economy went into a long and deep recession. Political violence was only one factor, and according to some economists not necessarily the most important factor of the decline. Oil price shocks, the world recession, and the way the province was historically incorporated into the international capitalist division of labor in the nineteenth century were listed as significant factors. "Dependence on exports to Britain and a distorted over-specialized industrial structure set the parameters of the North's development. Britain's own decline since around the First World War took the North of Ireland with it and left it particularly vulnerable to the external economic shocks of the 1970s" (Munck 1993, 67–68).

The impact of the Troubles, however, cannot easily be discounted. The escalation of the conflict combined with the world recession handed a devastating blow to the economy of Northern Ireland. The violence led to a decline of business confidence and the withdrawal of foreign investments as between 1973 and 1990 the number of externally owned manufacturing plants declined from 351 to 207. Most of the remaining companies, and the few that entered, concentrated in traditional and declining low-technology industries that required a semiskilled work force. Despite the attempts to attract new modern forms of international investments, the Troubles tarnished the image of the province in the eyes of international investors, and the economy remained largely outside the orbit of the global economy (Teague 1987). The Irish Republic, on the other hand, where the political situation was stable, was able to attract foreign investment associated with more modern industries, and the region rapidly industrialized. The adverse political situation in the north seems to make much of the difference between the north's decline and the Republic's growth (Hamilton 1993).

Several attempts were made to quantify the cost of the Troubles. The cost in human lives and injuries between 1969 and 1995 amounted, respectively, to 3,196 and 37,617. Economic losses of the Troubles are based upon estimates, some controversial. Taking into account costs of injuries, discouraged business and tourism, damaged property, and higher law-and-order spending, the combined loses have been estimated by economists somewhere between £14 to £23.5 billion (Birnie and Hitchins 1999). In terms of employment, it has been estimated that the conflict destroyed or prevented the creation of some 46,000 manufacturing jobs in Northern Ireland. This loss was somewhat compensated by some 36,000 jobs related to the conflict in the public sector (police, prisons, education, and so on) and about 5,000 security related jobs in the private sector (Rowthorn and Wayne 1988, 94).

Protestants, who dominated the industrial workforce in the peak years of the economy, suffered most from its decline but were compensated by jobs that became available in the public sector and were mostly obtained by Protestants. Catholics lost fewer jobs but received less in the public sector. All in all, therefore, the conflict led to redistribution of employment within each community but had limited effect on the share of each community in the total number of jobs available. Unemployment among Catholics remained greater, and they remained crowded into low-paid and insecure forms of employment (Rowthorn and Wayne 1988, 95). Also, the trade-off between jobs lost in industry and jobs created in the public sector created a relationship of dependency between the province and the British economy as the expanded public sector was largely financed by the British taxpayers.

The British government, concerned about the political and social consequences of the economic crises, chose to finance the Northern Irish economy. Thus, contrary to the fiscal restraint imposed in the rest of the UK, public expenditures constantly rose in Northern Ireland. The Labor government (1974–79) created about fifty thousand jobs in the public sector and the Conservative government, in spite of its neoliberal agenda, also treated the province carefully. While Northern Ireland was adversely affected by the Conservatives' reconstruction of the welfare system, it was relatively protected compared to the rest of the UK. In 1980–81, public expenditure per person in Northern Ireland was about 33 percent greater than in the rest of Britain; by 1986 it had increased to 42 percent. Manufacturing jobs continued to decline despite direct or indirect subsidies by the state, and as a result the province became more and more dependent on public sector employment (Morrissey 2000).

The assessments of the social and political impact of the subventions are related to general perceptions of the conflict. One view considers the relationship of dependency as anomalous and holds that the enlarged public sector turned the region into a "workhouse economy" that simply sucks imports from the outside and exports little in return (Rowthorn 1993). The second view, held by more traditional unionists, claims that the subvention is not exceptional. Because Northern Ireland is a part of the United Kingdom, it is only natural that it would come to the rescue of a region troubled by a combination of political and economic difficulties (Gudgin 1995a).

The economic decline had several consequences for the dynamics of the conflict. First, among lower-class Protestants, unemployment drove many young males toward political extremism. Middle-class unionists, on the other hand, benefited from the expansion of public employment that accompanied direct rule, which created opportunities that facilitated the emergence of a Protestant middle class with a standard of living similar to their counterparts in the rest of the UK. The benefactors included not only those in the public sector but industries that have enjoyed generous assistance from the UK government and rates of profit unrelated to actual performance (Coulter 1997).

Second, members of the province's professional and business classes were drawn increasingly into channels of communication and career advancements that encompass the UK and center upon the British state. It was reflected in patterns of travel, studying in the UK, and consumption style (Coulter 1997, 121–22). Politically, this middle class desired "minimalist integration" and was gradually prepared for compromises over the status of the region. Their integration with Britain sheltered this Protestant professional middle-class from many of the adverse economic effects of the conflict. But this dependency made it difficult for this group to resist the joint initiatives of the British and Irish governments, since by the mid-1980s subventions from Britain were providing 25 to 30 percent of the disposable income of Northern Ireland's population (Kennedy-Pipe 2000).

Finally, and central to this work, like in Israel, a growing part of the business community and middle—and upper-middle-class unionists reached the conclusion that in order to restore the economy and integrate globally, compromises had to be made in order to end the conflict. This business class was detached from party politics and chose to exercise their influence through participation in the broader sphere of civil society and professional organizations that gave voice to their specific, sectional interests. This method of involvement proved to have important advantages as it both kept the business community "above" local politics and let their voices be heard where it was necessary. Speaking from a "professional" position gave their ideas the stance of an enlightened civic conscience and of working for the public good (Coulter 1997, 132). From this vantage point and, in their eyes, a nonpolitical point, the Northern Ireland transnational class sought to promote peace.

Transnational Class and Global Incentives

In the early 1990s, the business community in Northern Ireland, frustrated with economic stagnation, was ready to become politically involved in order to promote peace it perceived as a precondition for economic development and global integration. Jim MacLaughlin describes the rise of new hegemonic groups in Ireland who were set on Europeanizing and modernizing the country and actively contributed to the devaluation of "old nationalism" both in the Republic and the north. "In this new Ireland there is an abiding concern for the country's *international status* in Europe and in the modern world system, there is far less concern for the purity of the original ideals of the Irish state and the Irish economy" (McLaughlin 1999, 62).

Essentially, the borders that partitioned the island and the internal boundaries that separated the two communities seemed for many businesspeople incompatible with world developments. John McGuckian, the chairman of the Northern Ireland Industrial Development Board, explained the economic logic behind pulling down borders, especially the ones that separated Northern Ireland from the Republic much against the economic logic of the era of globalization and, more concretely, contrary to the practices of many multinational corporations that operated in the region. "One very simple thing, which is happening, is that the international marketing community is beginning to look at the island of Ireland as one unit. Companies like Coca-Cola, Mars and Unilever have now started to look financially at Ireland as one unit" (Social Democratic and Labour Party 1993).

Global business practices were therefore already operating across the island, but the business community realized that economic logic by itself would not open borders because of the sensitive political issues involved. Enabling the economy to operate across borders would require them to become involved in Northern Ireland's politics, something they avoided for a long period. Before the 1990s, the business community maintained distance from the political events because businesspeople felt there was little that could be done and much to lose. "During the Troubles, one of the best ways of staying alive was keeping your head down and one of the best ways to protect your business was keeping quiet," explained one senior businessman, ". . . that's what businesspeople did" (Anonymous 2, 2000).

But when leading businesspeople and business organizations perceived the economy had to "go global" and sensed changing perceptions among politicians and general weariness of conflict, they began to advocate conflict resolution.

> When the gun ran the country, the business community was not willing to put its head above the parapet. But once there was a little light at the end of the tunnel and one or two of the political parties started to talk to get the gun out of politics, that is when the business community has come out to say, gently, but at every occasion that this is a good thing [the talks] and that we have got to think about the future. We did not get out there to lecture but to state the obvious. But this was an obvious that was missing for years because we were not willing to risk our lives saying it. (Anonymous 6, 2000)

Businesspeople interviewed for this study were active supporters of the peace process: all were prominent members or headed business organizations involved in the process. All businesspeople interviewed had professional affiliations outside of Northern Ireland; many of them lived in Europe or the United States for long periods. Only one of the twelve interviewed was Catholic, the rest Protestant.[2] All saw themselves as Northern Irish but declined either to be identified with any political party or to define themselves as unionist, a political affiliation.

> I wouldn't identify myself at all. I spent much of my career outside Northern Ireland . . . I could scarcely tell the difference when I wake up in the morning of whether I am working in an international or any particular national environment . . . the issue is how to make business successful, how to deliver to your customers, your shareholders, and staff and how to make the absolute advantage out of the opportunities there are . . . my political priorities are private. (Anonymous 3, 2000)

> I am not a unionist. I am a Protestant. Basically my politics is business . . . I do not enjoy that whole situation of Protestants and Catholics; there are more important things in life than killing for Ireland . . . my politics are that I want to see a country at peace with itself and an economic community enlarged. (Anonymous 6, 2000)

Businesspeople's cosmopolitan perceptions and global practices were combined with local patriotism as all of them described themselves attached and committed to the province and to a lesser extent or more ambiguously also to Britain. They supported the integration of Ireland within the European Union, but an overarching European identity in place of an Irish identity appealed only to some of them; most preferred to have a local Northern Irish identity with some attachment to Britain. Yet all of them supported compromise over the issues that divided Northern Ireland that would both open borders to the wider world and allow the two communities to coexist. They believed that most members of the business community shared their views and attributed this moderation to a "business culture" that is based upon rationality, pragmatism, orientation toward the future, and compromise. They were convinced that this type of thinking, adopted by more people and the political

2. Interviewees were located by their public involvement in the peace process. Their religious identities were unknown to the author before the interviews.

elites who would see the "bigger picture" could end the conflict. Identity, explained one businessman, could be resolved with a new setting. "I am an Irishman, a British citizen, and a European. The EC will protect the minority on the island and I think people here don't want revenge . . . Eventually we will become a part of an all-Ireland and I don't have a problem with that" (Anonymous 6, 2000).

Another businessman more inclined toward unionism (with a "small U," in his words) argued that his unionist identity is perfectly compatible with compromise. "My Irishness is a broad, expansive, and welcoming tradition that has Protestant background and wishes to be a part of the UK as a part of a uniting Europe and wishes to put an arm around my Catholic cousins with which we share a common heritage" (Anonymous 2, 2000).

Despite their economic status and wide business connections, most of the businesspeople interviewed, unlike their Israeli counterparts, had little or no relations with the local politicians. The networks easily observed in Israel were practically nonexistent in Northern Ireland for several reasons. First, since 1972 when the Stormont government was dissolved, the important political and economic decisions were made in London. The important address for business needs and demands, therefore, was the Northern Ireland Office (NIO) rather than the local parties. As one businessman explained, "We ignored the politicians . . . they were only fighting among themselves. The only way for us to get things done was to talk to the civil service and through them to the government ministers" (Anonymous 6, 2000). And second, for the sake of their business operations, most businesspeople wanted to remain neutral and not be dragged into the conflict and risk their business.

> Politics was all about "what about the border?" "what about terrorism?" "which community you were a member of" . . . terribly divisive politics. Business people cannot afford that because at the end of the day shareholders don't lend money to you to go and spend it on political objectives but to make more money for them. Similarly, what your employees want is to work in an environment that is not threatening. (Gibson 2000)

During the 1990s, especially when the peace process began, new relationships, mostly working ones, between the business community and local parties and politicians developed, but according to interviewees a distance remained. On the one hand, businesspeople saw the need to educate politicians about the economy, a subject they had ignored for a long period. But, on the other hand, suspicion and some resentment toward local politicians were still held by several businesspeople for the unconstructive role they played in the conflict. Also, politicians were blamed once and again for their general indifference toward the economy. "Politicians here in Northern Ireland are a unique bunch. Not only do we work on shades of orange and green as distinct from Great Britain's party system, but we're also lumbered with a group of MPs with precious little interest in the business life of the province" *(Ulster Business,* March 18, 1994).

The relationship of the business community with the British government was also difficult. While the Northern Ireland Office was available to address concerns and many of their businesses were enmeshed in the British economy, the businesspeople felt, in spite of the subventions, that they were not treated fairly by the government and pointed to the low state of infrastructure in Northern Ireland. The British government, who searched for support among Protestants for the peace process, attempted to use its relations with the business community to encourage it to speak for peace. Sir Patrick Mayhew, Northern Ireland secretary, in an address to the Confederation of British Industry in Northern Ireland (April 12, 1995) explained that peace and economy are dependent upon each other, and therefore it is the role of business to become involved.

> Nothing could be more important for the building of a strong economy than the achievement of that long-term political settlement that we all seek. May I urge that more business and professional people make their voice heard, as some most notably and rightly have already. And I mean not only through the CBI, very valuable though that is, but *individually* too. You are the people who provide the jobs that alleviate the drab hopelessness and waste of unemployment, that dispel the sense of unfairness that is hard but not impossible to root out, that bring contentment and self respect, the prosperity that we politicians talk about so much, but cannot ourselves create. So make your voices heard, you have a right, and more than a right—a duty to do so. And we politicians have a duty to hear you. (Confederation of British Industry 1998)

This embrace of businesspeople by British politicians and the NIO, however, has proven to be problematic for the businesspeople, who were accused, especially by the DUP, of being "lackeys" of the Northern Ireland Office. But since the early 1990s, as a result of the local, regional, and global changes discussed below, businesspeople began to perceive peace as central to both their own interests and wider societal ones and gradually became involved. "Business has begun to see that if you want to get anywhere in economic terms you have got to be integrated into the global economy. In order to become integrated you must play that international game, to present yourself to the world so they want to do business with you" (Quigley 2000b).

Integration in the European market and in the evolving global economy seemed for businesspeople an important opportunity that should not be missed. Like in the Israeli case, the changes associated with globalization fostered the development of a self-conscious transnational class to whom the relationship between peace and economic development was obvious. But the interaction between global and local has not been similar as a different set of opportunities, constraints, and historical path dependencies operated in Northern Ireland and influenced the choices made by the business community and others. Specifically, as the business community gradually entered the political arena to promote and support peace, a different path of political intervention than that of the Israeli business community was pursued and different outcomes were achieved. This gradual political involvement, with its opportunities and constraints, will be described in the following pages.

Regional Opportunities: The Role of the EU

The development of the EU and the single European market, formally completed in 1992, had a significant influence on the dynamics of the conflict in Northern Ireland by the introduction of a new "nonterritorial" logic concerning it and the emergence of new incentives that eventually made it easier to "sell" the agreement (P. Gillespie 1998). The changes in concepts of citizenship and boundaries within Europe offered new possibilities for the resolution of territorial conflicts. With a common European citizenship, individual Europeans could consider themselves both as citizens of a local area for some purposes (such as the provision of certain social services) and as part of a linguistic or other cultural grouping for political purposes; in the specific case of Northern Ireland, it became possible to imagine a future in which all the citizens of the island would be European citizens for the more important purposes (Leavy 1999). The potential integration within Europe also had significant economic aspects that enabled the transnational class to make a strong case for a compromise. The EU was not only a favorable setting but also became an active player involved in the resolution of the conflict. It provided support for cross-border cooperation between north and south and for peace and reconciliation programs within Northern Ireland.

Because Northern Ireland's per capita GDP was below 75 percent of the EU average it was granted an "Objective One" status—that is, given high priority for support from the EU. After the cease-fire in 1994, the European Commission deepened its involvement in the peace process with a special support program of a £240 million budget (Teague 1996). The program has set out the following priorities: employment creation, urban and regional regeneration, cross-border development, social inclusion, and investment and industrial development. The program was based upon a "decentralized approach" that focused on grassroots citizen organizations and the promotion of social inclusion for those at the margins of economic and social life and to exploit the opportunities and address the needs arising from the peace process. Despite the fact that by the late 1990s Northern Ireland's economy no longer qualified for this status, the EU decided to continue its support. The regional policy commissioner of the EU, Monika Wulf-Mathews, stated, "We know that the peace process needs support to become self-reliant. Therefore, Northern Ireland will benefit from generous transitional arrangements in the period 2000/6" (Wolf-Mathews 1999).

The changes related to the development of the EU influenced not only the parties to the conflict within Northern Ireland but also its wider cycles, Britain and the Irish Republic. In the Republic, a wide gap had formed between traditional nationalist aspirations and the new realities. If old-style nationalists dreamed of fighting for a united Ireland, more and more citizens of the Irish Republic saw their future in acquiring an education and either working in Europe or exploiting new opportunities at home. The Irish Republic, which began to enjoy significant economic growth, was focused on attracting new investments and multinational companies and less concerned with the dream of a united Ireland. The changes in the Republic were matched by the growing weariness in Britain over the issue of Northern Ireland and with a general improvement in the relations between the two states the EU helped to foster. In the 1980s, when both governments reached the conclusions that the spillover effect of the conflict in Northern Ireland was a threat that outweighs their interests in that region, they were ready to cooperate to try and resolve the conflict. These joint efforts led to the Anglo-Irish agreement of 1985 and the Downing Street Declaration of 1993 (M. Cox 2000).

Finally, the developments in the EU created mutual economic interests and shared concerns across the island. The rationale behind the single European market (SEM) was that free trade in Europe would deliver to EU member states the benefits that the United States' large market delivers. Yet it was reasonable to expect that the richer areas of the EU, possessing larger firms and economies of scale as well as access to technological innovation, would be more efficient in a free market and that the poorer regions would suffer from underinvestment and their economic growth would be stunted (Tannam 1999, 100). The increased competition from stronger European economies, therefore, threatened both parts of Ireland and especially the unstable north with "peripheralization." Moreover, after the completion of the Channel tunnel between Britain and Europe, the two Irish regions were the only ones separated by sea from continental Europe.

The new economic realities led businesspeople to the conclusion that cooperation between north and south were necessary and to argue that if the two did not swim together, they might both sink separately. The idea of integrating Ireland, which will be elaborated upon below, was supported by EU funds for cross-border cooperation and by business organizations who lobbied to access those funding regimes and to influence policy makers in London, Dublin, and Brussels (Anderson and Goodman 1997).

> I don't have a problem with an all-Ireland economy. I would not have said that twenty-five years ago, but now with the EC we are all a part of a broad European community. The laws of the EC are going to protect the [Protestant] minority. In the Chamber of Commerce, I would not come out and say we should have a united Ireland; what I would say is that economics suggests that we should treat this country as one. If you talk politics you might get into trouble, if you talk economics that is another matter. (Anonymous 6, 2000)

Catholics in Northern Ireland were also encouraged by the developments of the EU and its growing involvement in the region. This was especially true of the SDLP, which in the 1990s advocated a policy of a "United Ireland in an EC context." Its leader, John Hume, even proposed that the EU play a part in the governance of Northern Ireland. The EU was part of the SDLP's idea of "internationalizing" the conflict. International forces, it argued, had two roles to play in regard to conflict resolution in Ireland: arbitration and the attraction of international capital. The EU had another potential role as its supranational bodies and pooling of sovereignty could provide new solutions that would take into account the three strands of the conflict: Catholic-Protestant, North-South, Ireland-UK (Farren 2000). The possibility of attracting multinational capital and supranational subsidy (via the EU), according to the SDLP, changed the conflict from a zero-sum game to "the prospect that bitter conflict be replaced by cooperation and partnership without anyone being cast as victor or vanquished and without anyone losing distinctiveness or identity" (Hume 1993, 231). Hume and the SDLP were quick to catch on to the rhetoric of the EU and globalization to advance their cause, resembling the "New Middle East" slogans described in the previous chapter.

> As we enter the 21st century, the world around us is changing fast. The old social and economic model of individual nation states is being superseded in the West by a model of a Europe of the Regions, with those Regions vying with one another for business and wealth. The North of Ireland [rather than NI] has to recognize it does not yet have the necessary infrastructure to seize the opportunities that this new situation affords: unless we develop that infrastructure, we will not attract inward investment and will not be able to retain our homegrown entrepreneurs. (Social Democratic and Labour Party 2000)

> If the strategy is to be meaningful, it must be set firmly in an all-island and, indeed, a European context. It could even be argued that it should be set in a global context.(Social Democratic and Labour Party 2000)

Hume's arguments were also directed toward Sinn Fein, which was initially reluctant to join the EC. In an increasingly integrated Europe in which the very notion of sovereignty was being put into question, argued Hume, the IRA campaign and the premodern assumptions that underpinned it were basically irrelevant (M. Cox 1998). Sinn Fein on socioeconomic matters remained critical of EC policies, and demanded decentralization, democratization, and greater social provisions, but gradually perceived the EU as a "key terrain for political struggle and one which we can use to advance our republican aims of national independence and economic and social justice" (Sinn Fein 1999). Already in 1992, in its document "Towards a Lasting Peace in Ireland," Sinn Fein seems to have reached conclusions close to that of Hume that included the perception that traditional sovereignties are being eroded and that there are new opportunities to solve the Irish problem through the transformations in Europe

(Arthur 1999). Similarly, two years later, the Sinn Fein manifesto of 1994 argued that the EU provides new important opportunities: "The concept of European Union and open borders is at odds with a divided Ireland. Sinn Fein believes the EU can have a constructive role to play in facilitating a peace process in Ireland . . . The political and economic transformation of Europe provides a golden opportunity for Ireland to finally resolve its British problem and embark on a process of economic and political reunification to the benefit of all our people" (Sinn Fein 1994).

The SDLP also attempted to direct its arguments across the dividing lines and persuade the Protestant community and especially businesspeople, who were cautious in their response to the EC's involvement. Protestants remained concerned that there was a hidden agenda behind the development of the EU to unite Ireland, and, consequently, make them a minority. Statements made by nationalist politicians in Northern Ireland and in the Republic since the early 1970s that the European Union would "likely be uniformly directed towards that path to a united Ireland" (Fitzgerald 1993) made many unionists concerned about the growing EU involvement. In response, unionists highlighted the significance of borders for the preservation of national sovereignty and identity and the danger of membership in a body whose "raison d'etre is to eliminate frontiers or make them more permeable" (Meehan 2000).

In its party manifesto of 1997, the UUP explained that it objects to an extended EU that would eventually compromise the status of Northern Ireland as an integral part of the UK. "Our belief is that a European 'super state' could hamper the benefits which increased cooperation already bring to the citizens of the nations that make up the EU. Therefore, we oppose any move toward European federalism, which infringes upon our liberty and status as citizens of the United Kingdom" (Ulster Unionist Party 1997). The UUP supported the economic aspects of the EC, like trade liberalization, but argued that national state sovereignties are to be respected and preserved. Similarly, the DUP came around to support the economics of the EU and argued for "cooperation in Europe without incorporation" (Goodman 1996).

A survey of attitudes toward the EU, taken in 1993, showed that respondents in Northern Ireland were more pro-European than respondents in Britain. This support for the EU largely reflected the nationalist position, but it also correlated with younger age, higher education, and to some extent employment in sectors likely to benefit from integration in the EC (Smith and Corigan 1995). Like in the issue of north-south integration described below, the business community found that, even if for different reasons, it had shared interests with the moderate nationalists and that its views were closer to that of the SDLP than to a large part of the UUP and certainly of the DUP.

Internationalization of the Conflict

The conflict in Northern Ireland always had international dimensions that related to British and Irish foreign policies and the active Irish diaspora. For a long time, the influence of outside forces on the conflict was considered mostly negative for two main reasons. First, the paramilitaries received support from abroad that helped them to arm and maintain the violent struggle. And second, the general international view that Northern Ireland was a hangover from the colonial era made most outsiders favor a unified Ireland. Consequently, the unionists' insecurities and siege mentality grew and nationalists' incentives to compromise were reduced (Guelke 1988; McGarry 2001). Developments associated with globalization and the global exposure of human rights transgressions, however, made British presence in Northern Ireland problematic and placed its policies under critical observation. Britain was brought several times before the European Commission of Human Rights and the European Court of Human Rights for its treatment of detainees and prisoners in Northern Ireland (McGarry 2001, 309). In addition, Britain was criticized by various international agencies for its policies in Northern Ireland.

The adoption of the MacBride principles by several U.S. states in the 1980s that tied investments in Northern Ireland to antidiscrimination and affirmative action measures signaled a new form of international involvement. Since the 1970s, American administrations have joined forces with Europeans to try and influence the British policy toward Northern Ireland. The role of the United States in the conflict resolution expanded in the 1990s under the Clinton administration, which began to intervene directly in the conflict. Not only did Clinton sent envoys, advisers, and, most importantly, the former senator George Mitchell to Northern Ireland, his decision to grant Sinn Fein's leader Gerry Adams a visa to the United States enabled Adams to bring his party and the IRA to the cease-fire in 1994. Particularly important was U.S. administration assistance when the negotiations were deadlocked over the disarmament dispute. Clinton pressed the British to include Sinn Fein, allowed Adams to raise money in the United States, and personally met with Sinn Fein's leaders. Clinton's visit to Northern Ireland in November 1995, during which he met with Protestants and Catholics, was described as a spectacular success (Holland 1999, 272). On April 9, 1998, the deadline set by the British government to reach an agreement, the parties, in spite of intense negotiations, were unable to meet the deadline. Again, it was the intervention of President Clinton that, together with Blair and Ahern's efforts, enabled the parties to reach the Good Friday Agreement. The new international setting, therefore, provided not only economic opportunities but also political pressures to resolve the conflict. But it was the combination of the two and the corresponding internal changes that turned international intervention into a positive factor that, eventually, facilitated the agreement achieved.

An Island Economy: The North-South Corridor

With the development of the EU and the SEM described above and the similar economic problems (despite important differences)[3] the north and south were sharing, uniting the island, according to many, made perfect sense from an economic point of view. Arguments that there were grounds for cross-border cooperation have been voiced since the 1920s but became more compelling in the 1990s (Tannam 1999, 131). With both parts of Ireland being small in size and lacking a solid industrial base, it was argued that "the removal of barriers of trade would open the floodgates to highly competitive imports from abroad with adverse consequences for both economies" (132). Cooperation between the two parts could, for example, enable the development of Irish multinational companies that would draw on the strengths of a coordinated island marketplace to grow domestically and progress to export markets (Bradley 1996, 143). But despite the economic logic, the issue of cross-border cooperation was far from simple and it was unlikely that it could happen by itself. In a region bitterly divided over the question of its constitutional status, a part of the United Kingdom or of a united Ireland, borders mattered greatly. The business community, mostly in favor of cross-border cooperation, discovered that it had to act politically in order to make the economic change happen.

3. Despite some similarities, the economies of the north and the south have diverged since the mid-1970s. Following world recessions and the decline of indigenous industries, the south continued to attract a high proportion of the available inward investment, particularly from the United States. This contrasted sharply with the difficulties faced by the north, not all of which were related to the Troubles.

During the 1990s, Northern Ireland business decided that it was time to strengthen economic relations with the Irish Republic. This new perception was especially significant because businesspeople of unionist background were traditionally dismissive of the supposedly "backward" south (Anderson 1998). These motivations and changed perceptions were the result of, on the one hand, the influence of externally based multinational enterprises that were regarding their Irish operations in island-wide terms and, on the other hand, shared concerns in Ireland, north and south, that increased competition from the EU threatened their "peripheralization." A conference that was held in Belfast in 1990 titled "Selling into the Republic" was indicative of the growing interest in cross-border business interactions. The conference was planned with facilities for sixty to seventy company representatives, but to the surprise of the organizers three hundred company representatives attended (Tannam 1996). More important, the Confederation of British Industry (CBI) in Northern Ireland and its Irish counterpart, the IBEC, formed a joint steering group with a four-part agenda that included the development of infrastructure, public-sector—and private-sector-led opportunities, and the facilitation of joint activities. The CBI and IBEC lobbied their governments to improve the rail link between Belfast and Dublin and the EU to support the project. The Chambers of Commerce in Northern Ireland and the Republic followed the CBI/IBEC initiatives and began their own cooperation to improve business contacts (Tannam 1996).

For the first time, business took an initiative they described as "nonpolitical" that had, despite their claims of "business only," important political ramifications. Sir George Quigley, chairman of the Ulster Bank and the Institute of Directors (IOD), proposed in 1992 that "Ireland, North and South, should become one integrated 'island economy' in the context of the Single European Market." Quigley argued that the SEM necessitated more economic cooperation between north and south as "an exercise in synergy, not a zero-sum game where a wholly insufficient quantity of existing island wealth is simply redistributed" and that north and south could form together an economy of 5 million people that would enable the achievement of larger-scale economics. The proposal for a united Ireland, he warned, must remain purely economic: "making a reality of the island economy is dependent on their being no political agendas, overt or hidden" (Anderson 1993). The professional position adopted at this stage by businesspeople would be replicated in later interventions when the business community kept at a distance from politics.

The highlight of the "Island Economy" proposal was to create a Belfast-Dublin "economic corridor" with coordinated government investment policies in science and technology parks, research facilities, roads, public transportation, and other facilities. The corridor, Quigley argued, would serve as the initial focus for a growth strategy that would expand to encompass other areas (Pollak et al. 1992, 294). A feasibility study conducted for the CBI in 1994 confirmed that the development of a "Dublin-Belfast economic corridor" would have important benefits for both economies and potentially lead to a substantial increase in annual output. In its conclusion, the study recommended that resources to "improve the prestige of the corridor, adequately market its identity and to build business confidence in the corridor" be allocated (Coopers and Lybrand/Indecom 1994).

Estimates of the overall gains of greater trade and increased connections between the two Irelands varied, either because they were related to political positions or because it was difficult to estimate the all-Ireland implications of peace and political stability (Gorecki 1995). The Confederation of Irish Industry (CII) estimated in 1990 that the gains would increase trade flows from £1.3 to £4.5 billion and as a result the creation of some 75,000 jobs in both economies (Bew, Patterson, and Teague 1997, 174). Conversely, Scott and O'Reilly estimated the advantages of integration to be much lower than the CII estimates and predicted an increase in employment by 7,500 jobs, one-tenth of the CII estimate (quoted in Bradley 1995)! The economist and now UUP MP Esmond Birnie argued that there were in fact no reasons to believe that greater economic integration would generate sufficient extra prosperity to underpin a "creeping political unification." Specifically, he doubted whether much, if any, gains would be achieved from more cooperation or from creating economies of scale. Employer organizations from north and south, he argued, have widely (or wildly) exaggerated the effects of cooperation and stated unrealistic figures of numbers of jobs that might be created. Therefore, he concluded, it would be best to leave for individual businesspeople to determine the extent of cross-border cooperation (Birnie 1995). Gerard O'Neill doubted economic predictions regarding the future of the island's economy. Most prognostications, he argued, are based on redundant models that ignore important variables. "It is the vision inside the heads of business people and citizens on both parts of the border that is the most important variable shaping the future for the island" (P. Gillespie 1996).

Naturally, nationalists who were in favor of strengthening ties with the Republic were strong supporters of cross-border cooperation. Hume and others expected that deepened cooperation between political and economic elites would create a "spillover dynamic" and expand the boundaries of integration (Bew, Patterson, and Teague 1997, 198). The SDLP, like the business community, argued that a united Ireland was economically sensible and a way must be found so that "the full potential of both parts of Ireland can be exploited and developed to achieve benefits that each separately could never achieve" (SDLP 1997). The party, despite its social-democratic foundations, was quick to adopt the economic, and to some extent also the neoliberal, logic of the regional and global developments and stressed the need to rejuvenate an economy characterized by underemployment, underachievement and "an under-developed private sector" (SDLP 1997). "Through the European market, 323 million consumers will be open to Northern Ireland business, the Northern Ireland market will be just as open for European firms. The most efficient, most competitive companies will be the winners—those badly prepared will be the losers" (quoted in Munck 1993, 124–25).

In the paper submitted in 1997 to the multiparty talks, the SDLP argued that there is hardly a socioeconomic sector where coordination was not likely to be beneficial, from improved infrastructure, to agriculture, environmental protection, and attraction of inward investment. All this would require political intervention and strategic planning through joint institutions (quoted in Munck 1993, 124–25). In an address to the Chambers of Commerce in 1998, Hume repeated the economic logic of the island economy and argued that it transcends political matters. His arguments resembled those of the business class quoted above.

> Most international firms therefore structure their operations around this reality. They are not interested in the political divisions within this island. As citizens, we are all perfectly entitled to have very different political views and aspirations. But as economic actors, it is futile to let our political differences get in the way of economic realities. It is simply senseless to let outsiders behave in an economically rational fashion while we allow our political differences to stop us behaving rationally in economic terms. (*Ulster Business,* April 4, 1998)

For many unionists, the economic idea of integration promoted by the business community, and embraced by the SDLP, was perceived as an attempt to undermine the union, intentionally or unintentionally. Robert McCartney of the United Kingdom Unionist Party (UKUP) warned against "arrangements [that] are being made to create an economic infrastructure that would ultimately make the giving of consent to a united Ireland the only answer to economic destruction" (quoted in J. Doyle 1997). Similarly, Esmond Birnie of the UUP argued that "the unspoken political aim is that such economic integration will give momentum to a process of political integration which may prove unstoppable." Jim Nicholson of the UUP was more explicit and warned that the majority of unionists "would not like to see the large business interests North and South . . . carve up the cake for their own benefit" and that business, therefore, had to realize that "to continue to overlook the political interests within Northern Ireland would not bring long term success" (Anderson 1993).

Even after the Belfast agreement, which instituted the north-south cooperation in a joint ministerial council, unionist politicians and especially loyalists remained suspicious of what they considered too intensive and politically inclined north-south connections. "Once you establish the principle of an all-Ireland authority," explained Nigel Dodds of the DUP, "you have undermined Northern Ireland's position as part of the United Kingdom in a very fundamental and radical way" (quoted in Aughey 2000). Similarly, Ian Paisley argued that the economy was a zero-sum game and therefore "the all-Ireland economy is a false concept. Dublin has no interest in seeing Northern Ireland flourish because that would be at the expense of the Republic." But even David Trimble, a senior partner to the agreement, was cautious that cooperation would not endanger the status of Northern Ireland, "what we oppose is not any useful economic contact, but cross-border institutions devised for political rather than economic purposes" (*Business Telegraph,* April 7, 1998).

While the (Catholic) SDLP's agenda seemed closer to the (mostly Protestant) business community than the (Protestant) UUP's, this convergence was not translated into any form of cooperation. The business community maintained that their agenda was economic, not political and kept their distance from the SDLP and other political parties. A series of interviews conducted with economic and political figures in Northern Ireland in 1992 confirmed that cross-border cooperation was done more for economics than for any other reason. "Enthusiasm is . . . for economic integration as an end in itself, not as means to another end. It is explicitly distanced from nationalist hopes . . . business people north and south were building cross-border links for sound economic, not ideological reasons" (Anderson and Shuttleworth 1993).

But already in the earlier stages of cross-border cooperation, it was obvious that the political reality made it difficult for an island economy to be created through private economic initiatives without macro political changes. First, the two economies were separated by currency and tax systems that required some coordination and, second, the ongoing conflict in the north impeded economic integration. Not only would the north, still under conflict, find it difficult to compete with the stable south, but important sectors in the south like tourism were reluctant to become associated with the Troubles. Thus, with different institutional arrangements, political culture and interests, and with a lack of common institutional framework and a political program, economic integration remained limited (Anderson and Shuttleworth 1992). In 1993 the two economies were far from integrated; only about 4 percent of the Republic's imports came from Northern Ireland and 5 percent of Northern Irish imports came from the south (Anderson 1993). Economic cooperation has expanded since the early 1990s, however, much of it resulting from initiatives taken by the business organizations. In 1991 the Irish Business and Employers Confederation (IBEC) and the CBI of Northern Ireland set up a joint business council with the aim of taking a number of practical initiatives at European level to maximize north-south trade and to make Irish industry more efficient vis-à-vis international competition. In 1993 the Joint Business Council agreed on a common approach to EU funds to strengthen the infrastructure, industrial base, and human resources on the island (Brennan 1995).

In 1995, partly with the help and encouragement of the EU, several all-Ireland firms were established, usually with their headquarters based in Dublin. Irish banking became more integrated, agribusiness organizations were established, and joint ventures in tourism, especially after the cease-fire, began to operate (Anderson and Goodman 1997). Multinational companies selling into Ireland reorganized on an island basis and producers and retailers constructed north-south partnerships. Also, there was a surge in mergers and rationalization of production as well as growth in the number of employees working for all-Ireland companies. Greater integration has also been reflected in governmental bodies like utilities and tourism, strengthening of noneconomic networks—women's rights, environmentalists—and social and cultural practices (Anderson 1998).

The economic opportunities of a unitary Ireland naturally appealed to the Catholic community, who for a long time desired integration, as well as to the business community, operating on economic rationality, but the wider Protestant community had yet to be convinced. If the benefits were not evenly divided, there was a danger that the Protestant community would experience the unification of Irish economic life as a project that offered few instrumental rewards but threatened to undermine the status of Northern Ireland within the United Kingdom (Coulter 1997, 137). Businesspeople engaged in cross-border cooperation stressed not only that an island economy benefited all, but also that the initiatives they engages in were economic and posed no threat to the status of Northern Ireland. A chamber of commerce representative explained that "business organizations have to spend a lot of time avoiding getting caught up in politics . . . we would always put the emphasis on jobs and growth" (Morrow 2000). Most businesspeople interviewed for a study conducted in 1997 expressed their want of a firmer partnership, embedded in institutions, but believed that this would happen only when Northern unionists become aware of the practical necessity for it (Anderson and Goodman 1997).

Suspicions toward cooperation and the intentions of the south were greater among the lower-middle—or the working-class unionists, while the middle class favored European integration and viewed the borders and the conflict as relatively irrelevant (Anderson 1993). Businesspeople interviewed in 2000 for this work generally perceived the development of an island economy as inevitable, the reality of a globalized economy and an evolving European market.

> I think there is already an all-island economy. I don't see any tension with issues of identity. The UUP stance is nonsense; it's all around defending what they believe is a union that has changed. In the UK of the twenty-first century and in a globalized world we cannot have that sort of a union. . . . an island is an island, and it is natural that with no barriers there would be more flows. It's natural, nothing to do with politics and a united Ireland does not necessarily follow from this. (Anonymous 2, 2000)

> An all-island economy is my business and the only people that would blame you for doing business with the south are bigoted loyalists. (Anonymous 5, 2000)

Businesspeople's interest in cooperating with the Irish Republic was also based on wanting to be part of its success. Frustrated with the economic stagnation of the province and disappointed with Britain's inability to create economic growth, joining forces with the south made perfect economic sense.

They [the Republic] have done everything right and at the end of the day it makes good sense to say that they are the best partners in terms of doing business. We are on the same island, speak the same language, and we are reaching a stage that we have to be involved in a wider economic community. Therefore, my politics suggest . . . that an all-Ireland economy can be much more successful than a Northern Ireland economy . . . Britain maintained troops on the street but have not pumped investment, our infrastructure has gone to hell, all things are falling apart. We are actually a third-world country. We are being treated very poorly by Westminster and people get blindsided to that. If you look at the success in Dublin, that's the model . . . We have a better chance of having a successful economic future by being a one-island economy and forgetting about [the] Westminster link. (Anonymous 6, 2000)

There is evidence that the message the business community was sending, that it is engaged in economics rather than in politics, has largely been successful. The creation of the north-south corridor has been perceived also among the wider public as nonpolitical and therefore acceptable. A survey conducted by Irwin in February 1999 found that resistance to north-south bodies diminished among the Protestant population as their benign nature became apparent. A majority of Protestants considered north-south economic cooperation to be "important" or "very important" (Irwin 2000). But what is no less important is that the initiatives the business community undertook to promote the north-south corridor mark the formation of a self-conscious business community with growing self-confidence, prepared to become involved in the resolution of the conflict.

Business Initiatives, Peace Dividends: The 1994 Cease-Fire

With the economic and political developments in the 1990s, businesspeople could not avoid the conclusion that economic development would be difficult if not impossible without the resolution of the conflict. Initially, in spite of this realization, businesspeople were reluctant to come out and take a position, but gradually this has changed. In December 1993, the *Financial Times* surveyed Northern Ireland businesspeople, chief executives of major companies, on the issue of the conflict. The fifty-three respondents to the survey, out of eighty that were approached, insisted on anonymity. The majority of those interviewed expressed a firm belief that the province would enjoy an economic boost if peace was achieved and said they are ready for political concessions. About two-thirds of them thought that the IRA and the loyalist paramilitaries could not be defeated militarily and supported the inclusion of Sinn Fein in the political process, something the unionist parties consistently opposed (*Financial Times*, December 15, 1998).

The change of perceptions had occurred among businesspeople but a willingness to become actively involved was yet to come. An important step was

8.1 Financial Times Survey

Do you think the military defeat of the IRA is:

Possible?	21%
Impossible?	70%
Don't Know	9%

Which of the following concessions would you be prepared to see the British government offer to achieve an end to the violence, assuming that the right of majority consent in Northern Ireland to any change in the current status of the province remains fully guaranteed by both governments? (more than one answer allowed)

Acknowledgment of the aspiration of Irish unification	32%
Enhanced north-south structures for political cooperation	61%
Enhanced north-south structures for political cooperation	20%
None of these/don't know	14%

Please assess the effect an agreed settlement that achieved an end to the violence would have on business and economic opportunities for Northern Ireland. Would it have:

A very positive effect?	52%
A fairly positive effect?	38%
Neither a positive nor a negative effect?	2%
A fairly negative effect?	5%
Don't know	3%

Regardless of the progress of a political settlement, do you think new north-south structures to enhance economic and business co-operation on the island:

Are necessary?	61%
Are useful but not essential?	36%
Are unnecessary?	3%

Source: Financial Times, Dec. 15, 1993

taken in the summer of 1994 when the Northern Ireland branch of the CBI published a paper titled "Peace: A Challenging New Era." The paper argued that, after the joint statement of the SDLP and Sinn Fein in April 1993 and the Downing Street Declaration of the Irish and British government in December 1993, an opportunity to achieve a permanent cessation of violence was the closest it has been in years. The Troubles, the paper argued, have cost the economy of Northern Ireland in jobs and prosperity, hurt its image, deterred potential foreign investors, and caused talent to migrate away. Ending the violence, therefore, could significantly change the economic fortunes of the province. "The impact of a permanent cessation of violence would be profound. There are clearly significant benefits principally relating to inward investment opportunities, tourism, the indigenous industrial base and the freeing up of public expenditure for wealth creation activities and social needs" (Confederation of British Industry, Northern Ireland, 1994).

The CBI paper was an important step in the growing involvement of the business community in the conflict's resolution by use of its leading organization and professional status. The paper steered away from political questions, analyzed the difficulties of the economy, and put numbers on the potential investments and employment that peace (or, used interchangeably, "cessation of violence) could create. To begin with, argued the paper, money spent on law and order could, if violence ceased, be reinvested in wealth-creating activities and infrastructure. Additionally, stability could bring the foreign investments Northern Ireland required. The CBI delivered a clear message to policy makers, that they must do everything they could to put an end to the conflict. It is "vital that Government thinks through *now* the strategic implications of a permanent cessation of violence and develop policies and priorities to ensure that the benefits are maximized . . . the realization of the full potential of the Northern Ireland economy and the provision of more opportunities for its citizens will require a political settlement" (Confederation of British Industry, Northern Ireland, 1994).

The paper also made some wider public impact as the explicit link it established between peace and economic prosperity became popularized in the term "peace dividends," often used since then by the media. The paper could not have had better timing, as shortly after its release in August 1994 the IRA declared a cease-fire, followed six weeks later by a loyalist cease-fire. The cease-fire confirmed business expectations of what a permanent peace could bring, and the wave of optimism became a self-fulfilling prophecy. Tourism increased within the space of a year, unemployment was down to 11.5 percent, and over £30 million in investment ventures were announced.

The CBI and the Institute of Directors (IOD) followed the cease-fire with optimistic economic forecasts. They estimated that up to 50,000 jobs could be created by the end of the decade and predicted large inward investments, especially from the United States (*Irish News,* September 1, 1994, 20). The British government also delivered optimistic messages. John Major in his address to the IOD in 1994 stated that "peace will give a massive boost to Northern Ireland's economy. Equally, the chance of more jobs, better security for families, must be the most powerful incentive for peace. I know that the business community is already preparing for new opportunities. So is the government in partnership with you" (quoted in Shirlow 1997). Also, as mentioned above, the EU set up a Special Support Program for Peace and Reconciliation with a five-year disbursement of almost £400 million targeted directly at cross-community cooperative projects. More investments, investment plans, and aid came from Australia, New Zealand, and Canada, all with a purpose of advancement of prosperity in the region and strengthening support for the peace process (McSweeny 1998).

The overall result was a growth of business confidence indicated in press interviews and in a survey the CBI conducted.[4] Sir George Quigley, the chairman of the Institute of Directors, described in an interview the new business state of mind: "When you talk to business people they are in a very buoyant mood—surprisingly bullish, not a lot of pessimism around" (*Independent,* October 31, 1994). Northern Ireland was having its own "peace festival" after the cease-fire, with the support of the business community and the press, that resembled the euphoric mood in Israel after the DOP signing. The media highlighted the peace dividends and the potential economic growth that seemed a reality. One paper, calling the cease-fire "Ulster Peace," described "investor pulses racing" with more than 150 companies that included names like Nissan, Du Pont, Nokia, and Bell Helicopters, who expressed an interest in investing in the region. The paper quoted an enthusiastic IDB executive who exclaimed, "There will never be a better time to invest in Northern Ireland than right now" (Rodgers 1994). The stock market also responded positively to the cease-fire that altered the perceptions of Northern Ireland and eroded the risk discount that was factored into investments (*Business Telegraph,* August 29, 1995).

---

4. Business confidence peaked during the cease-fire but then returned to the levels of the 1990s, probably because the cease-fire failed to produce permanent peace.

At the end of 1994, the consulting firm Coopers and Lybrand reviewed the peace dividends of the cease-fire and the perceptions of businesspeople. The review found local business to be very optimistic: almost 90 percent believed that the impact of the cease-fire would be quite positive or very positive, although on the "micro level" (the individual business unit), the optimism was somewhat smaller. Especially optimistic were the manufacturing sector and larger companies who believed that exporting their products would become easier under conditions of peace (Coopers and Lybrand 1997).

In May 1995, a White House investment conference on Ireland was held in Washington, D.C. Addressed by President Clinton and top-level politicians, bureaucrats, and business executives, the conference was designed to promote peace by investments in Northern Ireland. While Ian Paisley, the leader of the DUP, announced that the party would not attend the conference because it has been turned into a "political event," other politicians and business organizations attended the conference in large numbers (*Irish Times*, May 6, 1995). In this conference, and in another held in Pittsburgh in October 1996, the Northern Irish representatives sought to interest foreign companies in the province. They marketed the advantages the province held such as government incentives, a large employable pool of highly trained labor and competitive labor costs, easy access to the SEM, and an exit clause from the Social Chapter of the EU Treaty.[5]

In February 1995, the British and Irish governments introduced the Framework Document, which represented, according to the two governments, the "best assessment of where broad agreement might be found" between unionists and nationalists. This document was supposedly a basis upon which the Northern Ireland parties could directly negotiate. Both large unionist parties, the UUP and the DUP, rejected the proposals and stated that they were "designed to trick the Ulster people into themselves ending the union and their British identity" (Aughey 2000). In the business community, other voices were heard. The CBI strongly supported the document, its chairman Doug Riley explaining that from their point of view, a professional economic and pragmatic one, the framework document was the right direction to follow. "Where an all Ireland economy is seen to be the most effective approach, then we will support it. Where it delivers more jobs, more wealth, a competitive infrastructure or greater social benefits, we will support it" (*Financial Times*, February 23, 1995).

5. This was the U.S. Conference for Trade and Investment in Northern Ireland, held in Pittsburgh, Penn., Oct. 6–8, 1996.

1996 Breakdown of the Cease-Fire and the G7

In February 1996, negotiations between the Northern Ireland parties reached a dead end over the issue of weapons decommissioning as a condition for Sinn Fein entry into the all-party talk. Following the deadlock, the Provisional IRA ended the cease-fire with the bombing of the Canary Wharf in London. The renewed violence was perceived as a serious setback that risked everything that had been achieved so far and threatened to put the province where it was before the cease-fire. While investment intentions remained generally positive, the security situation, warned one economic review, could have a considerable influence on whether investment intentions would be translated into real projects (Coopers and Lybrand 1997). Pessimism began to overshadow the optimism of the past two years. Sir Patrick Mayhew, the Northern Ireland secretary, declared that the peace dividend "has been reversed," and announced that funds for training, education, and welfare would be cut to meet the increased cost of law and order after the breakdown of the IRA cease-fire (*Financial Times,* December 11, 1996).

In retrospect, businesspeople described the breakdown of the cease-fire as a "moment of truth," a time in which all gains achieved in the past two years were in danger of being eroded. "Business had a resilience which was a 'business as usual' approach. During the troubles, level of expectation was quite low. But after the cease-fire, when people [had] seen what it was like [to live in peace], it was very difficult to accept that we are going to return to the period before the cease-fire" (Kingdom 2000).

With so much at stake, the business community was ready to become more politically involved, make bolder statements, sharpen and amplify its call for peace. Essentially, it asked the parties to the conflict to consider the consequences of the breakdown of the cease-fire and the necessity to resume the peace process. "We had a simple message, that no society that wants to prosper can afford the 'luxury' of violence and destruction. The continuation of violence sends a wrong message to the outside world and it leads to a loss of [business] confidence" (Quigley 2000b).

The escalation of the violence in the summer of 1996 during and after the Protestant annual marches of Drumcree was the catalyst for the formation of the Group of Seven (G7). The group, which consisted of representatives of business organizations, trade unions, and civic society organizations,[6] was

6. The group included the CBI, the Hospitality Association, the Northern Ireland Chamber of Commerce, the Institute of Directors, the Northern Ireland Growth Challenge, the Northern

formed in order to put pressure on all parties to return to the negotiating table. The importance of this coalition was the cooperation it engendered among different groups to promote peace. Business organizations and trade unions, despite their deep disagreements over many economic issues, could unite around the issue of peace. The trade unions, who for a long time attempted to draw members from the two communities, were largely supportive of the peace process. Like the business community, trade unions came to the conclusion that peace is required for economic regeneration, but also that both economic growth and social inclusiveness could be achieved.

The Drumcree march, in which the Protestant Orange Order annually marches through Catholic neighborhoods to commemorate the siege of Drumcree, was an especially troubling issue. In July 1995 a confrontation occurred when Orangemen were prevented by the authorities from marching through a nationalist neighborhood in Portadown, considered by them a traditional marching route. Eventually, the marches were let through, something many unionists considered a significant victory (Hennessey 1997, 296). The Drumcree standoff in the following summer of 1996 was even more intense and, according to one report "brought Northern Ireland close to anarchy" (Tomlinson 1998). Two years later, in the summer of 1998, the G7 became closely involved in preventive mediation between the Orange Order and the Catholic residents. Its message to the parties was clear: the confrontations between the communities over the marches are detrimental to the economy and must be stopped: "Northern Ireland is on self-destruct: action is imperative. The present madness cannot continue. Northern Ireland cannot credibly, on the one hand, hold itself out as a prime location for investment and tourism and, on the other hand, indulge in behavior that gives the investor and the tourist reason to shun us . . . People talk frequently about ensuring that their children have a better future. Is this it?" (G7 press statement 1998). Meeting face to face with both sides and encouraging the two to find a compromise, the summer of 1998 was quiet.

Going back to the summer of 1996, the group was mostly concerned with the collapse of the peace process and with attempts to bring the political parties back to negotiations. The general message of the group reiterated the "peace dividends" concept to both politicians and the public at large. The group began to meet collectively with the political parties to try and influence them to re-

---

Ireland Economic Council, and the Northern Ireland Committee of the Irish Congress of Trade Unions.

sume the peace process. It avoided individual meetings in order not to become carriers of messages between parties or identified with any party's message. The collective meetings also ensured that all parties received the same message, namely that Northern Ireland could not realize its economic potential under the present tension and violence. The first meeting took place in September 1996, and five more meetings took place in the next twenty-one months. According to notes taken by Sir George Quigley and given to the author in May 2001, some of the parties were suspicious of the G7's motives, believing either that it carried the British government's agenda or that it was promoting an all-Ireland solution, both charges denied by the group, which claimed it had no political agenda. The G7 found the meetings to be useful, as all parties seemed to recognize the positive developments of the past two years and were attentive to the G7's warning of the "catastrophic" economic consequences if the peace process would collapse (G7 press statement 1996b).

The message delivered to the political parties in closed sessions also had to be delivered to the people of Northern Ireland in order to create more pressure on the parties. The public was targeted through a series of public statements made at critical junctures conveying the benefits of peace for the whole population. In August 1996 the G7 published a lengthy statement stressing the impacts of the renewed troubles on Northern Ireland's global integration. The message was clear and simple: people of Northern Ireland must make a choice, like the business class had already made, and like people in Israel had to make, between the continuation of the conflict and the economic betterment that compromise could bring.

> The world thought that we had turned a corner. It has been shocked—indeed we have surprised ourselves—by the public display of animosity and bitterness. . . . For Northern Ireland the moment of truth has arrived, when it must decide whether it wants to be regarded as a credible, serious, first division economic player or is prepared to accept relegation. . . . [business] is severely handicapped if it has to operate in an environment which destroys confidence. It is essential that those both inside and outside Northern Ireland who have to make investment decisions based on an assessment of risk should possess that confidence. Community stability is a crucial factor in the assessment. A society which does not eschew violence and turmoil—whatever the perceived justification—is on the road to nowhere. Surely the *entire* population on Northern Ireland can accept that whatever else divides it, it has a common interest in rapid economic growth and jobs. (G7 press statement 1996a)

In another statement distributed among employees, the G7 explained its objective of creating more jobs, greater prosperity, and better opportunities. Northern Ireland society faces the choice between "real opportunities and real potential for peace, progress, prosperity," or "more hostility, animosity and sectarianism if the right direction is not chosen" (G7 press statement 1997b). The G7 continued to deliver statements regarding the peace process and the severe economic implications of its destruction. In April 1997, it expressed concern over the slow progress of the peace process and encouraged the politicians to do more to advance peace and stability (G7 press statement 1997a). In June 1997, prior to the marching season, the G7 sent a message to employers, schools, and churches, with the hope it would reach 85 percent of households in the province. It warned that another summer of disruption and violence would be "economic suicide" for Northern Ireland (newsletter, June 3, 1997). During the summer of 1997, after Sinn Fein returned to the talks, it encouraged all parties to engage actively in the peace process, take into account the economic implications of the decisions they make and be determined that the disagreements will not "wreck the economic prospects which it is in everybody's interest to protect and enhance." The statement also called on others to actively support the process since "silence is not an option when so much is at stake" (G7 press statement 1997c).

A year after its establishment, the members of the G7 were cautiously optimistic in regard to the prospects of peace and stability. The group felt that its stance was helpful to support those politicians (particularly of the UUP) who were hesitant to participate in talks alongside Sinn Fein. According to Quigley (2000a), the G7 made it harder for the parties to walk away by constituting a countervailing moral force to those who favored such a course. In another press release, the G7 stated: "Given peace and stability and a serious attempt to confront the difficult political issues, we have no doubt that lost ground can be regained and that Northern Ireland will be as well placed as any region in Europe—and better than most—to benefit from economic growth and jobs and to create worthwhile opportunities for all. That will assure the flows from it in terms of quality of life and standard of living, is the prize" (G7 press statement 1997d).

The difficulties the G7 encountered were less between business and trade unions over economic issues and more between the business organizations themselves. The CBI, who represents larger businesses, was more ready to make explicit statements of support for peace than the Chambers of Commerce, whose constituency of smaller business was more divergent in its views, some of them more traditional unionists or even loyalists. Accordingly, not all representatives of the Chambers of Commerce were comfortable with the position of the G7 and argued that it had extended its mandate and become overtly political. "One of difficulties with the business community here is that some time there is a feeling that the G7 does not have a mandate to speak for business . . . We don't have a mandate to speak on issues like decommissioning . . . we can say we need peace and stability but not beyond it" (Anonymous 4, 2000).

In 1998, because of its differences with the G7 position, the Chamber of Commerce decided to withdraw from the group and afterward held independent initiatives it found more acceptable to its members. In a series of lunches, the chamber members met with the leaders of the parties involved in the talks, including Sinn Fein. The invitations clearly emphasized that the speakers at those lunches would be addressing economic and not political issues *(Business Telegraph,* February 24, 1998, 15).

The return of the parties to the negotiating table and the deep involvement of the British, Irish, and American governments led to intensive negotiations that ended on April 10, 1998, with the Good Friday Agreement. The agreement was based on the three strands that appeared in earlier discussions. The first strand of the agreement provides for a new Northern Ireland assembly. The second strand was about north-south cooperation through the establishment of a North-South Ministerial Council. Finally, the third strand, east-west cooperation, proposed a new body, a British-Irish Council, linking the province with Britain. The parties to the agreement decided that on May 22, 1998, a referendum would be held in Northern Ireland and the Republic to ratify the Good Friday Agreement.

Strategy 2010: Prospects and Concerns

Business organizations and trade unions could mobilize around the issue of peace and share expectations for peace dividends but remained deeply divided on socioeconomic issues and on how dividends would be divided. But for these two sectors to maintain the cooperation for the long run, some common ground had to be found. The business community, on its behalf, declared again its commitment to social inclusiveness and trade unions agreed that structural economic changes are inevitable. Questions of social inequality were expected to become a pertinent issue in all stages of peace. Rowthorn and Wayne predicted in 1989 that peace would have mixed economic results as it could, on the one hand, draw multinational companies and, consequently, benefit the local professional class and skilled workers. But, on the other hand, peace would probably lead to a reduction of British spending on security as well as a possible reduction of the subvention that would have negative consequences for the lower classes.

With the advances made in the peace process, the unions remained generally supportive of the process but were more cautious about the dividends and the promises of economic betterment. Unison, the public service union, published an ad calling for "YES to peace, YES to healing, Yes to hope," but explained that the agreement "does not promise everything we want but we never have seen an agreement which did . . . It is a start." The trade unions supported peace because of the general adverse effects of the conflict and their realization that the economy was in dire need of investments. They insisted, nevertheless, that economic growth should be compatible with social needs. Economic plans, for the present and for the future, between the neoliberal-minded business and professional class and the concerned trade unions seemed harder to reconcile than the commitment to peace.

In 1997 the minister of the economy, Adam Ingram, appointed a steering group to conduct a fundamental review of Northern Ireland's economic development and to create a comprehensive strategy that would take into account anticipated national, European, and world economic trends. Published in 1999, this plan came to be known as "Strategy 2010." The steering group members appointed to direct the review were largely drawn from the private sector, but also from trade unions and the local government. Eighteen working groups established by the steering committee examined specific topics and industry sectors and submitted reports and recommendations. "Strategy 2010" provides an opportunity to examine not only the interaction between business and other parts of society but also the ability for them to find some common ground on economic issues.

The report identified the globalization of economic activity as the primary factor that will set the future context for accelerated growth and the restructuring of the region. The plan advocated a structural and cultural change in order to move Northern Ireland away from an economy "cushioned by public expenditure" toward a culture that "generates a common commitment to economic success." Northern Ireland had to become competitive, to promote technological development and a "knowledge driven economy," to develop an outward approach and create a winning economy. Peace and stability were considered indispensable for the economic takeoff and were, accordingly, the first topic discussed under "opportunities and constraints" (Northern Ireland Economic Development Strategy Review Steering Group 1999).

> The establishment of a stable political environment in Northern Ireland will be of critical importance to the speed and scope of the development of the economy. The civil unrest of recent years has adversely affected business confidence, leading to delay in or cancellation of investment strategies. It has also clearly had an effect on our ability to attract inward investment projects into the region, and this in turn has restricted our integration into the wider European and global economies. . . .
>
> Peace gives us our best chance in a generation to strike out on a new path to prosperity. We need to set the work of change in motion with new energy and urgency. The "wait and see option" is not an option, either. (Northern Ireland Economic Development Strategy Review Steering Group 1999, 101)

The document, despite a commitment to social inclusion, seemed for many to reflect the neoliberal vision of the business community as it highlighted the role of entrepreneurs and the private sector. To translate the potential of globalization and peace into real economic growth, it argued, a new economy based on different premises than the old one was required.

> The days of an economy cushioned by public expenditure are over. What we want to spend, we have to earn through our own enterprise and self help. We must take responsibility for our own future. . . .
>
> We need a culture which generates a common commitment to economic success based on inclusive and effective partnership; that honors the entrepreneurs and encourages others to emulate them; that is confident in its own abilities; that ensures that the fruits of economic success are widely and fairly shared throughout society. (Northern Ireland Economic Development Strategy Review Steering Group 1999, 3)

Critics of Strategy 2010 found it lacked a firm commitment to inclusion and equality. The West Belfast Economic Forum, an independent research and advocacy organization, argued that the principles on social cohesion and equality were vague and therefore meaningless and did not address the social economy in deprived areas of Northern Ireland, like West Belfast, which suffered from deep-seated long-term unemployment and received little inward investment benefits. The plan, it stated, failed to account for "economic discrimination, employment differentials and an overall deficit of economic democracy" (West Belfast Economic Forum 2001). Other critics argued that the plan ignored the political dimension of any economic change and the different perceptions held by the two communities. To begin with, the decision whether to interact with the south or maintain the ties with the UK is a political decision based not solely upon economic incentives (Bradley and Hamilton 1999). Furthermore, the massive restructuring the plan advocated was unlikely to be painless, and therefore might reevoke tensions between the communities, an issue that needed to be seriously addressed.

Trade unions complained they were only marginally involved in the production of Strategy 2010.[7] In a meeting held September 6, 2000, of its enterprise, trade, and investment committee, for example, Unison argued that social cohesion must be coherent in both the principles and the recommendations of the plan as there were no recommendations (out of sixty-two in total) covering social cohesion, equality, or social inclusion. The Irish Congress of Trade Unions (ICTU) applauded the goals of Strategy 2010 but claimed that there was a "failure to translate this bold approach into a practical and meaningful program" and asked "why not set targets for the reduction of inequality or low pay?" The response of the ICTU reflected the distance between the business community and the trade unions who were concerned with the "privatization ethos that underpins much of strategy 2010" and, conversely, the "lip service" being paid to social cohesion, equality, and inclusion. Finally, the ICTU warned that cutting down on public services, as the plan called for, in line with the "cul-de-sac slogan that the market place is good and the public sector bad," would have severe effects and intensify inequality and social exclusion (ICTU 2000).

The differences between the business community and the trade unions should not be underestimated but neither should the cooperation that the parties were able to achieve throughout the peace process. The decision made by the business community to approach the political arena through civic society rather than the political parties and, consequently, the cooperation with other active civic society organizations prevented the demands for peace from being associated with interests and demands of the transnational class and endowed it with wider circles of support.

7. See the testimony of Tom Gillen (ICTU) to the House of Commons Select Committee on Northern Ireland Affairs, May 9, 2000.

Spoilers

Globalization created new incentives and encouraged significant sectors of society to mobilize to support peace. But, like elsewhere, globalization has not erased competing identities and dissolved political differences, as those remained significant factors that had to be accounted for in the peace process. While spoiler actions have been mentioned above in the description of the events, it is useful to try to theorize and contextualize their presence and activities. The advancements made in the peace negotiations met with a growing opposition and the empowerment of the more extreme parties in both sides. In the election held in the summer of 1996, two years after the cease-fire and shortly after its collapse, both the DUP and Sinn Fein increased their support. Unionists were reluctant to adopt any resolution that would undermine the status of the province and were suspicious of the developments associated with the EU. Also, they were concerned with the question of political violence and, specifically, with the IRA. Loyalists, who rejected on principal the compromises suggested in the peace process, were able to draw on these concerns and increase their support. Potential economic benefits, therefore, were counterbalanced by security concerns and a lack of trust. Under these terms, with large parts of society cautious about the peace process, extremists from both sides of the divide held the potential to undermine any political achievements.

Extremists from both sides have often used illegal force to achieve political leverage, and republican and loyalist paramilitaries, despite the small number of their active members, have made their mark on the dynamics of the conflict (Fitzduff 2002, 89). The paramilitaries' survival was dependent upon wider cycles of support, often found in the more marginalized areas. Moderate politicians, from both sides of the divide, attempted to persuade the paramilitaries to end their campaigns and enter the democratic process; these persuasions proved significant in securing the cease-fire of 1994 (Fitzduff 2002, 111). After the cease-fire and during the peace process, some of the paramilitary groups did not give up entirely the use of violence. The IRA, frustrated with the delay of Sinn Fein's inclusion in the peace talks, called off the cease-fire in 1996 by exploding bombs in the Canary Wharf in London. After it returned to the talks, splinter groups dissatisfied with what they considered an IRA "sellout" emerged out of the organization and continued the armed struggle.

Loyalist paramilitaries also maintained their stance against the peace process. Shortly after the IRA broke off from the peace process, loyalist paramilitaries began their own campaign of terrorism, motivated not only by the IRA's action but also by the decision of the authorities to reroute some Orange marches from Catholic areas. But the large part of the opposition was done by the civic loyalist organizations. The Orange Order, a loyalist civic organization, greatly increased its activity from the late 1980s. Contrary to any ideas of deterritorialization and loosening of identity issues within an EU or a global context, the Orange Order greatly increased the number and the scope of its parades from the late 1980s onward, and took pride in marching through Catholic residency areas in order to symbolically reclaim territory (Anderson and O'Dowd 1999). Among the Protestant community, in spite of the developments and opportunities described above, a hard-core noncompromising element vehemently opposing any concession of the union maintained its position. Peter D. Robinson, MP for the DUP, described before the agreement the core the party was relying on. "Nationalists know they have the British government on the run. Equally, they know there is a section of the unionist community no longer prepared to fight but who appear to be resigned to defeat . . . Yet, as at every time of crisis in past generations, there is at the heart of unionism a solid, indefatigable and determined spirit to defend Ulster and the Union" (DUP Yearbook 1996).

The hard core of Protestant loyalism was unlikely to support any agreement that would compromise the union. Similarly, hard core republicans were predicted to remain in opposition to any agreement that would fall short of the unification of the island. Politicians were aware of the need to make the agreement attractive to all in order to minimize the influence of the extremists. Back in 1998, prior to the Good Friday Agreement, Gary McMichael of the proagreement UDP argued that the agreement must make a real, material difference in the life of all citizens so it would hold. As an editorial in the *Financial Times* put it, "The average person on the Shankill or Falls Road, in Lisburn or Londonderry or Strabane, must be able to see an improvement in his or her life beyond the absence of violence" (April 17, 1998).

But in the period prior to the agreement, beside the economic progress, improved business confidence, and the relative reduction of violence, paramilitary activity remained a threat to the process. Fractious loyalist parties embarked on a campaign of targeted and random killings of Catholics and splinter republican groups countered by murdering loyalists and placing bombs in predominantly Protestant towns (Farren and Mulvihill 2000, 193). Despite their relatively small numbers, the paramilitaries retained enough mil-

246 • Late Globalization and Deterritorialization

itary capacity to hurt the peace process. The question remained how society at large would react to the actions of spoilers and whether spoilers could set the agenda or would be marginalized.

The Referendum

The involvement of the business community and other parts of civil society in the peace process helped the moderate unionist politicians to remain within the negotiation process even when there were pressures to exit. Businesspeople believed that without their backing, the UUP, and especially David Trimble, who entered the UUP leader position a hard-liner, under pressure from within the party and from the DUP, would have withdrawn from the talks. The counterpressure of the business community and wider popular support for peaceful resolution helped convince Trimble and other unionist politicians that there is a significant constituency favoring compromise and, therefore, that negotiations should continue. The success at delivering their message was another boost to the growing self-confidence of the business class, who with its adaptation to global economic trends felt it could lead society to a better future.

The negotiations were finalized in the Good Friday Agreement, but the public had yet to give its support in the referendum. The Catholic community was largely supportive of the agreement, as it was an answer for many of their desires, but among the Protestant community was a large divergence and discontent over what they saw as a negative change of the status quo. Many unionists were reluctant to have the Irish government involved in the agreement and even more so in a resolution that hinted shared sovereignty. Other divisive issues were the acceptance of Sinn Fein as a partner (due to its relationship with the IRA) and the plan to release prisoners. Overall, there was a general feeling that the union was compromised and, therefore, unionists had to be persuaded to vote yes.

Supporting the Good Friday Agreement again posed the dilemma for the business community of how to support a peace initiative created by the political parties without becoming politically identified. In previous stages of the peace process, the business community maintained its professional position, called on the parties to be attentive of the economic consequences of the conflict, and avoided a discussion of the type of agreement that was to be left to the politicians to draft. The Good Friday Agreement required the business community, if it wanted to influence, to take a position on an agreement that was explicit on the price of peace. The CBI's statement published in the major newspapers prior to the referendum is the best example of the attempt of a major business body to maintain a "professional" opinion about the referendum. The statement followed the pattern developed in the past four years and made an explicit link between the success of the peace process and the economic future of Northern Ireland. "Our mission," it argued, is "to help create and sustain the conditions in which businesses in the United Kingdom can compete and prosper." Accordingly, a vote for the agreement is a vote for economic prosperity: "The CBI believes that a 'YES' vote in the Referendum is a major step toward creating a more favorable and positive environment in which business can grow and flourish and more jobs can be created. It is only industry and commerce that creates the wealth which allows us to support our families, schools, healthcare and environment." The CBI statement, however, carefully avoided saying to the public "vote Yes" explaining instead that the referendum is for individuals, who must make up their own mind based upon their own judgment values. "We hope that every individual will vote in the referendum and we encourage them to do so . . . we have the confidence that the people of Northern Ireland and the politicians they support can help make Northern Ireland a better place in which to live and work" (Confederation of British Industry 1998).

In an op-ed published in the same week, titled "CBI backs Stormont package," Chris Gibson, the CBI chairman, despite the title, repeated the statement almost word by word and again avoided an explicit statement on how to vote (Gibson 1998). The CBI also warned of the economic dangers of a "NO" vote and the failure of the peace process. Bill Tosh, the CBI's vice chairman, said in the *Observer*, "if we say NO, we will pay the price for a lack of agreement and ongoing political instability. My fear is that Gordon Brown [the British exchequer] will just get fed up pouring billions into our economy when we can't even make a political agreement together" (April 14, 1998). Nigel Smith, the director of the CBI, explained that the organization avoided taking part in the ongoing Yes campaign in order not to damage its integrity by telling people how to vote on a political issue (N. Smith 2000). Chris Gibson, the CBI chairman, in an interview given to the author two years later, explained that the statement was a necessary compromise the organization had to make. "While I said Yes personally and worked hard in the Yes campaign as an individual, we had on the council people who wished to say NO. We had to get a collective statement and this, to my judgment, was not a cop-out but a reasonable result" (Gibson 2000).

Other businesspeople maintained a similar stance. *Ulster Business* magazine stated that "it's hardly an appropriate time for business organizations to publicly espouse the virtues or otherwise of Agreement by which so much hinges either way" (May 5, 1998). The pressure increased when the British government through the Northern Ireland Office tried to mobilize the business community for support, and businesspeople, fearing that they would be marked as "government lackeys," attempted to distance themselves from the NIO. Their worries were confirmed when the document with the names of those approached was leaked to the press. "They were calling and asking us to publicly say 'Yes.' When the media got hold of a list of people the NIO put down as influence in the community . . . this whole attempt backfired on them . . . the one thing you don't do with Irishmen is try to dictate to them" (Kingdom 2000).

The business community continued to deliver its "professional" message that peace and prosperity are linked and attempted to circumvent the more sensitive and divisive issues. Business organizations that surveyed their members with questions concerning the level of involvement they should exercise received mixed messages that validated their beliefs over what can and cannot be done.

> We as a business community have always said we need peace and stability but the Good Friday Agreement had other elements in it that might have been against some people's conscience. I personally voted yes but I would not presume telling somebody who lost a relative how they should vote. All we could say as a business community is that in any economic scenario we need peace and stability. I did a survey among the members of the Chambers of Commerce and the message that came back was that they are happy as long as we stay in the economic stance, but there would be a big divergence once we move into the political. (Kingdom 2000)

While the business community, except a few individuals, hesitated to explicitly say "Yes," other parts of civil society took a different approach. The "Yes Campaign" that targeted the unionist community was an initiative taken by civic society, professionals, academics, and some businesspeople who proposed and conducted a nonparty and cross-party campaign. The campaign's priority target was "middle unionism" concentrated in and around Belfast (Oliver 1998). The people of the campaign found the business community, as well as some of the trade unions, less than supportive and were disappointed by their unwillingness neither to align with a "yes" vote nor to financially support the campaign. "The private sector kept its counsel too. Amongst those who had borne much of the economic burden of the troubles, they were also those amongst whom the most benefits would accrue most quickly. The economic case for political stability was overwhelming. We recalled Machiavelli's 1532 observation at this moment: 'only lukewarm support is forthcoming from those who would prosper under the new order' " (Oliver 1998).

The Yes campaign, explicit in its political message, did not make much use of the economic incentives, finding their appeal was limited and possibly even counterproductive. "We did weekly poling to determine what would make unionists vote yes. While they liked the idea of prosperity, stability, growth, etc., they said they would vote on issues of principle, on moral and religious guidance. They made a distinction, politics comes before economics and promises of forthcoming investment seemed like bribery" (Oliver 2000).

The campaign's message was nevertheless representative of its initiators' social standing and world outlook, as international Irish figures like actor and filmmaker Kenneth Branagh and Richard Needham, former economy minister for Northern Ireland, campaigned for the referendum aided by a multinational advertising company, Saatchi and Saatchi. Much of the campaign's funding, and at some stages the majority of the spokespeople, came from outside of Northern Ireland, enough to worry the directors that this could become a major weakness and delegitimize the campaign (Oliver 1998, 62).

If the political message was implicit in the business community's position, the economic was implicit in the "Yes" campaign's message of a "better future," or "Vote Yes, it's the way ahead." At times, the economic message was more explicit. In a 1998 press release by the "Yes" campaign, for example, the future benefits were laid out: "This is Northern Ireland's chance to build a stable, prosperous future . . . if the Good Friday agreement is agreed in the referendum and implemented through the assembly and the North-South bodies there will be huge goodwill towards the province from the British and Irish governments, the EU and the US. All have promised investments if the agreement succeeds."

The "peace dividends" theme driven by the business community was part of the debate, also reflected in the media. On May 18, 1998, the *Daily Telegraph* laid out the alternatives that faced the region. On the one hand, "Clinton and Blair warn voters of a 'nightmare scenario' " if the process fails. And, on the other hand, "They [Clinton and Blair] held out the prospect of a 'good life' backed by international investment if Ulster's people made a leap of faith to support the Good Friday Agreement." Clinton's pledge of a $100 million aid package to help turn the political agreement into lasting peace also received media attention, including a front-page article in the April 11, 1998 issue of the *Belfast Telegraph*. One week before the referendum Britain's chancellor of the exchequer, Gordon Brown, announced a £315 million program for economic development of the province. Although it was not made conditional on accepting the agreement, and was stressed that this had been planned for a long time, Brown was quite explicit on the relation. "Having created a framework for peace," he explained, "We can now create a framework for prosperity" (quoted in McSweeny 1998). On February 24, 1998, the *Belfast Telegraph,* while noting that knowledge of this package should have been available long beforehand and that the package was designed to effect referendum voting, expressed hope that this was a taste of what help might be available from outside sources if the agreement was endorsed. While many remained unconvinced in the coincidence of the plan release, it was generally welcomed. About two and a half months later, on May 13 and 15, the *Irish Times* reported "business delight" at the cash pledge well-planned for addressing the problems of the Irish economy. John Major, in an interview published in the May 12 *Irish Times,* stated his confidence that a vote "Yes" would herald a new future of economic prosperity for the north.

The promise of peace dividends at times backfired and was attacked as bribery, especially the promises coming from Britain and the Northern Ireland Office. Gordon Brown's announcement was seen by some as a dishonest attempt to persuade people to vote "Yes." Added to the leaked NIO list of people within Northern Ireland that could mobilize support for the agreement, it tainted the message of peace and prosperity. The opposition attacked those promises as particularistic interests unlikely to benefit the province. Ian Paisley, in an address to the Chambers of Commerce before the referendum, discarded the prosperity promise and the willingness of the business community to be "bought off."

> The fact is that the future of the Northern Ireland economy will remain the victim of those who bomb, kill and bully but only if you and I are prepared to pay the ransom demanded. Unfortunately there are those—some in this very room—who seem to have thrown in the towel and who are willing to settle for prosperity on terms of those who hold democracy to ransom. . . . Those who waste energy and time on concepts such as the economic corridor are more

interested in political destination than hard-headed economic opportunities. (Paisley 1998)

The referendum result was strong support for the Good Friday Agreement, but with a large Protestant minority voting against it. The desire to end the conflict, the changing context of world politics, and the evolving EU all made it easier to "sell" the agreement. But such support was not inevitable, nor unconditional. In a poll conducted by the NIO in mid-May, just before the referendum, only 30 percent of Protestants were for the agreement, with 38 percent against and 33 percent undecided (Oliver 1998). It seems reasonable to assume, therefore, that the mobilizing of civil society for support and the use of the dividends argument, explicit or implicit, played an important part in the transformation. Two years after the agreement, on the other hand, support was in decline.

Post-Referendum: Peace, Spoilers, and Potential Spoilers

Despite the successful "Yes" campaign and the referendum results, the agreement did not satisfy the demands and desires of many republicans and even more loyalists. The fact that Sinn Fein was a part of the agreement and the new government indicated that republicans gave up on their demand for a united Ireland. But, in practice, the splinter groups of the IRA vowed to continue the struggle, and the IRA itself was reluctant to decommission before substantive progress in the implementation of the agreement be made. Sinn Fein leadership found itself under criticism from its own supporters and challenged by republican extremists. Bernadette Sands-McKevitt, the sister of the hunger-strike hero of the IRA, Bobby Sands, denounced the agreement as a sellout. "Bobby did not die for cross-border bodies with executive powers. He did not die for nationalists to be equal British citizens within the Northern Ireland State" (quoted in Tonge 2002, 180). Sands McKevitt became the leader of the "32 County Sovereignty Committee" that united Sinn Fein members opposed to the agreement. The IRA splinter groups constituted themselves into the Continuity Army Council under which umbrella terrorist attacks and killing continued to take place (Farren and Mulvihill 2000, 197). The Protestant leaders of the UUP were also under severe pressure and criticism from the DUP, but also from within the party, over the agreement and were forced to take a hard stand on the issue of decommissioning. Loyalist paramilitaries also maintained their capabilities to strike violently and to threaten stability.

The continuous use of violence began to backfire upon the paramilitaries, who discovered that society was no longer tolerant of terrorism. In August 1998, the "Real IRA" group detonated a bomb in the city of Omagh that killed twenty-nine civilians, most of them women and children. The response to the attack included an unequivocal condemnation of the act by Sinn Fein that led to a first meeting between Gerry Adams and David Trimble to discuss the issue of violence. The Real IRA declared not long after the attack that it was calling a cease-fire. In July 1998, during the Drumcree crisis and the standoff between the Orange marchers and the police, the Loyalist Volunteer Force, an extremist Protestant paramilitary group, set fire to the house of a Catholic woman who lived in a loyalist district and killed her three sons. After the public reaction, the last Protestant paramilitary groups still defying the peace process declared an end to their campaign (Holland 1999, 296).

While violence was reduced, the agreement was yet to be implemented. The results of the referendum were encouraging to the business community and the larger transnational class as they indicated that Northern Ireland was on the right track. *Businessweek* triumphantly declared that Northern Ireland was normalizing and would soon match other European societies. "Northern Ireland is fast becoming a consumer society like the rest of Europe. Its business leaders have been twisting politicians' arms to end the conflict. And its young people consider the sectarian war an anachronism" (Reed 1998, 52).

In June 1998, shortly after the referendum, U.S. secretary of commerce William Daley came to Northern Ireland with a group of businesspeople from high-profile companies. "These business people came here on a business mission, not a mission of mercy," declared Daley. "When they are deciding where they may invest, they can be convinced that there is no better place to use as a platform for Europe than Ireland" (*Accountancy Ireland*, August 1998). Several months later, in October 1998, leading Northern Irish businesspeople went on a large marketing campaign across eleven North American cities with the message that "there has never been a better time to invest in Northern Ireland." The editor of *Ulster Business* returned from the tour deeply impressed with the global potential for the region, concluding that "never before has a generation in Northern Ireland had the opportunity to so totally determine its economic future" (Baxter 1998, 5).

But, in spite of business enthusiasm, wide parts of society, especially

Protestants, remained suspicious of the future. Only 57 percent of Northern Ireland Protestants voted "Yes" and the large minority that voted "No" was enough for the DUP to claim victory, as it was able to maintain its opposition to the agreement in spite of the external pressures from Britain, the EU, and the United States. The result of the referendum were replicated in the elections held a month afterward: of the fifty-eight unionists elected, thirty were from proagreement parties. Trust had to be built and major issues had yet to be settled. The Protestant community expected a swift decommission of the IRA and the Catholics a reform of the RUC security force. Implementation of the agreement was proven difficult as each side was waiting for the other to make a move and both were reluctant to do so.

A public opinion survey conducted by Irwin in May 2000 found that security is the clear number one priority for the whole community of Northern Ireland.[8] But, another recent survey found that most people when asked about expectations from the new assembly put higher priority on day-to-day issues than on decommissioning (*Northern Ireland Life and Times Survey* February 2000). Overall, the combination of all unfulfilled promises led to a decline in support of the agreement and growing support for the DUP, the leading antiagreement power. A poll conducted by the *Belfast Telegraph* in February 1999 indicated that, despite 60 percent support, there was an 8 percent shift from the Yes camp to the No.

Peace dividends were often mentioned in regards to the peace process, but the economic developments following the referendum did not provide sufficient "cement" to hold the agreement in place. The coalition of business and the other sectors of civil society was based on a balance between economic development and social justice. But, as often quoted by participants, in practice this was a balance difficult to hold. Economic issues were not discussed in detail during the previous period, first, in order not to split the peace coalition, but second, because economic decisions were still made in London. The delegation of authority to a Northern Ireland assembly, as agreed in the Good Friday Agreement, required that these issues be debated and responsibility transferred to the assembly.

---

8. The survey found differences between constituencies. Unionists and SDLP voters gave the highest priority to "commitment to nonviolence" and "paramilitary decommissioning." The Sinn Fein electorate gave high priority to "reform of the RUC," "early release of prisoners," and "Northern Ireland demilitarization" (Irwin 2000).

The rhetoric of peace dividends had to be translated into tangible benefits. Economic indicators since the early 1990s and especially after the cease-fire of 1994 showed continuous economic growth and reduction of unemployment. The IDB economic overview of the Northern Ireland economy shows that Northern Ireland enjoyed the fastest growth among the UK regions. Manufacturing grew by almost 22 percent over five years, investment increased by 66 percent, GDP increased by 11.6 percent between 1990 and 1995 and 6.3 percent between 1996 and 1997. Unemployment fell from 17.2 percent in 1986 to 6.7 percent in 2000. Also, new inward investment projects were secured, offering the prospect of over 2,500 jobs. Major food chains from the UK established themselves; significant hotel developments were nearly completed, as were other major developments. Despite the growth, there are indicators that the effects on the lower classes were insufficient and that the economic developments will offer limited employment opportunities, low paying and insecure, for the socially marginalized. "They may well be restricted between the options of labor market inactivity or the acquisition of futile and low paid jobs in which the socially deprived will merely be required to 'toss the burgers' " (Shirlow and Shuttleworth 1999b).

The forthcoming economic benefits and opportunities, according to Shirlow, were likely to be reaped by the middle—and upper-income groups of Northern Ireland. Those groups possess the skills and training that allow them to integrate in contemporary labor recruitment strategies and enjoy new consumption patterns and investment opportunities. These patterns were also supported by the government's policies. The government, argued Shirlow, "equates job creation with conflict resolution but continues to support conventionalist growth-led strategies of economic renewal which perpetuate the very social marginalization and alienation which they are supposedly intent upon removing" (Shirlow 1997). The industries that historically formed the basis of

Table 8.2 Economic Statistics, 1992–1996

Year (£m)	1992	1993	1994	1995	1996
Gross Domestic Product	11,600	12,434	13,091	13,890	14,470
Consumer Spending	9,373	9,805	10,475	11,222	
Personal Disposable Income	11,081	11,887	12,541	13,236	

Source: *Irish Almanac and Yearbook of Facts 1999* (Dublin: ArtCam Publishing, 1999).

economic well-being, namely textiles and shipbuilding, were likely to continue their decline, especially if Britain stopped protecting them. While blue-collar jobs were expected to be lost, many of the new jobs created were professional, managerial, or administrative positions and expected to be occupied mainly by upper and middle classes of both communities. The overall result was growing insecurity among the working class, especially the Protestants, and growing animosity funneled into sectarian competition, antagonism, and a perception among the socially alienated that, whether there is peace or war, nothing was going to change (Shirlow 1997). The potential marginalization and alienation among the Protestant and Catholic working class, the sections of the community who were most actively engaged in the conflict, threatened to re-create a sectarianized "underclass" (McGovern 1997).

The DUP's continued and increased support indicated that the economic growth has not changed the perceptions of many Protestant constituencies, especially among the working class.

> Peace might be good for the businessmen. But for the ordinary men there has been a massive increase in oil prices, in housing costs . . . It is okay for a businessman who is making more money, but is it filtering down to the ordinary person? The average person will tell you he is making more for petrol, insurance, for his house . . . [On the one hand] there are people who are very principled and support the DUP because of that. They see themselves as British. This is something you can't explain or change. We are British; we can't be bought or bullied. [On the other hand] . . . there are other people who don't think as strongly about their identity, but feel the agreement has not delivered what they were promised. They believed Trimble, they believed the government, they believed the American government and now they are turning to the "No" camp. There is a sea change in Ulster. People say this is not working. (McAlister 2000)

The party's rhetoric took advantage of the combination of economic uncertainties and the ongoing difficulties with decommissioning to convince the public that they had been cheated by the government.

> It was a deceptive package sold by the government. If you lived in Belfast, you have seen that the shipyards were reduced 600 people, that other companies were closing down. We were promised a lot of jobs but they haven't been forthcoming and those that did come would probably come anyway regard-

> less of the agreement . . . some of them, like the call centers, are jobs on a shift system . . . the companies are getting grants but they can leave anytime they want. These are not long-term viable jobs. (McAlister 2000)

It was only a question of time, argued the DUP, until the real nature of the agreement would be revealed to the wide Protestant community.

> Big business paid for the Yes campaign, publishing big ads and full pages in the *Belfast Telegraph* costing three to four thousand pounds. We estimate conservatively that the government and business spent 3 or 4 million pounds on the campaign; we spent around 87 thousand; it was a David and Goliath situation. Ordinary people were deceived into thinking "if these businessmen say so . . . they are running the country, they are smart men, if they are saying that it is good, maybe it is good." But if this agreement was good and there was peace in the streets, we wouldn't have won the South Antrim by-election and we wouldn't have the majority of unionists in this house and people in the street would be deserting us. But on all those the reverse is true. (McAlister 2000)

"Peace dividends" were supposedly the cure to the economic and social ailments of Northern Ireland, but some of the forecasts seem to be overly optimistic. For example, the prediction of 58,000 new jobs was based upon the generosity of Britain and the EU, continuing to funnel the subventions and the European funds into Northern Ireland (Gudgin 1995b). Paradoxically, however, if the conflict subsided, there was little reason to suppose that the money would continue coming. Britain has its own economic priorities and potential new members to the EU from Eastern Europe might attract more attention and funds. Hopes were raised, especially by the SDLP, that there was a possibility that the EU involvement in the region would grow and that delegation of some authority to the EU would solve issues of territorial identities in Northern Ireland. Not only was this scenario highly unrealistic because of unionist opposition, but also the money that the EU transfers to the region is approximately £200 million, compared to the £3.7 billion the British exchequer transfers, and it was unlikely that the EU could fill this gap (Teague 1996).

The peace process fueled high hopes, which, in the short run, became self-fulfilling prophecies and translated into impressive growth. Yet all these, as several political economists noted, could be temporary effects. Once peace becomes permanent, the early enthusiasm that fueled economic growth will subside and Northern Ireland will have to contend with serious structural problems. "Northern Ireland would lose its novelty value for tourists, inward investors would begin looking elsewhere; the wallets of European and American would close; and slowly but inexorably the fundamental economic weakness would peep out. The brutal reality is that, under peaceful conditions, Northern Ireland becomes just another part of the European periphery, with no particular reason to perform better than anywhere else" (Bew, Patterson, and Teague 1997, 118). With the reduction of the subventions and the resolution of the conflict, job losses were also expected. The security services, for example, were expected to be reduced in size and to cease being almost exclusively Protestant. Similarly, the relatively large public sector, funded by British subventions, will be reduced, especially in the event that the neoliberal, small government agenda remains in the lead. Also, the declining industries that, for political reasons, were spared adjustment to competition now will be subjected to market dynamics. The quality of the new jobs created might not match that of jobs lost. Bew and Patterson described the change as a "move from joblessness to penniless" (109). Many of the new jobs created during the 1990s were part-time or low-grade jobs and a part of a new form of labor market, deregulated and flexible (109). Inward investment was unlikely to benefit the poorest members of society or bring good quality work to disadvantageous areas (Shirlow and Shuttleworth 1999a). Rather, it would increase social exclusion since the "unemployed tend not to gain these jobs and the track record of the economy has been such that the 'haves' tend to gain at the expense of the 'have nots' " (Shirlow and Shuttleworth 1999b).

Violence has been significantly reduced since the Good Friday Agreement but political and economic uncertainties remain. A survey of Northern Ireland's economy in September 1999 concluded that despite overall positive economic prospects, the region is unlikely to fulfill its economic potential in an environment of continuing political uncertainty (Bonner, Elliott, and Rea 1999). Another survey of 300 local companies conducted between February and May of 2000 indicated that firms were reducing their planned investments because of the suspension of the Northern Ireland assembly (O'Gorman and Harding 2000). The February 11, 2000, issue of the *Wall Street Journal* reported on the concerns of businesspeople and the danger that the period of unprecedented foreign and domestic investment will end if the peace process does not get back on track. The business community issued statements that expressed their concern with the political environment. In a press release on March 9, 2000, Mark Ennis, the CBI chairman, stated, "All the obligations under the Good Friday Agreement must be met, including decommissioning. Every effort must be made by all stakeholders in Northern Ireland to help find a resolution to the current impasse." According to the *Financial Times* of June 26, 1999, the G7 also declared that "the present uncertainty is conducive to instability and is highly detrimental to Northern Ireland's economic prospects" The parties, however, remained trapped in the debate and, in spite of some progress, unable to implement fully the agreement.

Conclusion

The external changes associated with globalization and the development of new forces within Northern Ireland created new opportunities to resolve a conflict previously considered intractable. A growing transnational class, and especially the business community, has realized that economic development and global integration require a resolution of the conflict and, that it could mobilize to promote peaceful resolution. As in Israel, the business community has exercised its "voice" rather than its "exit" option and used its professional status to promote political change from within. Unlike the Israeli business class, however, Northern Irish businesspeople had little or no relations with local politicians and the business community chose to maintain its distance from politics and remain "professional" even when it mobilized to promote peace. The business community's distance from politics limited its influence (as demonstrated by the position taken during the 'Yes' campaign), but, inadvertently and possibly aided by its cooperation with civic society groups, business did help the peace camp maintain its universal image.

The economic incentives associated with globalization combined with a favorable regional setting and domestic changes to enable the negotiations and the peace agreement. The decision of Britain and the Irish Republic to cooperate to foster an agreement in Northern Ireland, the involvement of the U.S. government, and the encouragement of the EU, combined to positively influence the negotiations among the parties. The Good Friday Agreement, within the context of the European Union, was able to meet the demands of both sides regarding citizenship and sovereignty. Nevertheless, even though violence was significantly reduced, political and economic uncertainties remain significant for the future of the peace process, as the events that followed the 1998 referendum demonstrate. The continuing difficulties of decommissioning, Orange marches, sectarian violence, the need for police reforms, and the continuing existance of a large Protestant minority opposed to the peace process and suspicious of Catholic intentions have created several crises, temporarily stalling implementation of the agreement more than once. The suspension of the institutions of self-rule and the empowerment of Sinn Fein and the DUP after 1998 at the expense of, respectively, the SDLP and the UUP are indications of the difficulties that still lie ahead.

9

Conclusion

Trajectories of Peace and Conflict

VISIONS OF PEACE IN ISRAEL and Northern Ireland, emerging in the early 1990s and the following peace agreements, seemed to lend support to the arguments that globalization creates new opportunities to transform seemingly intractable conflicts. The peace processes in Northern Ireland and Israel shared a common vision, associating conflict resolution with global integration, but differed profoundly in their structures, dynamics, and outcomes. Both conflicts were influenced by globalization processes, yet in different ways. While macro, world-systemic, and global developments created opportunities, incentives, and constraints for conflict resolution, it was the interaction with micro, local preferences, social structures, and choices that set in motion the actual dynamics of the peace processes and, eventually, determined their outcomes.

The purpose of this work has been to elucidate the micro-macro relations of globalization to the two conflicts in order to explain their trajectories. The theoretical framework established in chapter 1 set out a threefold comparison: first, between two periods of globalization, one at the turn of the nineteenth and other at the turn of the twentieth century; second, between the two conflicts, which are different but also share enough characteristics to justify comparison; and third, between the influences of the two periods of globalization on each conflict, providing a comparison across time of the development of the conflict from its crystallization along ethnic lines and national agendas to the unfolding of its deterritorialization and reterritorialization.

Globalization One—Territorialization

In both periods of globalization discussed in this work, a systemic hegemonic crisis occurred: the decline of the British laissez-faire system at the end of the nineteenth century and the decline of American embedded liberalism at the end of the twentieth century. Britain and the United States developed the capacity to lead the system in the direction of new forms of interstate cooperation and division of labor, and to provide system-level solutions to system-level problems. These capacities enabled them to credibly claim that they represented a general interest and, henceforth, establish their hegemony. The hegemonic world orders provided relative political and economic stability but eventually were challenged by intensified competition that was beyond the regulatory capacities of the system. Globalization, the decline of these established world orders, entailed a change of territorial perspectives and new sets of constraints and opportunities for states and nonstate actors (Arrighi and Silver 1999, 28–30).

The decline of the Pax Britannica was characterized by fierce competition among European powers that challenged British hegemony. Free trade was replaced by protective tariffs and exclusive control of territories, and the balance of power system, formerly operating to prevent major wars, was replaced by alliances whose purpose was to win in the event of war. Britain's unilateral insistence on free trade was an attempt to reflate its power by turning itself into a financial center. Until the outbreak of the World War I, the strategy enabled global flows and international organizations to coexist with intense interstate competition. Three important macro or systemic changes arising from the decline of Britain's hegemony had important implications for our two case studies. First, the period was marked by a growing popular sense of national identity based upon exclusiveness and the identification of a nation with a "homeland" territory. Second, world affairs were perceived to be a competition among states over territories and resources, entailing cooperation between a state and its business elite against their competitors for the acquisition of new territories. And third, this competition reinforced the perception of the world beyond Europe as a legitimate field for European nations to expand into.

It was during this period that Jewish and Irish nationalism crystallized and developed their territorial agendas. Influenced by the changed atmosphere these emerging national movements sought to take advantage of new perceived opportunities. Although both movements started from a minority position among the people they claimed to represent, they grew continuously, expanding their influence and power by relying on, among other things, support from their diaspora communities. Globalization spelled not only incentives and opportunities but also constraints not only in the form of major powers but also in the form of competing territorial claims and rival national movements.

The development of exclusionary nationalism in Europe undermined the position of Jews, particularly in Eastern Europe, and forced them to seek alternatives for their marginalized—but until then relatively stable—status. The majority of Jews who made changes chose to become part of the wide migration of the period to America, but a minority, influenced by the nationalist zeitgeist, chose a territorial solution that, they claimed, would make Jews a nation like all nations. Zionists attempted to take advantage of the developments in Europe, first, by a diplomatic effort among European powers to receive a charter for settlement and, second, by land acquisition that would make their settlement in Palestine a fact.

The Irish national movement was likewise a product of the zeitgeist, during which it crystallized along clearly defined ethnic-religious lines and achieved the required momentum to make its territorial claims. Unlike the Jews, the Irish lived on the land they claimed, but they sought to overthrow what they considered foreign rule. Britain's shift to formal imperialism highlighted another difference between the two movements. Formal imperialism created an opportunity for Zionism to try to become a part of Britain's expansion and exploit its interest in the Middle East. Conversely, the Irish were largely a victim of Britain's domino theory, which all but ruled out compromise over the status of the island.

As these Jewish and Irish national movements developed and established territorial demands, they encountered opposition from, respectively, an indigenous Palestinian population and a powerful Protestant minority backed by Britain. In both cases, the struggles for exclusive territoriality turned into zero-sum games in which each party attempted to establish sovereignty and prevent its rival from establishing any competing claims. Partition, in Palestine and Ireland, was a solution that represented the spirit of the times by aiming to create nationally homogeneous territories, but in the event it created problematic entities rather than long-term and stable solutions. The partitions also "turned around" the analogies: if in the previous period Jewish and Irish national movements seemed to share some characteristics, in the later period the Jewish majority of Israel had become comparable to the Protestant majority in Northern Ireland.

Both Israel and Northern Ireland shared the problem of a large ethnic minority who saw the borders as arbitrarily and unjustly drawn and the entities in which they were trapped as illegitimate. Palestinians and Catholics perceived the new entities as depriving them of the possibility of belonging to a more favorable political entity, instead confining them to one in which they were treated unfairly by the majority. In Northern Ireland, when the Catholic minority became frustrated with its ability to achieve equality, the region descended into a violent ethnic conflict. Until 1967, through various measures of coercion and co-optation, Israel managed to avoid an internal ethnic conflict between Jewish and Palestinian citizens. The densely occupied territories unofficially annexed to Israel after the 1967 war, with Palestinian populations not granted citizen status, soon brought Israel and the Palestinians to a direct conflict.

Globalization Two—Deterritorialization

As long as the Protestant and the Jewish majorities, as well as their political and economic elites, continued to adhere to the traditional concept of territoriality and ascribed a high value to territory, both conflicts seemed intractable. For an overwhelming majority of Jewish Israelis and Northern Irish ("Ulster") Protestants, the struggles in which they were enmeshed seemed beyond their control, an imposed reality they had to accept. Their determination and resilience were derived from the perception of being societies under siege, a situation in which questions of security and collective values overrode economic considerations and individualistic values. But at the turn of the twentieth century, macro, world-systemic changes created new incentives and opportunities that seemed to alter the rigidity of the conflicts and introduce new interests and ideas.

These changes were related, first and foremost, to a globalization associated with the demise of American embedded liberalism that introduced new conceptions of space, territory, and sovereignty. The American hegemony, formed after World War II, had "laid new tracks" for the world system, significantly different from the Pax Britannica. American embedded liberalism sought to strike a middle way between free markets and stable political entities, departing from British laissez faire in favor of domestic stability and subjecting free trade to the objectives of the cold war. The modern state became the principal type of political rule, supported by international financial and military institutions. The decline of this world order, like the decline of the previous one, was the result of the hegemonic power being emulated by other states and of the growing competition from state and nonstate actors that undermined the capacity of the United States to lead the system. This hegemonic crisis—the advent of globalization—differed significantly from the crisis that eroded the

Pax Britannica. First, the decline of the hegemonic order of embedded liberalism did not entirely overlap with the declining power of the United States; its
military supremacy has hardly been challenged. Second, unlike the previous
period when capitalists and states converged on territorial expansion and formal imperialism, the rise of contemporary globalization has caused a divergence, with an empowered capitalist class seeking to forge more flexible
relations with the state. And third, the breakdown of embedded liberalism has
not led to a closure of borders to trade but to an accelerated liberalism and, in
some respects, to a decline in the importance of territoriality.

The deterritorialization of politics arising from globalization, discussed in
chapter 5, implied a new set of constraints and opportunities that underscored
the new trajectories of the two conflicts. Embedded liberalism established regulations and control over flows of capital that could undermine domestic
stability. Its rupture—a process of deregulation and disembedding of markets—changed the shape of politics and created new incentives for those seeking to break away from fixed territorial structures and explore opportunities
beyond them. This transnational class, whose interests and affiliations transcend state boundaries, has the assets, skills, and capital to reap the available
benefits, as well as the political leverage to help facilitate the changes. Thus, on
the one hand, it contributed to the erosion of the world order by influencing
states to liberalize, deregulate their economies, and open borders to international flows, and on the other hand, it was positioned to be the greatest
beneficiary of the erosion. The disembedding of markets and the rise of nonterritorial forms of power (multinational firms, offshore economic spaces, and
macroregional blocs), all beyond the direct control of the state, have introduced a new geography, culminating in what has been described as an "unbundling of territoriality" (Ruggie 1993) or deterritorialization.

The optimistic liberal scenario of globalization was quickly adopted by
Israel's business and political elites, who perceived the opportunities it created to
lead the way toward peace and economic growth. These elites shared the desire to
integrate globally and reap the potential economic and other benefits available;
they also shared the frustration of being trapped in a conflict that prevented this
successful integration. Accordingly, these groups sought to create an environment conducive to economic development that included economic liberalization, globalization, and peace. Similar hopes and expectations also developed in
Northern Ireland, though they were less explicitly pronounced.

The initial developments of the peace processes in Israel and Northern Ireland seemed to confirm the optimistic economic and political expectations of the business community and the planners of the peace. Israel, in the early 1990s and especially since the Madrid conference, enjoyed positive business confidence and economic growth. Likewise in Northern Ireland the cease-fire announced in 1994 led to growing business confidence and prospects for foreign investment. The signing of the agreements, between Israel and the Palestinians in 1993 and in Northern Ireland in 1998, created waves of euphoria as promises of a bright future, made by local and foreign businesspeople and politicians, captured the news media's attention. Yet in both cases the agreements proved to be the starting rather than the end point; wider support for the processes and the compromises involved was still lacking. To the business and political elites associated with the transnational class, territorial compromise seemed the logical path to follow. Other parts of society still needed to be convinced.

Globalization and Discontent—Reterritorialization

Deterritorialization is only a part of the picture of global politics at the turn of the twenty-first century. The transnational class operating across the globe to disembed the economy and deterritorialize the state has so far fallen short of a hegemony capable of creating a stable and legitimate world order. Deterritorialization, therefore, has been matched by growing discontent and, consequently, reterritorialization. For those threatened by globalization's course of events—those who lack the skills, the mobility, or the desire to integrate globally—territory and the nation-state have become ever more important. Their discontent is manifested in rising ethnic tensions, xenophobic nationalism, and a reassertion of territoriality. As a result, globalization had been unfolding not as a linear process that erases local identities and renders territorial conflict obsolete but rather as a disjunctured process and a double movement in which projects of deterritorialization and reterritorialization are carried out by different groups for different ends and often clash with one another.

Globalization raises new opportunities for the management and/or resolution of conflicts but also breeds new tensions and challenges encapsulated in the double movement described by Polanyi. While new incentives can help set in motion a peace process, its actual outcome is determined by specific global-local interactions: macro changes associated with globalization on the one hand, and on the other, local politics, institutions, historical path dependencies, and strategies pursued by political agents. Specifically, the success of entrepreneurs promoting their agenda of peace depends on their ability not only to reach agreement with former enemies but also to maintain sufficient support from within. For the process to win legitimacy, the incentives associated with globalization and the dividends of peace (economic and other) must be perceived as universally beneficial. The ending of violence is a necessary step toward peace but the creation of institutions and support structures strong enough to discourage the parties from taking up arms again is necessary for its survival. Globalization, therefore, provided a new context and new incentives for the resolution of ongoing conflicts in Israel and Northern Ireland. As described in chapters 6 and 7, these opportunities were taken by political and economic elites in Israel and Northern Ireland who were part of, or becoming part of, the transnational class and consequently were influenced by the deterritorializing trends outlined above.

The double movement of globalization, in which liberalization and deterritoralization is countered by a defensive reaction, encapsulates the inherent tensions of the peace processes. Optimistic scenarios for peace based on global integration and economic growth rest on two problematic tenets: first, that globalization and peace are universally desirable and, second, that their dividends are universally available. These assumptions ignore the possibility that fundamentalist groups may act as "spoilers," ready to derail a peace process if compromises seem extreme to them. They also ignore the likelihood that globalization's dividends will benefit some groups but marginalize others. In other words, although global incentives for peace can create the initial momentum for resolution, the darker side of globalization may provoke opposition to both globalization and peace.

Initially, both regions seemed to follow a similar course, in which steps toward reconciliation and economic development based on global integration cross-fertilized each other and created an expanding virtuous cycle. After the initial euphoria, however, it became obvious in both cases that peace was yet to be achieved. To begin with, Ulster loyalists were not impressed with the scenario of an Ireland within a federal "Europe of the regions"; likewise, Jewish settlers were not convinced by visions of a "New Middle East." Moreover, other sectors less ideologically committed to the conflict also remained skeptical. The peace dividends were intended to capture the latter groups: constituencies not part of the peace camp but that might be persuaded to support the process if convinced that peace would bring a better future for them and their children. Consequently, the influence of globalization and peace dividends depended on their availability not only to the elites geared to take advantage of new opportunities but also to wider sectors of society.

The new incentives associated with globalization provided an important starting point for the negotiations between Israelis and Palestinians in Israel and between Catholics and Protestants in Northern Ireland. But both agreements reached were vague on various contentious issues, issues that had been left for later stages of the process, and were therefore vulnerable to threats of derailment by opposition. Both peace processes faced not only spoilers determined to prevent compromise but also wide sectors of society who were skeptical and suspicious both of the other side and of the intentions of their own leaders and elites. Accordingly, the peace processes encountered obstacles, uncertainties, setbacks, and discontent. As the two processes unfolded, however, it became clear that globalization created different sets of opportunities and constraints in each that translated into different trajectories and outcomes.

Global and Local—Different Trajectories

The peace processes in Northern Ireland and Israel shared a common vision that associated conflict resolution with global integration, but they took very different routes toward peace. The Good Friday Agreement in Northern Ireland was based on a complex power-sharing model between Protestants and Catholics intended to give each group an opportunity to express its national identity and at the same time to build joint institutions for self-rule. Unlike this agreement, which defined success in terms of coexistence the peace process between Israel and the Palestinians, despite the vision of the globalized "New Middle East," was based on a partition that would lead to the formation of two separate states. Power-sharing agreements foster cooperation and thus have a greater transformative potential then partition agreements, which can easily turn into zero-sum negotiations that replicate the conflict. Power-sharing and partition are not necessarily à la carte choices available to leaders. Rather, the choice is shaped by histories, political economy, third parties and other factors beyond leader's control (Ben-Porat, 2005).

Northern Ireland's regional setting and internal structure have made partition unlikely and power-sharing possible. The Good Friday Agreement, within the context of the European Union, was able to provide each side to the conflict with a potentially satisfactory formula for citizenship and sovereignty. For the Protestants, the agreement provided legitimacy for the existence of

Northern Ireland and hope for an end to the violence, economic regeneration, and an improved quality of life. For Catholics, it provided a chance for the ending of structural inequality, stronger links with the Republic of Ireland, and a greater respect for their culture. But even though this formula was enough to allow the drafting, signing, and approval of an agreement through a referendum, actual implementation has proven difficult. Questions regarding the decommissioning of arms and police reforms, combined with lingering opposition to compromises, present a continuous challenge to policymakers involved in implementation. The agreement has likewise failed to change the sectarian nature of politics and society in Northern Ireland, as the limited success achieved by parties outside the ethno-national blocs and the lack of swing voting between the two blocs attest.

The balance sheet for the Good Friday Agreement is, therefore, mixed. On the one hand, it has achieved significant steps toward reconciliation; on the other, unresolved issues still threaten to derail the peace process. The difficulties in the agreement were reflected in the continuous difficulties encountered by the elected assembly. In October 2002, the political difficulties seemed so great that the institutions of self-rule were suspended indefinitely and direct rule from Westminster was restored. The political difficulties were matched by public perceptions, as the Catholic Sinn Fein and the Protestant DUP increased their shares of the vote at the expense of the more moderate parties. In July 2005 an important breakthrough seemed to occur when the IRA declared an end to its armed campaign and called on its volunteers to dispose of their arms. By September 2005, however, sectarian violence was on the rise again when the traditional Orange marches raised Loyalists' frustration after they were forbidden to march through Catholic neighborhoods. Then, in October, the IRA declaration was confirmed when the Independent International Commission on Decommissioning announced that the IRA had put all its weapons beyond use, in accordance with its statement in July. Despite the optimism after decommissioning was achieved, however, uncertainties remain about the IRA's intentions. Overall, the agreement's ability to accommodate, even if temporarily, the territorial demands of the parties and to initiate cooperation, drawing on global and regional resources, has succeeded in curbing violence and establishing dialogue.

The Israeli-Palestinian peace process, unlike Northern Ireland's, was essentially an attempt to create two separate entities by partition. Regional and cross-border cooperation were discussed and attempted, but they suffered from the lack of a supportive regional framework and the deep structural inequalities between Israelis and Palestinians. Under these terms, cooperation became dependent on and secondary to, partition. Partition seemed to be the logical solution, answering both Israel's desire to maintain its Jewish status and the Palestinian demands for independence. Three significant obstacles challenged the possibility of partition, however. First, since the 1970s Israel had built a system of settlements across the West Bank and Gaza, so that by 1993 more than one hundred thousand Israelis were living on the land of what was supposed to be a Palestinian state. Second, Palestinians who fled or were deported from Israel in the 1948 war were demanding, for themselves and their progeny, "the right of return" from the refugee camps and other places of habitation to their original homes. And, third, both sides were laying uncompromising national and religious claims to the city of Jerusalem.

The deferral of contentious issues such as future borders, settlements, Jerusalem, and the refugees to a later stage of negotiations, possibly in hope of more confidence building, proved a failure. With limited cooperative measures, the peace process between Israel and the Palestinians has gradually narrowed its focus to partition and developed a zero-sum dynamic of territoriality that neither approaches transformation nor brings the sides any closer to agreement on the issues not subject to partition. As a result of these obstacles, the peace process has turned into a zero-sum dynamic, which replicated the conflict as each side has attempted to secure maximum territorial gains. Policymakers, who were under pressure from domestic opposition that delegitimized territorial concessions, found it more and more difficult to compromise, so a comprehensive agreement was perceived to be impossible. The core of the peace processes became a series of interim agreements based on Israeli redeployments, the extent of which has been a constant source of tension because of Palestinian demands for sovereignty and Israeli demands for security. The zero-sum dynamic, limited trust, and the remaining distance between Israelis and Palestinians left the process exposed to spoiler actions.

The violent collapse of the Camp David negotiations in 2000 was a direct result of the previous seven years of negotiations as the attempt to resolve all issues at once was a colossal failure. The continuing reality of, from the Palestinian perspective, checkpoints, economic instability, and expansion of settlements, and from the Israeli perspective, anti-Israeli propaganda, terrorism, and lack of action against Palestinian fundamentalists groups has left both publics skeptical of the other's commitment to peace; this skepticism has, consequently, limited the leaders' ability to make peace.

The violence that followed the Camp David talks led Israeli policymakers to adopt unilateral measures. In the summer of 2002 the Likud government, headed by Ariel Sharon, decided to the construct a separation fence between Israel and the Palestinian territories. The growing numbers of Israeli casualties from suicide bombers infiltrating Israel from the West Bank and the growing public pressure for security caused the Likud government to support the construction of a fence it had previously opposed. This unilateral measure received no support from the Palestinians, who claimed that the fence encroached on their territories. Palestinian demands received international support, including from the International Court of Justice, which ruled against the fence. Domestic and international pressure caused Israel to modify the fence's route, but the project continued. Israel's disengagement from Gaza was a continuation of this unilateral strategy and an attempt to reduce friction points between Israelis and Palestinians. Israel's execution of the plan in summer 2005 was hailed by the world but left Palestinians frustrated as Israel indicated it will unilaterally determine future and final boundaries. The limited cooperation between the sides during the engagement was short lived as it was followed by another cycle of suicide terrorism and mortar attacks on the one hand, and on the other, targeted killings and closures.

Between Relative Success and Obvious Failure

What obviously differentiates the two peace processes was the higher level of violence impeding the Israeli-Palestinian peace process and the important role played by religious fundamentalist spoilers in its derailment. The ability of spoilers to derail the Israeli-Palestinian peace process and the relative stability of the Northern Ireland peace, however, is less an explanation for the collapse of former than an outcome of the structural differences between the two processes and the different global-local interactions affecting them. Several important differences between the two peace processes have been described in this work. First, Northern Ireland held significant regional advantages relative to those of Israel/Palestine. Regional institutions can play a vital role in peace processes if they can create incentives for peace, offer nonterritorial alternatives, or even moderate the adverse effects of globalization. The development of the EU had a significant impact on the dynamics of the conflict in Northern Ireland by providing both economic incentives and a "safety net" of a European citizenship, eventually making it easier to "sell" the peace agreement. Unlike the emerging reality of European Union, however, the "New Middle East" was at most a vision for the future dependent upon the development of the peace process. Not only did regional developments provide limited support for the Israeli-Palestinian peace process, they were largely dependent on the advancement of the peace process for their own existence. The wide gaps between the Israeli and Arab economies created fears among the latter that Israel would use its economic power to dominate the region and limit the opportunities for equal cooperation.

A second important factor that explains the different trajectories is the greater difficulties experienced by the Israeli propeace coalition in appealing to major constituencies in the geographical and political periphery. In both Israel and Northern Ireland, the combination of peace and globalization appealed to the business and other elites who perceived themselves capable of taking advantage of the new opportunities. Turning this vision into a political reality, however, required the mobilization of a wider coalition by convincing others of its universal advantages. In Israel, the peace process was largely identified with the elites and, as such, left significant constituencies alienated or hostile to the developments. In Northern Ireland, it is still to be assessed whether the promise of "social inclusion" delivered during the peace process was anything more than rhetoric, but, nevertheless, unlike in Israel, there were no indications in Northern Ireland of significant class differences in support/opposition to the process. The lack of wide support in Israel was not only a question of image and perception but also of "real" unequal distribution of dividends. While in Israel economic growth was accompanied by growing disparities between center and periphery, among Palestinians peace dividends were practically nonexistent. Peace dividends, therefore, offered limited inducements to participate in the process, leaving large segments of society indifferent or hostile to it, and consequently making the process vulnerable to the actions of spoilers.

Third, the influence of the business community and the transnational class on the peace process is also significant. Neither in Northern Ireland nor in Israel has this class achieved hegemony but, paradoxically, it seems that the relative political power of the Israeli business community has backfired. With its direct channels to the political elite, the Israeli business community felt no need to cooperate with other sectors of civic society or compromise over economic issues. This approach and the dual agenda of the transnational class—peace and economic liberalization—contributed to the perception among wide sectors of society that peace was an elite interest and possibly alienated potential supporters of peace. The limits of the business-political nexus and of the legitimacy of the peace process were revealed in the 1996 elections, when the Labor Party was ousted. Conversely, the relatively weak Northern Irish business community had to search for partners in order to make its mark on the process. Its partnership with civic society required compromises, even if temporary, on other issues, such as economic policy. These compromises have paid off in the wider support the peace process engendered across society and in an avoidance of an association of peace with the limited interests of the elites.

Fourth, while the building of wide coalitions described above determines the support for peace within the community, the structure of the peace agreement determines the level of interaction and reconciliation between the parties as well as the distribution of the dividends. Essentially, while incentives were somewhat similar, the two peace process and the agreements that followed were aimed toward very different goals. The peace process in Northern Ireland attempted to redefine issues of sovereignty and democracy in a way that would allow Protestants and Catholics to live together and maintain their identities. The Good Friday Agreement embedded the governance of Northern Ireland in an array of regional, national, and transnational institutions that created many spaces for interactions, debate, and cooperation between Catholics and Protestants that created the potential of future reconciliation. Whereas in Northern Ireland since the 1970s, Catholics and Protestants have been, despite the gaps and inequalities, encountering one another more and more as equals or partners in work or civic organizations, in Israel such engagements between Israelis and Palestinians have been rare. The encounters between Israelis and Palestinians, who since 1967 have been under Israeli occupation, typically have been between soldiers and civilians or between employers and low-wage workers. The peace process has not significantly changed these relations. Moreover, given the wide economic gaps between the underdeveloped West Bank and Gaza and the booming Israeli economy, opportunities for cooperation as equals have been limited. Encounters on environmental and other issues, either in bilateral or multilateral settings, have involved mainly government officials and professionals. Overall, therefore, Israelis and Palestinians remained distant from each other, if not hostile.

Globalization, Peace and Discontent

Can any practical, policy-making conclusions be drawn from all the above? Northern Ireland, despite the continuing difficulties in implementing its peace agreement, seems generally better positioned to capitalize on the new opportunities associated with globalization. Factors like geographical regional advantages, economic conditions, and histories are often beyond the influence of policy makers, who operate within limits imposed upon them. Yet the choices made by policy makers within these limitations remain significant. During the last decade Israeli policies shifted between two equally untenable shortcuts: a new Middle East based on market principles and partition (unilateral or by agreement) based on a demographic logic. The failure of liberal economics to provide a path out of a protracted conflict was described in detail in this book. Not only are some issues and constituencies not susceptible to economic incentives and some conflicts incapable of reduction to economic gains, but the inherently unequal nature of liberal economics is likely to create significant disincentives. Partitions carry a promise of finality but rarely deliver on that promise, since the division of territory involves issues of identity and security and often entails difficult decisions. Territorial compromises require creative solutions and trust, and consequently entail cooperation between the parties and the creation of mutual interests, elements the zero-sum dynamics of partition do not foster.

To become a reality, a legitimate and stable peace between Israel and the Palestinians would have to be based on social inclusion within and between parties for significant cooperation to become a reality. The promise of economic growth created some momentum in the early, euphoric stages of peace, especially in Israel, but it failed to carry the process forward. Among Israelis, a new propeace coalition would have to encompass measures of social inclusion and create an economically viable alternative that would distribute peace dividends throughout the wider public, including its peripheries. Only the combination of peace and social equality could dissociate peace from its current elite interest image. Given the wide gaps between Israelis and Palestinians, it is even less likely that markets would create cooperation on equal levels that could help transform the conflict. Rather than being spontaneous and based solely on market rationality, therefore, cooperation and common interests would have to be carefully planned and initiated at both elite and grassroots levels and supported by governments and civic society organizations. Finally, while it is unlikely that in the near future a formula similar to the Northern Ireland peace could be implemented between Israel and the Palestinians, neither should Israelis and Palestinians rely on magic formulas of partition that would permanently separate them from each other. Regardless of global incentives and local partition peace plans, Israelis and Palestinians would have to find ways to cooperate and share the resources available. If any lesson can be culled from the past decade, it is that there are no real shortcuts to peace.

REFERENCES
INDEX

References

Newspapers

Accountancy Ireland
Belfast Telegraph
Business Telegraph
Businessweek
Daily Telegraph
Financial Times
Haaretz
Independent
International Trade Finance
Irish News
Irish Times
Maariv
Newsletter
Observer
Ulster Business
Wall Street Journal
Yediot Achronot

Books, Articles, and Interviews

Agnew, John. 1989. "Beyond Reason: Spatial and Temporal Sources of Ethnic Conflicts." In *Intractable Conflicts and Their Transformation,* ed. Louis Kriesberg, Terrell A. Northrup, and Stuart J. Thorson. Syracuse: Syracuse Univ. Press.

————. 1995. *Mastering Apace: Hegemony, Territory, and International Political Economy.* New York: Routledge.

Ahad Ha'am. 1931. "Emet Me-Eretz Israel" (Truth from the Land of Israel) [in Hebrew]. In *Al Parashat Derachim* (On a Crossroad). Berlin: Perlag.

278 • References

Aharoni, Yair. 1998. "The Changing Political Economy of Israel." *Annals of the American Political and Social Science* 5, no. 555 (January): 127–46.

Aharonson, Ran. 1999. "The First Aliyah Settlement: Colonialism or Colonization?" [in Hebrew]. In *One Land, Two Peoples,* ed. Dany Jacoby. Jerusalem: Yad Ben-Zvi.

Akenson, Donald H. 1992. *God's People: Covenant and Land in South Africa, Israel, and Ulster.* Ithaca, N.Y.: Cornell Univ. Press.

Amery, Julian. 1951. *The Life of Joseph Chamberlain.* Vol. 4, *1901–1903.* London: Macmillan.

Anderson, James. 1993. "A United Irish Economy: Economic and Political Aspects of Economic Integration." *Regional Studies Series, European Society for Irish Studies* 1, no. 2.

———. 1998. "Integrating Europe, Integrating Ireland." In *Dis/Agreeing Ireland,* ed. James Anderson and James Goodman. London: Pluto Press.

Anderson, James, and James Goodman. 1997. "Problems of North-South Economic Integration and Politics in Ireland: Southern Perspectives." *Irish Journal of Sociology* 7:29–53.

———, eds. 1998. *Dis/Agreeing Ireland.* London: Pluto Press.

Anderson, James, and Liam O'Dowd. 1999. "Contested Borders: Globalization and Ethno-National Conflict in Ireland." *Regional Studies* 33, no. 7:593–604.

Anderson, James, and Ian Shuttleworth. 1992. "Currency of Co-operation." *Fortnight,* no. 311 (November): 18–20.

———. 1993. "Bordering on the Difficult." *Fortnight,* no. 313 (Janauary): 26–27.

———. 1998. "Social Change and Conflict Resolution in Northern Ireland." *Political Geography* 17, no. 2:187–208.

Angell, Norman. 1911. *The Great Illusion.* London: William Heinemann.

Anonymous 1. 2000. Interviewed by Guy Ben Porat. Belfast.

Anonymous 2. 2000. Interviewed by Guy Ben Porat. Belfast.

Anonymous 3. 2000. Interviewed by Guy Ben Porat. Belfast.

Anonymous 4. 2000. Interviewed by Guy Ben Porat. Belfast.

Anonymous 5. 2000. Interviewed by Guy Ben Porat. Belfast.

Anonymous 6. 2000. Interviewed by Guy Ben Porat. Belfast.

Appadurai, Arjun. 1990. "Disjuncture and Difference in the Global Cultural Economy." *Public Culture* 2, no. 2:1–23.

Arian, Asher, and Michal Shamir. 1995. "Two Reversals: Why 1992 Was Not 1977." In *The Elections in Israel 1992,* ed. Asher Arian and Michal Shamir. Albany, New York: State Univ. of New York Press.

Arnon, Arie, Israel Luski, Avia Spivak, and Jimmy Weinblatt. 1997. *The Palestinian Economy: Between Imposed Integration and Voluntary Separation.* Leiden: E. J. Brill.

Arthur, Paul. 1993. *Northern Ireland: A Crucial Test for a Europe of Peaceful Regions?* Oslo, Norway: Norwegian Institute of International Affairs.

———. 1999. "Quiet Diplomacy and Personal Conversations." In *After the Good Friday Agreement*, ed. Joseph Ruane and Jennifer Todd. Dublin: University College Press.

Arrighi, Giovanni. 1982. "A Crisis of Hegemony." In *Dynamics of Global Crisis*, ed. Samir Amin, Giovanni Arrighi, Andre Gunder Frank and Immanuel Wallerstein. New York: Monthly Review Press.

———. 1994. *The Long Twentieth Century*. London: Verso.

———. 2000. "Globalization, State Sovereignty, and the Accumulation of Capital." In *The Ends of Globalization: Bringing Society Back In*, ed. Don Kalb, Marco van der Land, Richard Staring, Bart Van Steenbergen, and Nico Wilterdink. Lanham, Md.: Rowman and Littlefield.

Arrighi, Giovanni, and Beverly Silver. 1999. *Chaos and Governance in the Modern World System*. Minneapolis: Univ. of Minnesota Press.

———. 2002. "Polanyi's 'Double Movement': The Belle Epoques of British and U.S. Hegemonies Compared." *Politics and Society* 31, no. 2:325–55.

Ashworth, William. 1975. *A Short History of the International Economy since 1850*. London: Longman.

Atwood, Alex. 2000. SDLP. Interviewed by Guy Ben-Porat. Transcript. September.

Aughey, Arthur, ed. 1995. *The Idea of the Union*. Vancouver, Canada: Balcouver Press.

———. 2000. "The 1998 Agreement: Unionist Responses" in *A Farewell to Arms? From 'Long War' to Long Peace in Northern Ireland*, ed. Michael Cox, Adrian Guelke, and Fiona Stephen. Manchester: Manchester Univ. Press.

Avineri, Shlomo. 1997. "From the 'Jewish Issue' to the 'State of the Jews" [in Hebrew]. In *The Jewish Cause: Herzl's Diaries, 1895–1904*, by Theodore Herzl. Jerusalem: Bialik Institute.

Azar, Edward E., and Stephen P. Cohen. 1979. "Peace as Crisis and War as Status-Quo: The Arab-Israeli Conflict Environment." *International Interactions* 6, no. 2:159–84.

Azaryahu, Maoz. 2000. "McIsrael? On the 'Americanization of Israel.' " *Israel Studies* 5, no. 1:41–65.

Bank of Israel. 1998. Annual Report.

Barber, Benjamin. 1995. *Jihad vs. McWorld*. New York: Random House.

Barbieri, Katherine, and Gerald Schneider. 1999. "Globalization and Peace: Assessing New Directions in the Study of Trade and Conflict." *Journal of Peace Research* 36, no. 4:387–404.

Barnet, Richard, and Ronald Mueller. 1974. *Global Reach: The Power of The Multinational Corporations*. New York: Simon and Schuster.

Barnett, Michael. 1996. *Israeli in Comparative Perspective*. Albany, New York: State Univ. of New York Press.

Bar-On, Mordechai. 1996. *In Pursuit of Peace*. Washington, D.C.: United States Institute of Peace.

Barrat-Brown, Michael. 1963. *After Imperialism*. London: Heinemann.

Bar-Siman-Tov, Yaacov. 2001. "Peace Policy as Domestic and Foreign Policy." In *Peace-making in a Divided Society,* by Sasson Sofer. London: Frank Cass.

Bauman, Zygmunt. 1989. *Modernity and the Holocaust.* Ithaca: Cornell Univ. Press.

Baxter, Carlton. Editorial. 1998.*Ulster Business* 8, no. 11 (November).

Beilin, Yossi. 1997. *Touching Peace* [in Hebrew]. Israel: Yediot.

Bell, Eric. 2000. Institute of Directors. Interviewed by Guy Ben-Porat. Transcript. September.

Beloff, Max. 1987. *Imperial Sunset.* Vol. 1, *Britain's Liberal Empire, 1897–1921.* London: Macmillan.

Ben-Porat, Guy. 2000. "In a State of Holiness, Rethinking Israeli Secularism." *Alternatives* 25:223–45.

———. 2005. "A New Middle East?: Globalization, Peace, and the Double Movement." *International Relations* 19, no. 1:39–62.

Ben-Simon, Daniel. 1997. *A New Israel* [in Hebrew]. Tel-Aviv: Modan.

———. 2000. "A Journey to the Heart of Israelis." *Haaretz,* January 7.

Bentsur, Eytan. 1997. *The Road to Peace Crosses Madrid* [in Hebrew]. Tel-Aviv: Yediot.

Benvenisti, Meron. 1990. "The Peace Process and Inter-Communal Strife." In *The Elusive Search for Peace,* ed. Hermann Buhr Giliomee and Jannie Gagiano. Oxford: Oxford Univ. Press.

Bergsten, Fred. 1982. "The United States and The World Economy." *Annals of the American Academy of Political and Social Science* 460:11–20.

Bew, Paul, Henry Patterson, and Paul Teague. 1997. *Northern Ireland—Between War and Peace: The Political Future of Northern Ireland.* London: Lawrence and Wishart.

Birnie, Esmond. 1995. "Economic Consequences of the Peace." In *The Idea of the Union,* ed. Arthur Aughey. Vancouver, Canada: Balcouver Press.

———. 2000. UUP, MP. Interviewed by Guy Ben-Porat. Transcript. September.

Birnie, Esmond, and David Hitchins. 1999. *Northern Ireland Economy: Performance, Prospects, Policy.* London: Ashgate.

Blaut, James. 1993. *The Colonizer's Model of The World.* New York: Guilford Press.

Blyth, Mark. 1999. "Globalization or Disembedded Liberalism? Institutions, Ideas, and the Double Movement." Unpublished manuscript.

Bonner, Karen, S. Elliott, and D. Rea. 1999. "Governance, Demographic and Economic Facts and Statistics for Northern Ireland." *Economic Outlook and Business Review* 14, no.3 (September).

Boyce, David George. 1988. "One Last Burial": Culture, Counter-Revolution, and Revolution in Ireland, 1886–1916." In *The Revolution in Ireland, 1879–1923,* ed. David George Boyce. London: Macmillan.

———. 1990. *Nineteenth-Century Ireland: The Search for Stability.* Dublin: Gill and Macmillan.

———. 1991. *Nationalism in Ireland*. London: Routledge.

———. 1996. *The Irish Question and British Politics, 1868–1996*. London: Macmillan.

———. 1999. "Ulster Unionism: Great Britain and Ireland, 1885–1921." In *The Northern Ireland Question: Nationalism, Unionism, and Partition*, ed. Patrick J. Roche and Brian Barton. Aldershoot: Ashgate.

Bradley, John. 1995. *An Island Economy*. Dublin: Economic and Social Research Institute.

———. 1996. *An Island Economy: Exploring Long-Term Economic and Social Consequences of Peace and Reconciliation in the Island of Ireland*. Dublin: Forum for Peace and Reconciliation.

Bradley, John, and Douglas Hamilton. 1999. "Strategy 2010: Planning Economic Development in Northern Ireland." *Regional Studies* 33, no. 9:885–90.

Brasted, H. V. 1983. "Irish Nationalism and the British Empire in the Late Nineteenth Century." In *Irish Culture and Nationalism*, ed. Oliver MacDonagh, W. F. Mandle, and Pauric Travers. New York: St. Martin's Press.

Brennan, Peter. 1995. "The European Union: The Island's Common Cause." In *Border Crossings*, ed. Michael D'Arcy and Tim Dickson. Dublin: Gill and Macmillan.

Bull, Hedley. [1977.] 1995. *The Anarchical Society*. New York: Columbia Univ. Press.

Cafruny, Alan W. 1990. "A Gramscian Concept of Declining Hegemony." In *World Leadership and Hegemony*, ed. David Rapkin. Boulder, Colo.: Lynne Rienner.

Cain, P. J., and A. G. Hopkins. 1993. *British Imperialism: Innovation and Expansion 1688–1914*. London: Longman.

Calhoun, Craig. 1997. *Nationalism*. London: Open Univ. Press.

Calleo, David P., and B. M. Rowland. 1973. *America and the World Political Economy*. Bloomington: Indiana Univ. Press.

Camilleri, Joseph A. 1995. "State, Civil Society and Economy." In *The State in Transition: Re-imagining Political Space*, ed. Joseph Camilleri, Anthony Jarvis, and Albert Paolini. Boulder, Colo.: Lynne Rienner.

Campbell, David. 1998. *National Deconstruction: Violence, Identity, and Justice in Bosnia*. Minneapolis: Minnesota Univ. Press.

Carr, Edward Hallett. 1945. *Nationalism and After*. London: Macmillan.

Caspi, Arie. 1993. "We Did Not Win the Lottery." *Haaretz* Weekend Supplement, September 10.

Castenada, Jorge. 1996. "Mexico's Circle of Misery." *Foreign Affairs*, July/August.

Catterall, Peter, and Sean McDougall. 1996. *The Northern Ireland Question in British Politics*. New York: St. Martin's Press.

Center for Palestine Research and Studies (CPRS). 1996. "The Peace Process after Netanyahu's Election, Freedom of Expression, Democratization under the PNA, the Recent Arab Summit, the Performance of the Legislative Council." http://www.cprs-palestine.org.

Center for Palestine Research and Studies (CPRS). 2003. www.cprs-palestine.org, accessed July 2003.

Central Bureau of Statistics. 2001. *Israel 2000: Social Report,* no. 3. Jerusalem: CBI.

Cerny, Philip G. 1990. *The Changing Architecture of Politics: Structure, Agency, and the Future of the State.* London: Sage.

———. 1995. "Globalization and The Changing Logic of Collective Action." *International Organization* 49, no. 4 (Autumn): 595–625.

———. 1997. "Paradoxes of The Competition State: The Dynamics of Political Globalization." *Government and Opposition* 32, no. 2 (Spring): 251–74.

———, ed. 1993. *Finance and World Politics: Markets, Regimes, and States in the Post-Hegemonic Era.* Aldershot, Hants.: Edward Elgar.

Chan, Steve. 1995. "Grasping the Peace Dividend: Some Propositions on the Conversion of Swords into Plowshares." *International Studies Quarterly* 39, no. 1:53–95.

Clark, Ian. 1997. *Globalization and Fragmentation.* Oxford: Oxford Univ. Press.

Cohen, Benjamin. 1996. "Phoenix Risen: The Resurrection of Global Finance." *World Politics* 48, no. 2 (January): 268–96.

Cohen, Yinon, and Yitchak Haberfeld. 1998. "Second Generation Jewish Immigrants in Israel: Have the Earning Gaps in Schooling and Earnings Declined?" *Ethnic and Racial Studies* 21, no. 3:507–28.

Collins, Peter, ed. 1994. *Nationalism and Unionism Conflict in Ireland 1885–1921.* Belfast: Institute of Irish Studies, Queen's Univ. of Belfast.

Conaty, Ann. 2000. Department of Enterprise and Trade, Northern Ireland. Interviewed by Guy Ben-Porat. Transcript. September.

Confederation of British Industry, Northern Ireland (CBI NI). 1998. Press statement, F.S. July 5.

Confederation of British Industry, Northern Ireland (CBI NI). 1994. "Peace: A Challenging New Era." Belfast: CBI NI.

Connolly, William E. 1996. *The Ethos of Pluralization.* Minneapolis: Univ. of Minnesota Press.

Coopers and Lybrand (economic consultants). 1997. *The NI Economy: Review and Prospects.* January.

Coopers and Lybrand/Indecom (economic consultants). 1994. "A Corridor of Opportunity." In *Study of Feasibility of Developing a Dublin-Belfast Economic Corridor.* Report Prepared for the Confederation of British Industry (NI) and the Irish Business and Employers Confederation. Belfast and Dublin: CBI (NI) and IBEC.

Cortright, David. 1997. "Incentive Strategies for Preventing Conflicts." In *The Price of Peace,* ed. David Cortright. New York: Rowman and Littlefield.

———, ed. 1997. *The Price of Peace.* New York: Rowman and Littlefield.

Coulter, Colin. 1997. "The Culture of Contentment: The Political Beliefs and Practice of the Unionist Middle Classes." In *Who Are 'The People'?* ed. Peter Shirlow and Mark McGovern. London: Pluto Press.

Cox, Michael. 1998. "Northern Ireland: the War That Came in from the Cold." *Irish Studies in International Affairs* 9:73–84.

———. 2000. "Northern Ireland after the Cold War." In *A Farewell to Arms? From 'Long War' to Long Peace in Northern Ireland,* ed. Michael Cox, Adrian Guelke, and Fiona Stephen. Manchester: Manchester Univ. Press.

Cox, Michael, Adrian Guelke, and Fiona Stephen, eds. 2000. *A Farewell to Arms? From 'Long War' to Long Peace in Northern Ireland.* Manchester: Manchester Univ. Press.

Cox, Robert. 1983. "Gramsci, Hegemony, and International Relations: An Essay in Method." *Millenium* 12, no. 2: 73–84.

———. 1996. "Perspective on Globalization." In *Globalization: Critical Reflections,* ed. James Mittelman. Boulder: Lynn Rienner.

Crick, Bernard. 1990. "The High Price of Peace." In *The Elusive Search for Peace: South Africa, Israel, and Northern Ireland,* ed. Hermann Gilomee and Jannie Gagiano. Cape Town: Oxford Univ. Press.

Crocker, Chester A., and Fen Osler Hampson. 1996. "Making Peace Settlements Work." *Foreign Policy* no. 104 (Fall): 54–72.

Cronin, Sean. 1980. *Irish Nationalism: A History of Its Roots and Ideology.* New York: Continuum.

Crumm, Eileen M. 1995. "The Value of Economic Incentives in International Politics." *Journal of Peace Research* 32, no. 3:313–30.

Devetak, Richard, and Richard Higgot. 1999. "Justice Unbound? Globalization, States, and the Transformation of the Social Bond." *International Affairs* 75, no. 3:483–98.

Doyle, John. 1997. "Ulster Like Israel Can Only Lose Once: Ulster Unionism, Security, and Citizenship, 1972–1997." *Dublin City Univ. Research Paper* 31.

Doyle, Michael W. 1986. *Empires.* Ithaca: Cornell Univ. Press.

Drake, Laura. 1999. "Arab-Israeli Relations in a New Middle East Order." In *The Political Economy of the Middle East,* ed. J. W. Wright, Jr. London: Routledge.

Dreier, Peter. 1982. "Capitalists vs. the Media: An Analysis of an Ideological Mobilization among Business Leaders." *Media, Culture, and Society* 4:111–32.

Dumas, Lloyd J. 1995. "Finding the Future: The Role of Economic Conversion in Shaping the Twenty-First Century." In *The Socio-Economics of Conversion from War to Peace,* ed. Lloyd J. Dumas. New York: M. E. Sharp.

DUP Yearbook. 1996. Belfast: n.p.

Elazar, Daniel J., and Shmuel Sandler, eds. *Israel at the Polls, 1992.* Jerusalem: Jerusalem Center for Public Affairs.

Ellis, John S. 2000. "The Degenerate and the Martyr: Nationalist Propaganda and the Contestation of Irishness, 1914–1918." *Eire/Ireland* 35, no. 3/4: 7–33.

Epstein, Isaac. 1907. "The Hidden Question." *Hashiloah* 17.

Etzioni-Halevy, Eva. 1997. *A Place at the Top* [in Hebrew] Tel-Aviv: Cherikover.

European Commission. 1998. *Peace and Reconciliation: An Imaginative Approach to the European Programme for Northern Ireland and the Border Counties of Ireland.* Luxemburg: Office of the Official Publications of the European Commission.

———. 1999. *Northern Ireland in Europe.* Published by the EC Representation in the UK.

Evans, Peter. 1997. "Eclipse of the State?" *World Politics* 50, no. 1 (October): 62–87.

Evron, Yair. 1973. *The Middle East: Nations, Super-Powers, and Wars.* London: Elek Books.

Farren, Sean. 2000. "The SDLP and the Roots of the Good Friday Agreement." In *A Farewell to Arms? From 'Long War' to Long Peace in Northern Ireland,* ed. Michael Cox, Adrian Guelke, and Fiona Stephen. Manchester: Manchester Univ. Press.

Farren, Sean, and Robert F. Mulvihill. 2000. *Paths to a Settlement in Northern Ireland.* Buckinghamshire: Colin Smythe.

Federman, Michael. 2000. Dan Hotels. Interviewed by Guy Ben-Porat. Transcript. August 1.

Field, James, Jr. 1971. "Transnationalism and the New Tribe." In *Transnational Relations and World Politics,* ed. Robert O. Keohane and Joseph S. Nye. Cambridge, Mass: Harvard Univ. Press.

Fieldhouse, David Kenneth. 1982. *The Colonial Empires.* London: Macmillan.

Fitzduff, Mari. 2002. *Beyond Violence: Conflict Resolution Process in Northern Ireland.* Tokyo: United Nations Univ. Press.

Fitzgerald, Garrett. 1993. Quoted in *Northern Ireland: A Crucial Test for a Europe of Peaceful Regions?* by Paul Arthur. Oslo, Norway: Norwegian Institute of International Affairs.

Flynn, Mary Katherine. 2000. *Ideology, Mobilization, and the Nation: The Rise of Irish, Basque, and Carlist Nationalist Movements in the Nineteenth and Early Twentieth Century.* London: Macmillan.

Foster, Roy F. 1988. *Modern Ireland, 1600–1972.* London: Allen Lane.

Fraser, Tom. 1994. "Partitioning India, Ireland, and Palestine." In *Nationalism and Unionism: Conflict in Ireland, 1885–1921,* ed. Peter Collins. Belfast: Institute of Irish Studies.

Freedman, Robert. 1972. "The Partition of Palestine: Conflicting Nationalism and Great Power Rivalry." In *The Problem of Partition: Peril to World Peace,* ed. Thomas Hachey. Chicago: Rand McNally.

Frieden, Jeffrey A. 1991. "Invested Interests: The Politics of National Economic Policies in a World of Global Finance." *International Organization* 45, no. 4:425–51.

Friedman, Isaiah. 1977. *Germany, Turkey, and Zionism, 1897–1918.* Oxford: Oxford Univ. Press.

Friedman, Thomas. 1999. *The Lexus and the Olive Tree.* New York: Farrar, Straus, Giroux.

Fukuyama, Francis. 1989. "The End of History?" *National Interest* 16:3–18.

G7 press statement. 1996a. August.

G7 press statement. 1996b. October.

G7 press statement. 1997a. April 15.

G7 press statement. 1997b. June 3.

G7 press statement. 1997c. July 4.

G7 press statement. 1997d. August.

G7 press statement. 1998. July.

Gabai, Yoram. 1996. "The Peace Process and Market Economic Developments" (in Hebrew). *Bank Hapoalim,* November.

Gallagher, John. 1981. "Nationalisms and the Crisis of Empire, 1919–1922." *Modern Asian Studies* 15, no. 3:355–68.

Gamble, Andrew. 1994. *Britain in Decline.* London: Macmillan.

Gaon, Benny. 2000. Interviewed by Guy Ben-Porat. Transcript. June 11.

Gaon, Benny. 1997. "We Need to Bring Back the Pink Color to the Economy's Cheeks." *The Industrialists* [in Hebrew], January.

Garvin, Tom. 1981. *The Evolution of Irish National Politics.* New York: Holmes and Meier.

———. 1987. *Nationalist Revolutionaries in Ireland 1858–1928.* Oxford: Clarendon Press.

———. 1988. "Revolutionary Activists, 1890–1922." In *The Revolution in Ireland, 1879–1923,* ed. David George Boyce. London, Houndmills and Hampshire: Macmillan.

Gellner, Ernest. 1983. *Nations and Nationalism.* London: Basil Blackwell.

Gibson, Chris. 1998. "CBI Backs Stormont Package." *Belfast Telegraph,* May 12.

Gibson, Chris. 2000. Interviewed by Guy Ben-Porat. Transcript. September.

Giddens, Anthony. 1981. *A Contemporary Critique of Historical Materialism,* vol. 1. London: Macmillan.

Giliomee, Hermann. 1990. "The Elusive Search for Peace." In *The Elusive Search for Peace: South Africa, Israel and Northern Ireland,* ed. Hermann Gilomee and Jannie Gagiano. Cape Town: Oxford Univ. Press.

Giliomee, Hermann, and Jannie Gagiano, eds. 1990. *The Elusive Search for Peace: South Africa, Israel and Northern Ireland.* Cape Town: Oxford Univ. Press.

Gill, Stephen. 1990a. *American Hegemony and the Trilateral Commission.* Cambridge: Cambridge Univ. Press.

———. 1990b. "The Emerging Hegemony of Transnational Capital: Trialetralism and Global Order." In *World Leadership and Hegemony,* ed. David Rapkin. Boulder, Colo.: Lynne Rienner.

———. 1996. "Globalization, Democratization and Indifference." In *Globalization: Critical Reflections,* ed. James Mittelman. Boulder, Colo.: Lynne Rienner.

Gill, Stephen, and David Law. 1989. "Global Hegemony and the Structural Power of Capital." *International Studies Quarterly* 33: 93–124.

Gillespie, Alan. 2000. Interviewed by Guy Ben-Porat. Transcript. September.

Gillespie, Paul. 1996. "The Northern Dimension." In *Britain's European Question: The Issues for Ireland,* ed. Paul Gillespie. Dublin: Institute of European Affairs.

———. 1998. "European Context Helps Underpin Northern Accord." *Irish Times,* April 11.

Gillespie, Paul, ed. 1996. *Britain's European Question: The Issues for Ireland.* Dublin : Institute of European Affairs.

Gilligan, Chris, and Jon Tonge, eds. 1996. *Peace or War? Understanding the Peace Process in Northern Ireland.* Brookfield, Vt.: Ashgate.

Gilpin, Robert. 1975. *U.S. Power and the Multinational Corporation.* New York: Basic Books.

———. 1981. *War and Change in World Politics.* Cambridge: Cambridge Univ. Press.

———. 1987. *The Political Economy of International Relations.* Princeton: Princeton Univ. Press.

Girvan, Brian. 1999. "The Making of Irish Nationalism: Between Integration and Independence." In *The Northern Ireland Question,* ed. P. Roche and B. Barton. Aldershot, Hants.; Brookfield, Vt.: Ashgate.

Goodman, James. 1996. "The Northern Ireland Question and European Politics." In *The Northern Ireland Question in British Politics,* ed. Peter Catterall and Sean McDougall. New York: St. Martin's Press.

Gorecki, Paul. 1995. "Peace and Political Stability: All-Ireland Implications." In *The Two Economies of Ireland,* ed. John Bradley. Dublin: Oak Tree.

Gorny, Yosef. 1987. *Zionism and the Arabs, 1882–1848: A Study of Ideology.* Oxford: Oxford Univ. Press.

Groffman, Shlomo. 2000. Interviewed by Guy Ben-Porat. Transcript. June 10.

Grovogui, Siba N'Zatioula. 1996. *Sovereigns, Quasi Sovereigns, and Africans.* Minneapolis: Univ. of Minnesota Press.

Gudgin, Graham. 1995a. "The Economics of the Union." In *The Idea of the Union: Statements and Critiques in Support of the Union of Great Britain and Northern Ireland,* ed. John Wilson Foster. Vancouver: Belcouver Press.

———. 1995b. "Northern Ireland after the Ceasefire." *Irish Banking Review,* Autumn.

Guelke, Adrian. 1988. *Northern Ireland: The International Perspective.* Dublin: Gill and Macmillan.

Gutwein, Daniel. 1994. "Socio-Economic Aspects of Tsarist Jewish Policy 1881–1905." *International Review of Social History* 39:197–221.

Haber, Deborah. 1990. "The Death of Hegemony: Why 'Pax Nipponica' Is Impossible." *Asian Survey,* September.

Haber, Ethan. 2000. Interviewed by Guy Ben-Porat. Transcript. June 30.

Hall, Peter. 1993. "Policy Paradigms, Social Learning, and the State." *Comparative Politics* 24:275–96.

Halliday, Fred. 1983. *The Making of the Second Cold War*. London: Verso.

Hamilton, Douglas. 1993. "Foreign Investment and Industrial Development in Northern Ireland." In *Beyond the Rhetoric: Politics, Economy, and Social Policy in Northern Ireland*, ed. Paul Teague. London: Lawrence and Wishart.

Hampson, Fen Osler. 1996. *Nurturing Peace: Why Peace Settlements Succeed or Fail*. Washington, D.C.: USIP.

Hannerz, Ulf. 1996. *Transnational Connections*. London: Routledge.

Haren, Patrick. 2000. Interviewed by Guy Ben-Porat. Transcript. September.

Hareven, Aluf. 1978. "The Non-Hidden Question" [in Hebrew]. In *The Second Aliyah, 1903–1914*, ed. Mordecai Naor, 111–20. Jerusalem: Bialik Institute.

Harkavi, Yehoshafat. 1969. "The Arab-Israeli Conflict" [in Hebrew]. In *Between Israel and Arab*, ed. Y. Harkavi. Tel-Aviv: IDF.

Hartley, Stephen. 1987. *The Irish Question as a Problem in British Foreign Policy, 1914–1918*. New York: St. Martin's Press.

Hassner, Pierre. 1993. "Beyond Nationalism and Internationalism: Ethnicity and World Order." *Survival* 35, no. 2:49–65.

Hayes, Bernadette, and Ian McAllister. 1999. "Ethnonationalism, Public Opinion, and the Good Friday Agreement." In *After the Good Friday Agreement: Analysing Political Change in Northern Ireland*, ed. Joseph Ruane and Jennifer Todd. Dublin: University College Press.

Hayes, Carlton J. H. 1963. *A Generation of Materialism, 1871–1900*. New York: Harper and Row.

Hechter, Michael. 1975. *Internal Colonialism: The Celtic Fringe in British Industrial Development, 1536–1966*. Berkeley: Univ. of California Press.

Held, David, Anthony McGrew, David Goldblatt, and Jonathan Perraton. 1999. *Global Transformations: Politics, Economics, and Culture*. Cambridge: Polity Press.

Helleiner, Eric. 1993. "When Finance Was the Servant: International Capital Movements in the Bretton Woods Order." In *Finance and World Politics: Markets, Regimes, and States in the Post-Hegemonic Era*, ed. Philip G. Cerny. Aldershot, Hants.: Edward Elgar.

———. 1994. *States and the Reemergence of Global Finance*. Ithaca: Cornell Univ. Press.

———. 1997. "Braudelian Reflections on Globalization." In *Innovation and Transformation in International Studies*, ed. Stephen Gill and James H. Mittelman. Cambridge: Cambridge Univ. Press.

Hennessey, Thomas. 1997. *A History of Northern Ireland, 1920–1996*. New York: St. Martins Press.

———. 1998. *Dividing Ireland: World War I and Partition*. London: Routledge.

Hermann, Tamar, and David Newman. 2000. "A Path Strewn with Thorns: Along the Difficult Road of Israeli-Palestinian Peacemaking." In *The Management of Peace Process,* ed. John Darby and Roger MacGinty. London: Routledge.

Herzl, Theodor. 1988. *The Jewish State: An Attempt at a Modern Solution of the Jewish Question.* Reprint: New York: Dover. Originally published in German as *Der Judenstaat: Versuch einer Modernen Lisung der Judenfrage* (Wien: M. Breitenstein's Verlags-Buchhandlung, 1896).

―――. 1997. *The Jewish Cause, Herzl's Diaries, 1895–1914,* vol. 1 [in Hebrew]. Jerusalem: Bialik Institute.

Hildebrand, K. 1993. "The Transformation of the International System: From the Berlin Congress (1878) to the Paris Peace Treaty (1919–1920)." In *The Quest for Stability: Problems of West European Security, 1918–1957,* ed. Rolf Ahmann, Adolf M. Birke, and Michael E. Howard. Oxford: Oxford Univ. Press.

Hirschfeld, Yair. 2000. *Oslo: A Formula for Peace* [in Hebrew]. Tel Aviv: Yedioth.

Hirschman, Albert O. 1970. *Exit, Voice, Loyalty: Responses to Decline in Firms, Organizations, and States.* Cambridge, Mass.: Harvard Univ. Press.

Hirst, Paul. 2000. "The Global Economy: Myths or Reality?" In *The Ends of Globalization: Bringing Society Back In,* ed. Don Kalb et al. Oxford: Oxford Univ. Press.

Hirst, Paul, and Graham Thompson. 1999. *Globalization in Question.* Cambridge: Polity Press.

Hobsbawm, Eric. 1969. *Industry and Empire.* London: Penguin Books.

―――. 1983. "Mass-Producing Traditions: Europe, 1870–1914." In *The Invention of Tradition,* ed. Eric Hobsbawm and Terence Ranger. Cambridge: Cambridge Univ. Press.

―――. 1989. *The Age of Empire.* New York: Vintage Books.

―――. 1990. *Nations and Nationalism since 1780.* Cambridge: Cambridge Univ. Press.

―――. 1994. *The Age of Extremes: A History of the World, 1914–1991.* New York: Vintage.

Hobsbawm, Eric, and Terence Ranger, eds. 1983. *The Invention of Tradition.* Cambridge: Cambridge Univ. Press.

Holland, Jack. 1999. *Hope Against History.* London: Hodder and Stoughton.

Horowitz, Eli. 2000. Interviewed by Guy Ben-Porat. Transcript. May 25.

"How to Buy Peace with Money." 1994. *Nativ: A Journal of Politics and the Arts.* April.

Hume, John. 1993. "A New Ireland in a New Europe." In *Northern Ireland and the Politics of Reconciliation,"* ed. Dermot Keogh and Michael H. Haltzel. Cambridge, U.K.: Cambridge and Woodrow Wilson Center.

Hutchinson, John. 1996. "Irish Nationalism." In *The Making of Modern Irish History: Revisionism and the Revisionist Controversy,* ed. David George Boyce and Alan O'Day. London: Routledge.

Ikenberry, John G. 1989. "Rethinking the Origins of American Hegemony." *Political Science Quarterly* 104, no. 3: 375–400.

Ikenberry, John G., and Charles Kupchan. 1990. "Legitimation of Hegemonic Power." In *World Leadership and Hegemony*, ed. David Rapkin. Boulder, Colo.: Lynne Rienner.

Imlah, Albert. 1958. *Economic Elements in the Pax Britannica*. Boston: Harvard Univ. Press.

Inbar, Efraim. 1994. "The 'No Choice War' Debate in Israel." In *The Conflict with Israel in Arab Politics and Society*, ed. Ian S. Lustick. New York: Garland Publishing.

Irish Congress of Trade Unions (ICTU). 2000. "Submission, no. 3: Submissions to the DED's Consultative Document on 'Strategy 2010.' "

Irwin, Colin. 2000. "The People's Peace Process: 2—Priorities for Peace." Belfast. Unpublished manuscript. (The author wishes to thank Dr. Irwin for the data.)

Israel Democracy Institute. 1993. Caesarea Conference, June.

———. 1994. Protocols of the Caesarea Conference, Summer.

Jacobson, David. 1997. "New Frontiers: Territory, Social Spaces, and the State." *Sociological Forum* 12, no. 1:121–34.

Jervis, Robert. 1978. "Cooperation under the Security Dilemma." *World Politics* 30, no. 2:167–214.

Joll, James. 1992. *The Origins of the First World War*. New York: Longman.

Kacowicz, Arie M. 1996. "The Process of Reaching Peaceful Territorial Change: The Arab-Israeli Conflict in Comparative Perspective." *Journal of Interdisciplinary History* 27, no. 2:215–45.

Kadosh, Orna. 2000. "An Interview with Padan" *Maariv*, Weekend Supplement, June 23.

Kalb, Don, Marco Van der Land, Richard Staring, Bart Van Steenbergen, and Nico Wilterdink, eds. 2000. *The Ends of Globalization: Bringing Society Back In*. Lanham, Md.: Rowman and Littlefield.

Kant, Immanuel. [1795] 1957. *Perpetual Peace*. New York: Liberal Arts Press.

Katz, E., and E. Haz. 1995. "Twenty Years of Television in Israel: Do They Have Long-Term Effects?" [in Hebrew]. *Zmanim* 52 (Spring).

Katz, Jacob. 1979. *Anti-Semitism: From Religious Hatred to Racial Rejection* [in Hebrew]. Jerusalem: Academon Press.

Kearney, Hugh. 1989. *The British Isles: A History of Four Nations*. Cambridge: Cambridge Univ. Press.

Keck, Margaret E., and Kathryn Sikkink. 1998. *Activists Beyond Borders*. Ithaca: Cornell Univ. Press.

Kennedy-Pipe, Caroline. 2000. "From War to Peace in Northern Ireland." In *A Farewell to Arms? From 'Long War' to Long Peace in Northern Ireland*, ed. Michael Cox, Adrian Guelke, and Fiona Stephen. Manchester: Manchester Univ. Press.

Keohane, Robert. 1984. *After Hegemony: Cooperation and Discord in the World Political Economy.* Princeton: Princeton Univ. Press.

Keohane, Robert, and Joseph Nye. 1977. *Power and Interdependence: World Politics in Transition.* Boston: Little, Brown and Co.

Keren, Michael. 1993. "Economists and Economic Policy Making in Israel: The Politics of Expertise in the Stabilization Program." *Policy Sciences* 26:331–43.

———. 1994. "Israeli Professionals and the Peace Process." *Israel Affairs* 1, no. 1:149–163.

Kern, Stephen. 1983. *The Culture of Time and Space.* Cambridge, Mass: Harvard Univ. Press.

Khalidi, Rashid. 1997. *Palestinian Identity: The Construction of Modern National Consciousness.* New York: Columbia Univ. Press.

Kimmerling, Baruch. 1983. *Zionism and Territory.* Berkeley: Univ. of California Press.

———. 1999. "Elections as a Battleground over Collective Identity." In *The Elections in Israel 1996,* ed. Asher Arian and Michal Shamir. Jerusalem: Israeli Institute of Democracy.

———. 2000. "The Formation of Palestinian Collective Identities: The Ottoman and Mandatory Periods." *Middle Eastern Studies* 36, no. 2:48–82.

Kimmerling, Baruch, and Joel S. Migdal. 1993. *Palestinians: The Making of a People.* New York: Free Press.

Kindelberger, Charles P. 1969. *American Business Abroad.* New Haven: Yale Univ. Press.

———. 1973. *The World in Depression, 1929–39.* Berkeley: Univ. of California Press.

Kingdom, Stephen. 2000. Interviewed by Guy Ben-Porat. Transcript. September.

Klein, Yitzhak. 1993. "Political Economy and the 1992 Elections." In *Israel at the Polls 1992,* ed. Daniel Elazar and Shmuel Sandler. Jerusalem: Jerusalem Center for Public Affairs.

Klier, John D. 1992. "Russian Jewry on the Eve of the Pogroms." In *Pogroms: Anti-Jewish Violence in Modern Russian History,* ed. John D. Klier and Shlomo Lambroza. Cambridge, U.K.: Cambridge Univ. Press.

Knox, Colin, and Joanne Hughes. 1995. "Cross-Community Contact: Northern Ireland and Israel—A Comparative Perspective." *Nationalism and Ethnic Politics* 1, no. 2:205–28.

Kobrin, Stephen. 1998. "Back to the Future: Neomedievalism and the Postmodern Digital Economy." *Journal of International Affairs* 51, no. 2:361–86.

Krasner, Stephen D. 1999. "Globalization and Sovereignty." In *States and Sovereignty in the Global Economy,* ed. David A. Smith, Dorothy Solinger, and Steven Topik. London: Routledge.

Krugman, Paul. 1998. "America the Boastful." *Foreign Affairs* 77, no. 3:32–45.

Kumar, Radha. 1997. "The Troubled History of Partition." *Foreign Affairs* 76, no. 1:22–34.

Lake, David. 1995. "British and American Hegemony Compared." In *International Po-litical Economy: Perspectives on Global Power and Wealth*, ed. Jeffrey A. Frieden and David A. Lake. New York: St. Martin's Press.

Lambroza, Shlomo. 1992. "The Pogroms of 1903–1906." In *Pogroms: Anti-Jewish Vio-lence in Modern Russian History*, ed. John D. Klier and Shlomo Lambroza. Cam-bridge: Cambridge Univ. Press.

Landes, David. 1969. *The Unbound Prometheus: Technological Change and Industrial Development in Western Europe from 1870 to the Present*. Cambridge: Cambridge Univ. Press.

Lautman, Dov. 2000. Interviewwd by Guy Ben-Porat. Transcript. March 23.

Leavy, James. 1999. "Europe: A Key to Developments in Northern Ireland." *Irish Studies* 89, no. 353.

Lesch, Mosely Ann. 1979. *Arab Politics in Palestine, 1917–1939: The Frustration of a Na-tionalist Movement*. Ithaca, N.Y.: Cornell Univ. Press.

Levy, Shlomit, Hannah Levinson, and Elihu Katz. 1997. "Beliefs, Observances, and So-cial Interactions Among Israeli Jews: The Guttman Institute Report." In *The Jew-ishness of Israelis: Responses to the Guttman Report*, ed. Charles S. Liebman and E. Katz. New York: State Univ. of New York Press.

Levy, Yagil. 1997. *Trial and Error*. New York: State Univ. of New York Press.

Levy, Yagil, and Yoav Peled. 1994. "The Utopian Crisis of the Israeli State." In *Critical Es-says on Israeli Social Issues and Scholarship, Books on Israel*, vol. 3, ed. R. A. Stone and W. P. Zenner. New York: State Univ. of New York Press.

Lipkin, David. 1993. "Economic Catch." *Maariv* Sept. 15, 1993.

Lipson, Charles. 1985. *Standing Guard: Protecting Foreign Capital in the Nineteenth and Twentieth Centuries*. Berkeley: Univ. of California Press.

Lissak, Moshe, and Dan Horowitz. 1989. *Troubles in Utopia: The Overburdened Polity of Israel*. New York: State Univ. of New York Press.

Long, William J. 1996. *Economic Incentives and Bilateral Cooperation*. Michigan: Univ. of Michigan Press.

Lory, Aviva. 1994. "The Peace Fog of the Businessmen" [in Hebrew]. *Haaretz*, Sept. 5.

Loughlin, James. 1998. *The Ulster Question since 1945*. New York: MacMillan.

Lustik, Ian. 1990. "Becoming Problematic: Breakdown of a Hegemonic Conception of Ireland in Nineteenth-Century Britain." *Politics and Society* 18, no. 1:39–73.

———. 1993. *Unsettled States, Disputed Lands: Britain and Ireland, France and Algeria, Israel and the West Bank-Gaza*. Ithaca, N.Y.: Cornell Univ. Press.

MacDonagh, Oliver. 1977. *Ireland, the Union, and Its Aftermath*. London: G. Allen and Unwin.

MacLaughlin, Jim. 1999. "The 'New' Intelligentsia and the Reconstruction of the Irish Nation." *Irish Review* 24:53–65.

Maguire, Joseph. 1999. *Global Sport: Identities, Societies, Civilizations*. Oxford: Polity Press.

Makovsky, David. 1996. *Making Peace with the PLO: The Rabin Government's Road to the Oslo Accord.* Boulder, Colo.: Westview Press.

———. 2001. "Middle East Peace Through Partition." *Foreign Affairs* 80, no. 2:28–45.

Maman, Daniel. 1997. "The Elite Structure in Israel: A Socio-Historical Analysis." *Journal of Political and Military Sociology* 25, no. 1:25–46.

———. 1999. "The Social Organization of the Israeli Economy: A Comparative Analysis." In *Israel: The Dynamics of Change and Continuity,* ed. David Levi-Faur, Gabriel Sheffer and David Vogel. London: Frank Cass.

Mandel, Neville L. 1976. *The Arabs and Zionism before World War I.* Berkeley: Univ. of California Press.

Manley, Lester. 2000. Interviewed by Guy Ben-Porat. Transcript. September.

Mann, Michael. 1986. *The Sources of Social Power,* vol. 1. Cambridge: Cambridge Univ. Press.

Mansergh, Nicholas. 1965. *The Irish Question, 1840–1921.* London: Allen and Unwin.

McAleavey, Seamus. 2000. Interviewed by Guy Ben-Porat. Transcript. September.

McAlister, St. Clair. 2000. Interviewed by Guy Ben-Porat. Transcript. September.

McCall, Cathal. 1999. *Identity in Northern Ireland.* London: Macmillan.

McClure, Alan. 2000. Interviewed by Guy Ben-Porat. Transcript. September.

McCormack, Feargal. 2000. Interviewed by Guy Ben-Porat. Transcript. September.

McCusker, Jim. 2000. Interviewed by Guy Ben-Porat. Transcript. September.

McGarry, John. 2001. "Globalization, European Integration, and the Northern Ireland Conflict." In *Minority Nationalism and the Changing International Order,* ed. John McGarry and Michael Keating. Oxford: Oxford Univ. Press.

McGarry, John, and Brendan O'Leary. 1995. *Explaining Northern Ireland.* Oxford, Mass.: Blackwell.

McGovern, Mark. 1997. "Unity in Diversity? The SDLP and the Peace Process." In *Peace or War? Understanding the Peace Process in Northern Ireland,* ed. Chris Gilligan and Jon Tonge. Brookfield, Vt.: Ashgate.

McKeown, Patricia. 2000. Interviewed by Guy Ben-Porat. Transcript. September.

McMahon, Deirdre. 1999. "Ireland and the Empire-Commonwealth, 1900–1948." In *The Oxford History of the British Empire.* Vol. 4, *The Twentieth Century,* ed. Judith Brown and William Roger Louis. Oxford: Oxford Univ. Press.

McNeill, William H. 1982. *The Pursuit of Power.* Chicago: Univ. of Chicago Press.

McSweeny, Bill. 1998. "Interests and Identity in the Construction of the Belfast Agreement." *Security Dialogue* 29, no. 3:303–14.

Meehan, Elizabeth. 2000. "Europe and the Europeanization of the Irish Question." In *A Farewell to Arms? From 'Long War' to Long Peace in Northern Ireland,* ed. Michael Cox, Adrian Guelke, and Fiona Stephen. Manchester: Manchester Univ. Press.

Megged, Aharon. 1994. "The Israeli Suicide Drive." *Haaretz,* June 10.

Meidan, Anat. 1997. "Until the Last Cheeseburger." *Yediot Achronot,* Weekend Supplement, Jan. 1.

Memorandum. 1993a. Subject: "Material State and Mental State." Chambers of Commerce files, Israel.

———. 1993b. Chambers of Commerce files, Israel. Aug. 31.

———. 1993c. Chambers of Commerce files, Israel. Sept. 12.

———. 1993d. Chambers of Commerce files, Israel. Sept. 28.

Miall, Hugh, Oliver Ramsbotham, and Tom Woodhouse. 1999. *Contemporary Conflict Resolution: The Prevention, Management, and Transformation of Deadly Conflicts.* London: Polity Press.

Miller, David, ed. 1998. *Rethinking Northern Ireland.* London: Longman.

Ministry of Economic Planning. 1995. "Israel as a Strategic Center in the New Era." Jerusalem. Internal document.

Mitchell, Claire. 2003. "Protestant Identification and Social Change in Northern Ireland." *Ethnic and Racial Studies* 26, no. 4:612–31.

Mittelman, James. 2000. *The Globalization Syndrome.* Princeton: Princeton Univ. Press.

Mjost, Lars. 1990. "The Turn of Two Centuries: A Comparison of British and U.S. Hegemonies." In *World Leadership and Hegemony,* ed. David Rapkin. Boulder, Colo.: Lynne Rienner.

Modelski, George. 1999. "From Leadership to Organization: The Evolution of Global Politics." In *The Future of Global Conflict,* ed. Volker Bornshier and Christopher Chase Dunn. London: Sage.

Mommsen, Wolfgang J. 1980. *Theories of Imperialism.* New York: Random House.

Morgenthau, Hans. 1985. *Politics among Nations.* New York: McGraw-Hill.

Morris, Benny. 1987. *The Birth of the Palestinian Refugee Problem, 1947–1949.* Cambridge: Cambridge Univ. Press.

Morrissey, Mike. 2000. "Northern Ireland: Developing a Post-Conflict Economy." In *A Farewell to Arms? From 'Long War' to Long Peace in Northern Ireland,* ed. Michael Cox, Adrian Guelke, and Fiona Stephen. Manchester: Manchester Univ. Press.

Morrow, Ian. 2000. Interviewed by Guy Ben-Porat. Transcript. September.

Mosse, George. 1993. *Confronting the Nation: Jewish and Western Nationalism.* Hanover: Brandeis Univ. Press.

Munck, Ronnie. 1993. *The Irish Economy: Results and Prospects.* London: Pluto Press.

Murray, Robin. 1971. "Internationalization of Capital and the Nation State." *New Left Review* 67:84–109.

Nagid, Chaim. 1993. "The Americanization of Israeli Culture." *Skira Hodshit* [in Hebrew], nos. 8–9 (January): 20–39.

Nitzan, Jonathan, and Shimshon Bichler. 1996. "From War Profits to Peace Dividends: The New Political Economy of Israel." *Capital and Class,* Autumn: 61–94.

Northern Ireland Economic Development Strategy Review Steering Group. 1999. *Strategy 2010,* Belfast: Ministry of the Economy.

Northern Ireland Life and Times Survey, February 2000. www.ark.ac.uk/nilt/.

Nye, Joseph S. 1990. *Bound to Lead: The Changing Nature of American Power.* New York: Basic Books.

O'Connor, Tim. 2000. Interviewed by Guy Ben-Porat. Transcript. September.

O'Dowd, Liam. 1998. "Coercion, Territoriality, and the Prospects for a Negotiated Settlement in Ireland." *Political Geography* 17, no. 2:239–49.

O'Gorman, E., and D. Harding. 2000. "Is This the Man to Know in Northern Ireland?" *Business Voice,* September.

O'Hearn, Denis. 2000. "Peace Dividends, Foreign Investment, and Economic Regeneration: The Northern Irish Case." *Social Problems* 47, no. 2:239–49.

Ohmae, Kenichi. 1995. *The End of the Nation-State.* New York: Free Press.

O'Leary, Brendan, and John McGarry. 1993. *The Politics of Antagonism: Understanding Northern Ireland.* London: Athlone Press.

———. 1999. *Policing Northern Ireland: Proposals for a New Start.* Belfast: Blackstaff Press.

Oliver, Quintin. 1998. *Working for "Yes": The story of the May 1998 referendum in Northern Ireland.* Belfast: Referendum Company.

———. 2000. Interviewed by Guy Ben-Porat. Transcript. September.

O'Mahony, Patrick, and Gerard Delanty. 1998. *Rethinking Irish History: Nationalism, Identity, and Ideology.* Hounmills, Basingstoke, Hampshire: Palgrave.

O'Rourke, Kevin H., and Jeffrey G. Williamson. 1999. *Globalization and History.* Cambridge, Mass.: MIT Press.

Owen, Roger. 1981. *The Middle East in the World Economy, 1800–1914.* London: I. B. Tauris.

Oye, Kenneth A. 1985. "Explaining Cooperation under Anarchy: Hypotheses and Strategies." *World Politics* 38, no.1 (October): 1–24.

Oz, Amos. 1983. *In the Land of Israel.* London: Flamingo.

Paisley, Ian. 1998. Address to the Northern Ireland Chambers of Commerce, Linen Hall Library, Doc. 8983.

Palgi, Arie. 1979. *Peace and Nothing More* [in Hebrew]. Israel: Poalim.

Pamuk, Sevket. 1987. *The Ottoman Empire and European Capitalism, 1820–1913: Trade, Investment, and Production.* Cambridge: Cambridge Univ. Press.

Parker, Geoffrey. 1998. *Geopolitics: Past, Present, and Future.* London: Pinter.

Peled, Yoav. 1989. *Class and Ethnicity in the Pale.* London: Macmillan.

———. 1998. "Towards a Redefinition of Jewish Nationalism in Israel? The Enigma of Shas." *Ethnic and Racial Studies* 21, no. 4:703–27.

Peled, Yoav, and Gershon Shafir. 1996. "The Roots of Peacemaking: The Dynamics of Citizenship in Israel, 1948–1993." *International Journal of Middle Eastern Studies* 28:391–413.

Pensler, Derek Jonathan. 1990. "Zionism, Colonialism and Technocracy: Otto Warburg and the Commission for Exploration of Palestine 1903–1907." *Journal of Contemporary History* 25, January:143–60.

Peres, Shimon. 1993. *The New Middle East*. New York: Holt and Co.

———. 1997. "Propelling the Peace." *Harvard International Review* 19, no. 2:38–40.

Peres, Yochanan, and Ephraim Ya'ar-Yuchtman. 1999. *Between Agreement and Disagreement: Democracy, Security and Peace in Israeli Consciousness* [in Hebrew]. Jerusalem: Israel Democracy Institute.

Pinsker, Judah Leib (Leon). [1882] 1951. *Autoemancipation* [in Hebrew]. Jerusalem: Histadrut.

Platt, D. C. M. 1968. "Economic Factors in British Policy During the New Imperialism." *Past and Present*, no. 39:120–38.

Plotzker, Sever. 1993a. "Koor's Secret Peace Project." *Yediot Acharonot*, Sept. 15.

———. 1993b. "Who Is Afraid of a Palestinian Union?" *Yediot Acharonot*, Weekend Supplement, Sept. 10.

———. 1995. Editorial. *Yediot Acharonot*, Nov. 7.

Poggi, Gianfranco. 1990. *The State: Its Nature, Development, and Prospects*. Stanford: Stanford Univ. Press.

Polanyi, Karl. 1957. *The Great Transformation*. Boston: Beacon Press.

Pollak, Andy, ed. 1992. *A Citizens Inquiry: The Opsahl Report on Northern Ireland*. Belfast: Lilliput Press.

Pollard, Sidney. 1974. *European Economic Integration, 1815–1970*. London: Thames and Hudson.

Porath, Yehoshua. 1974. *The Emergence of the Palestinian-Arab National Movement, 1918–1929*. London: Frank Cass.

Proper, Dan. 2000. Interviewed by Guy Ben-Porat. Transcript. April 6.

Puchachevsky, Nehama. 1908. Editorial. *Hashiloha* 18.

Putnam, Robert D. 1988. "Diplomacy and Domestic Politics: The Logic of Two-Level Games." *International Organization* 42, no. 3:427–60.

Quigley, George. 2000a. "Background Notes: Role of G7 in the NI Peace Process." Unpublished manuscript.

Quigley, George. 2000b. Interviewed by Guy Ben Porat. Transcript. September.

Rabinowitz, Dan. 2000. "Postnational Palestine/Israel? Globalization, Diaspora, Transnationalism and the Israeli-Palestinian Conflict." *Critical Inquiry* 26: 757–72.

Ram, Uri. 2000. "The Promised Land of Business Opportunities: Liberal Post-Zionism in the Glocal Age." In *The New Israel: Peacemaking and Liberalization*, ed. Gershon Shafir and Yoav Peled. New York: Westview Press.

———. 2004. "Glocommodification: How the Global Consumes the Local—McDonalds in Israel." *Current Sociology* 52, no. 1:11–31.

Rapkin, David. 1990. "The Contested Concept of Hegemonic Leadership." In *World Leadership and Hegemony*, ed. David Rapkin. Boulder, Colo.: Lynne Rienner.

Razin, Assaf, and Efraim Sadka. 1993. *The Economy of Modern Israel: Malaise and Promise*. Chicago: Univ. of Chicago Press.

Reed, Stanley. 1998. "Business Jumps in to Help Tame the Troubles." *Business Week,* May 25.

Reich, Robert. 1991. "What Is a Nation?" *Political Science Quarterly* 106, no. 2:193–209.

Reshef, Tzali. 1996. *Peace Now* [in Hebrew]. Tel-Aviv: Keter.

Retzky, Allan. 1995. "Peace in the Middle East: What Does It Mean for Israeli Business?" *Columbia Journal of World Business* 30, no. 3 (Autumn): 26–32.

Robertson, Roland. 1990. "Mapping the Global Condition: Globalization as the Central Concept." In *Global Culture: Nationalism, Globalization and Modernity,* ed. Mike Featherstone. London: Sage.

Robinson, Glenn E. 1997. *Building a Palestinian State: The Incomplete Revolution.* Bloomington: Indiana Univ. Press.

Robinson, Ronald, and John Gallagher. 1981. *Africa and the Victorians.* London: Macmillan.

Rodgers, Paul. 1994. "Ulster Peace Sets Investor Pulses Racing." *Independent on Sunday.* December 11.

Rodman, Kenneth A. 1995. "Sanctions at Bay? Hegemonic Decline, Multinational Corporations, and the U.S. Economic Sanctions Since the Pipeline Case." *International Organization* 49, no. 1:105–37.

Rodrik, Dani. 1997. *Has Globalization Gone Too Far?* Washington: Institute for International Economics.

Rogger, Hans. 1986. *Jewish Policies and Right-Wing Politics in Imperial Russia.* London: Macmillan.

Rogowski, Ronald. 1989. *Commerce and Coalitions: How Trade Affects Domestic Political Alignments.* Princeton, N.J.: Princeton Univ. Press.

Rolnik, Guy. 1993. "Gaza and Jericho, but the National Bank First." *Haaretz,* Oct. 6.

———. 1999. "A Different Country." *Haaretz: A Hundred in Economy.* Special supplement, Dec. 12.

Rosenau, James N. 1990. *Turbulence in World Politics: A Theory of Change and Continuity.* Princeton: Princeton Univ. Press.

Rosecrance, Richard. 1996. "The Rise of the Virtual State." *Foreign Affairs* 75, no. 4:45–61.

Rossant, John. 1989. "Israel Has Everything It Needs—Except Peace." *Business Week,* Dec. 4.

Rothstein, Robert L. 1999. "In Fear of Peace: Getting Past Maybe." In *After the Peace,* ed. Robert Rothstein. Boulder, Colo.: Routledge.

Rowthorn, Bob. 1987. "Northern Ireland: An Economy in Crises." In *Beyond the Rhetoric: Politics, Economy, and Social Policy in Northern Ireland,* ed. Paul Teague. London: Lawrence and Wishart.

———. 1993. Foreword to *The Irish Economy: Results and Prospects,* by Ronnie Munck. London: Pluto Press.

Rowthorn, Bob, and Naomi Wayne. 1988. *Northern Ireland: The Political Economy of the Conflict*. Boulder: Westview Press.

Roy, Sara. 1998. "The Palestinian Economy after Oslo." *Current History*, January.

———. 1999. "De-Development Revisited: Palestinian Economy and Society since Oslo." *Journal of Palestine Studies* 28, no. 3 (Spring): 64–82.

Rozen, Yossi. 2000. Interviewed by Guy Ben-Porat. Transcript. May 9.

Ruane, Joseph, and Jennifer Todd. 1996. *The Dynamics of Conflict in Northern Ireland: Power, Conflict and Emancipation*. Cambridge: Cambridge Univ. Press.

———. 1998. "Irish Nationalism and the Conflict in Northern Ireland." In *Rethinking Northern Ireland*, ed. David Miller. London: Longman.

———, eds. 1999. *After the Good Friday Agreement: Analysing Political Change in Northern Ireland*. Dublin: University College Press.

Ruggie, John Gerard. 1982. "International Regimes, Transactions, and Change: Embedded Liberalism in the Postwar Economic Order." *International Organization* 36, no. 2:379–415.

———. 1993. "Territoriality and Beyond: Problematizing Modernity in International Relations." *International Organization* 47, no. 1:139–74.

Rupert, Mark E. 2000. *Ideologies of Globalization: Contending Visions of a New World Order*. New York: Routledge.

Rupert, Mark E., and David Rapkin. 1985. "The Erosion of U.S. Leadership Capabilities." In *Rhythms in Politics and Economics*, ed. Paul M. Johnson and William R. Thompson. New York: Praeger.

Russet, Bruce. 1985. "The Mysterious Case of Vanishing Hegemony; or, Is Mark Twain Really Dead?" *International Organization* 39, no. 2:207–32.

Sachar, Howard. 1996. *A History of Israel*. New York: Knopf.

Sack, Robert David. 1986. *Human Territoriality: Its Theory and History*. Cambridge: Cambridge Univ. Press.

Sagi, Eli. 1996. "The Israeli Economy in the Era of Peace" [in Hebrew]. In *Israel in an Environment of Peace*, ed. R. Bar-El et al. Israel: Technion.

Said, Edward. 1979a. *Orientalism*. New York: Vintage Press.

———. 1979b. *The Question of Palestine*. New York: Times Books.

Salfiti, Farida. 1997. *Israel's "Peace Dividend": The Jordanian Case*. Nablus, Palestine: CPRS.

Sandler, Shmuel, and Hillel Frisch. 1984. *Israel, the Palestinians, and the West Bank*. Lexington, Mass.: Lexington Books.

Sartre, Jean-Paul. 1948. *Anti-Semite and Jew*. New York: Schocken Books.

Sassen, Saskia. 1998. *Globalization and Its Discontents*. New York: New Press.

Savir, Uri. 1998. *The Process* [in Hebrew]. Israel: Yediot Acharonot.

Sayigh, Yezid. 1989. "Struggle Within, Struggle Without: The Transformation of PLO Politics since 1982." *International Affairs* 65, no. 2:247–71.

Schama, Simon. 1978. *The Two Rothschilds and the Land of Israel.* New York: Knopf.

Scholte, Jan Aart. 1996. "The Geography of Collective Identities in a Globalizing World." *Review of International Political Economy* 3, no. 4 (Winter): 565–607.

———. 2000. *Globalization: A Critical Introduction.* New York: St. Martin's Press.

Schroeder, Paul W. 1994. "The New World Order: A Historical Perspective." *Washington Quarterly* 17, no. 2:25–43.

Schultz, Helena Lindholm. 1999. *The Reconstruction of Palestinian Nationalism: Between Revolution and Statehood.* Manchester, U.K.: Manchester Univ. Press.

Social Democratic and Labour Party (SDLP). 1993. "Inter-Regional Economic Development in Ireland in an EC Context." SDLP Conference, Wellington Park Hotel, Belfast, Linen Hall Library document, p. 6368.

———. 1997. "Submissions to the Multi-Party Talks, 1997." Belfast: Linen Hall Library document.

———. 2000. "Regional Development across the North." SDLP discussion paper.

Sela, Avraham. 1998. *The Decline of the Arab-Israeli Conflict: Middle East Politics and the Quest for Regional Order.* Albany: State Univ. of New York Press.

Sella, Amnon. 1994. "Custodians and Redeemers: Israeli Leaders Perceptions of peace, 1967–1979." In *Arab-Israeli Relations,* ed. Ian Lustik. New York: Garland Publishing.

Semyonov, Moshe. 1996. "Open Borders, Co-Existence, and the Future of the Social Schisms in Israel." In *Israeli Society and the Challenges of Transition to Co-Existence,* ed. Tamar Hermann and Ephraim Yuchtman-Yaar. Tel-Aviv: Steinmetz Center, Tel-Aviv Univ.

Shafir, Gershon. 1989. *Land, Labor, and the Origins of the Israeli-Palestinian Conflict, 1882–1914.* Cambridge: Cambridge Univ. Press.

———. 1998. "Business in Politics: Globalization and the Search for Peace in South Africa and Israel/Palestine." *Israel Affairs* 5, no. 2:102–19.

———. 1999. "Zionism and Colonialism." In *The Israel/Palestine Question,* ed. Ilan Pappe. London: Routledge.

Shafir, Gershon, and Peled, Yoav. 2000. "Peace and Profits: The Globalization of Israeli Business and the Peace Process." In *The New Israel: Peacemaking and Liberalization,* ed. Gershon Shafir and Yoav Peled. New York: Westview Press.

Shalev, Aryeh. 1990. *The Intifada: Causes and Effects* [in Hebrew]. Tel-Aviv: Papyrus.

Shalev, Michael. 1992. *Labour and the Political Economy in Israel.* Oxford: Oxford Univ. Press.

———. 2000. "Liberalization and the Transformation of the Political Economy." In *The New Israel: Peacemaking and Liberalization,* ed. Gershon Shafir and Yoav Peled. New York: Westview Press.

Shamir, Michal, and Asher Arian. 1982. "The Ethnic Vote in Israel's 1981 Elections." *Electoral Studies* 1, no. 3:315–31.

Shapira, Anita. 1992. *Land and Power: The Zionist Resort to Force, 1881–1948*. Oxford: Oxford Univ. Press.

———. 1999. "Herzl and the Irony of History." In *The Age of Zionism* [in Hebrew], ed. A. Shapira, Y. Reinhartz, and Y. Harris. Jerusalem: Merkaz Shazar.

Sharony, Yehuda. 1995. Editorial. *Maariv,* Nov 7.

Sheves, Shimon. 2000. Interviewed by Guy Ben-Porat. August 14.

Shikaki, Khalil. 1996a. "The Future of the Peace Process and Palestinian Strategies." *Journal of Palestine Studies* 26, no. 1:82–88.

———. 1996b. "The Peace Process, National Reconstruction, and the Transition to Democracy in Palestine." *Journal of Palestine Studies* 25, no. 2:5–20.

Shirlow, Peter. 1997. "The Economics of the Peace Process." In *Peace or War? Understanding the Peace Process in Northern Ireland,* ed. Chris Gilligan and Jon Tonge. Aldershot, Hants.: Ashgate.

Shirlow, Peter, and Ian Shuttleworth. 1999a. "Inward Investment and the Politics of Peace in Northern Ireland." *Regional Studies* 33, no. 1:79–83.

———. 1999b. " 'Who Is Going to Toss the Burgers?' Social Class and the Reconstruction of the Northern Irish Economy." *Capital and Class* 69:27–46.

Shlaim, Avi, and Avner Yaniv. 1994. "Domestic Politics and Foreign Policy in Israel." In *Arab-Israeli Relations,* ed. Ian Lustik. New York: Garland Publishing.

Shostack, Yossi. 2000. Interviewed by Guy Ben-Porat. Transcript. July 31.

Sicker, Martin. 1992. *Judaism, Nationalism, and the Land of Israel.* Boulder: Westview Press.

Sinn Fein. 1994. Election Manifesto. Belfast: Linen Hall Library document.

———. 1999. "Peace and Independence in Europe." Belfast: Linen Hall Library document.

Sklair, Leslie. 1995. *Sociology of the Global System.* Baltimore: Johns Hopkins Univ. Press.

———. 1997. "Social Movement for Global Capitalism: The Transnational Capitalist Class in Action." *Review of International Political Economy* 4, no. 3:514–38.

———. 1999. "Global System Theory and the *Fortune* Global 500." *International Journal of Politics, Culture, and Society* 12, no. 3:435–50.

Smilansky, Zeev. 1909. "From the Dream to Reality." *Ha'Olam* [in Hebrew], Aug. 28-Sept. 22.

Smith, Anthony D. 1999. "Zionism and Diaspora Nationalism." Chap. 8 in *Myths and Memories of the Nation.* New York: Oxford Univ. Press.

Smith, Charles D. 1992. *Palestine and the Arab-Israeli Conflict,* 2nd. ed. New York: St. Martin's Press.

Smith, Mike L., and James Corrigan. 1995. "Relations With Europe." In *Social Attitudes in Northern Ireland,* ed. R. Breen, Paula Devine, and Gillian Robinson. Belfast: Appletree Press.

Smith, Nigel. 2000. Interviewed by Guy Ben-Porat. Transcript. September.

Smooha, Sami. 1994. "Arab-Jewish Relations in the Peace Era." *Israel Affairs* 1, no. 2:51–66.

Sofer, Arnon. 1998. "From 'One Dunam and Then One More' to 'Territory for Peace.' " *Ariel Center for Policy Research Policy Paper,* no. 4.

Sofer, Sasson. 2001. "Israel in the World Order: Social and International Perspectives." In *Peacemaking in a Divided Society,* ed. Sasson Sofer. London: Frank Cass.

Sokolov, Nachum. 1907. Editorial. *Ha'Olam.* Apr.

Solingen, Etel. 1995. "The New Multilateralism and Nonproliferation: Bringing in Domestic Politics." *Global Governance* 1, no. 2 (August): 205–27.

Starr, Harvey. 1999. "Introduction." In *The Understanding and Management of Global Violence,* ed. H. Starr. New York: St. Martin's Press.

Stedman, Stephen John. 1997. "Spoiler Problems in Peace Processes." *International Security* 22, no. 2 (Autumn): 5–53.

Stein, Arthur A. 1984. "The Hegemon's Dilemma: Great Britain, the United States, and the International Economic Order." *International Organization* 38, no. 2 (Spring): 355–86.

Stein, Leonard. 1961. *The Balfour Declaration.* London: Vallentine Mitchell.

Steinberg, Gerald. 1993. "A Nation That Dwells Alone? Foreign Policy in the 1992 Elections." In *Israel at the Polls, 1992,* ed. Daniel Elazar and Shmuel Sandler. Jerusalem: Jerusalem Center for Public Affairs.

Sternhell, Ze'ev. 1998. *The Founding Myths of Israel.* Princeton: Princeton Univ. Press.

Strange, Susan. 1987. "The Persistent Myth of Lost Hegemony." *International Organization* 41, no. 4 (Autumn): 451–74.

———. 1995. "The Defective State." *Deadfalls* 24, no. 2:55–74.

———. 1996. *The Retreat of the State.* New York: Cambridge Univ. Press.

Strauss, Michael. 2000. Interviewed by Guy-Ben-Porat. Transcript. May 30.

Swirski, S., E. Konur, and Y. Yecheskel. 1999. *Israel: A Social Report, 1999.* Tel-Aviv: Adva Center.

Tannam, Etain. 1996. "The European Union and Business Cross-Border Co-Operation: The Case of Northern Ireland and the Republic of Ireland." *Irish Political Studies* 11:103–29.

———. 1999. *Cross-Border Cooperation in the Republic of Ireland and Northern Ireland.* Great Britain: Macmillan.

Teague, Paul. 1987. "Multinational Companies in the Northern Ireland Economy: An Outmoded Model of Industrial Development?" In *Beyond the Rhetoric: Politics, Economy, and Social Policy in Northern Ireland,* ed. Paul Teague. London: Lawrence and Wishart.

———. 1996. "The EU and the Irish Peace Process." *Journal of Common Market Studies* 34, no. 4: 549–70.

————, ed. 1987. *Beyond the Rhetoric: Politics, Economy, and Social Policy in Northern Ireland.* London: Lawrence and Wishart.

————. 1993. *The Economy of Northern Ireland.* London: Lawrence and Wishart.

Telhami, Shibley. 1996. "Israeli Foreign Policy." In *Israel in Comparative Perspective,* ed. M. Barnett. New York: State Univ. of New York Press.

Tessler, Mark. 1994. *A History of the Israeli-Palestinian Conflict.* Bloomington: Indiana Univ. Press.

Therborn, Goran. 2000. "Dimensions of Globalization and the Dynamics of (In)equalities." In *The Ends of Globalization: Bringing Society Back In,* ed. Don Kalb et al. Lanham, Md.: Rowman and Littlefield.

Thornton, Archibald Paton. 1959. *The Imperial Idea and Its Enemies.* London: Macmillan.

Tilly, Charles. 1975. *Coercion, Capital, and European States, A.D. 990–1992.* Cambridge, Mass.: Blackwell.

————. 1995. "Globalization Threatens Labor's Rights." *International Labor and Working Class History* 47:1–55.

Tomlinson, Mike. 1998. "Walking Backwards into the Sunset." In *Rethinking Northern Ireland,* ed. David Miller. London: Longman.

Tonge, Jonathan. 2002. *Northern Ireland: Conflict and Change.* London: Longman.

Trevor-Roper, Hugh. 1961. *Jewish and Other Nationalisms.* London: Weidenfeld and Nicolson.

Ulster Unionist Party. 1997. General Election Manifesto, 1 May. Belfast: Linen Hall Library document.

Usishkin, Menachem. 1907. Editorial. *Ha'Olam.* August.

Vasquez, John A. 1995. "Why Global Conflict Resolution Is Possible." In *Beyond Confrontation: Learning Conflict Resolution in the Post-Cold War Era,* ed. John A. Vasquez, Linda Stamato, James T. Johnson, and Sanford Jaffe. Ann Arbor: Univ. of Michigan Press.

Vital, David. 1975. *The Origins of Zionism.* Oxford: Clarendon Press.

————. 1988. *Zionism: The Formative Years.* Oxford: Oxford Univ. Press.

Vogel, Ezra. 1986. "Pax Nipponica?" *Foreign Affairs* 64, no. 4:752–67.

Wade, Robert. 1996. "Globalization and Its Limits: Reports of the Death of the National Economy Are Greatly Exaggerated." In *National Diversity and Global Capitalism,* ed. Suzanne Berger and Ronald Dore. Cornell: Cornell Univ. Press.

Walker, Brian M. 1994. "The 1885 and 1886 Elections: A Milestone in Irish History." In *Nationalism and Unionism Conflict in Ireland, 1885–1921,* ed. Peter Collins. Belfast: Institute of Irish Studies.

Weisbrod, Robert. 1966. "African Zion: The Attempt to Establish a Jewish Colony in the East Africa Protectorate, 1903–1905." Ph.D. dissertation, New York Univ.

Weiss, Linda. 1998. *The Myth of the Powerless State: Governing the Economy in a Global Era.* Ithaca: Cornell Univ. Press.

West Belfast Economic Forum. 2001. "Response to the Committee Enquiry on 'Strategy 2010.'" http://www.wbef.org.

Wolfsfeld, Gadi. 1997. *Constructing News about Peace: The Role of the Israeli Media in the Oslo Peace Process.* Tel-Aviv: Tami Steinmetz Center for Peace Research, Tel-Aviv Univ.

Wulf-Mathews, Monica. 1999. Quoted in "Northern Ireland in Europe." Regional brochure by the European Commission Representation in the United Kingdom.

Ya'ar, Ephraim, Tamar Hermann, and Arie Nadler. 1996. *The Peace Index Project: Finding and Analysis.* Tel-Aviv: Univ. of Tel-Aviv Press.

Yiftachel, Oren. 1997. "Israeli Society and Jewish-Palestinian Reconciliation: 'Ethnocracy' and Its Territorial Contradictions." *Middle East Journal* 51, no. 4:1–15.

Zilberfarb, Ben-Zion. 1994. "The Effects of the Peace Process on the Israeli Economy." *Israel Affairs* 1, no. 1:84–95.

———. 1996. "The Israeli Economy in the 1990s: Immigration, the Peace Process, and the Medium-Term Prospects for Growth." *Israel Affairs* 3, no. 1:1–13.

Zuckerman, Mortimer B. 1998. "A Second American Century." *Foreign Affairs* 77, no. 3 (May/June): 18–31.

Index

Abusharif, Bassam, 161
Adams, Gerry, 223, 252
African colonization: British reasoning
    behind, 27n. 1; European struggle over,
    29, 42; legitimization of, 39–41; as
    solution for Zionists, 62–63
agricultural crisis (1879–82), 84
Ahad Ha'am, 69–70, 71
Aharonson, Ran, 44
Ahern, Berti, 223, 224
Alexander II (Czar of Russia), 49
Allon, Yigal, 145
Altneuland (Herzl), 68
American hegemony, 263; British vs., 7–9,
    112–14, 130; debate over loss of, 113–14;
    decline of, 8–9, 113, 118–20, 131, 262,
    263–64; difficulties of, 118–23;
    embedded liberalism of, 8, 109–10,
    112–18; maintenance of, 118n. 3;
    reflation of, 122–23; rise of, 112–18. *See
    also* embedded liberalism
Americanization, 155–56, 193–95
Amman Business summit, 179
Anglo-American Committee, 104
Anglo-Irish Agreement (1985), 208, 219
Anglo-Palestinian Company (APC), 73
antiglobalization movements, 10–11,
    134–35, 138
anti-Semitism: in Eastern Europe, 49–52;
    emergence of in late nineteenth century,
    8, 37, 46; emigration as solution, 41;
    Herzl on, 53–55; Herzl's use of, 56, 61; in

Ireland, 87, 90; as motivation to
    Zionism, 55; nationalism and, 39;
    Pinsker on, 52–53; rise of Jewish
    nationalism and, 45–55; in Western
    Europe, 47–49
APC. *See* Anglo-Palestinian Company
    (APC)
Appadurai, Arjun, 133
Arab Executive Committee, 77
Arab-Israeli conflict: Egyptian-Israeli peace
    treaty and, 140, 147–48; impact on 1992
    elections, 163–64; Israeli-Palestinian
    conflict as element of, 5, 139, 144–45;
    nature of, 139–40; 1967 war and, 145,
    150. *See also* Israeli-Palestinian conflict
Arabs: Ahad Ha'am's view of Arabs, 69–70;
    declaration of war on Jewish state, 105;
    development of political identities, 74,
    76–77; end of boycott, 170, 173;
    evacuation of, 70, 75, 76; income levels in
    Israel, 187; Jewish perceptions of, 69–70,
    72; partition of Palestine and, 103–4;
    promise of Arab state, 77, 104; resistance
    to Jewish settlement, 73–78, 104; second
    aliyah and, 71–72; view to Israeli peace
    process, 178–80; willingness to negotiate
    after 1967 war, 145; as workers for first
    aliyah Jews, 71; Zionist view of, 67–72.
    See also Palestinians
Arafat, Yasir, 160–61, 189, 191, 192
arms race, 27–28, 168
Arrighi, Giovanni, 2, 6, 113

303

21–24; principles of, 8, 19–24, 41, 116; reflation of, 123. *See also* balance of power; free-trade imperialism; laissez faire; Pax Britannica

British identity, 206, 207

British-Irish Council, 240

British mandate, 76, 77, 104–5

Brooke, Peter, 209

Brown, Gordon, 247, 250

Bruno, Michael, 171

Buchanan, Patrick, 134

Bull, Hedley, 131

Bülow, Bernhard von (German secretary of state), 60

business community: at Casablanca business summit, 179; cross-border cooperation in Ireland and, 224–25, 227, 228, 230–31, 232; development of autonomy in Israel, 152; differences between trade unions and, 240–41, 243; divisions on socioeconomic issues, 240; early globalization and, 31, 33; economic policy in Palestinian Authority and, 180–83; effect of uncertainty of social space, 3; effects of economic problems in Northern Ireland, 213; establishment of G7, 236–40; EU developments and, 223; globalization of in Israel, 152–53, 264; Good Friday Agreement and, 246–48, 252; investment in peace in Israel, 201; investments in Palestinian Authority, 180–81, 189; Israeli election (1992) and, 163–67; Israeli election (1996) and, 199; and Israeli politics, 157–60, 164–66, 198, 271; Madrid conference and, 162; Northern Ireland's politics and, 213, 214, 216–17, 218, 231–33, 236, 237–40, 246–48, 258; opportunities provided by peace process, 154, 175–77, 178, 188; opposition to, 125–26; in Palestine, 189–90; peace dividends and, 137–38; perceptions/practices of in Ireland, 215–18, 271; promotion of

deterritorialization, 9, 160, 183–84; Protestant relationship with Britain, 212–13, 217; requirements of success, 35; role in globalization and fragmentation, 154, 185; role in peace process in Israel, 5, 141, 166, 171–74; role in peace process in Northern Ireland, 5, 204, 213–14, 218, 231–40, 246, 258; solutions for hatred, 168; Strategy 2010 and, 241; territorial expansion and, 9, 20, 28–29; Tone's nationalism and, 81; view of renewed violence in Ireland, 236; vision of New Middle East, 167, 180–83; Yes Campaign and, 247, 248–49. *See also* multinational corporations; transnational class

Butt, Isaac, 83–84

Caesarea conference, 166, 176–77

Cairo accords, 170, 192

Camp David negotiations, 139, 148, 201, 269

capital: global production networks and, 132; Israeli use of stock exchange for, 153; liberalization initiative and, 126–27; new formulation of world economy and, 122, 124

capitalism, 8, 25–27, 46–47, 110, 117, 124

Carr, Edward Hallett, 37–38

Casablanca business summit, 179

Castenada, Jorge, 128

Catholic Association, 81, 82

Catholics: Anglo-Irish Agreement and, 208; armed conflict in 1960s, 207–8; attempts at unification with Protestants, 81–84; changes in perceptions of conflict, 204; contacts with Protestants, 5; cost of conflict to, 211–12; cross-border cooperation and, 228, 229; demands of, 42, 87–88, 203; discrimination against, 5, 88, 93, 205–6, 209, 210, 211–12; Drumcree marches and, 237; effects of partition on, 100–101; EU developments

and, 85–86; Jewish "separatist" approach
to Arabs and, 71; national boundaries
and, 37; in Northern Ireland, 202;
objections to McDonald's in Israel over,
193–95; as point of conflict, 4; revival of
and Irish nationalism, 87–90;
transnational class and, 127, 138

Curragh Mutiny, 96

Daley, William, 252
Davis, Thomas, 82
de-Anglicization, 84–85
Declaration of Principles. *See* Oslo
    Declaration of Principles
decommissioning, 1, 251, 252, 253, 255, 259,
    268
decommodification of social-economic
    order, 10–11, 135, 185–89
defense industry, 158
democracy: aftermath of 1967 war in Israel
    and, 150; communist challenge and, 117;
    conflict over in Northern Ireland, 272;
    globalization and, 167; of Israel, 151;
    shift in balance of power from nation-
    states and, 114, 136
Democratic Party for Change (DMC),
    155–56
Democratic Unionist Party (DUP):
    accusation against business community,
    217; cross-border cooperation and, 228;
    empowerment of, 259; EU developments
    and, 222; Good Friday Agreement and,
    251–52, 253; lack of peace dividends
    and, 255–56; opposition to peace
    process, 244, 245; rejection of
    Framework Document, 235;
    tactics/position on identity, 207; United
    States conferences on Ireland and, 235
depression: of 1870s, 8, 24, 41; hegemonic
    leadership and, 6, 113; of 1970s, 120–21;
    rise of anti-Semitism during, 46–47, 48
deterritorialization: American hegemony

and, 8; by business community in
    Northern Ireland, 214; contemporary
    globalization and, 113, 263–65;
    definition of, 132; by EU, 218–21; groups
    carried by, 133–34; in Israel, 184, 185,
    188; opportunities for conflict resolution
    and, 115; promoters of in Israel, 160;
    pursued by Israelis, 154–55; struggle
    with reterritorialization, 9, 113–14, 133,
    134–35, 138, 265–67; by transnational
    class, 129, 160, 184, 185. *See also*
    territoriality
Devoy, John, 96
diffusionist myth of emptiness, 40–41
direct aid, 12, 162–63, 250
DMC. *See* Democratic Party for Change
    (DMC)
Dodds, Nigel, 228
DOP. *See* Oslo Declaration of Principles
double movement of globalization:
    antiglobalization movements, 134–35;
    collapse of nineteenth-century liberal
    order and, 10; deterritorialization vs.
    reterritorialization, 265–66; in Israeli-
    Palestinian peace process, 139, 186–88,
    195–96, 200–201; in Northern Ireland,
    204
Downing Street Declaration (1993), 219, 233
Doyle, Michael, 35
Dreyfus, Alfred, 48
Drumcree marches, 236, 237, 245, 252, 259,
    268
Dubnow, S. M., 54

economic autarchy, 89
economic incentives: as force for peace,
    11–14, 136; interdependence and, 11–14;
    to Irish peace, 203–4, 209–10, 233,
    238–39, 246–48, 249–50, 258; to Israeli-
    Palestinian agreement, 140–41, 152–54,
    162–63, 166–67, 168–69, 170–73; limited
    acceptability/uneven distribution of,

Israel (*cont.*)
negotiate after 1967 war, 145. *See also*
Israeli-Palestinian conflict; Oslo
Declaration of Principles; Palestine
Israeli-Arab conflict. *See* Arab-Israeli
conflict
Israeli-Palestinian conflict: Camp David
negotiations, 139; causes of, 3; cease-fire
in 1981, 148; complexity of, 139–40;
constraints on economic globalization,
154; contemporary globalization and, 5,
9; early globalization and, 4, 9, 100–101;
Egyptian-Israeli peace treaty and, 148;
international aspects of, 4–5; as interstate
conflict, 144; during interwar years, 143;
Israeli view of, 140; nature of, 139–40;
Northern Ireland conflict vs., 3–6, 260,
261–63; partition and, 3–4, 143–44,
262–63; renewal of violence in, 6,
269–70; separation fence, 269–70;
territoriality and, 112; transnationals'
hope for resolution, 156–57; unfolding
of, 9, 78. *See also* Oslo Declaration of
Principles; peace process
Israelis: Americanization of, 155–56,
193–96; under British mandate, 142–43;
contact with Palestinians, 272; formation
of national identity, 9; perception of war,
140; response to peace talks, 139; spoilers
of peace, 184–88; treatment of
Palestinians, 5; view of peace process,
171–73, 184–86, 201. *See also*
Ashkenazim; business community; Jews;
Labor Party (Israel); Likud; Mizrahim

Jewish nationalism: context of formation of,
9; cooperative settlement, 72–73;
crystallization of, 4, 19, 261; Herzl as
advocate of, 53–55; influences on
development of, 44–55, 89; motivations
for, 55, 78; Pinsker as advocate of, 52–53;
as reaction to anti-Semitism, 42;

redefining of, 189; of second aliyah in
Palestine, 71–73
Jewish State, The (Herzl), 54, 68
Jews: emigration from Eastern Europe, 51,
262; exclusion from European politics,
39, 42, 45–55, 262; first aliyah, 71;
German intervention with Ottoman
Empire on behalf of, 65; immigration
into Palestine, 63–64, 71, 104, 142–43;
life in Eastern Europe, 45–46, 49–52; life
in Western Europe, 47–49; opposition to
peace process, 188, 266; partition of
Palestine and, 103–4; pogroms in
Ireland, 87, 90; pogroms in Russia,
50–51; relations with European society,
47; relations with Palestinians, 5; second
aliyah, 51, 63–64, 71–73, 76, 102;
territorial demands of, 42; territoriality
and, 112, 263. *See also* Ashkenazim;
Israelis; Mizrahim; Zionism/Zionists
jihad, 111, 191
Joint Business Council, 229
Jordan, 149, 161, 179
Junker aristocrats, 25

Kahn, Zadoc, 68
Kant, Immanuel, 11
Keohane, Robert, 118n. 3
Keren, Michael, 170
Kern, Stephen, 36
Keynesian paradigm, 117, 126
Khalidi, Rashid, 74, 75
al-Khalidi, Yusuf, 68
Khartoum summit conference, 145
Kimmerling, Baruch, 44–45, 72, 74
Kindelberger, Charles, 6, 110n. 1
Koor, 173, 181

labor. *See* working class
Labor Party (Israel), 146; DOP legitimacy
and, 184; election of 1977, 146–47;

election of 1992, 140, 163–66; election of
1996, 198–200, 271; supporters of, 150,
151, 159
Labour Party (Britain), 204
laissez faire: American rejection of, 115,
116–17; British hegemony and, 8, 23;
crisis of Pax Britannica and, 109, 113,
260; depression of 1970s and, 25;
international trade and, 20, 22;
replacement by geopolitics, 21;
resurgence of protectionism and, 30
Lake, David, 116n. 2
Landes, David, 24
language, 37, 38, 85, 86, 88–89
Lansdowne, Lord, 62
Lautman, Dov, 163, 166, 171, 198
Lebensraum theories, 39
left wing: Egyptian-Israeli peace treaty and,
147; Israeli election of 1992 and, 165;
Israeli election of 1996, 198–200;
opposition to globalism, 10–11;
supporters of in Israel, 151, 152
Leroy-Beaulieu, P. Paul, 39
liberalism, 11–12, 21. *See also* embedded
liberalism
Likud: building of separation fence, 270;
election of 1992, 163–67; in election of
1996, 198–200; goals of, 163; ideology of,
159; response to Oslo DOP, 184–85;
supporters of, 150, 151; victory in 1977
and 1981, 146–47
Lissak, Moshe, 150, 151
List, Friedrich, 89
Literary Revival, 85–86
Lloyd George, David, 64–65, 96
local developments: globalization and, 111;
hegemonic leadership and, 119; impact
on peace process, 1–3, 13–14, 224;
leading to Good Friday Agreement,
203–4; in Palestine under British
mandate, 143; transnational class and,
10, 124, 128
loyalists: armed conflict in 1960s, 207; cross-

border cooperation and, 228; doubts
about military defeat of, 232; Drumcree
marches and, 236, 237, 245, 252, 259,
268; Good Friday Agreement and, 252;
1994 cease-fire, 234; opposition to peace
process, 244, 245, 266; renewed violence
by, 244–46; representation of, 207;
response to Anglo-Irish Agreement, 208;
view of Good Friday Agreement, 251. *See
also* paramilitaries
Loyalist Volunteer Force, 252

MacBride principles, 223
Mackinder, Halford, 35
macroregional blocs, 8, 114, 264. *See also*
European Union (EU)
Madrid Conference, 140, 162, 169
Major, John, 209, 234, 250
Mallon, Seamus, 203
Mann, Michael, 26
Manufacturers Association of Israel, 163,
171, 172, 173, 175, 181, 182
market economy: American structuring of
global economy, 116; countermovements
against, 134–35; disembedding of,
126–27; hierarchical compression and,
113; Israeli shift to, 152–54; Peres's faith
in, 168; regulation of, 117; as
replacement of territorial sovereignty,
109
markets: American competition in, 123;
British control of, 22; disembedding of,
9–11, 113, 264; embedding of, 116–17;
globalization of, 2, 6, 32; interstate
competition for, 28–31, 132; for Irish
goods, 92; for Israel's products, 175, 178;
liberalization of in Israel, 155–56, 273;
neoliberalization and, 132; open access
to, 23–24; overexpansion of, 24–25, 28;
self-rule of under British hegemony, 22
Marx, Karl, 100
Mashov group, 164

conference, 162; negotiations with Israel, 139, 140, 161; Oslo Declaration of Principles, 169, 189; readiness for negotiations, 160

Palestinian Authority: and economic development, 189; economy of, 189, 190, 196; establishment of, 170–71, 190, 193; investments in, 180–81; Paris Agreement, 182–83; peace dividends in, 189–91; priorities of, 189–90; spoilers in, 190; terrorist attacks and, 196, 197

Palestinian identity, 74–75

Palestinian nationalism, 73–78

Palestinians: alignment with Iraq in Gulf War, 162, 169, 180; attacks on Israel, 148–49, 161–62, 180, 183, 190, 191, 196–97, 198–99; under British mandate, 142, 143; citizenship of, 5; and closure of Israeli borders, 180, 183, 190–91, 192, 194–95, 196; collective identity of, 74; contact with Israelis, 272; development of national identity by, 74; discontent of with peace process, 191–93; economic status of, 153, 180–81, 183, 192; identity of, 73–74; and intifada, 149, 160–61, 162, 163, 180, 191; Irish Catholics compared to, 100–101; in Israel following 1948 war, 144; Jewish relations with, 5, 44, 144; Madrid conference, 162; marginalization of, 4; national identity of, 74–75; after 1967 war, 145; Paris Agreement, 183; peace dividends for, 189–92; and renewed violence, 192; resistance by to Jewish settlement, 73–78; response of to partition, 144; response of to peace talks, 139; and spoilers of peace, 190, 191; status of after Camp David negotiations, 148; territorial demands of, 42; territoriality and, 112; view of partition, 4, 262–63; view of peace process, 183, 201. See also Arabs; Palestine Liberation Organization (PLO); Palestinian Authority

paramilitaries, 206, 207, 223, 232, 244–46, 252

Paris Agreement, 180–83

Parnell, Charles Stewart, 81, 83–84, 85

partition: Catholic resentment toward, 206; change in concept of, 102–3; development of conflict and, 3–6, 262; effects ofon Irish Catholics/Palestinians, 100–101; as goal of DOP, 6, 192–93, 267, 268–69, 273; incompatibility of with new world order, 213–14; of Ireland, 103, 105, 202; of non-European/non-American regions, 20, 27n. 1, 31; of Palestine, 103–5; Peel Committee recommendation for, 143; as a problem, 105; as a solution, 102

Patterson, Henry, 257

Pax America. See American hegemony

Pax Britannica: effects of decline of, 20–21, 24–31, 45, 113, 261; end of, 115; establishment of, 21–24, 41; force behind, 35. See also British hegemony

"Peace: A Challenging New Era" (CBI), 233

peace dividends: for Catholics, 267; cease-fire of 1994 in Northern Ireland and, 231–35; for Israel, 140–41, 171, 178–79, 183–84, 185, 186–87, 189, 197, 201, 266; liberal view of, 11–14; limited acceptability/uneven distribution of, 12–14, 112, 137, 169, 184–85, 186–87, 197, 204, 240–41, 264–65 (see also spoilers); in Northern Ireland, 203, 233–35, 236, 246–50, 252–57; for Palestinians, 179–80, 189–91; for Protestants, 267; studies concerning, 11–12, 136; virtuous cycle of, 13, 136, 196. See also economic incentives

Peace Now, 151, 157, 193

peace process: antiglobalization movements and, 11, 134–35; breakdown of cease-fire in Ireland, 236; as breakpoint in protracted conflicts, 139–40, 191; changes in Northern Ireland facilitating,

252; identity of, 138; ideology of in Israel, 200; influence on globalizing process, 111–12, 124–26; integration of Ireland with Europe and, 218–19; interest in peace process in Israel, 141, 266, 271; interest in peace process in Northern Ireland, 213–18, 258, 266, 271; and Israeli politics, 198; opposition to, 111–12, 125; Padan as representative of, 194; perceptions/practices of in Ireland, 214–15; politics and, 10, 124–29, 138; politics in Israel and, 157–60, 198, 271; politics in Northern Ireland and, 213, 216–17, 231–33, 236, 237–40, 246, 258; practices in Israel, 154–57; promotion of deterritorialization, 160, 184, 185; role in peace process, 135, 171–74, 204; view of normalization process, 197–98; vision of New Middle East, 167. *See also* business community

transnational companies. *See* multinational corporations

Trimble, David, 141, 228, 246, 252, 255

Troubles, the. *See* Northern Ireland conflict

Truman Doctrine, 115

"Truth from the Land of Israel" (Ahad Ha'am), 69

Turkey. *See* Ottoman Empire

two-level games, 3

two-nation theory, 103

Uganda Plan, 62–63

Ulster Unionist Party (UUP): cross-border cooperation and, 228; EU developments and, 222; Good Friday Agreement and, 251–52, 259; influence of G7 over, 239; opposition to peace process, 266; rejection of Framework Document, 235; tactics/position on identity, 207. *See also* Protestants; unionists

Ulster Volunteer Force, 99

Ulster Workers Council, 208

unionists: concerns/methods of, 98–100; control of Northern Ireland's government, 205; cross-border cooperation and, 225, 227–28, 230; Curragh Mutiny and, 96; Drumcree marches and, 237; effects of economic problems, 212; EU developments and, 215–16, 222; Good Friday Agreement and, 1, 253n. 8; identity issues, 204–5; international intervention and, 223; measurement of success/failure of region, 204; opposition to home rule, 96; opposition to peace process, 245; opposition to Sunningdale Agreement, 208; partition and, 103; representation of, 207; response to Anglo-Irish Agreement, 208; role in peace process, 246; view of peace settlements, 244; view of subventions, 212; Yes Campaign and, 248–49

United Kingdom. *See* Britain

United Nations: charter of, 116; partition of Palestine, 143–44; Resolution 181, 161; Resolutions 242 and 338, 170; Special Committee on Palestine (UNSCOP), 104–5

United States: antibusiness mood, 125–26; antiglobalization movements in, 134–35; brokering of Israeli-Palestinian cease-fire and, 148; economic cooperation with Britain, 26; Good Friday Agreement and, 240, 253, 258; industrialization of, 25; investment conference on Ireland in, 235; investors in Ireland, 252; involvement in Jewish affairs, 104; Irish diaspora in, 83, 95–96; Jewish emigration to, 51; loan gaurantees to Israel, 162; Madrid conference, 162; McDonald's in Israel, 193–95; negotiations with Palestinians/Israelis, 5, 161, 169; role in Irish peace process, 5, 223–24; signing of DOP in, 171; unchallenged military power, 120; as